THE INSIDERS' GUIDE TO BECOMING A YACHT STEWARDESS

I did it!!!! A big thank you to Julie!!!! This book guided me every step of the way. I ordered the book on 3-17-08, and on 6-3-08 I was on my first boat!! Julie not only gives you an accurate view of what working on a yacht is truly like, she includes her own personal accounts out at sea (which, by the way, are quite funny!!). Julie includes EVERYTHING you will need from training, accommodations, to local spots to network in various ports. I bought this book with no real intention on changing my career. I had always wondered about the industry, and once I got the book, I couldn't put it down. The very next day I started taking the steps toward making this dream a reality. You will find Julie's stories entertaining and the book will engage you from page one. If you have ever thought about becoming a yachtie, you MUST HAVE THIS BOOK!!!!!!!!!!

—**Caresa Brown (Marti)** via Amazon.com, Key West, FL

So funny… and a blueprint too. This book is absolutely a JOY to read. From the Preface to the back cover this book is entertaining from beginning to end! The lovable reading makes the application and instructions that Julie, the author, walks you through actually exciting to follow through with. I took it everywhere until I'd covered everything. I was compelled and frankly didn't want to put it down. It's the best reading I've done lately. This book is robust with instructions and real life application so direct that anyone can apply them to their lives seamlessly!

—**M. Palmer**, via Amazon.com, Los Angeles, CA

Hi Julie, I would just like to say thank you so much for all your BRILLIANT advice in your book!!! My name is Leanne… and I have always wanted to get into the yachting industry, so after a holiday to the South of France I decided that it was time to fulfill my dream, however I had no idea where I start. So one day while researching I came across your website, I read a caption of your book and decided to order it. My first best decision I have made so far!

I started reading your book and just couldn't put it down, I found it so informative but at the same time very interesting and it had me giggling very often! I really enjoy the way if felt like I'm listening to a friend giving me advice, I really felt like I got to know you. Towards the end I started sparing my reading times so I didn't have to come to the end of the book I was enjoying it so much! The more I read the book the more driven I got to do it! I ordered your book on the 7th October 2011 and you will be happy to know you have encouraged me so much that I will be arriving in Fort Lauderdale on the 28th December to start my job search!

So I just felt like I owe you a thank you as you have been so instrumental in helping me understand a whole new world! I love absolutely EVERYTHING about your book and have already told so many other women that are interested in being a Stewardess to read it. I just thought I'd let you know how I feel. I'm sure it must be invigorating for you to find out how you have completely changed someone's life! Thanks again!

—**Leanne Roos**, South Africa

This book is amazing. Funny, informative, entertaining, and meticulously detailed. I don't think anyone has done such a good job of actually putting the facts down on paper. This woman is talented! I am a writer in the yachting industry myself, and I am amazed at all of the details of the industry she has brought to life. I really appreciate and admire the tremendous amount of work that went into this. Great balance of info and entertainment.

—**Alene M. Keenan**, via Amazon.com, Ft. Lauderdale, FL

Detailed, information, and useful: This book was so well-researched and detailed. I recommend it for anyone considering a career in the yachting business. I wish I had found it sooner! The author includes humorous, personal stories which make it entertaining as well. I especially appreciated the detailed salary information, descriptions of each crew member's responsibilities, and a detailed sample of a typical daily schedule as well as a pronunciation guide to luxury menu items. She thought of everything you need to know and presents it in an easy-to-read format.

—**Shannon C Kelly** via Amazon.com, Los Angeles, CA

Julie, My husband and I just arrived to Ft. Lauderdale and we have begun the job search. We are very experienced in the hospitality industry, and we are excited to bring our skills to the yacht scene. We just finished our first temporary job out of Seattle together. It was a week cruise through the San Juan Islands up to Vancouver and Victoria, B.C. on a 92' MY. It was a three-person crew including my husband as chef and the captain. I just want to thank you for your guidance. Your book prepared me for the level of service and dedication needed to be successful as a "green" sole stewardess. We did very well and are now in Ft. Lauderdale with a great reference! The "job hunt" section in the book is also very useful! My book is about to fall apart from the heavy use for reference purposes. I feel like we have been able to plunge ahead with a good head start thanks to your insight. Take care and wish us luck!

—**Connie Navarre**, Fort Lauderdale, FL

Dear Julie, I feel like I know you well enough to be my best friend. I just read your book cover to cover in 3 days. And one morning I literally woke up really early with excitement to read more of it. That Christmas Eve feeling… I cannot express to you (though I'll sure try) how perfectly your book came into my life and how much it has changed things since I've read it. It is exactly the document I needed to make me launch into this next step of my life with 100% confidence.

I imagine you get a lot out of changing people's lives, so that they might have their own experiences similar to yours. It is obvious that you have a genuine passion for the industry and for the people running it in the future. I also wanted to say that loved your writing style. You left none of my questions unanswered. And I loved reading your stories. I literally laughed out loud multiple times while I was reading them. I've shared multiple excerpts from your book with my family.

—**Kelly Robinson**, Chicago, IL

I found your site a few weeks ago and ordered your book. I read it in one day! I couldn't take my eyes away from it. You have totally convinced me that I HAVE to do this. I bought my ticket to go to St Maarten on October 13 (I have family there) to take the STCW course and then I'm going to start my quest for work on a yacht! Your book is ideal! Thank you so much!

—**Brit Frashier**

Julie, I received your book as a gift last spring. I am just now getting ready to head south (I'm from Ohio). I thought the book was GREAT! I come from a sailing background and was invited to cook/stew on a private 65' yacht for six months in 2007. I wish I knew an inkling of what you share in this book before I took off. Since then, I captained a sailboat in the Bahamas for a year in 2008 and took 2009 off for health reasons. I'm ready to get back into the industry and will need all the insight I can muster to find the right gig. I head to Fort Lauderdale January 30th. Wish me luck.

—**Laurie Sampson**, Ohio

Hi Julie, I love your book! I am following your advice completely. I will be coming to Ft. Lauderdale to actively begin my search for a job as a yacht stew and go to school per your suggestion. I am also planning on attending the Triton's March event. Thank you very much for writing such an excellent guide. Your book has helped me immensely. You have given me hope that I might be able to get a job on a yacht.

—**Donna C.**, Wisconsin

A must read for those aspiring to become yacht crew. This would have been invaluable to me a few years ago when I took the overnight sleeper to the South of France with a tent and box of CVs to seek a career change onto large yachts. Full of practical advice but entertaining as well this book is an excellent read even if the closest you will ever get a large yacht is standing on the dock.

—**Malcolm C. Barraclough** via Amazon.com, The Netherlands

Hi, my name is Emily and I live in Montana. I am 17 years old and I attend my local high school. My strong desire to travel has led me to your book and I absolutely love it! It's hard for me to find a better way to travel the world, than on a luxury yacht. I understand that the stewardessing work will be very tough, but who would be crazy enough to pass up an opportunity like this? You are a great role model to people like me who have a dream to see the world.

—**Emily Samson**, Bozeman, MT

I am 19 years old and met a crew in Savannah, GA while attending Savannah College of Art and Design. Once I heard about the yacht industry I knew I had to do it! I cannot be more excited. I know this will be an amazing experience. I ordered your book which has helped me so much in planning for this adventure.

—**Anna Haldewang**, Savannah, GA

I bought your book, it has been both helpful and useful but also VERY encouraging! Can't wait to get moving on this exciting new adventure. Thank you,

—**Jess Arbour**

Hi Julie, I bought your book a couple of months ago and cannot believe how amazing and insightful it has been. I had already made the decision to pursue work on a yacht before purchasing your book, however since reading it I am so excited and must admit I would have been totally clueless without it, so thank you very much. I am planning on heading to Florida (from Australia) in October to begin my courses and the big job hunt. Thank you for your assistance

—**Bree Madigan**, Australia

Hi Julie, My name is Laura and I just finished reading your book and would like to tell you thank you, because this will be my bible while I try to break into the yachting industry. Thank You,

—**Laura Nash**

A fantastic insight for anyone interested in this career! This book is not only a "How To" it's a very good insight on how things really are once you get out on the big sea. The author does a great job by not leading you on that everything is fantastic all the time and tells it like it is. The "I must Confess…" are great additions and I found myself sometimes skipping ahead just to read some of those. I bought this book because I was interested in the profession and couldn't find anything worth reading about it. This is the book to read! And after reading it, I am certain that I am going to Ft. Lauderdale and becoming a Yacht Stew.

—**Heather A. Morris** via Amazon.com

Hi Julie, I have been reading your book and am excited to break into the role of a stewardess in the yachting industry! You have written such a wonderful and informative book and I hope that our paths cross sometime in the future! All the best,

—**Stacy Stephens**

Hi Julie, I used to work on yachts in the Mediterranean myself for about one year, and then another season whilst already at university. This is about 6 yrs ago now. Now I got the degree, got the work experience and had enough of 9-5 office jobs, therefore I am considering of going back into yachting for a while, for a bit of adventure. To "freshen up my memory" I ordered your book the other day. Your work is very inspiring, thanks a lot for that, and keep up the good work!

—**Anne-Jasmin**, Germany

Hi Julie, I just received your book last week and read it in one day!! It was GREAT! I really enjoyed reading it and it provided me with some very valuable tips and information. I am a 26 (almost 27) year old, American female with a background in medical marketing. I have been laid off since May and decided I would get out of the corporate world and become a yacht stewardess since it has always been my dream to live at sea. Best regards,

—**Ashley R.**, Dallas, TX

Hi Julie, I've just read your book, twice, it was an amazing insight and well worth the read. Thank you. In September I will be completing the Maritime Hospitality course with UKSA here in the UK and plan to travel to Fort Lauderdale in October to look for employment onboard a superyacht as a Stewardess! I'm hoping my new career onboard will be as colourful as yours!! Best wishes,

—**Saskia K.**, **Norfolk**, U.K.

Hello Julie, I recently purchased your book (which is fabulous by the way!). I am very serious about starting a career as a stew in the fall. I will be looking for work in Ft. Lauderdale. Your book has become my "Bible" so to speak.

—**Donna-Lisa Morin**

Hi Julie, I recently purchased and read your book and must say while I had already made the decision to pursue becoming a yacht stewardess your book made it very real. Thank you, thank you, and thank you Julie!

—**Briana K.**, Washington

Hi Julie: Let me firstly say that you are my personal hero and have saved and my interest in the yachting industry!!! I have always been interested in working on yachts but up until recently I have had very little luck in finding someone who could help me get started!! I heard about Matt Brown's blog and it was through this that I came to learn about you!!! I then went straight onto amazon to order your book. My name is Emma, I am 23 years old and am a recent university graduate. I am now in the UK working. So my story seems very similar to yours when you started out in the industry and this has made all the difference to me!!

—Emma Boxall, United Kingdom

Hi Julie, thanks to your book, I'm heading to Ft. Lauderdale to become a yacht stew. A career change is severely in order for me! Thanks for writing!

—Kelli Sanders

Hi Julie! My name is Christina Kotseas and I've just read your book and moved to Ft. Lauderdale today! I am so excited to begin my job search and have a meeting set up with Lynne at LuxYachts tomorrow morning.

—Christina Kotseas, Fort Lauderdale, FL

A fun ready and gets me excited about my new career: This is a great book if you are considering work in the industry. [It] is very fun and exciting to read. I would recommend it to anyone who is curious. I'm sure all life on a Yacht will not be exactly like the books says but I believe it is a very realistic description of the industry.

—A Walker, via Amazon.com, New York

Recently I had the pleasure of running into a yacht crew in New Orleans and hanging out with them for several months. These guys opened my eyes to a world that I didn't know existed. Now, I've bought your book and am planning to come to Ft. Lauderdale at the beginning of April to start taking the necessary training classes and do the job hunt. Just so you know - the book was very helpful and will be a great asset when I start doing all the preparations and planning for the move to Ft. Lauderdale. I'm very excited about starting fresh in a new industry and travelling the world!!! Thanks,

—Janie Irvine, Houston, TX

Hey Julie, GREAT BOOK. Too bad I rarely have a chance to read it. I keep it on the yacht, and my stew keeps reading it on her breaks, so I never get to touch it. I wish I had that book when I got started on the yachts.

—Captain Michael Elliston

THE INSIDERS' GUIDE TO BECOMING A YACHT STEWARDESS

Confessions from My Years Afloat with the Rich and Famous

Julie Perry

—— 2nd EDITION ——

NEW YORK

THE INSIDERS' GUIDE TO BECOMING A YACHT STEWARDESS
Confessions from My Years Afloat with the Rich and Famous

ISBN 978-1-61448-785-2 paperback
ISBN 978-1-61448-786-9 eBook
Library of Congress Control Number: 2013944420

Morgan James Publishing
The Entrepreneurial Publisher
5 Penn Plaza, 23rd Floor,
New York City, New York 10001
(212) 655-5470 office • (516) 908-4496 fax
www.MorganJamesPublishing.com

For my parents,
JACKIE SCANLON and BOB PERRY
I love you.

TABLE OF CONTENTS

ACKNOWLEDGEMENTS

Writing this book was a labor of love. In the process of creating it, there are many circles of family, friends, colleagues, and in this case, even students, who made contributions. I wish here to express my most sincere appreciation for these amazing individuals:

My deepest gratitude goes to Captain Carl Sputh, Chris Sputh, Captain Ted Sputh, and Captain Ryan Sputh, without whom I never would have known about this industry, and whose support, encouragement, and love has touched my life in many ways over the years.

To Megan Fernandez, who planted the seed that would blossom into this book, I thank you a million times over. To Diane Byrne of Megayacht News who assisted me with editing this second edition: words can only suggest my profound appreciation for her editing skills, perennial patience, and generous collaborative spirit. To Kate Chastain, thank you for assisting me with research (and for being one of my favorite success stories so far). A tremendous amount of gratitude goes to Heidi Newman, my editor on my first edition of *The Insiders' Guide*, who magnificently assisted as a midwife to birth my book into this polished, professional reality back in 2006. And a thank you to my sister in survival, Suki Finnerty of YachtingToday.TV., for her unwavering friendship, and of course, all of the incredible yacht-crew photos she provided for both my book cover and my website.

To Jenny Banner, my best friend and confidante, who, in many ways, was my first publisher—compiling a year's worth of my emails-from-sea into book form and giving me the idea that I could one day do this. To the entire staff at Morgan James Publishing, especially David Hancock, Jim Howard, Margo Toulouse, and Bill Barrett. To Adrienne Gang for writing the Foreword to this book and for becoming such a close friend and cheerleader as I wrapped up this second edition. To my dearest friends Jim Clinger, Erin Jump Fry, and Tiffany Benedict-Berkson for their help on the book cover design and all-around moral support. And a huge thank you to Jason Bean for his work on my website.

This guide originally took shape back in 2006 with the help of Kristen Cavallini-Soothill of American Yacht Institute, an angel disguised as a human being. And my sincerest gratitude goes to the following yacht industry professionals and companies for assisting with content and commentary: Ami Ira and Heather Adams of Crew Unlimited; Tish Owen George; Joy Weston at Crew Pacific, Lynne Cottone of Luxury Yacht Group, Michael French and Claire Murray French at ICT; Julie Liberatore, Amy Morley Beavers, and Lisa Morley of MPT, Debra Blackburn Boggio of Fraser Yachts Worldwide, Theresa Morales of Liquid Yacht Wear, Peter Vogel of Warsash Superyacht Academy, and Martin Redmayne of The Superyacht Group. To Mark Rutterford of Viking Recruitment, Dorie Cox and Lucy Reed at *The Triton*, Lauren Beck and Steve Davis at Dockwalk, the entire staff at Bluewater Books & Charts, Tim Thomas at *Boat International*, Beverly Grant of IMA Yacht Crew Solutions, and Victoria Allman for her great contributions to the book and blog. Several people have offered their support in a variety of ways: they are Jim Bray, Amanda and Chris Hilfer, Gordon Connell, Hope Yonge, Shelley Furse, Norma Trease, Joyce Goll Clear, Dhardra Blake, and all of my colleagues at BLASTmedia. And thanks to Jill Smith Hinke, my hero over the years, for paving the way.

To some extra special people who deserve my most heartfelt gratitude for our time together—when wit, love, laughter, and learning were never in short supply: Captain Ian, Chef Jules, Mr. Bini, Yuko Duko, Johnny G., Andrea B., Jason W., Heather Hartley ("Haitch"), Sam P., Phil M., Miles, Ulf, Jennifer C., Julie L., Justin D., and Tara R.

To my dear family: Patty Perry; Jack "D.J." Scanlon; Robert Michael and Kathryn Perry; Peggy Perry; Amy Perry; my step bro and sis, Kevin and Kristin Cane; and my dear cuz, Kelly Merket. And most importantly, to Mom, Dad, and my brother, Robert, who abundantly supported and wholeheartedly encouraged me to follow my bliss: pursuing my dream of writing my first book, and now, seven years later, its updated sister, *The Insiders' Guide to Becoming a Yacht Stewardess*.

Front cover photography courtesy of Suki Finnerty of YachtingToday.TV.
Uniform provided by Liquid Yacht Wear, Fort Lauderdale.

FOREWORD
(Adrienne Gang)

Congratulations! I am excited for you! Getting this book in your hands may be the first step you are taking to explore a career in the incredible industry of yachting. If you have already jumped on board (pun intended) and are looking to deepen your understanding of yachting and pick up some useful information along the way, you have found what I believe is one of the best resources available to the yachting community to date.

My name is Adrienne Gang and I am a veteran chef and stewardess in this amazing industry. I am a huge advocate for the opportunity and adventure that a yachting lifestyle can offer to anyone wanting and willing to take on the pros and cons of the job. I can honestly say that I wasn't always so committed to or sold on the yachting lifestyle. I came into the industry as a chef with restaurant and catering experience but no real understanding of what the whole role of "stewardess" entailed on board. I assumed, like I'm sure many "green stews" do, that the interior maintenance portion of the job description was common sense or a no-brainer. I thought with my recreational boating experience and my home housekeeping skills I'd be just fine. I could not have been more wrong.

I was fortunate to have patient owners and even more patient crew at the beginning of my yachting career, but I still felt for a long time like I was missing some crucial pieces of the interior puzzle. I taught myself the best I (and the Internet) was able to come up with on how to "polish granite," "set and preform proper table service," and "do flower arrangements" (which, to this day, still remains the bane of my existence).

Following several years of improvisation, close calls, short cuts, and lucky guesses I was really beginning to wonder if I was ever going to put all of the pieces together. As if by divine design a captain of mine, seeing my obvious struggle, handed me a copy of Julie Perry's book *The Insiders'*

Guide to Becoming a Yacht Stewardess. I was ecstatic to finally have a resource in my hands that had so many of the answers to questions I had been scouring the earth for in the previous years.

Over the years, I have given or recommended this book to any woman or man thinking about getting into yachting, and I keep my own personal copy on hand at all times. I know that when living on a yacht, space can be limited for your personal effects, but this book is definitely worth its weight.

—**Adrienne Gang**, Chief Stewardess on Bravo TV's "Below Deck." June 2013.

PREFACE

I carry this quote **from Thoreau's *Walden* in my journal:**

> *"Why should we be in such desperate haste to succeed, and in such desperate enterprises? If a man does not keep pace with his companions, perhaps it is because he hears a different drummer."*

For nearly three years, I sailed the high seas with some of the world's richest people as my companions, and I certainly didn't keep pace with them…

I cleaned their toilets.

I Must Confess…
I never would have expected I'd become a yacht stewardess.

I'm a born-and-bred Midwestern girl from Indiana, and I began life marching to the same drummer as most of the people around me. My idea of a successful life was doing well in school and getting a good job. Well, actually, getting a GREAT job (in a "keeping up with the Joneses" sort of sense…with a briefcase to match). I finished high school at the top of my class and entered Indiana University, determined to come out four years later bound for law school or some high-powered corporate position.

But during my final year in college, while taking a schedule of both English Literature and Philosophy courses, I became inspired to seek a more unique route than just the safe and secure. Ancient Greek philosophers were encouraging me to question everything around me, to look for answers beyond the obvious, and to step out of my "cave" and seek a more enlightened perspective on life. The brave works of bohemian Modernist writers were inviting me to get out and explore the world and to travel to far-off places, namely Europe.

As I contemplated these messages, I realized I had fallen into the habit of defining my career goals based upon what others expected of me. My life felt generic, and I yearned for a more adventurous path. I even began to question the motives behind my plan up until then: *Who was I,* I wanted to know, *away from the things that defined me—my family, my friends, my academic record?*

I ended up graduating Phi Beta Kappa (a national academic honorary society) with two degrees... but when it came time either to submit my law school applications or to interview with the Procter & Gambles of the world, I passed on both. Instead, I decided it was time to do a little soul-searching. I yearned to be an "American in Paris," to lounge around the fashionable ports of the Côte d'Azur (the South of France) like Hemingway and Fitzgerald, or to be *Down and Out in Paris and London,* as George Orwell had once done.

Bottom line: **I wanted to travel!**

First I went to England under the auspices of a six-month work abroad program. I spent four months struggling to make ends meet in London, working for a marketing firm (because it would look good on my résumé when I got back to the States—old habits die hard, you know). I had a tough time admitting it, but I was miserable. This was just not the adventure I had imagined. I was playing it too straight and narrow and not getting what I could out of my short time living abroad.

One day, a total stranger—the sort of character few Midwestern mothers would want their daughters taking advice from—approached me on the street (literally, out of nowhere) and told me to **"take a leap in the dark and never look back."** I was open-minded enough and romantic enough to listen: I quit my job the next day and hopped a bus to Edinburgh, Scotland the following week.

Once in Edinburgh, I was left with only £7 to my name. I lived in a hostel (inexpensive, dormitory-style accommodations) for a short time, working the front desk in exchange for room and board until I could afford a flat. To survive the next five months, I managed to find and juggle three jobs (bartending, waiting tables, and telemarketing), and I actually overstayed my work visa by an extra three months. It was struggle, it was strife, it was a game of survival in a foreign environment—and I loved every minute of it! In the end, I had managed to save enough money to finish my year abroad backpacking through Europe, 14 countries in under three months.

Talk about a rite of passage journey! Back home in Indianapolis, I realized that law school was no longer something I wanted to pursue. I felt I'd seen something on that other continent, and I wanted to go another round. Oh, I pretended like I was ready to get serious about finding a "real job" (as my parents would put it): I enrolled in an advertising course, signed on to run a few local political campaigns, and swore to my mother that I was researching the market for PR jobs.

But deep down, I longed for another chance to travel. I secretly began spending every spare moment possible investigating work abroad programs online. I desired something completely out of the ordinary and hoped that, maybe this time, I could even make some killer money. Yeah, the student loans had kicked in.

Opportunity knocked the day I was scheduled to interview for a coveted position with a national political party's office in Washington, D.C. A friend of mine from high school called and asked me to come to Florida. He was the captain of a luxury yacht, and a position had just come open on his crew. He wanted me to come work for him: as a **stewardess.**

I Must Confess...
It's all Carl's fault.

If it weren't for my friend Carl, I never would have known about this career option. In fact, even with that connection, I was still pretty clueless about what I was setting off to do.

Carl and I grew up together. His dad had worked in the yachting industry for years, as a captain and later as a yacht charter broker based out of Indianapolis. While my friends and I all knew that, we still had little clue what it meant exactly. We just knew to call him "Captain Ted." And boy, did Captain Ted have great travel stories.

When we graduated from high school, Carl followed in his father's footsteps by heading off to Fort Lauderdale to obtain entry-level work as a deckhand on megayachts. There again, my friends and I thought, "Okay, sure, whatever that means." During the years I was slaving away in college, Carl used to come home from places in the Caribbean and the Mediterranean with tons of crazy stories about working aboard these "palaces on water." He would tell me how he was working on this classy boat owned and visited by some really big-named people. But that wasn't the crazy part. What blew my mind was his exact job function.

"So what is it that you *do* as one of these deckhands?" I would ask.

He would respond with things like, "Oh, I clean the yacht by washing it down each morning and evening" or "I take the guests out and teach them how to water ski." And my favorite: "I run the Jet Skis daily to make sure they are working properly and have enough fuel for the guests to play on them."

In awe, I would ask, "And you are getting PAID to do this?"

That's where it got really crazy. Not only was Carl getting paid a salary, but that money he made was never really touched; it just went straight into his bank account and sat there because he made enough income in TIPS to live off that money alone! Crazier still, he had no living expenses: no rent, no utility bills, no car payment. Even his meals and basic toiletry items were provided.

Over the course of the next three years, Carl worked his way up from entry-level deckhand to a more experienced deckhand and then to a licensed first mate. By the age of 22, he became one of the industry's youngest yacht captains, taking command of a 114-foot megayacht and sailing it all over the world.

I always thought it sounded too good to be true.

So years later, when he called up inviting me to come work for him—to serve rich people food and iron their underwear while they vacationed on these glamour vessels—I knew it was something I had to consider.

As it turns out, the job with Carl didn't come to fruition. He needed a stewardess by the following week, and I had too many loose ends to tie up before I could leave. He hired someone else.

"Oh Julie, you should still give it a shot… It will be easy for you to land a job on your own," Carl encouraged me over the phone. "Just fly down to Fort Lauderdale, take a five-day stewardess training course, register with some crew agencies, and you'll be hired in no time. There are a ton of yachts desperate for stews right now. You can do it by yourself… you don't need me!"

Carl had planted a seed. For the next several weeks, I could not stop thinking about all the extraordinary adventures I might experience working as a luxury yacht stewardess. I would wake up in the middle of the night and start researching online all the places yachts travel. I even began analyzing my bank account, trying to determine how much money I could scrounge together to get my air ticket to Fort Lauderdale, pay for training, and support myself while I looked for a job.

Of course, I then ran through my mind all the reasons why I shouldn't try it (but then again, why I should!): *What would I do with my apartment?* (Break the lease.) *Who could take care of my car?* (Sell it.) *Where would I put my stuff?* (Storage units are cheap, as are parents' basements.)

Suppose I get down there and can't find a job? (It's called commitment and determination—try it.) *Suppose I don't like it once I get there?* (You'll never know unless you give it a whirl.)

Yes, despite my reservations, something was working deep down inside, and like a wave on the sea, it gathered momentum before hitting me full force with a message that was nostalgically familiar: **Take a leap in the dark and never look back.**

Within three weeks, I had turned down the interview opportunity in Washington, moved out of my apartment, sold my car, and moved every item I owned into my father's basement. The next thing I knew, I was on a plane to Fort Lauderdale instead. I was off to become a yacht stewardess!

(And until I got there and saw things with my own two eyes, I still didn't get what it was all about.)

But Carl was right. One month, a five-day, intensive stewardess training course, and a handful of interviews (all arranged by some very helpful crew recruiters) later, and I landed a job on a 164-foot megayacht owned by a European billionaire. It would be chartered out for $25,000 per day, which would mean that our 10-person crew could make between $1,700 and $3,500 per person in tips on a weeklong charter, on top of a healthy salary. I'd be one of only two Americans onboard this colossal cruising castle as we sailed to chic ports throughout the Caribbean and Mediterranean, catering to some of the most powerful individuals in the world.

As you can imagine... ***I never looked back.***

------◆------

"I shall be telling this with a sigh
Somewhere ages and ages hence:
Two roads diverged in a wood, and I—
I took the one less traveled by,
And that has made all the difference."
—from *The Road Not Taken* (1916)
Robert Frost, American poet

(Now c'mon, you knew that quote was coming.)

Author's Note: Portions of this Preface originally appeared in the May 2003 issue of *Indianapolis Monthly* magazine, in an article entitled "Cabin Girl: Confessions of a Hoosier Turned Yacht Stewardess," co-written with Megan Fernandez.

INTRODUCTION

"While there's no such thing as a guarantee in this life, Julie Perry's guidance is as near to fail-safe as a person can get. As a fellow traveler, I was shown by Julie, step-by-step and in detail, exactly what needed to be done to make the dream of working in luxury yachting a reality. She was insightful, accurate, and hilarious at every turn and hurdle, explaining precisely what obstacles and adventures lay before me as I started from NOTHING. Thanks to Julie and her wealth of information, I was able to work, live, and play on one of the more prestigious charter yachts in the world and explore some of the most fabulous destinations throughout France and Italy. If you've ever wanted to change your world, see the world, and have an incredible time doing it, this is the book you NEED to read. Thanks, Julie… I OWE YOU."

—**Jim Bray**, a former deckhand and mate in the yachting industry

I Must Confess…
The first step was a little traumatic for me.

"OH my, *please*, take your shoes off!"
Those were the instructions given to me during my devastatingly embarrassing first moment ever stepping foot on a megayacht. Mind you, these words were directly followed by the statement, "You must ALWAYS remove your shoes when stepping onboard a yacht; even the guests know that!"

I was there to interview for my first job as a stewardess. What an entrance, huh? I didn't even know Rule #1. *(The most formal setting I'd ever encountered, and they wanted me barefoot?)*

And you wondered if this book would deliver helpful advice…. Well, *voila!* You've just learned one of the most basic, international laws of this industry: Always remove your shoes upon boarding a yacht, unless you are a crewmember who is wearing deck-approved footwear. Simply look down… there will be a shoe basket at the entrance or exit to the passerelle (also known as a gangway, this is the footbridge that leads over the water and connects the boat to the dock) into which you can deposit your pair.

Welcome Aboard!

Let me begin by offering you a HUGE congratulations! I opened with the previous confession to convey to you that I've been where you are. So, too, have many of the people I have helped over the years to launch successful careers in the luxury yachting industry. Like us, you reached out for this book—this information—for one of possibly many reasons:

- ❧ You want to travel the world.
- ❧ You seek adventure and a sense of accomplishment.
- ❧ You want to explore a less conventional career path.
- ❧ You're on a quest to make and save great money, while also living life to the fullest.
- ❧ You have a background in hospitality and are looking for a new way to apply it. (Or you have none whatsoever, but you think you'd be great at it!)
- ❧ You've always loved the sea and desire to break into the maritime industry.
- ❧ Maybe you've never even been on a boat, but you have nothing tying you down and wish to try something completely new.
- ❧ You yearn for a change in your life's path, or to take some time out from the one you're currently on—challenge yourself, expand your horizons… maybe even do a little soul-searching.

And I am sure there are many others.

I therefore congratulate you on taking a first step toward your own personal objective. Becoming a crewmember on a luxury yacht is a career move that not only can grow your bank account, but also can enlarge your worldview. It's about travel, it's about providing service, and it's about stepping outside of your comfort zone to become more knowledgeable about the world, its customs, and its diverse people. I know from firsthand experience that when you take on an adventure such as the one offered in this industry, you can discover an entirely new perspective on life.

My yacht stewardess career spanned from 1999 to 2001. Since that time, while I've managed to remain involved in the yachting industry as a freelance writer and a digital-media executive, it has in no way been a substitute for the glorious life at sea I left behind. But I've carried my stories with me—tales of my days providing five-star service to some of the world's richest and most famous people—and have quite often found myself reading these stories aloud from the pages of my mind… reminiscing and sharing my memories with individuals who have not only asked to hear them, but who've also asked how they, too, could have similar adventures.

Whether it was the daughter of my mother's co-worker in her second year of college, confused and needing a break; the dear friend struggling in the corporate world at age 30 and desiring a change; or one of my former marketing interns who felt she didn't know what she wanted to do with her life and was looking for an opportunity to travel abroad, I served as an unpaid career consultant, selling these young women (and men) on the idea of pursuing a job in luxury yachting. I then sat them down and outlined the A-to-Z steps to take to make it happen. In fact, I've "sent off" many individuals who once languished in perhaps the same position you might be in right now.

That's why in 2005, it finally occurred to me: I've been helping individuals one at a time… why not broadcast my coaching method to the masses? *Why not write a book?*

And ta da! I did.

From the moment the first edition of my book came out in October 2006, the response was tremendous. Not only have I met and corresponded with dozens upon dozens of hopeful yacht crew from around the world, but I've seen many of them go on to have terrific careers. In addition, several of the top yacht-crew training schools tell me that, to this day, they have students walking in the door with my book tucked under their arms. Captains and chief stews tell me they keep a copy onboard for all crew to read. And believe it or not, a few yacht stews have even contacted me to report sightings of my book on the bedside stands of their yachts' owners, perhaps a sign that these owners endeavor to learn more about the day-to-day work it takes to keep everything running smoothly aboard their most prized possessions.

Of course, no industry stays static, which is why I decided to update the book and release this second edition. So much has happened since the original version in terms of the growth of the yachting industry, the number of people applying for jobs, the performance and safety standards to which yacht crew are held, and more; I therefore felt it was crucial to provide the most up-to-date information possible.

The book you are holding in your hands is the result. In other words, ta da, again!

Within the pages that lie ahead, you will gain an in-depth understanding of one of the world's most exciting industries. More important, you will learn how you, too, can become a part of it. I realize that, similar to my first day stepping onboard a yacht, the thought of embarking upon a new career path—be it for the long- or short-term—can be daunting, if not a bit intimidating. So, the good news is that you can relax. This book is dedicated to outlining that path and making your journey as easy and hassle-free as possible.

Hundreds of hours went into researching and writing this guide, and hundreds more went into bringing everything up to date seven years after I wrote the first edition. I met with and interviewed more than two dozen industry professionals, from crew recruiters and training experts to current and former crew and captains. Thanks to these individuals and the contributions of their insider knowledge, I can say with confidence that you will receive all the exclusive advice and practical guidance you need to get started—and succeed!—as a luxury yacht steward/ess.

But this is not *just* a guidebook to getting a job on a yacht. Sitting down in 2005 to write exactly that—a how-to book about getting into this fabulous industry of unbounded opportunity—the project soon became something else. What also began to trickle onto the page were many of those stories I've carried around with me over the years: stories of what it was like living and working aboard one of these palaces at sea, tending to the ever-changing needs of our wealthy and eccentric guests, learning to get along with a multinational crew with whom we lived in such close proximity, and then packing in as much adventurous living as we could during our downtime, when the crew had the vessel all to ourselves and the world became OUR playground. I believe those stories will help bring this experience you're exploring to life.

The result is a hybrid: What you have before you is a how-to guide, but what you will also find are bits and pieces of a young woman's memoir. Nestled among all of my instructional "do this, do that, and oh yeah, don't forget to do this," I think you will hear the fondness I have for my years spent as a yacht stewardess calling out from the pages. For some, perhaps my anecdotes—my "confessions" (innocent, though they are)—are distracting, but my hope is that they will illustrate some of the adventures one can look forward to in this industry, if not also add a little comic relief.

I hope that my book's second edition release will continue to serve not only to educate, but also to entertain and inspire. I finally hit on the exact way to pay homage to the years I spent as a luxury yacht stewardess, and I am thrilled at the prospect that it will carry on helping others discover similar life-altering experiences and fulfillment.

The State of the Crew Job Market

The opportunity that exists to work aboard luxury yachts is one of the best-kept secrets around. This is not intentional; it has just not been necessary to promote the industry widely to the public. In fact, due to the privacy concerns of many well-known yacht owners and guests, the industry often tries harder to conceal its existence, shunning attention rather than attracting it. Consequently, most people eager to get paid to travel the world do not understand that the option is available.

Furthermore, the yachting industry has never really advertised for crew, because up until about 2005, when I sat down to write the first edition of this book, it didn't have to. Starting in the late 1990s and continuing into the mid-2000s, the number and size of megayachts being built each year was growing at the fastest rate in the industry's history, and with that building boom came job openings. As a matter of fact, yachting experts were noticing a shortage of qualified personnel to fill the positions available. That's why in the first edition of this book, I talked about how yacht crew jobs were therefore plentiful. In the years that followed, industry groups like the International Superyacht Society began holding informational and introductory training seminars at boat shows in major yachting ports like Fort Lauderdale, to help get the word out.

Unfortunately, though, the global economic crisis that began in 2008 caused a lot of yacht owners and would-be yacht owners to hold off on signing contracts to build new boats. Orders are still down, too. *ShowBoats International* magazine, which surveys shipyard order books each year for its *Global Order Book*, reports that in 2012, there were 629 yachts over 80 feet long on order to be built worldwide, which is about five percent less than in 2011 and still 31 percent less from the high (1,008) reported in 2008. Still other owners put their yachts up for sale. All of this has led to a reduction in job openings.

But, that does not mean there's no chance you'll land a job. In fact, like any industry, the yachting business is always looking for hard-working, dedicated people. With well over 6,000 megayachts over 80 feet (24.4m) in the world today, believe me, there are a lot of crew jobs to be had. And, even though the yacht construction boom of the last decade went bust, there still are some super-size yachts being built in need of new crew with the right attitude. (You'll learn more about this trend in Chapter 2.) Keep in mind the following great information that one experienced crewmember gave *The Triton*, a leading crew newspaper, in early 2012 when it asked readers to share their advice for newcomers to the industry: "It's OK to be green. Entry-level jobs are more about diligence than skill. Having a can-do attitude and performing all tasks to a high level is important. You have to earn responsibility, and this comes when you show you can take pride in any job."

So crank up that desire for a challenging, but awe-inspiring and rewarding adventure. And welcome aboard the world of luxury yachting!

A Quick Note on Gender and Terminology

I will be using the word "stewardess" or just plain "stew" throughout this book. Please note that this is for simplicity, my preference over the bulky slash mark (steward/ess) each time the term is applied. In doing so, I do not mean to rule out any of you male readers or lead you to think this job is not for you. On the contrary, two or three decades ago, the standard in the industry was for stew positions to be held by only males—especially when sailing in Europe, where the standards of service indicated that there was something more prestigious or acceptable about men serving guests.

Times have certainly changed, for today, 80-85 percent of stews in the industry are female. However, there are still plenty of men working as stewards in yachting. I worked with one myself; he was involved more with food service and bartending than he was making beds and doing laundry (and he was the chief, or head stew, so that was typical anyway), but he knew the entire job inside and out and was available to help in any capacity at a moment's notice. So guys, if you're reading, I'm not trying to slight you: In this book, "stewardess" and "stew" refer to you, too.

How to Use This Guide

My wish is that you use this book in the way best suited for your individual needs. With regard to my more anecdotal Confessions, I have attempted to sprinkle a few in each chapter, although you will find they are much more prevalent in the first half of the book. To make them easy to locate, each one is sectioned off and preceded by the lead-in "I Must Confess…"

Additionally, each chapter is carefully designed to walk you step-by-step toward finding a great job as a luxury yacht stew. To help you navigate your way through the information, the overall guide is divided into two parts. **Part I, "The *What* Industry?"** and comprised of Chapters 1 to 5, is devoted to giving you an overview of luxury yachting and what makes this industry, and the jobs within it, unique:

- ↝ **CHAPTER 1: *Shhh… I've Got a Secret*—Luxury Yachting Defined** explores what types of yachts exist that can, and perhaps will, employ you in the near future. You'll gain insight into how big these vessels are, who owns them, how much they cost, where they travel, what they're like inside, and more important for you, who works on them.
- ↝ **CHAPTER 2: What Has Yachting Done for Crew Lately?—(a.k.a. The Benefits!)** covers what is probably of even more interest to you from the perspective of working onboard, and that is how much money you can make as a yacht stew, as well as what other benefits accompany this job. From the pay to the people and back to the travel,

you'll be exposed to all the perks that make yachting such an exciting and dynamic career path.

↝ **CHAPTER 3: There's No "I" in CREW—Meet Your Fellow Crewmembers** gives you a look at job descriptions for the various other crew positions onboard a luxury yacht. This job involves interacting with and being part of a team, so it's important that you learn about whom you will work alongside… because on a yacht, you live alongside them as well!

↝ **CHAPTER 4: Around the World With a Silver Tray—What Becoming a Yacht Stew Entails** answers what will probably be your most burning question at this point in the book: *So what do I have to do in return for all these great experiences and benefits yachting can offer?* This is where you are introduced to the actual work. (Hey, the good news was in the previous chapter!) You'll gain exposure to what your daily duties may include.

↝ **CHAPTER 5: A Stew's Job Is Never Done—(Beyond The Big Three)** offers an even more in-depth look at a yacht stew's job functions. The focus in this chapter is on host/hostessing responsibilities, household management tasks, and elements of providing overall guest care.

By the end of **Part I,** you should have a good grasp of what being a yacht stewardess is all about. If you feel you're up for the challenge, you will be perfectly primed to begin the process—and that's where **Part II, "Getting Hired"** (Chapters 6–11), picks up: the actual "how to."

Part II opens with **The Quick Start Guide: The A to Z of How to Become a Yacht Stew.** This helpful reference outlines each separate step along the way to getting your first job and tells you in which chapter you will find further information. Use this as a checklist during your search for employment. You'll find more detailed advice in the chapters that follow:

↝ **CHAPTER 6: The Recipe for a Great Stew—The Skills and Traits Required to Get Hired** exposes you to the broad range of skills and personality traits future employers will want you to have. You'll also read about what previous work and life experiences will make you more marketable as a job candidate (which will be things to highlight on your résumé/CV when you begin putting that together).

↝ **CHAPTER 7: Learning the Ropes—Essential Training for Entry-Level Stews** provides information on the training and education that is required of entry-level crew. Along with suggested programs and courses to enroll in, this chapter also offers recommendations for non-mandatory training classes to best prepare you for the work that lies ahead and will increase your chances of getting hired quickly.

↝ **CHAPTER 8: Picking Up Anchor—Choosing and Moving to a Hiring Port** covers one of the most important steps to beginning your job hunt, and that is moving to a hiring port. *What are your options? How do you choose?* This chapter not only provides a list of crew house options in the four key hiring ports around the world—Fort Lauderdale, Florida; Newport, Rhode Island; Antibes, France; and Palma de Mallorca, Spain—but also offers key information on obtaining passports and travel visas.

↔ **CHAPTER 9: Let the Job Hunt Begin!—Crew Agencies, Day Working, and Networking** focuses on crew-placement agencies, as well as other means for obtaining your first job onboard a yacht. *Who do you contact? How do you begin?* All of these questions will be answered, along with specific advice on how to look for day work and how you can conduct your job search online. I also include insider advice on how and where to network in the hub hiring ports around the world.

↔ **CHAPTER 10: Fit to Be Hired—Résumés/CVs, Interviews, and Accepting Your First Job!** is one of the most important chapters of this guide if you are serious about embarking on a new career in yachting. Here, you will find key advice on how to put together a winning résumé/CV, how to gather references, how to prepare for and handle interviews… and even how to choose which job you want after you've become bombarded with employment offers!

↔ **CHAPTER 11: All Aboard—Life "Out There"** examines what it's like to live onboard a yacht. Okay, you're making lots of money now: *How do you save it? And what about "the afterlife"… after yachting? What are your options, and what type of opportunities will you have been prepared for as a yacht stew?* Ahhh, not to worry—the future will be very bright, indeed.

A brief **Conclusion** offers my final thoughts on what it's like to work as a yacht stew.

Throughout the guide, I have included bits of advice from numerous industry experts that are sure to save you time and help you land a job quicker and with less effort than you would otherwise have to expend. For especially key advice from these professionals, look for the **INSIDER TIP** icon: ❖.

Due to limitations in the length of this book, information that I do not include with regard to resources will be placed on my accompanying website: www.WorkOnAYacht.com. This industry changes quickly, and with so much up in the air with regard to crew training requirements and school offerings, you will also want to check my website for updates.

Now for What You Won't Find…

This is a how-to guide on finding and obtaining work in the yachting industry, but it is not a textbook on how to perform the actual functions of a yacht stew (although, you will pick up some helpful tips!). Rather, I leave this more detailed instruction to the training schools that specialize in this type of education. What I do provide you with is information on what skills you need to acquire, where to go for various types of training, and how to contact and enroll in these schools. Supplemental guides are also recommended. Over the years, more and more on-board yacht stew guides have come onto the scene, and most are great! But before you need to worry about acquiring and developing skills, it's best to make sure this is a type of work and lifestyle change you are ready to pursue. This book can help you assess that.

You also will not find dishy gossip about the owners and guests who travel aboard these boats. For an industry that brought me so much joy, satisfaction, and life-long memories, and for it to remain the institution it is, I honor the privacy of the people who travel aboard these vessels— without whom this opportunity would not exist. They don't deserve to have their private lives and intimate details splattered out on the page for all to read. This is the reason I have kept my confessions innocent, lighthearted, and, I hope, fun for you as a reader.

Setting Sail for New Horizons

This guide may leave you so thrilled at the prospect of becoming a yacht stew that you'll want to drop everything and sail off tomorrow. And how fantastic it would be if I could one day run into you at one of the crew bars—commonly referred to as "yachtie" bars—during the Fort Lauderdale International Boat Show (I still attend every year!) and have you tell me that you've just come in from a season in the Mediterranean on a 150-foot yacht and are out blowing your last charter tip!

On the other hand, you might read through this guide and decide, *no, I can't do that—yachting is not for me.* And hey, this is not an industry for everyone; it takes a very adventurous and open-minded type of individual, and the work itself can be incredibly demanding… But at the very least, I hope you walk away with a larger message: I hope that this book encourages you to take a journey—any journey—to discover some other destination or to explore more of who you are. In my life, travel has shown me that the world is a magical place, filled with opportunities beyond what most individual societies teach. When you take such a leap as to transplant yourself to a situation or place where you can be challenged and inspired to think, learn, know and do more, you gain a tremendous feeling of controlling your own destiny.

Somewhere out there, there is a match, and if yachting is not for you, I encourage you to keep searching. I learned a long time ago that you can talk all you want about wanting to do, to act, to make something happen… but in order to accomplish that, you have to take a step, even if it's just a small one. If purchasing this book was a step for you—but you find that it's not your cup of tea—keep stepping. There are myriad other opportunities out there waiting for you. Congratulations again for taking the time to explore one such opportunity.

Regardless of what you are looking for, and where you hope to find it, may travel and exploration of any kind transform your life for the better. Now, get out there and see the world!

> *"Twenty years from now you will be more disappointed by the things you didn't do than by the ones you did. So throw off the bowlines. Sail away from the safe harbor. Catch the trade winds in your sails. Explore. Dream."*
>
> —attributed to **Mark Twain**, American novelist and humor writer

PART

I

"THE *WHAT* INDUSTRY?"

1

SHHH... I'VE GOT A SECRET.
—LUXURY YACHTING DEFINED—

Referred to by many who work within it as a "closed" or "secret" society, the yachting world has flown somewhat under the general public's radar over the years. When I interviewed industry professionals for this book and asked them to describe what working aboard luxury yachts is all about, the answers I got carried this common theme:

- "It's a well-kept secret. People are just now starting to hear about it, but it's a shame that most don't have a clue they could have this type of opportunity."
- "Yachting is its own little microcosm. But few people outside this circle are aware of it."
- "This has been such a closed society. It's like the movie industry, really. It's a little underground world going on—the marine world is its own little secret world."

Despite what you haven't heard or didn't know before, I promise there's a sea of opportunity that awaits you if you decide to take the plunge. (Ah, me and my bad puns.) This chapter is dedicated to taking you inside this world and showing you what you can experience by becoming a part of it.

"The yachting industry provides opportunities beyond any I've ever seen before:

- ↔ **"The traveling.** You may be working your tail off, but when you get 10 minutes off, you're going to be in Portofino or Venice. You are going to be seeing seagulls in St. Tropez! It's just amazing all the places you'll go.
- ↔ **"The money** you make on a yacht is yours to keep. You don't have any expenses. You can live in a uniform for however long you want to stay in this career; you don't have a need to buy new clothes. You don't have a house payment, or any living expenses. The money you make is your allowance!
- ↔ **"The people you meet.** The contacts you make! Not that you can really sit down on the yacht as you're working and say, 'Okay, I'd like to make a connection with you, Donald Trump.' You can't play like the businessman on there making all your contacts... BUT, you lay low and sometimes there will be that opportunity—or they may remember you down the road!
- ↔ **"The crew.** You're in a protected environment while being on your own. But you're not really alone. You've got a captain, who's the law, but who's also like a surrogate parent. You've got a whole new family in the crew you work with. You'll walk away with friends for life—from all over the world!
- ↔ **"And the perspective...** that you gain on the world. Meeting different people, experiencing different cultures. Getting over yourself is also a real big benefit. Talk about growing up! It's just a brilliant education.
- ↔ **"Great food, great food, great food!** You get gourmet everything working on a yacht. And you don't have to cook it yourself; there's an onboard chef who handles that. I'd never even heard of some of the stuff I learned to eat on a yacht.

"... If I had the opportunity that kids have today to go do this for five or 10 years, ah, I wouldn't miss it. The whole experience is beyond comparison."
—**Kristen Cavallini-Soothill**, owner and operator of American Yacht Institute,
a stewardess training organization in Fort Lauderdale, Florida

"Is That Like Working on a Cruise Ship?"

"Yachting is sexy. Cruise ships? Not so much."
—**Julie Perry**, the author of this book (Yeah, that's right, I said it.)

I can remember coming home during my vacation time from yacht jobs, back to my land-locked hometown of Indianapolis, Indiana—in the heart of America's Midwest. I would run into old friends or acquaintances, and when I told them where I'd been and what I'd been doing, their reaction was always one of confusion:

"The *what* industry?"

No matter how distinct and straightforward I tried to put it—"I work in the luxury-yachting industry"—this answer was always met with blank stares.

I would rephrase my response to be more specific: "I'm a stewardess on a luxury megayacht."

"Ohhh," they would nod (un)knowingly, "like a cruise ship."

Ugh! That dreaded comparison. It was inevitable. I could never just state my vocation and have people "get it" right away.

I suppose it makes sense that my friends back home wouldn't be familiar with the yachting industry, or at least that it wouldn't pop readily into their minds. Let's face it: Everyone knows about employment opportunities that exist on cruise ships. But the same opportunities (and I call them golden opportunities) to work aboard luxury yachts seem to remain unheard of. I would suspect this was a foreign world to you, too… at least until you picked up this book.

Why is that?

Even if you have never traveled on a cruise ship before, you have no doubt been subjected to the trillions of dollars worth of advertising done by the large cruise lines, inviting the masses to come aboard and "live the life of luxury." Nearly everyone has been exposed to the all-affordable cruise line vacation and knows what it must be like to travel on these floating resorts.

So, when I told my friends I worked on a luxury megayacht, cruise ships were their most obvious point of reference. They clearly picked up on some key similarities between the two types of jobs. When I said I was "a yacht stewardess," they gathered that:

a) I worked on some type of boat.
b) that boat was a pleasure cruising vessel on which people vacationed.
c) I provided service for the vacationing guests aboard this pleasure cruiser.

What my friends perhaps *didn't* pick up on was that:

a) the boat I worked on was privately owned and privately chartered: more like a floating palace than a floating resort.
b) the pleasure cruising vessel I worked on was owned and visited by some of the world's wealthiest, and oftentimes most famous, people—the type for whom money is no object. And note: Most of them wouldn't be caught dead on a cruise ship.
c) the service I was hired to provide for guests was expected to be as top-notch as it comes—five-star quality, if not six. Sure, the duties might be similar to working on a cruise ship: serving food, making beds, cleaning, and doing laundry… But as a stewardess on a yacht, I handled *all* of these tasks, not just some of them. I also carried them out to much higher standards; nothing short of impeccable pampering was delivered. And the most unique part: I was providing this service to only a small number of people—a maximum of 12 on any given trip, with a crew-to-guest ratio that was nearly 1:1.
d) oh yeah, and I got paid boatloads of money to travel by sea to some of the most beautiful and exotic ports in the world.

Cruise Ships vs. Luxury Yachts—A Vast Sea of Difference

To explain the differences a bit more thoroughly, what distinguishes commercial cruises from luxury yachting is that they are *public* pleasure cruising vessels vs. *private* pleasure cruising vessels. The massive cruise ships are filled with hordes of tourists being shuttled around from port to port and periodically herded off and on for shotgun sightseeing opportunities. Private yachts, by contrast, carry the owner and his or her guests exclusively. That owner may live onboard or, as is more often the case, simply vacation onboard—but in either instance, the vessel is most certainly one man's (or woman's!) mobile castle. (Note that private yachts can be owned by one individual or by a corporation or group of individuals; either way, they are deemed private vessels.)

Yachting, then, in the case of private pleasure yachts, is a noncommercial boating activity. Well, *sort of.* In recent years, many private yacht owners have offered their yachts over to the charter market to help cover the maintenance costs. In other words, when these owners are not using their yachts, they let other people rent them for various durations of time. The line between commercial and noncommercial is blurred when private luxury yachts are put on the charter market.

I will talk more about yacht chartering later in the chapter, but for now, the important thing to know is that when yachts are chartered, it is still for private use. The distinguishing point here is that cruise ships take by-the-cabin bookings from multiple parties at once, whereas on a luxury yacht, one person pays for the private use of the entire vessel, not just a cabin.

Usually, the maximum number of guests you will have onboard a yacht is 12. To carry more than 12 guests on a chartered voyage requires that a vessel follow an entirely different and more cumbersome set of safety rules and regulations. As the race to build larger and larger yachts continues among today's multi-millionaires and billionaires, there are now charter yachts available that will take on these extra safety requirements. While still in the minority, these larger boats can be cleared to transport 18, and in a few cases, up to 36 guests at a time. (And note: These particular yachts will have larger crews to meet the demand.) With such restricted passenger numbers, you therefore have a small crew-to-guest ratio. Cruise ships, on the other hand, while they often manage a 1:3 or 1:4 ratio, haul around as many as 3,000 guests at a time. (And holy cruise ship! Royal Caribbean International's MS *Allure of the Seas*, launched in 2010, now holds the record for the largest passenger ship ever constructed—Capacity: 5,400 passengers at double occupancy, 6,296 maximum; Crew: 2,384 as of July 2012. Yikes.)

Another major difference between cruise ships and luxury yachts is the clientele. The guests traveling on a megayacht are among the most well-heeled people on earth. These individuals would no more consider boarding a cruise ship than they would take a public bus. Granted, there are luxury commercial cruise lines in existence, and several of them, such as Cunard, Seabourn, and Regent Seven Seas, are incredibly expensive and offer ultra-luxury accommodations and first-rate service. And yet, even the wealthy travelers who can afford these "six-star" (as they call them) cruise ship voyages cannot begin to afford the price tag of owning or chartering a luxury megayacht. We'll get to those astonishing price tags later in this chapter.

In the past, size was the first thing used to distinguish yachts from cruise ships. Yachts were always smaller, and the difference between them was obvious to the eye. As yachts have gotten bigger over the last 30 years, some are now as big as, or bigger than, their commercial counterparts. Even so, luxury yachts are still going to be more complex and have a blend of extravagance that sets them well apart from other floating creations. To further clarify, even the highest caliber of cruise ship in the world, such as Cunard's *The Queen Mary II,* cannot rival the craftsmanship that goes into building a luxury mega- or superyacht, as they are also often called. (Definitions of the various yacht categories, as in luxury, mega-, super-, or gigayacht, will be covered later in this chapter.)

Luxury yachts offer passengers another advantage that eludes travelers aboard big cruise liners, in that they can reach more remote destinations—the unspoiled islets and inlets, tranquil beaches, and intimate coves and harbors that are inaccessible to their gargantuan commercial cousins. Furthermore, on a luxury yacht, it is up to the guests where the vessel travels, and plans can change at a moment's notice. This is different than cruise ships, which offer guests pre-arranged itineraries to choose from—and these are set in stone (except when weather turns).

Cruise Ships vs. Luxury Megayachts		
	COMMERCIAL CRUISE SHIPS	**LUXURY MEGAYACHTS**
Ownership	Commercially owned and operated	Privately owned and used
Charter Formula	Passengers rent by cabin or block of cabins	One person or group of people charter the entire vessel
Size and Style	Floating Resorts: Sizes vary greatly depending on the line, but averages for some of the larger cruise lines are in the 800- to 900-foot range	Floating Palaces/Hotels: 80 to 500 feet in length, with an average of about 170 feet
Number of Guests	Hordes: Averages hover around 1,000 and can reach 3,000 on the larger ocean liners	Up to 12. In rare cases, 18 to 36
Number of Crew	Crew ranges from 300 to around 1,200	Crew ranges from 1 to 36, but the average for megayachts is around 6 to 10
Crew-to-Guest Ratio	1:3 and higher (1:2 in the case of the higher-end lines)	Small, often 1:1 or 1:1.5
Destinations Visited	Well-known, with itineraries etched in stone	More remote, with itineraries that are determined by the guests and can change on a daily (if not hourly!) basis
Clientele	A mixed bag of John Does	A well-to-do bunch of heavyweights
Quality of Service	Average to high	The highest
Crew Pay	Varies	Varies, but tips are infinitely juicier

Table1-1

Why Work on a Cruise Ship When You Can Work on a Luxury Yacht Instead?

To me, this is a no-brainer. On luxury yachts, the posh clientele, the unique travel opportunities, and more important, the money you can earn and the luxurious surroundings you live within make for an entirely different work environment than on commercial cruise liners.

It is actually quite astonishing how popular cruise ship jobs are, not to mention how stiff the competition is to obtain them. In researching the first edition of this book, I looked into some of the how-to guides for obtaining work with the cruise lines, and I was shocked at how cut-throat it can be. I must admit, after having spent my working years at sea aboard megayachts, I really have to ask: why? Sure, the service expectations are much higher on yachts; but if you are dedicated and receive the proper training, you can land a job on a yacht just as easily as you can on a cruise ship.

I'm not putting down the cruise line industry. After all, given my income level, if I were to take a vacation at sea, it would be my wallet's best option. What I am trying to point out is that commercial cruises are for The Everyman. They are marketed to the masses, and therefore we are all familiar with them, both as a form of vacation and as a form of employment. So when comparing the cruise industry to the yachting industry—and more specifically, the jobs one would hold in either—then yes, yacht professionals do wish to remain in a far separate category.

Moreover, when it comes to payoffs for the crew, yacht jobs take the cake. Base salaries for stewardesses, when compared with those of food and beverage servers, cabin stews, and laundry staff on cruise ships, are slightly higher. But where the potential income differences become dramatic is when you consider the tips one can earn working on luxury charter yachts, or the bonuses and perks afforded the crew on solely private yachts. We'll cover the benefits to your bank account more thoroughly in Chapter 2. Meanwhile, I can tell you now with total confidence: The money and other perks you can obtain working on luxury yachts beats those offered on cruise ships hand over fist.

And there you go! If the pay and benefits that come from accompanying the rich and famous on their private journeys around the world is news to you—and appeals to you—then that's where I come in. Consider me your coach on how to become a part of it all.

But let's get one thing straight right now: I will make no attempt to hide my passion for what I consider to be one of the world's greatest jobs. *Oh*, and to all my dear friends back home in Indiana, I NEVER WORKED ON A CRUISE SHIP.

"Compared to cruise ship jobs, yacht jobs pay a lot better. You have higher standards of living. You work probably a lot less: You have guests onboard one to three weeks out of the month with more frequent down time instead of four weeks out of every month. And it's a much more intimate environment. Plus you are exposed to people who are a lot higher up on the food chain—for your afterlife, after yachts. On cruise ships, the opportunities to carry your career land-based are not really going to be there like with yachting connections. On yachts, qualified people get jobs through the owners all the time, either in their homes or in their companies."

—**Ami Ira,** owner and operator of Crew Unlimited, a yacht-crew placement agency headquartered in Fort Lauderdale, Florida

I Must Confess…
*We yachties sort of frowned upon what
life might be like aboard the ol' cruise ships.*

We were attempting to exit a small port in Bermuda when the yacht I was working on got stuck behind a massive cruise liner. Several of my fellow crewmembers and I were seated on the bow (that's the front end) of our boat observing as the cruise ship workers scrambled to herd on last-minute stragglers from their day's excursion ashore. A disembodied voice bellowed out from the speakers, instructing passengers to line up at "the starboard embarkation point on Deck DD-2 near the Happy Day Lounge." (Or something like that.)

We watched and listened in horror before one of our deckhands finally spoke up. He made the comparison between cruise ships and luxury yachts as being similar to Target vs. Neiman Marcus. To top that, one of my fellow stewardesses chimed in with, "Or perhaps even more appropriately: Walmart vs. the Gucci store on the Champs Élysées in Paris." I thought that was an accurate analogy. (*She* said it, I didn't.)

Yacht Definitions: The Superlative Confusion

You may already be a little confused. Up until now, I've used several terms interchangeably: just plain **yachts, luxury yachts,** and **luxury megayachts.** To confuse matters even more, let me now introduce some other industry favorites: **superyachts** and **gigayachts.**

Which is which and what is what, and which kind am I telling you to work on?

The answer: All of them. The last thing I want you to do is get bogged down in industry jargon, none of which will make much sense until you are in the midst of it all anyway. I do, however, want to expose you to each of these terms so that you aren't later confused when you hear industry folk throwing them around.

Luxury, Mega-, Super-, and Gigayachts… and How They Differ

Know this: All yachts are boats, but not all boats are yachts.

Now, know this: All luxury yachts and megayachts are also referred to as just yachts, but not all yachts qualify as luxury, mega-, or super-.

That's enough to make your head spin. Allow me to break it down.

I want to start with the most basic definition of… **a yacht.**

Yachta, Yachta, Yachta

The basics: A **yacht** is a water-going vessel used for pleasure purposes only, be it cruising to distant shores, day sailing along a coast, or racing. It can be propelled by either motor or sail, or *both* (motorsailers, a hybrid of sorts). Regardless, as we learned in the last section, the key characteristic all yachts have in common is that they are privately owned.

From a size perspective, the answer can often vary depending on whom you ask, but a good "loose" definition of when a privately used boat is called a yacht is at 40 feet and up (12 meters+) if it is motor-powered. For sailing yachts, that qualifying length is more like 30 feet+ (9 meters+). It is at these lengths that privately owned pleasure yachts must be officially registered with most governing bodies of the maritime industry.

However, at 40 feet in length, a boat just barely qualifies as a yacht and can actually be handled by an owner on his or her own, without any hired crew needed to help run it. Owners with no ability to drive their yachts may hire a single captain for outings, but it's not until we get into the larger vessels of 70 to 75 feet and up that we start to see professionally trained crew as a necessity onboard.

Note: If you are anything like me, conceptualizing distances and measurements comes about as naturally as walking on your hands in a straitjacket. When trying to grasp the size of these boats in your mind's eye, here is a method that's helped me: Picture a regulation American football field—it's 100 yards in length. There are 3 feet to 1 yard; therefore, a football field is 300 feet long. Use that to visualize the size of the yachts I talk about from here on out. A 30-foot sailing yacht measures from the goal line to the 10-yard line on an American football field (10 yards at 3 feet to a yard is 30 feet). As for a powerboat, it becomes a yacht once it reaches the 13.3-yard line (that's 40 feet divided by 3, if you are at all following me here). If you're a reader who uses the metric system (and in the yachting industry, meters are quite often the measurement of choice), you can follow along in this discussion knowing that, while there is no set size standard for a regulation soccer field (as in European football), most fields are 115 to 130 yards in length, or roughly 100 meters. In meters, a 40-foot yacht is roughly 12 meters in length.

For further guidance on Feet vs. Meter conversions, please see Appendix A in the back of the book.

Luxury Yachts—This Ain't Your Daddy's Boat

Next in line on the way up the totem pole of the world's most splendorous and exclusive cruisers is the luxury yacht. The line between what qualifies as a yacht, plain and simple, and a luxury yacht, is not easy to draw. In fact, several industry experts I interviewed explained that the term does not really have an official definition—that it is only a "tabloid label" or a "layman's term." So, since no one is able to nail down these classifications with any certainty, I will simply do my best to share the more obvious differentiations, as noted by some experts I queried.

A luxury yacht seems to typically earn such a distinction once it has entered into a certain size category, that being in the 70- to 80-foot (21.4 to 24.4-meter) range and beyond. I even find myself applying it to yachts 60 feet and up. It is at these lengths that yachts begin to have non-guest living areas, known as crew quarters, built into them so that a crew can live aboard. Some experts may tell you that earning the tag "luxury" depends on such factors as the build, finish, quality, and attention to detail on a yacht's interior. However, I think it's fair to say that any yacht over the 80-foot (roughly 24-meter) mark is called a luxury yacht by default.

Megayachts—Megalomania!

At 80 feet (roughly 24 meters) and above, say hello to the megayacht. To call it a luxury megayacht, as I often do, is actually somewhat redundant. By its very nature, a megayacht is luxury; in fact, it is probably one of the world's finest examples of a luxury possession—the acquisition of which is incomprehensible to most mortals.

When asked to offer a definition of a megayacht, one respondent said it was any yacht over 150 feet in length. Another defined it as 80 feet and up. Still another used 100 feet as the distinguishing marker at which a yacht passed from simple yacht to megayacht status. Diane M. Byrne, the founder and editor of MegayachtNews.com and a former editor at *Power & Motoryacht* magazine, lends a bit more insight. She says that an article in *Power & Motoryacht* from 1985 credits George Nicholson, founder of the renowned yacht-brokerage firm Camper & Nicholsons International, with coining the term. Interesting enough, an October 1990 article from the *Los Angeles Times* makes the same assertion.

For what's seemingly such a subjective matter, the international maritime community actually agrees on one thing: Professional crew requirements and training standards start to apply with a yacht of 80 feet, or 24 meters. Given that, though, why such debate over the definition? It largely stems from the boom in yacht construction that occurred last decade. If you looked at the pages of one of the yachting magazines back in the late 1980s and early 1990s, for example, an 80-foot boat was considered top of the line. But as luxury yachts began gaining in popularity, the average lengths began growing, too. Soon, 100- to 165-footers (30- to 50-meter yachts) started becoming more common. By the time I started researching the first edition of my book, many launchings were coming out in the 170- to 200-foot and up range (52 to 61 meters+). Still, by industry definitions, any yacht that is 80 feet or larger is a megayacht.

And mind you, at 80 feet, that is considered a small megayacht!

Superyachts—Not Super Easy to Define

On to the definition of a superyacht, where we find even greater debate. A superyacht and a megayacht are viewed as the same thing by most yacht enthusiasts, and the terms are often used interchangeably. The choice of one label over another really depends on the person using it; although I do tend to find that megayacht is the American standard, while superyacht is favored by Europeans and the like.

Some industry professionals adopted the name superyachts to describe the finest yachts built in the world after the development of the International Superyacht Society in 1998. The Superyacht Society (www.superyachtsociety.org) is an organization that gives the industry a unified voice and advocates on its behalf, further promoting good yacht design and craftsmanship by awarding yacht designers and builders through annual peer-review awards.

Unlike the superlative prefixes mega- and giga-, which are more size-oriented (and obviously influenced by the digital age we live in), some experts argue that the term superyachts is one geared more toward the quality of the boats than anything else. In 1988, an annual book featuring the most splendid superyachts built in the previous year, appropriately called *The Superyachts*, was first published by Boat International Publications. At that time it was more or less a new expression, and the editor, Roger Lean-Vercoe, explained it like this:

"In our view, a 'superyacht' is a vessel that is generally large—probably, but not necessarily, over 30 metres (100 feet) in length—but, most important, it is a yacht which meets the highest standards of design and construction. In addition, it is a yacht that excels in one or more particular fields, be it craftsmanship, the ornateness of the interior, or even the sheer size of the project."

In Volume 18 of *The Superyachts* (2005), Lean-Vercoe repeats this definition, except he has raised the "generally large" figure to 40 meters (130 feet) as the minimum cut-off—again pointing out, however, that quality trumps size in the nomination of a superyacht.

And yet, despite that definition's reference to a longer length, megayacht and superyacht are most often used interchangeably, and the length at which boats become designated as either is, at the very minimum, 80 feet/24 meters. Meanwhile... the debate continues.

Gigayachts—Going Overboard

Finally, in the last several years, we have had a new development in this confusing superlative naming game. The media as well as industry commentators tend to coin phrases for the yachting community to use, and with all due respect, they love choosing names to sexy things up a bit. It is a fact that yachts are being built bigger and bigger each year, and it would seem the larger-than-life owners who can afford to build them have gotten into an unspoken competition of "who has the largest toy." The term gigayacht was therefore born to describe mega- and superyachts well over the 300-foot (91-meter) mark, which is equivalent to a full-length American football field. How that term came to be, though, isn't entirely clear.

When Diane Byrne worked for *Power & Motoryacht*, she was the moderator for its popular Megayachts forum, and she recalls the first time she saw "gigayacht" used was an offhanded comment posted by one of the forum users. "He was talking about how yachts were getting so big that a new word was going to be needed," she says. "Gigayacht sounded like a funny word at first, like something out of computer technology, but it worked—'mega' was a phrase from the same technology, after all. Interestingly, a newspaper article a few weeks later quoted that forum post. The word gradually seemed to take on a life of its own in other mainstream media. Maybe the reporters saw the forum or the first newspaper article quoting it, or maybe they thought they themselves coined it. But some definitely seemed to think that everyone in the yachting industry used the term back then, which nobody did." Byrne says industry representatives still prefer using "megayacht" and "superyacht," though they do know exactly what someone means when they say "gigayacht." These mammoth structures end up being more like small cruise liners when we consider their size. Only again, they are still privately owned and are therefore yachts, nonetheless!

For simplicity's sake, I will be referring throughout this book to the vessels on which I want YOU to seek employment as either luxury yachts or megayachts. There will be job opportunities out there to work on yachts in the 70 to 80-foot range (21.4 to 24 meters), but you can assume that for your first job, you will be looking for a stew position where you are not the only interior crewmember onboard—which would be the case on vessels this size. (To help you understand this, I include a crew size chart showing how many crewmembers the various-sized yachts tend to carry in Chapter 3.) It's going to take working under another stew, known as a chief stew, on a larger yacht before you are able to handle a yacht's interior on your own. Therefore, you will more likely be searching in the megayacht or superyacht categories.

Confusing, huh? I have included a table of comparison in **Table 1-2** for your review.

Yacht Classifications Table	
SIZE IN LENGTH	**CLASSIFICATION**
10 to 22 ft. (3 to 6.7m) American Football Field Equivalent: 3rd–7th yard line	**NOT Yachts** Called "Runabouts" or just plain "Boats"
22 to 39 ft. (6.8 to 11.9m) American Football Field Equivalent: 8th–13th yard line	**Cabin Cruisers or "Starter Yachts"** Still not there yet.
40 to 70 ft. (12 to 21.3m) American Football Field Equivalent: 14th–23rd yard line	**Yachts (It's Official!)** Although not requiring crew, yachts in this size range may have 1–3 crewmembers on a part- or full-time basis.
70 to 80 ft. (21.4 to 24.4m) American Football Field Equivalent: 24th–26th or 27th yard line	**Yachts and Luxury Yachts** 80 ft. (24m) is where a yacht is officially subject to a special code of boat operations; however, some yachts falling just shy of this length will adhere to these standards anyway. Some 60–70 ft.+ yachts will also carry 1–2 crewmembers onboard full-time.
80 ft.+ (24.4m+) American Football Field Equivalent: 27th yard line and up	**Luxury Yachts, Megayachts, or Superyachts** (and you can still just call them Yachts) At 80 ft. (24m), yachts are held to certain safety regulations and standards, including requirements for full-time, professionally trained crew onboard.
100 ft.+ (30m+) American Football Field Equivalent: 33rd yard line and up	**Luxury Yachts, Megayachts, or Superyachts** Some industry experts argue that this is the point at which yachts enter into the Mega- or Superyacht category.
130 ft.+ (40m+) American Football Field Equivalent: 43rd yard line and up	**Superyachts** Some industry experts argue that this is the point at which they begin calling a yacht a Superyacht. Please note that still others say Superyachts can also be 80 to 120 feet. There is no official answer.
300 ft.+ (91m+) American Football Field Equivalent: an entire 100-yard football field and larger!	**Gigayachts** Due to their larger size, Gigayachts are subject to an entirely different set of safety regulations and building standards. They will carry more guests and more crew than the smaller Megayachts. Industry experts don't typically use this term, instead still referring to them as Megayachts and Superyachts. Mainstream media, however, sometimes use the word.

Table 1-2

Note: In the above chart, the American football field equivalent distances are marked from the starting point of the goal line.

A Yacht's Interior

"Champagne wishes and caviar dreams..."
—Robin Leach, host of *Lifestyles of the Rich and Famous*

So, let's admit it: Those of us over the age of 30 will be forever intrigued by the TV show named *Lifestyles of the Rich and Famous*. That show—and more hip versions of the same concept, such as MTV's Cribs and VH1's *The Fabulous Life* series—rivet us to our sets as we gain a glimpse inside the world these people inhabit. We peruse the gossip columns and tune in to showbiz news programs for the latest goings-on in their personal lives. We dote over the cars they drive, the exotic resorts they stay in, and the mansions they own.

Well, that's what yachts are: They are the homes and vacation places of the world's privileged few, only in this case, they float on water; therefore, they move. And if there's one thing yachts can give to members of the most elite and envied people on the planet, it is a safe haven to which they can escape—far, far away from the paparazzi and hordes of fans who flock to them wherever they go on land.

Floating Cribs

Itineraries and guests aside, yachts themselves are the epitome of luxury, filled with posh amenities synonymous with extravagant living. They are built to impeccable finish by craftsmen—considered artisans as opposed to simply boat builders—and customized using only the rarest and most exquisite materials available. The interiors are maxed out in majestic quality: ornate woodwork made from exotic timbers, decadent furnishings (most of them handcrafted), and the world's finest marbles and semi-precious stones adorning the walls, floors, ceilings, hand railings, and even the instrument panels.

Step inside to find what qualifies as "necessities" aboard these oceangoing toys of mankind's most affluent. You'll discover silver tea sets, gold faucets and fixtures, silk-padded wall coverings, gleaming brass, rare antiques, and fine works of art. Many of these superstructures are outfitted with fitness centers, saunas, wine cellars, and in some cases swimming pools and personal cinemas. There are even video libraries with a selection that would rival that of Netflix or Blockbuster.com. The more elaborate yachts may include onboard helicopters, submarines, and, if you can imagine, hydraulically powered platforms that fold down or slide out from the side of the vessel to form private beach clubs.

Your Future "Office"

Most of the rooms you typically find in the finest of homes are present on these boats; they truly are portable villas. The following "tour" explores a sampling of what makes up a luxury or megayacht's interior. (Oh yes, and please remove your shoes.)

- **Bedrooms**—Known on a boat as **staterooms** or **guest cabins,** on a yacht they are comfortably appointed, elegantly decorated, and complete with the little extras one would expect from a considerate host. There is a master stateroom, or master cabin (often called the owner's cabin), for the owner or lead charter guest. There are cabins designated as VIP, which are spacious and often come with elaborate bathrooms, not to mention en-suite dressing rooms and offices. And finally, there are standard guest cabins, with perhaps less room and smaller bathrooms than the master and VIP staterooms, but which are luxury suites nonetheless. Expect every cabin onboard to come equipped with an array of high-tech gadgets: plasma TVs, sophisticated stereo equipment, DVD players, and iPads that control them all.

↔ **Bathrooms**—Bathrooms on boats are called **heads.** Each stateroom has its own private head, and here again, the VIP and the master cabins have larger and more lavish accommodations. Many master-cabin heads come complete with large walk-in showers and saunas, Jacuzzi tubs, and sometimes even his-and-her toilets. European bidets are commonly found in all of the guest-cabin heads on a yacht. There are also one or two heads located in the public areas of the vessels, and these are often referred to as **day heads.** On one yacht I worked on, there were gold sinks in both the master-cabin head and the day head.

↔ **Living Room(s) and Lounges**—The equivalent of a living room on a boat is referred to as a **main salon** or **main saloon.** This is the area where guests congregate, and there is ample seating. Either term, salon or saloon, is correct, but salon (which is French for *living room*) is the more commonly used of the two. I have heard industry people speculate that the reason saloon (rhymes with *balloon*) ever came about was due to its reference to the bar area present in this room (as the word saloon can also mean *tavern*). But no, the word saloon is, in fact, a nautical term meaning "a room for socializing on a passenger ship." Less formal public lounging areas, appropriately called **lounges,** are also found onboard, and they are often named for the area in which they're located—such as a sky lounge, found in the upper deck areas of the vessel.

↔ **Dining Room(s)**—This room is a standard on any megayacht, and on the larger boats, you will probably find two—one formal and one informal. And that's just on the interior. Additionally, there are outdoor areas on various decks for alfresco (meaning "open air") dining.

↔ **Bar Areas**—There are typically a number of bars scattered around a yacht. Some are in public areas where stews fix drinks in front of the guests, and others reside in service areas outside of guest view. There is at least one public bar on the interior of a yacht—in or near the main salon—and at least one, but probably more, on the exterior.

↔ **Owner's Study/Office/Library**—A lot of owners do business on their boats, so you will likely find a private working area either in the master cabin or in a public area for other guests to share.

↔ **Private Cinema/Theater**—Another name for this is a media room, or it could be one of the vessel's lounges. If one exists, it is a public area designated for activities such as viewing movies or sporting events. A big-screen TV is a staple to this room, even if there is one already in the main salon. You'll also find extensive DVD, CD, and even digital media libraries, satellite TV access, fancy sound systems, and computers with all the bells and whistles.

↔ **Gym**—This is standard on larger vessels. And the good news is that the crew can sometimes use it. You'll find treadmills, elliptical trainers, stair climbers, weight machines, and free weights. Whatever this room has, you can count on it being the latest "in" machine.

- ↦ **Foyers/Atriums**—These are chambered areas that connect passageways or serve as a landing space between staircases. You will typically find one at both the side entrance to the vessel and on each deck in the guest areas. Expect marble floors.

- ↦ **Saunas and Hot Tubs**—Not only are you likely to have saunas and Jacuzzi bathtubs in the master and VIP cabins, but having a Jacuzzi hot tub on the top deck is a given.

- ↦ **Staircases and Elevators**—Yachts are equipped with staircases galore: inside and out, some even winding, or spiral (not installed with the stews in mind). Elevators have become common in recent years, too, with some being glass-enclosed, with murals rising alongside them, and topped by skylights to look and feel more luxurious.

- ↦ **Cloak Rooms/Closets for Storage**—This is self-explanatory. (What I wish had been self-explanatory was how to keep them neat and organized.)

- ↦ **Observation Areas**—These are places where the guests congregate for a view of the ocean or surrounding spectacles.

Note: The crew areas of a vessel, including work and living spaces, are covered in Chapters 5 and 11.

Who Onboard Can Afford All This?
—The Owners, the Guests… and Their Money—

"We had a very famous Hollywood couple on as guests of guests. They stepped off the boat one day, and that's when the crowds gathered… and that is what people will remember. As for who the primary charter guest was—the one who'd invited that couple onboard—no one would know who that person is… but it's HUGE money."

—**Tish Owen George**, a chief stewardess
and yachting professional for over 15 years

Before I entered the yachting industry, the only real reference points I had with regard to luxury yachts were that Aristotle Onassis had owned one, Natalie Wood drowned falling off of one, and that the British royal family often traveled on one, including the late Princess Diana and Dodi al Fayed.

I suppose those examples are a bit outdated now. In recent years, the paparazzi have become increasingly skilled at tracking down their prey and are cranking out photos of celebrities and dignitaries vacationing aboard these grandiose vessels more than ever before. You've perhaps seen the pictures in tabloid magazines that include some of the most breathtaking yachts in existence paired with such images as: Rihanna hanging out on a sundeck, Posh and Becks taking a dip in the sea, Prince William and his new bride Kate vacationing with their fellow royals, and Beyoncé being whisked ashore on a tender boat by an ever-helpful deckhand.

Lately, mainstream media sources have jumped on the bandwagon, producing exposés on the mind-boggling world of megayachts, their extravagant features, and their even more extravagant owners and guests. And they aren't all well-known people, either. I've talked about the guests you have heard of, but in this next section, we'll get to those who are less familiar.

Owner-ship: For the Hull of It

People often associate yachts with big-name superstars. In actuality, a majority of the owners and many of the people who charter these boats have nothing to do with Hollywood or its media circus. Rather, they are major industry tycoons and business giants: moguls, magnates, oil barons, and even sheiks and heads of state. A lot of their names most of us wouldn't recognize. They may have invented something that we all use on a daily basis, or they founded and own things like international shipping companies, steel corporations, or computer software empires. Even still, some of them inherited their fortunes—hundreds of millions of dollars, if not billions. It would be a mistake to lump them all into one category, for their backgrounds are diverse. But the one thing they all have in common: a boatload of disposable income.

Have you ever taken a peek at *Forbes'* annual "The World's Billionaires" list? I thought it might be interesting to conduct a small study of how many of the world's most financially well-endowed are yacht owners. It was not the easiest task, but I can report that there was a lot of crossover with *Forbes'* 2013 list and the 2012 list of "The World's 100 Largest Yachts," published annually by *Power & Motoryacht* magazine (and also known as the *PMY* 100)—where the owners are even mentioned, that is. (For some of the lesser-known vessels out there, the owners' names are kept anonymous.)

Here are some of my more interesting findings: Paul Allen, the co-founder of Microsoft (along with Bill Gates), and weighing in at #53 on *Forbes'* 2013 list with a mere 15 billion dollars, is the owner of not just one, but *two* megayachts. Only the larger of the two is big enough to make *Power & Motoryacht's* list of "The World's 100 Largest Yachts," and it actually qualifies as a gigayacht because it is 414 feet long. In fact, that yacht, M/Y *Octopus* (which, by the way, features a full-sized movie theater onboard), is also the world's tenth largest yacht. (Rather, it's the world's tenth largest that is not state-owned. *Power & Motoryacht's* list excludes yachts owned and maintained by heads of state—and several of those vessels are actually larger. Let it also be noted that the *Forbes* billionaires list does not include royal family members or dictators who derive their fortunes as a result of their position of power, nor does it include royalty who, often with large families, control the riches in trust for their nation.)

With regard to Allen's *Octopus*, it held the first place rank on *PMY's* annual list until 2004 when Oracle founder Larry Ellison (the world's fifth-richest man in 2013, with 43 billion dollars) launched his second megayacht, M/Y *Rising Sun*, which beat Allen's *Octopus* by nearly 40 feet. Funny enough, Ellison sold *Rising Sun* and built a smaller megayacht—no slouch, though, at 288 feet—because it was too difficult to pull something that big into a marina. (If you're familiar with the Internet meme #firstworldproblems, I'm sure you'll agree that's one of them.) Despite the recent economic downturn, the quest to build one of the largest private palaces on the water doesn't seem to have slowed much: Since Ellison's and Allen's yachts once held the top two positions on the *PMY* 100, by fall of 2012 they had slipped to 6th and 10th places, respectively, as new builds continue to increase in size year after year.

At the end of 2012, the world's largest yacht was the 533-foot M/Y *Eclipse*, built by Russian billionaire and owner of the U.K.'s Chelsea Football Club, Roman Abramovich. Abramovich ranked 107th on the 2013 *Forbes* billionaires list with an estimated net worth of 10.2 billion dollars. Wilder still, Abramovich seems to have a fondness for not only size, but quantity: three of his five yachts hold a spot on *Power & Motoryacht's* list of the 100 largest. Oh, those boys and their toys!

And yet, in April 2013, M/Y *Eclipse* was outranked (dare I say "eclipsed") by an even bigger boat, M/Y *Azzam*. Launched by Lürssen, a leading shipyard for large luxury yacht building, Azzam is now the largest yacht in the world at 590 feet (180 meters). (I would say "shazam!" is more like it.) A yacht that size—most definitely worthy of the gigayacht classification—will require a crew of 100! It is also rumored to have cost its would-be owner around 627 million dollars. While the Lürssen yard won't comment on the yacht's owner, it is rumored to be Sheikh Khalifa bin Zayed Al Nahyan, president of the United Arab Emirates. That has yet to be verified, but CNBC and other mainstream media sources have reported that the vessel is likely linked to the royal family of the United Arab Emirates (who, remember, won't appear on *Forbes'* billionaires list because the magazine excludes from consideration royal families and heads of state).

More examples of individuals who own some of the largest yachts in existence are: Steven Spielberg, the famous movie director; Leslie Wexner, the owner of Victoria's Secret and The Limited group of stores; Mark Cuban, the owner of the Dallas Mavericks basketball team; and the Latsis family (as in Paris Latsis, Paris Hilton's famous ex-beau). Oh, and remember when I mentioned before that Larry Ellison sold M/Y *Rising Sun* to someone else? Yeah, well that was to David Geffen, who, along with Steven Spielberg, is one of the three DreamWorks SKG founders. Geffen also owns the 377-foot M/Y *Pelorus*, #17 on the *PMY* 100, and he falls into the top 200 richest in the world with a ranking of #198 on *Forbes'* 2013 list due to his 6 billion dollar net-worth. But it's not simply a yachtMAN's world out there at sea, as M/Y *Carinthia VII* is the largest yacht owned solely by a woman: German-Austrian retail giant Heidi Horten. *Carinthia VII* is just under 319 feet and ranks 25th on *Power & Motoryacht's* 2012 list, while Ms. Horten herself came in #423 on *Forbes'* 2013 list with a 3.2-billion-dollar fortune to her name.

Note: When you see the names of luxury yachts in print, they will often be preceded by one of the following prefixes: "M/Y" or "S/Y." This stands for "Motor Yacht" or "Sailing Yacht."

Eye-Popping Price Tags

So what kind of money are we talking here? A realistic cost for an average megayacht, 80 to 100 feet in length, used or relatively old, and sort of, kind of, ready to go: a minimum of 5 million dollars. A brand new 100- or 120-footer, and you're now talking $10 to $20 million. Once we get into the 140- to 180-foot range, luxury yachts can set the buyer back $30 to $50 million+, new or used, depending on who the builder is and what bells and whistles are found onboard. There is no limit to what some of these yacht purchasers want, and shockingly, can afford. In fact, the new gigayachts that are launching onto the scene—these gigantic 300- to 500-foot behemoths—are costing their insanely wealthy owners hundreds of millions of dollars.

And that's just to take ownership!

Keeping the Ship Afloat

Buying or building a yacht is one thing, but then comes the cost of operating one of these multi-million-dollar playgrounds at sea. The rule of thumb is that it will cost a minimum of 10 percent of the yacht's price tag to keep it running. Yet, a lot is going to depend on size because needs tend to grow exponentially with a vessel's length, including the number of crew. Then, there is dockage, or the cost of keeping it "parked" somewhere. Here again, the more space required, the larger the financial burden. Maintenance expenses alone can be astronomical—including repairing, painting, or refitting parts of the interior. Next, we have fuel costs…

Need I say more?

There are a lot of variables. Still, buyers are advised that the operating cost of owning a luxury yacht is going to be, on average, 10 percent of the vessel's price, regardless of size. That means for the media magnate who owns a 50-million-dollar yacht, he's going to be shelling out an easy $5 million a year just to keep it running!

I Must Confess…

I knew very little about the high-society life when I entered yachting.

Louis Vuitton luggage, Christofle crystal, Prada pumps, Mont Blanc pens… What did I know of these things? *Nothing.* Make no mistake about it, my middle-class upbringing left me flat-out clueless when it came to this lifestyle I was now catering to as a yacht stewardess.

Case in point: We had the heiress to a multi-billion-dollar fortune onboard, and while we were docked in the chic port of St. Barts, she went on a shopping spree. Upon her return, she asked me, "Julie, would you run over to one of the boutiques and pick up the items I just purchased? They are preparing my bags now."

Not a problem.

She then proceeded to tell me the name of the shop. Here is what I heard: "Air-mayz."

Hmmm. I wasn't sure how to spell it, but I imagined it to be something like "Airmez" or "Airmais"… you know, something French-like. So, off I went to complete this seemingly simple mission.

There I was, wandering the streets of this posh celebrity mecca, dressed in my casual daywear yachting uniform: khaki shorts, Sperry deck shoes, and a white t-shirt, with only the name of my yacht adorning the left breast pocket to lend me credibility as a likely visitor to such a destination.

The brisk succession of shops along the harbor was like a scaled-down version of New York City's Madison Avenue: Dior, Tod's, Bulgari, Cartier. I kept scanning the storefront signs—one after the other… They came, and they went.

"Air-mayz, Air-mayz, Air-mayz," I repeated to myself as I walked back and forth, back and forth. But I didn't see it.

And then it dawned on me: *Hermès!*

Seven years of studying French, and even more years as a *Vogue* magazine subscriber, and it took me that long to realize it. I had walked past the Hermès storefront at least five times by that point, reading the name and thinking to myself, "Now there's Hermès (as in 'HUR-meeze'—like the Greek God)… Nope, keep going."

But yes, that was it: "Hur-meeze" was "Air-mayz" (and Hermès was Hermès), and with a snort of self-disgust, in I went.

The formidable-looking saleswoman standing guard over the locked-up case of thousand-dollar silk scarves looked me over, and I swear even crinkled her nose a bit. The only patrons perusing the shop were a small group of women at the front counter—each of whom looked as if she'd just stepped off a Paris runway—and they decided to stop and stare as well.

"Uh, good afternoon," I began, trying to sound as official as possible, "I am here to pick up some recently purchased items for Mrs. X."

Okay, that settled them down; I posed no threat. They knew I wasn't there to hold anyone at gunpoint, or worse off, breathe on their scarves. They turned back to what they were doing, and alas, another clerk appeared from the back, carrying with him not one, not two, not even four, six, or eight, but *10* large shopping bags!

"If you'll excuse me for just one moment," I said, backing up awkwardly, "there are more bags than I expected. I am just going to step outside here quickly and call another crewmember to assist me."

Once outside the door, I ducked into a nearby alley and pulled out my crew radio: "Steve, I'm going to need some help over here. I came to pick up Mrs. X's shopping bags, and there are too many for me to carry on my own. There are ten of them!" Steve came back: "Sure, where are you?"

"Um, well, I'm at the 'Air-mayz' store, but if you're looking at the shop signs, you'll want to look for 'Hur-meeze' because that's how it reads."

"I'm sorry, could you repeat that... where am I going?"

Not wanting to confuse the poor guy, I said, "Oh forget it, just look for 'Hur-meeze.'"

Then, this 23-year-old Australian deckhand—a real beer-drinking, man's-man type of guy—came back over the radio with, "Uh, Jewels... I think you got that wrong. It sounds like you're at the Hermès store—you're just pronouncing it wrong. Hold tight, and I'll be right there."

Even he knew!

(And can you believe that when I got those bags back to the boat and was asked by Mrs. X if I would kindly unpack them, remove the labels from the clothes, and store them in her closet, I calculated the total amount spent on scarves alone, and it was over $12,000! On scarves?)

Charter-ship: Boating with the Big Fish

The yacht-charter market emerged when owners realized they could offset the high running costs of their yachts by chartering them, or renting them out, to other parties and individuals for a fee. Today, it's become even more popular, as the tax benefits of placing a yacht into charter service can be significant. Owners are able to deduct certain expenses from their federal taxes because they are running their boats as businesses.

Another factor in the yacht charter business is that many wealthy people find it more convenient and economical to simply rent someone else's yacht than to take on the full brunt of buying and maintaining one themselves. Besides, most owners cannot find the time to use their yachts year-round. Many of the wealthiest are known for only spending about four to six weeks a year enjoying time on their own personal vessels. Why hassle with ownership when today a person can charter a $30-million yacht for $300,000 a week?

You did read that correctly: $300,000 a week is a not-uncommon megayacht charter fee. As with yacht purchases, a boat's length and the number and style of onboard amenities dictate pricing. Other factors that can come into play are the time of year and the location where a voyage will take place. Some of the highest-end boats go for $500,000 a week and up. In fact, according to *Power & Motoryacht* magazine's "The World's 100 Largest Yachts" 2012 article, at roughly 535 feet, M/Y *Eclipse* is one of most exclusive and most expensive charter yachts, going for $2 million per week! To put that into perspective, just seven years ago, the most expensive charter yacht available was the 245-foot M/Y *Leander*, at $490,000 a week. At 282 feet, Steven Spielberg's M/Y *Seven Seas* is also among the world's most expensive. With amenities such as a 15-foot infinity pool and adjacent indoor cinema, the yacht charges, for one week of splendor for 12 guests, a staggering $1.3 million! And can you imagine being able to control every function on a yacht, from the blinds to the lighting to the music, with the touch of an iPad? Well, the 197-foot M/Y *Solemates* has an app for that, and most recently Sean "Diddy" Combs paid $690,000 for a week spent enjoying that high-tech amenity.

Now here's what will really shock you: When a person or private party charters a luxury yacht, the price they pay is, in all but a few rare cases, *not* all-inclusive. The charter fee— that is these $300,000 and up weekly rates—is what it costs to rent time on the boat, and that's about it. The crew are salaried fixtures who live onboard, and thus are included in the charter package. But if the clients want to take the yacht anywhere (which requires fuel), to dock it in any fancy ports (which requires a docking fee), or if they want to eat or drink (gourmet cuisine, wine, and even soft drinks and bottled water), *that's all extra*. Other add-ons include any telecommunications costs, taxes, and the most important one (in my opinion): CREW GRATUITY!

The Chartering Types

Now *here* is where you get the celebrities. While most people whom we consider famous—successful recording artists, big-screen actors and actresses, best-selling authors, professional athletes, supermodels—do boast big bank accounts, few can afford to own and operate a megayacht. They can, however, spare the pretty penny or two to charter one.

And they do.

While guest privacy is vehemently protected in this industry, it is common knowledge (thanks to various media) that some of the more notable big-name yacht charterers include the following: Rihanna, Simon Cowell, Kim Kardashian, Jennifer Lopez, Lindsay Lohan, Jay-Z and Beyoncé, John Travolta, Paris Hilton, Rod Stewart, and the list goes on...

Now take note: Just because they're photographed traveling onboard does not mean they're footing the bill. The deal with a lot of the major stars is that they often get hosted by the more obscure, yet very noteworthy, yacht owners and charterers. It's one of the benefits of stardom, I suppose: Everyone, including the world's most powerful, wants to be associated with you when you're a celebrity. One prime example is supermodel Naomi Campbell, whom I recall seeing three times in one year—in St. Barts, Capri, and Cannes—on yachts docked either next to or just down from the one I worked on. And yes, that was on three *different* yachts. A gladly welcomed guest in each instance, I'm sure—adding a touch more glamour to some already glamorous scenes.

It's also not uncommon to find many world leaders and politicians traveling on yachts. Due to the privacy factor, and the ability to move from place to place, high-ranking officials and dignitaries find this environment perfect for holding top-secret meetings. Note that in most cases, these are not the people paying for the trip; rather, big-money yacht owners, again, love to rub elbows! I myself had the former Prime Minister of a country (not the United Kingdom) onboard during a charter. And a couple of my yachting colleagues have confided to me, years after the fact, that they once hosted United States senators, and two former Presidents.

So, that is much of what working on luxury yachts is about: offering superlative service to the world's most powerful people. That's not to say that it's all about worshipping the ground these individuals walk upon (or the water they float upon); however, you should know before we go any further that in dealing with the elite of the elite, you need to leave behind any "I'm too good for this" attitude. Okay, I'll admit that some of the demanding trophy wives can be a little tough to deal with, but for the most part, the owners and guests are worthy of the utmost respect. Crew need to take a pride in what they do and realize they are an integral part of the experience these people have onboard. After all, there are plenty of rewards to reap in return; thanks to these people, yacht crew are afforded incredible opportunities!

> *"Keep in your mind that you are more than just domestic help. As a yacht crew, you have finer training, you have received safety training, you know about the nautical side of things, and you also have a more intimate relationship with the guests than, say, the housekeeper at the Radisson. That's why they're paying $400,000 a week for your services. It's because you are a different echelon of hired help. Still hired help, mind you, and that is a concept hard for some people to overcome."*
>
> —**Tish Owen George**, a chief stewardess
> and yachting professional for over 15 years

I Must Confess...
It was amazing what some of our guests deemed a necessity.

When guests are paying $25,000+ per day—plus fuel, food, oil, and port charges—you give them what they want. And I quickly learned that they aren't shy about telling you what that is.

I once served some guests from a prominent investment brokerage family; they'd chartered us for two weeks in the Caribbean. Upon arrival, one guest noticed that we had only 100 DVDs onboard and immediately went to a video store on St. Barts and tried to buy every movie in stock. Another guest on that trip said she "needed" a down duvet, which isn't easy to come by in the islands.

Over time, I got used to these types of demands. I wouldn't be fazed by the guest who freaked out when we couldn't find Special K cereal in Croatia, or the guest who had Domino's Pizza helicoptered in while we were anchored out near a remote island in the Bahamas. But in the beginning, simple Hoosier (an Indiana native) girl that I was, I was surprised by what constituted a "necessity."

Another great example:

When I took a Stewardess Training Course at American Yacht Institute, two of my classmates had worked on the yacht of a well-known billionaire's family, and with little prompting, they were happy to share war stories. Once, they told me, a guest needed a $2,000 garment cleaned for an event a couple nights later. They were in the Caribbean, and the guest didn't trust the island dry-cleaners, so she flew a crewmember to New York with the garment so it could be dry-cleaned overnight and returned to the boat the next morning.

Oh, the Places You'll Go—The Travel—

"You'll be on your way up!
You'll be seeing great sights!
You'll join the high fliers
who soar to high heights..."
—from *Oh, the Places You'll Go* by Dr. Seuss

The World Is Their Oyster... and Their Playground

All in all, yachting is one of the most jet-set industries in existence. The owners and guests are the crème de la crème, and for these people, yachts are like toys. Likewise, they see the world as their playground.

There's no telling where you might go working on a yacht—probably places you could never afford on your own, even in a lifetime. We're talking St. Tropez, France; Portofino, Italy; Porto Cervo, Sardinia; the islands of Capri, Mykonos, Mallorca, Stromboli, and Corsica... In the Caribbean there's Anguilla, St. Barts, Antigua, Virgin Gorda, St. Kitts, St. Martin/St. Maarten, and Tortola... You'll find yachts in Martha's Vineyard; Cape Cod; Nantucket; Newport, Rhode Island; the Hamptons and in New York Harbor. They travel the Eastern Mediterranean, the Western Mediterranean, French Polynesia, Northern Europe, Alaska, Australia, Fiji, Malaysia, New Zealand, Thailand—the list is as long as the world is wide, so long as they are accessible by water.

Yes, you can literally work your way around the world in this industry.

'Tis All in the Seasons

While the variety of destinations is vast, a majority of yacht itineraries tend to follow a seasonal formula. Yacht goers favor heading to the Caribbean islands during the winter months, and they congregate there from around late November through April. In the summers, it's either over to the Mediterranean or, as some boats prefer not to cross the "pond" (as in the Atlantic Ocean), up the East Coast of the United States. The summer season generally runs from mid-May all the way to September, and in some cases into October.

These seasons I've outlined are typically dictated by climate (obviously boats head where it's warm), but also by necessity. The Caribbean, the Mediterranean, and the U.S. East Coast are simply where the yachting infrastructure—such as marinas, maintenance facilities, and yacht-provisioning houses—is most established, and therefore convenient for facilitating megayachts.

The charter market also has a big influence over the parts of the world that yachts frequent. These seasonal areas I've mentioned are where guests want to travel if they're keen on being seen. Yachts attract like magnets to destinations that host big-name, glamour events such as the Cannes Film Festival and the Monaco Grand Prix, and the bigger boat shows in Antigua and St. Martin/ Maarten in the Caribbean, Miami and Fort Lauderdale in Florida, Monaco in the Mediterranean, and Newport in Rhode Island—all of which fit with this "Caribbean in the winter, the Med or U.S. East Coast in the summer" routine. Charter boats flock to these destinations during such key times of year in order to attract the maximum amount of attention, and hence bookings, from high-rolling charterers—or even buyers if the vessels are for sale. (More information on yacht industry events and when they are held can be found in Chapter 9.)

That's not to say that all yachts stick to these routes. Those that do not charter tend to stray from the standard itineraries, and such boats travel strictly according to the wishes of their owners. These vessels are likely to follow more adventurous paths, such as heading to Alaska, Australia, New Zealand, the British Isles, Northern Europe, Micronesia, or the Pacific Rim. Even some well-known charter yachts are now opting to position themselves in these places, outside of the "back and forth across the Atlantic" pattern, which is spicing up the variety of vacations that charterers can choose to take.

So, you never know where you might end up. In fact, the final resting point for a yacht doesn't even have to be connected to land. "Anchoring out," or staying "on the hook," as it is sometimes called, is when a boat simply drops anchor and hangs out in the water. Land will most likely be nearby, and in most cases within sight, but the point is that vessels do not necessarily have to be docked in ports and marinas to be considered "visiting" a destination. I can't tell you how many places I've been where I never actually set foot on land. But hey, I enjoyed the scenery!

It's the Journey That Matters… But the Destinations Are Nice, too

"Land was created to provide a place for ships to visit."
—**Brooks Atkinson**, American journalist

This is a section that I realize can create a lot of excitement for would-be crew. In order to manage your expectations a bit, please allow me to preface what you are about to read with a cold splash of reality. Yes, megayachts travel to all of these exotic destinations. But, just because a yacht you work on docks somewhere, or anchors off of somewhere, does not mean you will ever step off the boat. I don't want to paint too rosy of a picture here. Working on yachts means a lot of travel, yes, but it also entails a heavy workload for the crew. For a lot of these destinations, you might be seeing them through portholes, never knowing you were ever there until the captain mentions it later. So, to amend that Brooks Atkinson quote above just a tad, we could say that "'land was created to provide a place for ships to visit'—but not necessarily for crew to visit." But don't worry, you'll still be able to experience some of it. (I was always the first to volunteer to run errands ashore.)

Here is a listing of destinations yachts frequent (by no means exhaustive), starting with the more popular and heavily visited regions and ports, especially by the charter vessels, which includes locations in the Western and Eastern Mediterranean, the Caribbean, the Bahamas, and the U.S. East Coast:

Western Mediterranean
- The French Riviera (Côte d'Azur)—St. Tropez, Cannes, Juan-les-Pins, Antibes, Nice, Monaco, Villefranche-sur-Mer, and St. Jean-Cap-Ferrat
- Italy—San Remo, Genoa, Portofino, La Spezia, Cinque Terre, Viareggio, Naples, Positano, Capri, Amalfi, Ischia, Sicily, Elba, the Pontine Islands, Civitavecchia, and Venice
- Corsica and Sardinia—Porto Cervo, the Maddalena Islands, Cala di Volpe, Girolata, Calvi, and Bonifacio
- Spain—Gibraltar, Alicante, Barcelona, El Ejido, Marbella, Benalmadena, the Balearic Islands (Mallorca, Menorca, Ibiza), and the Canary Islands
- Croatia—The Dalmation Riviera, including Losinj, Kvarneric, the Kornati Islands, Sibenik, Trogir, Split, Bol, Hvar, Korcula, and Dubrovnik
- Malta

Eastern Mediterranean
- Greece—Athens, Corfu, Crete, Aretsou, Rhodes, Santorini, Kos, Mykonos... a new port every day
- Turkey—Antalya, Göcek, Fethiye, Bodrum, Kemer, Marmaris
- Cyprus—Limassol
- Israel or Egypt (when it's safe to do so; lately, that hasn't been the case)

Eastern and Western Caribbean
- The British Virgin Islands (Virgin Gorda, Anegada, Jost Van Dyke, Salt Island), Tortola, St. Barts, St. Martin/St. Maarten, St. Kitts and Nevis, Antigua, Anguilla, the U.S. Virgin Islands (St. Croix, St. John, and St. Thomas), St. Vincent and the Grenadines, Carriacou, Mustique, Montserrat, Trinidad & Tobago, Guadeloupe, Dominican Republic, Iles des Saintes, Martinique, St. Lucia, Aruba, Curaçao, Bonaire, Saba, St. Eustatius, Barbados, Turks & Caicos, Puerto Rico, the Yucatan Peninsula, including Cancun and Isla Mujeres (Mexico), and Cuba

The Bahamas
- With over 700 islands and cays to choose from, here are but a few places yachts end up: Nassau, Freeport, Eleuthera, Andros, Exuma, Abaco, Bimini, Walker's Cay, Harbour Island, Cat Island, and Berry Island

U.S. East Coast and Canada
- The Florida Keys, Miami, Fort Lauderdale, West Palm Beach, Florida's Intracoastal Waterway, the Carolina coastline, the Outer Banks (Hilton Head, Beaufort, and Kitty Hawk), New York City, Block Island, the Hamptons, Newport, Martha's Vineyard, Cape Cod, Nantucket, Boston, Maine, more towns throughout New England, and Halifax, Nova Scotia (Canada)

↠ **The Atlantic Crossing**
- When yachts relocate from one side of the Atlantic to the other, there are several stopping points that they all must visit as fuel stops. These are destinations with which most yachties are familiar: Traveling from west to east, yachts will make "pit stops" in Bermuda, the Portuguese Azores, Gibraltar, and then onto a final destination. On the west-bound journey, the route typically includes the Canary Islands, as opposed to the Azores.

Not as frequently visited, but still popular as yacht cruising areas, are the West Coast of the U.S. and Canada, Alaska, and passing through the Panama Canal:

↠ **U.S. West Coast and Alaska**
- The American West Coast and Southeast Alaska—San Diego, Catalina, Seattle, San Diego, Los Angeles, Sausalito, San Rafael, Long Beach, San Francisco, Santa Cruz, Catalina, Seattle, Puget Sound, Vancouver and Sidney (Canada), Juneau, Kodiak, and throughout the protected waters of Alaska
- Mexican Riviera and Baja Peninsula—Puerto Vallarta, La Paz, Manzanillo, Mazatlan, Ixtapa, and Cabo San Lucas

↠ **Panama Canal, Central and South America**
- Panama, Costa Rica, Belize, Guatemala, Honduras, Venezuela, Brazil, Argentina, the Galapagos Islands, and Ecuador (note that South America is not a popular cruising ground due to the security risks in these areas)

↠ **The South Pacific and The Far East**
- The Hawaiian Islands
- French Polynesia—Tahiti
- Australia—Sydney, Brisbane, Darwin, Cairns, Mooloolaba, and cruising throughout the Great Barrier Reef
- New Zealand—Auckland, Whangaparaoa, Russell, Opua, Whangarei, Wellington, and Tauranga
- Fiji and Tonga
- Southeast Asia—Thailand and the Similan Islands

↠ **Indian Ocean and South Africa**
- The Seychelles, the Maldives, the Comoros Islands, Mauritius, Madagascar, and Mozambique
- South Africa—Cape Town, Durban, and the Islands of Zanzibar, Pemba, and Mafia

Turn to Appendix B to see a sample Mediterranean Itinerary.

Here's something fun: MarineTraffic.com displays real-time AIS vessels information and ships' movements throughout the seas and ports—including port arrivals and departures—over Google Earth maps. Choose to see only yachts, or look vessels up by name. Check it out now, and of course, once you're off on your first crew job, let your friends and family follow your voyage around the world virtually: www.marinetraffic.com/ais.

I Must Confess...

I had never even heard of some of the places I made it to working on yachts.

What attracted me to this industry was the seduction of travel... and I wasn't disappointed.

I was hired through a crew agency in Fort Lauderdale, Florida, to fly down and meet my first boat in San Juan, Puerto Rico (and yes, they paid for my flight). I had certainly heard of Puerto Rico, but it's a place I don't think I otherwise would have visited.

From there, our boat journeyed all over the Caribbean. I always thought I had a pretty thorough grasp of this part of the world, and sure enough, St. Martin/ St. Maarten, Antigua, and the U.S. Virgin Islands were on our itinerary—and were familiar to me. But when our captain announced we were heading to Nevis and then on to Anguilla, Tortola, and Anegada, my reaction was, *huh?... where?*

No less shocking was when we headed back to Miami at the end of the season to prepare for an upcoming trip across the Atlantic Ocean. I was given our itinerary: We would be spending one month hanging out at the Miami Yacht Club, getting the boat ready for our voyage and provisioning for the upcoming season (it's cheaper and easier to buy dry food and guest necessities in the States than it is in Europe). We'd then head out in early May for our two-week transatlantic journey, making our first pit stop in Bermuda. *(Okay,* I thought, *I've heard of Bermuda.)* Next, I was told we'd be stopping in the Portuguese Azores. *(Say it again?)* My captain showed me this one on the map; I encourage you to go check it out yourself. It's literally out in the middle of nowhere (far off the coast of Portugal, and in line with the Strait of Gibraltar); and if you do an Atlantic crossing on a yacht, which most crew experience at some point, you'll go there. Our final fuel stop was going to be Gibraltar (Spain) before arriving at our final destination in the seaside town of Viareggio, Italy (near Pisa and Florence).

When I looked at the itinerary for where we'd be headed later in the season, with guests onboard, I drew blanks with nearly every destination: Lindos, Simi, Gocek, Fethiye, Kastellorizon, Limassol, Spetses, Hydra, Kefalonia—all lovely ports in Greece and Turkey, I was told. Not only had I never planned to go to these places, I never knew they existed (little recall from having read Homer's epics in high school English class). And until we actually got to them, I had no way of knowing they would be slices of paradise: azure waters, white villas, and glamorous beaches—dreamscapes.

Of course, not all of our ports of call were unbeknownst to me. We had a charter later in the season that included the Cannes Film Festival, and another where we were docked in the heart of the port (front row seats!) at the Monaco Grand Prix. We later sailed to Dubrovnik, Croatia; Haifa, Israel; and Valletta, Malta. We went all over the coast of Italy (Capri, Portofino, Naples, Positano) and the South of France (St. Tropez, Cannes, Monte Carlo, Nice, Antibes)—so many times, in fact, that some ports began to feel like home.

But that's just it: This yacht was my home. And each day, as I climbed up the stairs from the crew quarters area below, I would emerge to find a different destination awaiting me. Odysseus, eat your heart out!

Mum's the Word
—The Crew—

The major media will continue to get shots of high society's poster children parading around the decks of these mobile monoliths, and the paparazzi will endeavor even harder to capture the unsuspecting stars lounging in retreat mode aboard their sanctuaries at sea. But pay attention to this: What you DON'T see in these photos that most of my yachting colleagues and I DO see is who's standing in the background—handing these high-profile people a towel and a martini when they emerge from the water or when they are relaxing on deck; driving that dinghy (small motorboat) shuttling Paris Hilton ashore to shop in St. Tropez; assisting Cindy Crawford and her husband Rande Gerber as they step off the aft deck of that megayacht parked dockside in Capri ("Oh, Miss Crawford, you forgot your purse!")—that's the **crew**… and that could be **you.**

The lifeblood of this industry is the crew. These are the individuals who live aboard the vessels and look after them year round, guests onboard or no guests onboard. Myriad companies exist to recruit and train, license and place, network and represent, and even consult and insure the crew. If you want to know what went on aboard a yacht on a particular trip, you could just ask them, for they're going to know better than anyone. Ahhh, but they'll never tell!

This is an industry where discretion is paramount. Yachting professionals place importance on being trusted by their clients not only for the service they provide, but for their integrity. If being a yacht stew sounds like a job you want to pursue, please let that be the first lesson. In this line of work, you become privy to a lot of personal details regarding an extremely private and powerful bunch of people, and it is expected that you will endeavor to protect that information and not go spreading it around. In fact, confidentiality agreements between guests and crew are pretty common. Even without those, though, for this industry to continue to thrive and for job opportunities to continue to be offered in abundance, crewmembers should always keep in mind the following warning: "Loose lips sink ships."

There's No Business Like Boat Business
—The Industry—

Yachting is an industry, and it is serious business. The people who make it run include the marine architects, boat builders, craftsmen, and interior designers who create and even refit these seafaring mansions. Then there are the suppliers and service vendors, equipment manufacturers, fuel-bunkering agents, and the chandlers who provision and maintain them. Of course, you have the yacht brokers who sell them, the management companies who help operate them, the charter brokers and managers who handle the renting of them, and the workers at the shipyards and marinas who house and harbor them. There are yacht-insurance companies, yacht-painting companies, yacht-engineering and electrical companies... and this is all in addition to the crew-placement agencies and training schools that I referred to earlier.

To top it off, professional associations and industry-specific publications abound. There are yacht trade shows (not your average boat shows), designed around displaying, marketing, and selling these objets d'art to buyers, charterers, and enthusiasts. Then there are international bodies to standardize the rules and regulations that govern these vessels and their crews. Even still there are societies and organizations that come together on an annual basis to honor and award the industry's finest—from the boats and their architects down to the maintenance workers and crew.

These are the people who make up the yachting community. And from my experience both working among them and interviewing individuals for the writing of this book, they project a monumental sense of pride in their work and the boats and owners they service. You need not concern yourself with much of this industry information now. Your objective for the moment is simply breaking in and working onboard your first yacht—I highly recommend that you try it!

"Every owner, guest, charter client and friend of these key investors in our market, whoever steps foot on board one of the 5,000-plus yachts, needs to be treated with the most incredible level of service, professionalism and attitude that cannot be experienced anywhere else on the planet. These well-oiled machines, both in interior and engineering terms, should be the ultimate escape and experience so that every owner loves spending time on board and tells his friends and colleagues that it's the most fun you can have in the world. If every crewmember can play their role in ensuring that our client base get the best out of yachts, then it is fair to say that crew will be one of the most important parts of the triangle that fuels our fire and makes our industry burn brightly."

—**Martin Redmayne**, Chairman of The Superyacht Group

2

WHAT HAS YACHTING DONE FOR CREW LATELY?
—(a.k.a. The Benefits!)—

"There isn't a specific type of person best suited for this type of lifestyle, in fact the beauty of yachting is the diversity of crew. The industry is a cosmopolitan tapestry taking in all types of people, regardless of age or nationality. There is a place for anyone with a positive attitude. It is most definitely hard work, but the experiences and camaraderie one can take away from working on a yacht are unmatched. It's a wonderful combination of pressure and excitement and a unique opportunity for those willing to put in the time and effort."
—**Mike French**, President of International Crew Training, a Fort Lauderdale-based crew training and placement facility

Professionally trained yacht stews are always in demand. This isn't because it's not an amazing job, but rather, people just don't know the job exists. I've gone over how industry professionals refer to work opportunities in yachting as well-kept secrets. In this chapter, you'll understand where these commentators are coming from when they say that. It's because the pay, perks, and other benefits that accompany yacht crew positions truly are outstanding!

Whether you are willing to commit to this industry for one year, two years (I recommend a two-year minimum), five years, or as a lifelong career, working on yachts can be extremely rewarding on many levels. Not only that, but the work you do, the skills you learn, and the people you meet can all pave the way to a slew of opportunities down the road.

And the best part is: It's relatively easy to get started. It just takes the right attitude and some basic skill level. We won't get into the necessary training it takes to jump into stewardessing until Chapter 7, but what you'll discover here in Chapter 2 is that the yachting industry needs you. And after you see all the great benefits this job can offer, you might even discover that you, too, need the yachting industry.

The Job Market: Boom to Bust, But Coming Back

According to the The Superyachting Index, an annual business report conducted by Camper & Nicholsons (C&N), the megayacht industry represented a figure of $15.12 billion in 2010. That's an astounding number, translating in turn to quite a number of jobs. But, the jobs accounted for in that figure are more than just crew jobs. They're also people employed by marinas, interior designers, naval-architecture firms, and more.

So, here's a better statistic, also from C&N's The Superyachting Index, to chew on: It reported that there were 3,800 megayachts measuring 80 feet (24.4m) and larger worldwide in 2008 and 5,750 units in 2010, with around 365 of the yachts from 2010 delivered during that year. The last report C&N did was in 2011, which listed the 2010 numbers. This means that, if things stayed relatively the same in terms of the number of vessels delivered each year—and heck, even if they dropped significantly—then as of 2013, we could project that there are easily over 6,000 megayachts 80 feet and up afloat.

In doing research on these numbers, I found that other superyacht-industry analysts report even higher quantities of superyachts in existence than that. Boat International Media (BIM) states in its 2013 media kit: "Boat International Database currently lists 9,004 superyachts over 24 metres which represents an astounding US$83.9 billion worth of assets." So, 6,000 vs. 9,000? That's a roughly 3,250-yacht difference. There's just no way there were that many yachts 80 feet and larger delivered from the beginning of 2011 to the beginning of 2013. A few hundred, for sure…but not well in excess of 1,000. So, unless C&N's Index mistakenly references the 24m+ market in that 5,750 figure, when it meant to reference 30m+, I cannot come up with any reasonable explanation as to why the numbers are so drastically different. Granted, C&N's total is just a projection based on numbers and trends from its 2011 report, but as both sources claim to be accounting for all superyachts over 80 feet (24m), that's a bit of a vast discrepancy. And try as I might, I had difficulty getting an answer out of those who I asked. To debate the hows and whys any further is really outside the scope of this book (I know you're thinking, "c'mon, Julie, just tell us how to work on the damn things!")… But here's my point: While the total number of megayachts employing crew worldwide today remains tough to nail down with any accuracy, we can trust that it's no greater than 9,000, and it's definitely well over and above 6,000. Either way, that's a lot of boats to staff!

Due to the superyacht industry's obscurity, it has struggled over the years to recruit enough qualified personnel to fill all the available positions; yet they have managed to get by. The task became more daunting when megayachts started becoming more popular among those who could afford them, especially during the economic boom years of the 1990s. For the boat builders, that meant business was booming, too. By the time the first edition of this book came out in 2006, the boom was so well entrenched that there were too many yachts and not enough crew. Many referred to it as a crew-shortage crisis.

Things took a dramatic turn for the worse, though, when the global economic crisis hit in late 2008. The Superyachting Index found that in 2009, the number of new megayachts delivered dropped by 18 percent. The figure was still down the following year, by 8.5 percent, which the researchers say was 195 yachts. New orders weren't the only things to decline. The Superyachting Index discovered than 33 percent more megayachts were put up for sale in 2010 than in 2008 and 2009.

So how did this affect yacht crew? There were plenty of anecdotes about yachts being mothballed, so to speak, and therefore crew losing jobs. One of the most famous stories involves an equally famous yacht, *The Highlander*, which had been owned by the Forbes family (of *Forbes* magazine fame) for decades. *The Highlander* was kept in New York City and, literally every weeknight, year after year, would head out for twilight cruises around the harbor, entertaining all sorts of advertisers for the magazine and other high-profile individuals that the family knew. That all stopped in early 2009, and *The Highlander* sat in a shipyard in Florida until she sold this summer. Some of her crew had worked aboard her for 20 years; only one retained his job following *The Highlander* being pulled out of service in 2009, kept on to make sure most things were still in somewhat good shape until she could sell.

While that story is an extreme example, the widely read crew newspaper *The Triton*, which regularly surveys captains and crewmembers, found that starting in 2008 and carrying through to the summer of 2009, more yachts were being left tied to the dock. Some captains also told *The Triton* that their owners were either putting their yachts up for sale, or spending only as much money as they really had to, to keep the yacht's systems operating properly. In fact, a survey by *The Triton* in 2007 found that 80 percent of the captains expected their yachts to undergo fall maintenance periods, whereas only a little more than half answered the same way in 2009. "The vessel is for sale, so we're doing only enough to keep her in pristine condition for selling purposes," reported one captain.

By the summer of 2010, though, there was some good news mixing in with the disappointing news. In yet another survey, this time on captains' sense of how the industry was doing, *The Triton* received responses like, "there are a lot of yachts looking for experienced engineers at the moment, and our salaries are getting higher," as much as "more and more yachts are asking for chef/stew positions but want to pay for less than a solo chef."

Contracts Are Still Coming

Even with the global recession continuing on, there is good news: There's a number of abundantly wealthy individuals who can afford this type of luxury. Unlike the general public, the people who have the resources to build or purchase a megayacht are generally outside the trends of typical society. Now, it's true that some among the superrich are keeping their checkbooks in their pockets for the time being, waiting for the economic situation to settle. However, others are essentially unaffected by the economy and continuing to spend their money.

For some hard facts, I turned to the 2012 *ShowBoats International* Global Order Book, an annual summary of new superyacht construction published by *ShowBoats International* magazine (a Boats International Media publication). The 2012 Global Order Book states that there are 629 yachts measuring more than 80 feet long on order to be built worldwide. While that's down nearly five percent from 2011, and still down 31 percent from back in 2009, the number of shipyards reporting new projects is actually *up*. In fact, 209 builders stated that they had contracts, compared with 139 builders in 2008. Some of the builders were new companies, too, especially in Turkey and China. Turkey's yachting industry has been growing steadily for several years, due to a long history of shipbuilding as well as a lower labor cost. As for China, its developing industries are making headlines on a weekly, if not daily, basis, plus it has a sharply rising wealthy class. "While some yards may exist for only one project, the increase of yacht-building venues supports the idea that many buyers are still shopping for value," the report stated. "Interest in yacht ownership by wealthy individuals from emerging nations may indicate a wish to build yachts nearer to their homes, often driven by heavy import duties levied on imported yachts."

Here's another positive tidbit: While we have less yachts under construction, the size of the yachts has grown (and with larger yachts comes larger crews, so it still equates to increased job openings). For example, of the 1,008 megayachts 80 feet and up being constructed in 2008, only 21 of them were over 250 feet. Compare that to 2012 with 692 yachts over 80 feet being built, but where 39 of them were over 250 feet. It would appear that a lot more owners are thinking, "looks like we're 'gonna need a bigger boat!'" (that's a line taken from the movie *Jaws*, if you weren't aware, and it's always a fun joke to pull out with yachties). All kidding aside, if we look beyond yacht length and actually count the fleet of boats in gross tonnage (GT), a bigger quantity of yachts were/ are under construction in 2012/2013 than in 2011, 2010, and 2009. And while the numbers were not finalized in time for the publishing of this book, a rough estimate for 2013 is that there are 670 yachts under construction around the world, including 40 yachts over 250 feet. So the trend continues to be quantity decreases, but size increases. In the meantime, according to statisticians at Boat International Media (BIM), which publishes both *ShowBoats International* and the *Global Order Book*, a lot of projects that were delayed are now being delivered, making the *Global Order Book* smaller, but more active. They also attribute much of the decline in quantity to there being less of the dangerous, speculative builds.

Another reason megayachts continue to be constructed is that technology has made global communications easier. Boat owners are able to remain connected to their businesses even while at sea, doing everything from sending a simple email to making phone calls, even when they're far from the dock. I talked to one yacht captain whose boss spends $25,000 a month for satellite Internet access anywhere in the world. Now that's an owner who wants to conduct business while on his yacht—and it sounds like serious business!

Crew Jobs—A Crisis?

As I mentioned earlier in this chapter, the surge in luxury yacht production last decade had many industry experts predicting a challenge in terms of finding good, qualified crew. As each new yacht came closer to completion and delivery, that meant there were going to be voids for all positions and levels—not just stewardesses, but engineers, captains, mates, chefs, and deck crew, too. While I was writing the first edition of this book in 2005-6, these circumstances represented a great opportunity for those wanting to break into this field as interior crew (which is what stews are).

Yet, as I also explained earlier, when the worldwide financial crisis hit in late 2008, that meant far fewer new construction projects—which, in turn, you might think has led to there being far less of a need for new crew. Thankfully, that's not the case. In fact, according to Australian Superyacht Crew Recruitment & Training Academy, which as the name suggests is an Australia-based crew company, captains and owners are looking for an even higher caliber of crew to work aboard their yachts. On its website, it states, "Those with professional training under their belts will definitely distinguish themselves from 'the rest.' Additionally, those with something extra to offer in terms of life experience and other skills—for example, massage therapy, nursing/medical experience, trades, sports instructing, cooking, childcare, musical ability, hairdressing, beauticians—will certainly be in higher demand due to their wider skill base."

Mike French of International Crew Training backs this up. He says:

> While some boats do offer continued training for crew, for the most part new crewmembers are expected to bring their qualifications with them. More than just a certificate for the sake of competitive advantage in the hiring process, formal training provides the necessary skills to be a better crewmember once hired. The STCW convention [a five-day course required for working on charter yachts, which you will learn about in Chapter 7] forms the very foundation for safety training in the yachting sector, as in any maritime sector, and should be viewed as an investment in your career. Those who become impassioned about learning and constantly improving their trade are the ones that will get the most out of yachting.

So, what should you take away from this entire discussion? Easy: There's still a job market here for you. If you are looking to secure a job in yachting, now's the time.

Ah, but do heed one warning from the owner and operator of American Yacht Institute, Kristen Cavallini-Soothill. Here is what she had to say about the type of crew the industry is looking for:

> Worldwide events have changed the yachting industry, and I am witnessing through teaching aboard and at the various yards that more professionalism is expected. We recruited people into the industry several years ago, and then the economy fell. The end result is that we 'weeded out' some of those who didn't take our industry seriously enough, and what has come about is a push for more professionalism, and a bit of class! Service can be formal or casual, but the professionalism is still expected.... Personal qualities that are needed: professionalism, accommodating, energetic, aware, team-oriented, imaginative, proactive but within guidelines, easy to be around.

One other thing to be aware of if you are an American citizen: Yachts that are registered in the United States (often referred to as "U.S.-flagged vessels") cannot hire non-U.S. workers. They can if they are out of U.S. waters, but even then, if they get boarded by immigration officials, they're looking at trouble. Because of this, American stewardesses are often at a premium—the industry needs more of them. That's not to say that other nationalities won't fare as well, for while a majority of yachts are owned by U.S. nationals, that doesn't necessarily mean that those vessels are registered in America. In fact, according to Camper & Nicholsons' SuperYachting Index, of the 213 megayachts measuring 100 feet and larger delivered in 2009, 16 percent were owned by Americans, and a good portion of those were registered in Grand Cayman (and were referred to, along with other non-U.S. boats, as "foreign-flagged vessels"). There are numerous reasons why owners would choose to register their yachts outside of the U.S., but I won't get into those since it's beyond the scope of this book. Regardless, my point here is: There are still many U.S.-flagged vessels out there, so if you are an American looking to pursue a career in the yachting industry, you are needed.

> *"If I could clone American stewardesses, I would do it. There just aren't enough of them to go around."*
>
> —**Lynne Cottone**, Crew Placement Specialist at Luxury Yacht Group

(Drum Roll): The Benefits

All this talk about serving others, who those "others" are, and the amount of training you might need to stand out from other stew prospects, and I bet you're bound to be wondering by now: "Yeah, so, what's in it for me?" (It's only natural.) The answer: LOTS, if you are willing to put in the work and bring the right attitude.

Salaries to Savor

Salaries for entry-level yacht stewardesses start out between $30K–$43K a year, or $2,500–$3,600 a month. The reason for the variance is that salaries increase in proportion to the size of the yachts, so a 100-foot yacht might not pay as well as, say, a 200-foot yacht. That's not always the case, but when it is, that's usually because the workload will be a bit more demanding—there are more guests and more space to tend to on larger vessels.

Too, as you move up to higher-level positions, the pay increases. When you get started, you enter at what are often called the 3rd Stew or the 2nd Stew positions (also known as Junior Stews) within a crew and make only, for example, $30K a year base salary. As early as three to six months later, however, you could get bumped up a notch on the ladder and find yourself making an additional $500 a month. Advancement really can happen that fast. Periodic performance evaluations are also standard, which can lead to pay increases. (For discussions of crew hierarchies and the rank of positions on a yacht crew, see Chapter 3.)

The first thing people always say after I give them these figures: "Gee, is that all? I thought you said it paid well?" And someone will always add, "Oh, well I can get paid that same amount to take an entry-level office job."

But here's the kicker: *no expenses.*

Most all positions on luxury yachts require you to live aboard and travel with the vessel, and therefore, your room and board are completely covered. It is customary and expected that everything you need on a daily basis is provided by the yacht owner—your meals, your uniforms, laundry detergent, linens, and on most boats, even your personal hygiene products, such as soap and toothpaste. Meanwhile, your earnings automatically go into your bank account.

What other job can you take where, at the end of the year, you have nearly your entire salary sitting in your bank account, relatively untouched? Most people in other industries are lucky if they save 1/10 of the amount they earn in a year. Why? Because they are paying rent and utilities, buying and maintaining cars, and purchasing all the clothes they wear to work each day. And let's not forget groceries.

Here's another kicker (#2, if you will): It won't happen overnight, but after about two years in the industry, stews can often work their way up to the level of chief stewardess (the top position in the interior department that oversees the other stews). I've seen it happen faster than that, but on the larger and busier yachts, it takes a good two to three years of experience to be able to handle a chief stew's responsibilities. Keep in mind as well that chief steward/ess is a management role, which entails a whole new level of leadership duties and requires a supplementary skill set.

But it's worthwhile to achieve such a goal. According to *Dockwalk's* annual Crew Salary Survey in September 2012, chief stews are making a wide variety of salaries these days, and the amount of experience and training they have makes a difference. Of course, the size of the yachts will also be a factor. Compensation for chief stews runs anywhere from $3,300 to $5,000 a month on smaller yachts to $5,200 to $8,000 a month on yachts over 140 feet. It is very common now to see $65K and $70K salaries, or even $90K+ on the much larger vessels.

STEWARD/ESS SALARY RANGES				
STEWARD/ESS RANK	UNDER 100 FT. (30M)	100–140 FT. (30–40M)	140–180 FT. (40–55M)	OVER 180 FT. (55+M)
TOTAL # OF CREW	1–4	4–8	6–12	12+
Chief Steward/ess (sometimes called a Head Steward/ess)	$3,300–$4,000 PM or $39K–$48K PA	$4,000–$5,500 PM or $48K–$66K PA	$5,200–$7,000 PM or $62K–$84K PA	$7,000–$8,000+ PM or $84K–$96K+ PA
2nd Steward/ess (sometimes called a 1st or Senior Steward/ess)	N/A	$3,000–$3,800 PM or $36K–$45K PA	$3,300–$4,500 PM or $39K–$54K PA	$4,000–$4,500+ PM or $48K–$54K+ PA
3rd Steward/ess (sometimes called a Junior Steward/ess)	N/A	$2,500–$3,200 PM or $30K–$38K PA	$2,800–$3,400 PM or $33K–$40K PA	$3,000–$3,600 PM or $36K–$43K PA

PM = per month • PA = per annual

Crew salary information taken from various online and agency sources and cross-checked against Dockwalk's annual Crew Salary Survey, September 2012.

Table 2-1

Keep in mind that with live-aboard positions, you are paid whether guests are onboard or not. That seems obvious since I'm talking salaries here, but you'd be surprised at the number of people who ask me that. Although, don't be fooled into thinking that no guests equates to no work. When no owners or charterers are onboard, the crew is busy doing maintenance work and getting the vessel prepared for the next batch of visitors. (Be ready to accept that the work is never really done on a megayacht, guests or no guests.)

Traditionally, salaries have tended to be a bit less on sailing yachts than on motor yachts. There is a more laidback lifestyle on sailboats, so the service expectations are usually not as high. According to many of the crew placement specialists I interviewed, this has been changing in recent years. Crew working on these vessels really do need to be more knowledgeable about seamanship. Too, there are some pretty spectacular sailboats coming out now for which highly qualified crew will be needed (and rewarded as such). So, while it is changing, you may still find a small variance in base salary averages between motor and sailing yachts.

Now, are you ready for kicker #3?

Tips Ahoy!

Good base salaries and no expenses—those are big benefits in this industry. But where you can make an even *bigger* financial score is with guest tips.

As we've been over (but I'll restate it because some people get confused by this): On charter yachts, when the owners are not using the boat, other guests can pay a fee to use the vessel for what is usually one to two weeks at a time. Now here's a big benefit to working on this category of boat: Charter guests usually tip 10–20 percent of the charter fee to the crew, which can be between $1,000–$4,000 per crewmember for a week, on top of their salary!

This means that, even for the beginners who start out at a $30–$43K base salary, if you can land a job on a charter yacht, you could earn an additional income of $10–$20K a year… In fact, I once made $18,000 in tips in one summer season alone!

Just think: If the boat you work on costs $25,000 a day to be chartered, and you have the guests onboard for, say, 10 days, then that means they paid $250,000 to rent that vessel. (And again, that's before paying for food, fuel, and docking fees; but tips are factored on the base fee.) Even if they only tip 10 percent, that's $25,000. If you have a crew of 10, when the tip is divided equally, you EACH receive $2,500 in tips on top of your salary… All for 10 days of work (albeit hard work and incredibly long days).

This kicker does have a small hitch, though. I don't want to give any false illusions that tips are guaranteed, nor do I want you to think they will always be super generous. I've received tips that sent me into shock (big ones), and I was tremendously let down on a few occasions.

To give you the most accurate scoop, I decided to ask one of the top charter brokers in the business, Debra Blackburn Boggio of Fraser Yachts Worldwide, to comment on how guest tips are handled. A charter broker is the person who books and handles all the logistics of a chartered trip; he or she deals directly with the guests (or in most cases, the guests' personal assistants).

My question to Debra:

I know the topic of tips can be a sensitive one, but if you feel comfortable commenting, a common question I receive from people looking into this industry are about the additional compensation they might expect by taking a job aboard a heavily booked charter yacht. Is tipping guaranteed, is there a standard, and how does the effort a crew puts into a charter affect the gratuity that is given at the end of a trip?

Debra Blackburn Boggio:

Tips are a touchy subject… We brokers recommend a guideline for tipping. Americans are a tipping nation, and therefore the standard of 10–15 percent of the charter fee is what we recommend. However, most countries around the world do not have a tipping environment. Therefore, these clients are not prepared to offer this level of tip, so they expect to offer less, and do. Also, as yachts are getting larger and more expensive, it becomes unrealistic to think that a charterer would spend $350,000+ expenses for a week aboard a yacht, and then give over $50,000 to the crew just as an extra thank you.

Since a gratuity is a gift, it is *absolutely* at the discretion of the client, and no matter what we recommend, the client will still give what he or she feels is appropriate. In some cases that is 5 percent, in some it is 20 percent. A crewmember cannot expect a guaranteed 15 percent every time a charter is aboard. My advice to any new people in the industry is *expect nothing,* and whatever you get will be a bonus.

Hard work is noticed. I recently had a charter client who told me, 'The rest of the crew did okay, but so and so, the stewardess, went above and beyond, so we left her an extra tip.' Clients are always watching. These are the most wealthy, successful people in the world. They did not get that way by being unaware of whom they surround themselves with.

From my experience working on a heavily booked charter vessel, while the tips can vary from 5–20 percent, we most often found they averaged out to 10 percent by the end of a season. Given that the charter fee was so high for our vessel, it meant a lot of extra money. With the tips I made in one season, I was able to pay off my college loans, have some money to play and shop in ports, and I never even touched the salaried income that was wired into my bank account each month by the owner.

Are Strictly Private Boats Strictly Salary?

If tips are only given on charter yachts, what's in it for the crew working aboard boats that are strictly for the owner's use? Good question (and I'm so glad you asked!).

Knowing that crew are motivated to take jobs on yachts that offer chartering because of the potential for tips, many owners who do not charter their boats out (these vessels are called private yachts as opposed to charter yachts) offer other types of added benefits to their crews, such as longer vacation times, handsome yearly bonuses, and even reimbursement for training-program tuition.

I worked on a solely private yacht where the owner liked surprising the crew with sporadic gifts, such as all-expenses-paid weekend trips or an out-of-the-blue gift certificate for online shopping sites. I had another owner who actually tipped the crew when he used his own boat—not the big chunk of cash you can earn off a charter trip, but it certainly wasn't expected, nor was it necessary. You may also have more downtime on a private-only vessel, for unless the owner lives onboard— which is rare—he or she may only use the vessel about one week per month (or less). The other weeks you are doing maintenance projects to ensure the vessel is 100 percent ready when the owner wants to use it.

Yachts that don't charter may also offer slightly higher base salaries. When you consult industry salary charts, such as the one I've included for stewardesses in Table 2-1, you can assume that private-only yachts will award the higher-end figures in the specified ranges. That's not an absolute, but it is most often the case.

Crew Packages Come With Big Benefits

As with any job package, there are other benefits you can expect to receive besides income. Most yacht positions require a minimum commitment of six months to one year. After a short trial period, which can be anywhere from 30 days to three months, additional benefits take effect.

Below is a list of what you might find included in your compensation. There are no set standards in the industry, and this list will vary from boat to boat. In Chapter 10, we will discuss how to inquire during a job interview about what is or isn't included:

1) **Vacation Time**—In regard to annual leave, it varies from yacht to yacht, but most boats will give senior or management-level crewmembers three days per month worked and two days for other crew, which works out to roughly four weeks' paid vacation a year. Several days per month are often given to handle personal affairs, and then a minimum of two weeks' annual vacation away from the boat is customary. The timing can be complicated, and the crew are usually not in control of when they get to take that time away.

   Extended vacations must often coincide with a vessel's schedule and be taken when no guests are onboard. There are some yachts that rotate crew (and this is becoming more and more common), but most just try to give the time off during downtime. For example, they may need to wait until the boat is between seasons, heading into a shipyard for maintenance work, or simply when guests will not be using the boat. That rules out peak season and all major holidays. (Sorry, Mom.) It also typically takes being onboard six months before a crewmember is allowed an extended time away.

   I know of quite a few private yachts that give the crew six entire weeks away from the vessel. During some of that vacation time, they encourage the crew to enhance their training through additional courses. For stewardesses, that could mean going in for more safety or silver-service training, or even better, a week in Napa Valley taking wine courses!

2) **Medical Insurance**—A fair amount of yachts provide basic health-insurance benefits (or reimburse you for your own individual policy). If so, this is usually offered after a probationary period of 60 to 90 days. Whether the yacht offers you your own policy or not, if you sustain injuries during an accident while on yacht business, you are nearly always covered.

   ❖ **INSIDER TIP:** I asked crew placement specialist and former yacht chef Lynne Cottone of Luxury Yacht Group about the standard in the industry with regard to health insurance. Here was her reply: "Some boats will give you medical and dental benefits, some don't even go there. I recommend to crew that they have their own policy anyway because otherwise, every time you change jobs, you lose your insurance. Whenever I carried my own policy, I was reimbursed by the boat—and most boats will agree to that. I think health insurance is something crewmembers need to think about. You know if you get hurt onboard, they'll pay for it, but basic health insurance is something that people need to have."

For a listing of health insurance programs catered toward professional yacht crew, please visit my website: www.WorkOnAYacht.com.

3) **Roundtrip Air Ticket**—It is common on a lot of yachts that, after one year of service, you are rewarded a free roundtrip air ticket to anywhere in the world—for vacation purposes. Not every boat does it, and if they do, it will often be written into your contract. It is also pretty standard industry-wide that if you are terminated from a vessel, they give you a free return ticket to your port-of-hire, or back to your home port. If you leave on your own accord, that could be a different story. It's always best to know your rights before you act.

4) **Bonuses**—Bonuses are a common benefit in the industry, especially on non-chartering yachts where the crew are not earning tips on top of their base pay. Another instance when bonuses are awarded is when crewmembers complete one full year of service on a given vessel. I've even heard of owners who like to give their crew this little extra show of gratitude at more frequent intervals, like every six months. Being rewarded this bit of cash could also be performance-based.

5) **Continuing Education**—To encourage crew retention and longevity aboard their vessels, many owners like to cover education and training expenses. For captains, engineers, and other positions for whom maritime licensing is required, the courses they would take are obvious. Chefs, too, can always find classes to learn new culinary skills. But for stewardesses, the list of additional educational pursuits is long and varied: wine and food courses, Advanced First Aid and other medical-related certifications, massage school, accounting courses, etiquette classes, language courses; and they can even choose to fit in some maritime or navigational training. I know several stews in the industry who actually hold captain's licenses. Others like to fit in classes where they learn to drive the tender or dinghy boats. Obtaining a job where your tuition and expenses are covered (and the time off is given) for advancing your skill set is indeed a major bonus. In the end, the more training you have under your belt, the more money you might make. It also bodes well for your job security.

6) **401K**—Some yachts offer 401K plans, but it is not the standard.

7) **Taxes**—There are instances in this line of work where you are not required to pay income taxes. I don't want anyone to bank on this being the case, especially since the rules and laws surrounding this subject are ever-changing. I can tell you that I once worked on a foreign-flagged vessel, owned by a non-U.S. citizen, that was registered in Gibraltar (a British Overseas Territory off the tip of Spain). Because of the vessel's registration, and also the fact that we were cruising international waters, I was exempt from U.S. taxation on my income. Rather, I had to set up an offshore account to which my income was wired. I did, however, need to pay Social Security tax on that money once I brought it back into the States years later. I know a few current yacht crew who work on American-owned and registered vessels who get to avoid similar income tax payouts if and when they spend more than a certain amount of time working outside of U.S. waters (last I heard it was 330 days out of the year). So, say, if the yacht employing

them spends five months in the Caribbean and five months in the Mediterranean, they may be able to claim back any taxes that were automatically withdrawn when paid by the U.S. owner.

It gets very confusing. In fact, I heard recently that foreign crew are now expected to pay U.S. taxes when cruising our waters, which apparently they can claim back at the end of the year. Like I said, the rules are always changing. Don't count on not having your income taxed, but if it works out that way, you'll probably feel like keeping that same job forever. I know I did!

❖ **INSIDER TIP:** The best advice I have regarding tax laws as they apply to crew is to consult a maritime tax specialist as soon as you've taken your first job. You may even want to do this before you accept an offer, so you know what you will have to look forward to, or not. In the end, you could get excited because you hear a yacht is planning to spend the entire year following one itinerary, and the reality is, that itinerary ends up much different. Yacht owners are notorious for changing their minds a lot (because they can).

There are plenty of tax experts who deal strictly with this industry who would be happy to advise you on any situation. For a listing of yacht-crew tax specialists, as well as financial planners, please visit my website: www.WorkOnAYacht.com.

The Perks

Yacht crew enjoy a tremendous number of perks that people in other jobs can't even imagine. Perhaps the greatest benefit is that you are exposed to a lifestyle you might otherwise never have known: You get to travel to glamorous ports, meet important and famous people, experience luxury, and enjoy a lot of disposable income all the while. For many crew, especially those with watersport hobbies, the biggest lifestyle plus is just being out at sea.

The list goes on, of course. Take a look:

Globetrotting in Yachting—the Travel

> *"It furthers one to cross the great water."*
> —**I Ching**, Chinese classic text

I now know this to be true.

When I came home for my first vacation from yachting, I got in touch with one of my former college professors. I remember his first question to me was, "So, how are you enjoying indentured servitude?" I laughed at the time, but I have to admit, I didn't quite know what that meant. Once off the phone, I grabbed my trusty Webster's:

Entry: Indentured Servant
Part of Speech: *noun*

Definition: a person who is bonded or contracted to work for another for a specified time, in exchange for travel expenses (as in to America back when the English were migrating to the New World).

Well, he got me on that one. And I thought, *Right, that is what I'm doing—but I'm also getting paid a helluva lot to do it… I'm getting paid to travel the world!* I couldn't have felt prouder of myself. Some people would give their right arm to be able to visit some of the places I've seen.

As a yacht stew, you are living and working upon the canvas of the world. But yes, the word "working" is a key factor. While guests coming onboard often prevent you from being able to experience every single destination your yacht visits, there will still be time along the way to enjoy many of them. Here's another reason that respect for your guests must remain in the forefront of your mind: You owe these very people for the ticket you are holding. Therefore, service to them becomes very much a feeling of obligation—and thanks—for allowing you the incredible opportunity to live a free and adventuresome lifestyle.

I had a crew recruiter say to me, "Yeah, but you don't always get to see these places for yourself, so it's not really about the travel." I couldn't believe my ears! For me, just getting a glimpse of a gondola race in Venice from the guest cabin window I was cleaning felt like the opportunity of a lifetime. The alternative? I could have been at some corporate desk job staring out at a busy city intersection with skyscrapers stretching up on every corner…people bustling about to run errands, catch buses, get to lunch appointments…horns honking, brakes screeching, garbage cans falling. No thanks!

While serving as a yacht stewardess, I always had a fascination with the staircase leading up from the crew living area below deck to the main level of the yacht. Some mornings I'd reflect: *At the top of those crew mess stairs lies your job, lies your obligation, lies your responsibility…but also lies your freedom in abundance.* And sure enough, just outside that door (okay fine, or even just that window), a glorious new part of the world always awaited me.

I Must Confess…
Times in port, with no guests onboard, are spent living life to the fullest.

For some, this means partying like there is no tomorrow. Yachties feel this need to maximize the time they get for themselves. Those times can be few and far between—a couple days in a port may be all they will get for several weeks if facing a big charter or an owner coming to live onboard for an extended period.

For others, time ashore with no guests on the horizon means seeking out an adventure, such as taking a weekend away to some random place nearby. Many crew I worked with were known for just "heading out" with no specific destination in mind: just renting a car or taking a train, only to stop when the time felt right. We all did this—even if we could only manage a day trip. Some went alone, some went in pairs, and sometimes we'd go in a big group.

Many of my fellow crewmembers, and this is true for a lot of the industry, had well-traveled or backpacker backgrounds—and, even if they didn't, we all shared a common trait of wanderlust. We were vagabonds at heart. We each wanted to find the most authentic place within a place, to experience a destination like a local, or to behave like explorers, seeking off-the-beaten-path locations and experiences in every port we visited.

When we lived in Palma de Mallorca for several months, our crew did something like this nearly every weekend. The boat was being painted, and so we only worked 8–5, M–F, with an occasional Saturday morning tossed in. Someone was always on the boat standing watch, but if you weren't scheduled for duty, you were GONE. In Mallorca, we had one island to explore, and I'd be willing to bet we discovered a side of it that most tourists—even locals—never see.

When we weren't on charter, I was known for disappearing up to the top deck of the yacht, plugging my laptop into the bar, and typing out my thoughts for hours by the light of the moon. I did this in so many wonderful places—San Juan, Puerto Rico; the island of St. Kitts; Gocek, Turkey; Amalfi, Italy; Golfe Juan, France…

Ah, and running…running was my escape and a way to get out and investigate some of the ports. They were empowering, my runs ashore; even if guests were onboard and I only had a two-hour break. I loved to get on land (when we were docked and I could sneak off, that is) and move by my own two feet. Running in ports like Bermuda, and then Viareggio, on to Genoa, Haifa, and then Palma—it was like one continuous journey in my mind… Feeling like Forrest Gump when he walked for years…I imagined that my feet had carried me all the way to that point…and in many ways, they had.

Even if I were just sent ashore to buy milk in a place like Dubrovnik, Croatia, I took this as an opportunity to soak up all I could of this perk to my job. Compare this to when I go to grocery stores in America, where I put my head down and focus on getting in, getting what I need, and getting out. In Dubrovnik and other ports, instead I was looking around for something to sense, making the effort to capture a memory or new idea, trying to learn a characteristic of the local people, or simply watching how the world carried on in a place that was so far away from what I'd always known. To think of all the lives that had been there just as long as I had been alive, and wondering what they'd been doing… and looking back, to wonder still what they are doing today.

So you see, while you might not be able to enjoy every port of call, or to step on land to explore and play in every destination, the opportunities do come—and when they do, you make the most of them. Meanwhile, you always have the sea.

"If you want to build a ship, don't drum up people to collect wood and don't assign them tasks and work, but rather teach them to long for the endless immensity of the sea."

—Antoine de Saint-Exupery

Making Connections—the People

In the August 19th, 2005 issue of the tabloid magazine, *OK!* (the U.S. version), hip hop music mogul, Sean "Diddy" Combs was interviewed about his summer 2005 charter trip aboard the *Christina O*—a classic motor yacht once owned by the late Aristotle Onassis and restored to its former glory in a massive 2001 refurbishment:

Question from *OK!*: "This $150-million yacht had a $54-million refurbishment. How much do you think it's worth now?"

Diddy's Response: "If you ask me, it's priceless. You will not get on a boat that's built like this or that has a staff like this. The 38-person crew are some of the nicest people I've met. They hung out with us and partied with us. I'm going home next week, and I already miss them."

Note: At 325 feet, M/Y *Christina O* qualifies as a gigayacht. The vessel accommodates up to 36 guests in 18 staterooms; hence, the abnormally large number of crew mentioned in Sean Combs' statement.

You know by now that if you get a job in yachting, you'll be mixing with a very eclectic group of people, most of whom are way up there in the world. Taking care of such individuals and making their trip special allows you to get to know them in a very intimate way. You can establish a relationship with them that perhaps few people even in their inner circles might have. Think about it: When you get them onboard, they are on vacation. You may have the occasional business-related trip, but more often than not, they are there to relax. You get to see the best in people for that reason. I always gained a sense of satisfaction in knowing I enhanced their experience in some way.

I don't want you to think this means you should take a job in yachting to try and schmooze and get favors from rich and famous people, but it is worth noting that this line of work affords you the opportunity to perhaps establish a good rapport with the owners and guests. There is, of course, a fine line. One rule we always had was not to open up too much to the guests or try and take advantage of the relationships we formed with them.

Crew often receive more than their fair share of invitations from guests to come visit them at their homes. Normally, those aren't offers you really take people up on—unless it's an owner or guest you've worked for on many occasions. I know a few crew who have worked for the same owners for years and are treated like family; they do take advantage of such opportunities. But otherwise, guests really don't expect you to call them up one day saying, "Okay, Mr. 'So-and-So,' my bags are packed, and I'm on my way!"

Future job opportunities, though… now that's a different story. It happens all the time where owners and guests solicit crew to come work for them in a different capacity, be it on their estates or in their companies. Again, another no-no: You don't go pushing for it. Being an opportunist when the guests are there to seek privacy is over-stepping the boundaries of this job. The point is to focus on working hard and with sincerity, and when you least expect it, opportunity comes along.

Gaining a Family Away from Home—the Crew

> *"Good company in a journey makes the way seem shorter."*
> —**Izaak Walton**, English writer

The guests aren't the only people you benefit from meeting in this industry. You've also got **the crew.**

People come into this industry from many different backgrounds. You will meet and work with crew from all around the world and from all walks of life. Some will have grown up near the sea, while others will be completely new to it. You'll meet veterans of the maritime industry with years in yachting behind them, and you'll meet "newbies" just like you—many of whom left other careers to do this, and at all different stages of life.

Living, working, and traveling the world together, it's easy to bond quickly. In many ways, you become like family. You'll no doubt walk away with friendships to last a lifetime, not to mention a list of addresses all over the world where you'll always have a free place to stay. Sir Gilbert Parker, the Canadian novelist, put it quite well in his book, *Mrs. Falchion (1893):* "It must be remembered that the sea is a great breeder of friendship. Two men who have known each other for twenty years find that twenty days at sea bring them nearer than ever they were before, or else estrange them."

To this day, I still keep in touch with most of my former crewmembers. I worked on one crew where I was the only American. Alongside me were people from Australia, New Zealand, Scotland, Canada, England, Holland, France, Japan, Spain, and Italy—they made up my family at sea. On other yachts, I worked with Bulgarians, Czechs, Hungarians, Swedes, and even someone from Tasmania. Many of them are friends for life. (Only two do I wish never to see or hear from again.)

And it's not just the crew you work with, either. Yachties run in a tight-knit circle, as they frequent so many of the same places. I know it sounds crazy, since the territory of this industry spans the entire globe. But remember: There are seasonal patterns as to where these boats travel. You may meet a new pal in some port in Bermuda who you later run into in San Remo. It happens all the time. And it can make for some very romantic tales later in life. Ahhh, but I digress...

Living on a Yacht—the Lifestyle

Hello? You get to live on a yacht! That's a huge perk. These boats are fitted to a degree of luxury and extravagance that was for me hard to believe... Well, that's not counting the crew quarters, but when we cover those in future chapters, I'm sure you won't be let down—they're not too shabby.

And don't think you are completely cut off from enjoying your surroundings just because you're there to work. When there are no guests onboard, you get to take advantage of some of the amenities. By this, I don't mean staying in the guest accommodations (although, I had one captain who, the night after a long and grueling charter, let each interior crewmember pick a guest bed to sleep in—we used our own sheets, of course, and cleaned the cabins from top to bottom the following morning), but using the boat toys, such as the Jet Skis, water skis, the Sea-Doos, and scuba or snorkeling equipment, is usually allowed. Then there's the hot tub, or watching one of the yacht's 1,000 or so movies on giant screens, accompanied by some of the most expensive sound systems going. On most of the yachts I know of, the owners are perfectly okay with the crew taking time out to enjoy themselves every once in a while. And let's not forget the food the guests leave behind. That's fair game!

One thing I always found funny was the attention we got in various ports from the tourists who would gather around our boat—my place of employment, and my home—to admire it from afar. If we stepped out on deck in crew uniform, we'd be interrogated by inquiring-minded people hurling questions at us from the dock: "Who owns that boat?"; "How much is it worth?"; "Do you have anyone famous onboard?"; and my favorite: "Wow, do you have a dishwasher on that thing?" Funnier still was when our crew stepped off the yacht in street clothes, on our way to a night on the town: People would take pictures of us, assuming we were guests onboard! I once worked with an assistant engineer who loved signing autographs for people. He would always say, "Oh, yeah, well, I was in the movie *Boat Life*" (fictitious, of course, as was the name he signed: "Engines R. Cooley").

And for all you inquiring minds out there, the answer to the dishwasher question was five. One in the crew mess, two in the galley, one in the stew pantry, and one in the top deck bar. Yes, washing glassware was a never-ending, albeit convenient, chore.

Charity: How the Lifestyle Lets You Give Back

Believe it or not, living and working on a yacht also exposes you to some of the most generous people around. And I'm not just talking about wealthy yacht owners regularly donating large sums of money to hospitals, charities, and more worthy causes, though of course you'll likely meet some of them. Rather, I'm referring to how you as a crewmember can help support some worthy causes that are directly tied to the yachting industry.

While there are many ocean-oriented charities that do great work, two organizations I particularly admire, and ones supported by a number of crew, are YachtAid Global (YAG) and the International SeaKeepers Society. YAG's slogan is "changing the world without changing course." Founded by a former yacht captain and current port agent, Mark Drewelow, YAG connects communities in need, especially isolated ones, around the world with megayachts that will be cruising there or at least nearby, coordinating the delivery of much-needed items like school supplies. Drewelow was inspired to create YAG after spending 20 years on the water and having had numerous memorable and heartwarming encounters with locals. Visit YAG's website, www.yachtaidglobal.org, to learn how you can do everything from donate items to (once you land a job aboard a yacht) get your fellow crewmembers involved in transporting items.

As for the International SeaKeepers Society, it was founded by a group of megayacht owners who were increasingly concerned about the health of the world's oceans. SeaKeepers bridges the gaps between good science and both the business and yachting communities. In fact, many yachts are outfitted with special data-collection devices that automatically send information on the ocean's pH levels, salinity, and more, as well as atmospheric conditions, to leading scientists around the world. The device, called the SeaKeeper 1000, has been endorsed by the United Nations and the World Meteorological Association. Many yacht captains and crew are SeaKeepers Professional members, attending networking events and learning how they can do their part to protect the ocean and assist SeaKeepers in its goals. Visit SeaKeepers' website, www.seakeepers.org, for more.

Ports of Cause (POC) is one of the newest and most progressive groups to emerge in this category and exists to assure clean water globally. POC leverages the yachting industry to effect measurable change around cleaning up the planet's oceans and drinking water so that all forms of life can be sustained. It's model is one that collaborates with and supports non-profits (POC Cause Partners) already doing work in these areas, including Plant A Fish, JoinThePipe, Thirst No More, WaterKeeper Alliance, and International SeaKeepers Society. POC's efforts include global education and awareness; unifying the efforts of like-minded organizations, governments, and communities; high-profile fundraising and experiential red carpet events, as well as rallying the yachting industry behind these causes to demonstrate social responsibility and leadership. In particular, the first measurable initiative that POC is focused on is addressing the Great Pacific North Gyre, the largest landfill in the world filled with millions of pounds of trash—most of it plastic—floating in the middle of the Pacific Ocean and killing our ecosystems. In addition, POC also exists to educate the world about the positive global impact the yachting industry has on the economy, technology, innovation, design, and philanthropy.

I Must Confess...

Sometimes, I felt more fortunate than the guests.

The crazy thing was, even though these guests spent more than my annual salary each day they were onboard, I always felt as though I was the one truly gaining—without spending a dime. Several of the individuals I had onboard commented that they envied my lifestyle and the fact that I'd get to stay, after all the guests disembarked, and sit in the hot tub enjoying champagne and strawberries (granted, it was the champagne and strawberries the guests left behind). And who knew where I'd go next? Maybe Italy, maybe Spain, maybe Egypt, or even Australia.

I worked for one owner who, on every Mediterranean trip, had Kobe beef shipped to the yacht from Japan. If you aren't familiar with it (I sure wasn't), Kobe beef is the most expensive beef in the world. It is a special breed of cattle, and these pampered cows are massaged with Sake and fed beer and special grasses (I've even heard they are played classical music), before they are slaughtered and their tender meat sold for over $300 or more a pound in Japan. The owner liked to order *lots* of it. He even flew in a special chef—one trained in the preparation of this delicacy—whose job throughout the trip was to focus only on cooking this meat.

The owner made a deal with the crew that, when each trip was over, whatever hadn't been cooked was for us to enjoy. If you think that means we kidnapped this Japanese chef and tied him up so he couldn't cook the entire supply, you're wrong. We didn't have to. The owner never went through his entire stock. After one of his visits, we had nearly 20 pounds left over (worth more than $6,000)!

Talk about crew perks: We had a feast!

On another occasion, that same boss suddenly decided he no longer cared for Italian wine. Funny, for at the time he bought his yacht, he loved it so much he had us stock the wine closet with over 100 bottles of it, ranging in price from $500 to $2,000 each. Now he wanted us to get rid of it, to make room for its replacement: French wine.

With less than a week to accomplish that task, we had no choice but to start giving the stuff away. We turned to the shipyard workers where we were staying in Palma de Mallorca—a Spanish island. Now, people in Spain know their wine, and they recognize the finer labels when they see them. As the other stewardess and I walked up to these hourly-wage shipyard painters and, even though neither of us spoke Spanish, managed to convey to them, "Yes, take it, it's a gift," I swear they left skid marks as they skipped off toward their homes, grinning ear to ear.

What we couldn't get rid of, we divided up and stored in the crew closets for ourselves (for days off, of course).

Random Perks

Here are some other perks that you can look forward to as yacht crew:

- ➥ I covered it in the discussion on salary, but it's worth mentioning again: NO EXPENSES. That makes all the difference.
- ➥ The room and board part I went over, but here's another thing: You aren't just getting any old average meals—you eat like a queen or king onboard these boats because you're living alongside a trained chef who is, in most cases, world-class.
- ➥ You have no need for a car, and that's a huge burden to get off your back. That's not to say that you won't be driving; rental cars are usually supplied for the captain and crew to use on yacht business.
- ➥ Uniforms, baby! It would be an extremely rare case for these not to be provided for you.
- ➥ Crew sometimes receive gifts from their owners and guests. I worked for one charter guest who gave each member of our staff a silver medallion with our yacht's image embossed on the face. Another guest visiting on a Christmas charter in the Caribbean gave us each a $50 international phone card to call our families and loved ones.
- ➥ You may become the recipient of hand-me-downs from the boat. Yachts frequently go through refurbishments where owners may decide to fully redecorate the interiors. So, it's out with items that were a part of the old décor. Where does that stuff go? Goodwill is a good place, and we all know that the rich like to give, give, give (and deduct, deduct, deduct). But too, if you've got a place to send it, it could be yours (with permission, of course): towels, sheets, candles, books, throw pillows, glassware… I know a few former yacht stewardesses whose homes today are decked out with items they inherited from boats they once worked on.
- ➥ You could get to live abroad (on land). When yachts go into shipyards, they are sometimes taken completely out of the water, meaning the crew cannot stay onboard. That doesn't mean you get left to fend for yourself, though. The owner will have the crew put up in land-based accommodations, such as hotel rooms or a short-term rental house, and usually give them a daily allowance for meals. I had the opportunity to live ashore in Viareggio, Italy and Palma de Mallorca (where I had my own apartment). And although not overseas, I also spent land-based living time in Savannah, Georgia and Miami, Florida… all on the boss's bill.

Resist Temptation—Your Saving Grace

"Quite simply, don't blow your earnings. You can never save enough to ensure security in the future. Relatively speaking, a yachting career is generally short-lived, the average stewardess

staying in the industry for 2-3 years. So, it's wise to enjoy the process and appreciate your time working on yachts for what it is; a great opportunity to save."

—**Mike French**, President of International Crew Training

I will never forget my friend Captain Carl's father, a yacht captain himself, saying to me during my first few months as a stewardess, "Stay in this industry for a good five years, save every penny, and when you walk away, you'll be set up to do whatever you please."

That was great advice.

The fact that you have no expenses in this job means you can save tremendous amounts of money. So, if you are making $30K, $50K, or even $100K (of course it can vary with tips), it's your allowance. Put it in the bank, and you have a down payment to buy a house if you decide to leave the industry after several years. You can pay off college loans. You can go back to school. You have a golden opportunity here to start off your life with a nice financial cushion.

My biggest piece of advice here is not to go on big spending sprees and waste your money. You might not think that's something you'll fall prey to, but believe me, once you become immersed in a world of gourmet and glamour everything, it can rub off on you to the point of desiring similar stuff. Most yachties are known for developing a refined palette and a love for blowing big money on dining and entertainment when they get time ashore. I'm telling you now, if you do this, do it infrequently.

"The originator of this school bought a plane at the age of 23. An airplane! She started when she was 19, and she saved every nickel she made. We try to educate people to save 90 percent of it. Spend 10 percent if you must—I mean, you're in Greece, you're in France, you're in Tahiti, you're all over the world—so spend a little bit, but save most of it. You'll be glad you did!"

—**Kristen Cavallini-Soothill**, owner and operator of American Yacht Institute

I Must Confess...
I spent a little too much of my earnings on playtime—but I didn't always regret it.

In many cases, when crew get time ashore, they haven't spent money in a while, so they play hard, showing little worry when they drop huge chunks of cash on lavish meals, rounds of drinks "for everyone," mega shopping sprees, and things of that nature. I'll admit to doing it, too:

My crew was on an 18-day charter, and mid-charter, when the guests left to spend five days ashore in Israel, we were given some time off. The female crew, including myself, booked an entire day of spa treatments at the Hilton Tel Aviv. The total per person for the day, after an expensive lunch and living it up in the hotel bar after visiting the beauty salon for hair and make-up, was nearly $1,500. Let's face it, as someone who went straight from college to backpacking to this boat life, I had never in my life dropped that kind of money on these types of things, especially in one day.

We wound up staying out all night partying with the locals in Haifa, Israel (looking and feeling great, might I add). While I did have feelings of guilt for the expense (I mean, c'mon, I still had college loans to pay off), once we were back in the thick of that charter, finishing off those last eight days of round-the-clock work, I knew it had been worth every penny.

"I'm on a Boat."
—The Lonely Island, featuring **T-Pain**

3

THERE'S NO "I" IN CREW
—MEET YOUR FELLOW CREWMEMBERS—

"The thing I enjoy most about working on yachts is the camaraderie… When you get a great captain leading the crew, and you get a hardworking crew where everybody works together as a team, then it's very special. A crew that's like family—it's one of the most wonderful things you'll ever have."

—**Jules Macnab**, yacht chef

I am coaching you to ultimately gain a stewardess position on a yacht, and I promise we are going to get to the specific duties and responsibilities of your intended position shortly. Yet, to fully grasp how your role as a yacht stew will play out, you need to see a larger picture. Before a yacht stew is a yacht stew, he or she is first and foremost a member of a yacht crew.

A Portrait of Captain and Crew

Every sea-faring yacht over 80 feet (24.4 meters and approximately 300 tons) is required by law to have a fully licensed and professionally trained captain and crew—a leader and company who manage the vessel and oversee her operation. Here are the various positions you might find onboard:

- ⤤ Captain
- ⤤ First Mate or First Officer
- ⤤ Mate and/or Bosun
- ⤤ Deckhand(s)—often a couple deckhands found on larger vessels
- ⤤ Chief Engineer
- ⤤ 2nd Engineer—on larger vessels
- ⤤ Purser—on larger vessels
- ⤤ Chief Steward/ess
- ⤤ Senior and Junior Stew(s)—1st, 2nd, even 3rd Stew on larger vessels
- ⤤ Head Chef
- ⤤ Sous Chef/Crew Cook—on larger vessels

Together, the captain and crew are a cohesive team. And note here that "crew" and "team" mean the same thing: a group of people working together. You've no doubt heard the common expression, "There's no 'I' in team"? Well, lo and behold, there's no "I" in "crew" either. Although, there is one in "captain"… but that's not important right now. (And forget I wrote it!)

The point I am making here is that each crewmember must be a team player and work with the others toward several common objectives, the most important being everybody's safety onboard. Not to create the impression that this industry is dangerous, but you mustn't forget we are talking about living and working on a boat here. Being responsible for one another's lives out at sea, as well as the safety and well-being of the owner and guests when they are on the yacht, is always the number-one priority. You will be trusting your fellow crew with your life, and vice versa.

On top of this, when guests come aboard, you will be expected to provide a well-orchestrated, flawless, and first-rate quality of service, the success of which requires the entire crew to rely on and trust one another. There is a lot at stake when you are attempting to exceed the expectations of people who have paid the premium to travel on a yacht. Expect to do whatever it takes to get your team's job done, even if that means assisting another crewmember in a job you don't normally do. Be prepared for long hours, hard work, and even the occasional mental and emotional strain; but at the same time, expect some of the most fulfilling experiences of your life to come out of accomplishing such tasks through teamwork.

The Key Ingredient = The Crew

There are two well-known sayings in the yachting industry when it comes to discussing crew. The first comes from the owner and the guests' perspectives, and it goes something like this: You can have the most extraordinary itinerary, the most lavish of amenities, and be traveling aboard the most famed and admired yacht in the world, but on any give trip, if you get a bad crew, the experience is a disaster.

Even charter brokers are well aware that the crew is one of the biggest selling points in offering a yacht to a valuable client—equally as important as the boat itself:

The crew can make or break the charter, period. If the crew is top notch, treats my guests with respect, and takes good care of them, we have a successful charter and happy clients…

We charter brokers spend months of each year traveling around to meet the crew and visit the yachts. We do this to be sure we can count on the crew to offer the best service possible to our clients. A professionally trained crew is imperative to the operation and success of a charter yacht. Our clients are used to five-star service in their homes and wherever they travel. The yacht crew must be trained to this level.

—**Debra Blackburn Boggio**, Charter Broker for Fraser Yachts Worldwide

You now understand just how important the captain and crew are considered to be in the whole mix. That can be a lot of pressure… but that's also what makes the job so fulfilling: To be part of a team working together toward a common goal—that of providing the owner and guests with a safe and enjoyable experience.

The second most common thing said in regard to crew is very similar, only it's from a crewmember's perspective rather than a guest's. When we stop to consider what makes a particular yacht a good one to work on, again, it all comes down to the crew. It's the team you have around you that makes the difference. And naturally so, for not only do you work alongside these other individuals, but you have to live with them as well. They are your fellow crewmembers, and they are your teammates, but they also become your family away from home. If the chemistry is right, it can make for an amazing experience for all involved.

Getting to know the other crewmembers' roles onboard will allow you to begin thinking in terms of the overall team picture. And you never know… at some point, you may have to jump in and assist these people in their jobs.

I Must Confess…
The pressure can be exhilarating.

There is always a lot of pressure just before an owner or group of charter guests comes onboard. Each item crossed off your "to do" list is inevitably replaced by another, and you can count on the fact that at least one crewmember will exhibit symptoms of a last-minute panic. You might expect all this rushing around to wear the crew down and cause them fatigue, but quite often, just the opposite is true. I personally found the team-wide commotion to be exhilarating.

It is rather like being backstage the night of a big Broadway production debut. The runners that have been down on all the carpets to protect them when no guests are onboard all come up. (Under the beds is where many of them get stored.) Once those are up, the boat feels much more open and alive. You can feel the carpet under your feet, hand-woven and soft, so clean that light reflects off the fibers.

The deckhands are arranging seat cushions on the outside decks. The chef is in the galley handling food preparations: The smells of bread and pastry dough, boiling chicken and beef stock, sauces of several varieties, and an array of spicy scents fills up the entire main deck—it always reminded me of Christmas morning.

The deck lights come on as the entire crew works into the night. The deckhands are putting finishing touches on their polishing and varnishing work. They remove any final fingerprints off the rails, dirt out of the scuppers (holes pierced in a boat's deck to allow surplus water to drain off), and scratches from the teak to get the yacht sparkling with cleanliness. Inside, the china is being washed, the silver polished, and the guest linens pressed and stored. Every light switch is tested and every inch of the interior double-checked for dust. A shipment of lobsters is to be delivered at midnight.

Each crewmember is playing a different type of music in his or her respective work areas: The chef has Motown on in the galley; the deckhands blast hip-hop from the sundeck; you are blaring Madonna as you hoover a VIP cabin, while the stew a room over is scrubbing a bathtub to a dubstep beat. The next thing you know, Bob Marley comes wailing up from the engine room; and in the wheelhouse, the captain jams to The Stones. It's fantastic! To have to run across the boat to get something sends you on a musical journey. (And you stop off in the galley to assist the chef, who is now dicing onions to Roy Orbison's "Crying.") Preparations continue well into the night.

With only five hours of sleep, the entire crew is up early the next morning to assist with carrying 15 fresh flower displays and four new deck trees from the florist's delivery van onto the boat. Next, the beverage delivery arrives: The crew forms a human chain up the passerelle to hand off case after case of beer and soda, bottled water and fruit juices, and dozens of bottles of fine wine. The yacht is gleaming, the champagne is chilling, and the crowds on the dock are staring.

Then, just when you've finished potting that last-minute tree on the aft deck, a call comes over the radio that the boss's plane has just landed and he and his entourage will be there shortly. You manage to shower and be on deck just two minutes before they step on—fresh plant soil still beneath your fingernails as you shake the owner's hand, and with a beaming smile and an energetic voice, say, "Welcome aboard, Sir."

Types of Crew Employment

The personnel onboard to assist the captain are the crewmembers, and they are classified as one of three types of employees:

1) **Permanent Crewmember**—A vast majority of crew positions are permanent. These are your live-aboard jobs. When you have guests on, the crew coordinate to keep someone available at all times. Without guests, the standard for the industry is that the full-time, permanent crewmembers work a 5½- or 6-day workweek (with occasional Saturdays off), usually 8 a.m. to 5 p.m., with an hour for lunch (prepared by the chef). This can vary depending upon the yacht's schedule.

2) **Temporary Crewmember**—Periodically, workers are hired to fill certain crew positions on a temporary basis. This is the same as working freelance in other industries. Temporary crewmembers are usually not entitled to any benefits except a wage that is agreed upon, and travel costs as discussed. I know many people who, after years

of consecutive live-aboard yacht jobs, turn to freelancing so they can set down roots somewhere permanently, yet still take on the occasional yachting gig to make some fast money. In fact, a good friend of mine recently ran off to Australia for two months to take on a temporary position. Freelancers are welcomed by the industry because, with some charter trips, the permanent crew aboard might not be enough to handle the number of people coming on. I was on a yacht where we knew we were not prepared to keep up with the amount of laundry a group of guests was going to have (12 guests, but six were kids), so we hired an extra stewardess just for that charter trip. She went away with a great wage from the two weeks, and she got to share in the tips, too. Not a bad deal! In the case of smaller yachts, it may only be a captain who is required full-time, while additional crew are hired on when the owner or guests decide to use the boat. The ability to get freelance jobs usually only comes after you've had a couple years' experience working in the industry.

3)   **Day Worker**—As a day worker you are not entitled to any benefits other than an hourly wage agreed upon for the work to be completed. Day workers are hired for very short periods of work, such as one to five days, and they are brought on to assist with tasks that the permanent crew cannot handle on their own. Sometimes they are used so the full-time crewmembers can take a short vacation. Yachts like to hire day workers when they are in maintenance mode, during shipyard periods, or before a visit by the owner or guests when preparations get overwhelming. We'll discuss day working more extensively in Chapter 9 when I cover how to look for a job; it's a great way to get started in the industry.

Rotational Crew

Since the first edition of my book came out, there have been a lot more experiments with a concept of what is being called rotational crew. Consider this a hybrid position between a permanent and a temporary crewmember. While still not across the board common, we are starting to see a lot more instances of this.

Rotational jobs for crew, mainly captains, are the norm on commercial vessels, but with regard to private yachts, the resistance to these types of work-sharing arrangements is that a yacht owner has a much more personal relationship with his/her crew and prefers the consistency it brings. Yet, the concept of rotational crew is becoming more of a need for all crew, especially senior positions. Megayachts that charter must have a crew that's "always on," and they travel much farther, which entails more maintenance due to more equipment and class specifications. Crew can very easily get burnt out. Another problem is that highly experienced captains and crew often drop out of yachting in order to move ashore to start families and lead a "normal life." With rotation, you forget about the boat when you are off, so splitting life aboard with life ashore is an attractive option for many crew.

And even junior-level crew are beginning to be considered for such rotational-employment arrangements. As Paul Rutterford, Marine Recruitment Manager at Viking Recruitment points out, "Rotation is becoming more popular across the superyacht industry, particularly for larger superyachts. With the introduction of MLC 2006, and the requirement for a minimum number of days leave, plus the flag states bank holidays also being 'leave' days, we are seeing a lot more junior stewardess/deckhands going onto at least five months on, one month off rotation."

Here's another example of how this might work: Rotate the entire crew—nine weeks on, four weeks off. A total of 17 rotating crew, with 11 on board at all times, with 12 rotations per year. There are many variations being tested.

If you interview for a job that entails crew rotation, here are a few questions to make sure you ask: How are things organized salary-wise? Do crew get paid when off? If not, it could leave you with a small paycheck. You can't necessarily expect the same salary and perks when you take a rotational position. But there are certainly some very fair arrangements out there, and while they aren't necessarily catered to entry-level crew at this point, it is at least good to know the industry has more of this in its future—for a longer term career path.

Crew Make-Up

Every yacht crew exhibits an organizational structure that mimics that of most businesses or companies. The captain is in the main position of authority and control over the entire yacht, and the chain of command flows down from there.

A captain's job ranges from being in charge of just one full-time staff member—himself or herself—to functioning as more like the CEO of a large corporation, which comes complete with many departments, personnel, and a complicated budget.

Departmental Fundamentals

The organizational structure of a yacht crew is built around five key departments, or areas of responsibility:

1) **Administrative Department** (The Captain)—Administration and supervision of the yacht's overall operation
2) **Exterior/Deck Department**—Oversight of exterior maintenance, navigational support, and water-sport activities
3) **Engineering Department**—Oversight of engine room and equipment needs
4) **Galley Department**—Food provisioning and meal preparations
5) **Interior/Hospitality Department**—Oversight of interior maintenance, service, and hospitality

The purpose of this structure is to provide clearly delineated lines of authority and accountability to ensure safety and the highest possible quality of service to the owner and guests. On smaller yachts, where fewer crewmembers are required, some of these departments are fused into one; however, the main areas of responsibility that need to be covered remain the same.

Department Heads

Each of the five departments is overseen by a department head, similar to a manager, who is responsible for the organization and operation of his or her specific domain on the yacht. Department heads are also responsible for overseeing the crewmembers who work under their management and making sure those people are duly motivated and trained. In addition, they are expected to maintain accounts, logs, and inventories, which are usually updated and given to the captain on a weekly basis, or as requested.

The crewmembers in each department should be regularly exposed to all aspects of their department head's duties and responsibilities. This is to assure continuity of service should a department head fall ill or need to be absent from the boat. Crew are consistently in a learning environment during their time onboard. That's also how you work your way up to chief stew faster: watch, listen, learn, and imitate.

Here is how the five departments are normally run:

→→ The **Captain** heads up the Administrative Department with assistance from the First Mate/Officer and perhaps also a **Purser.**

→→ The **First Officer,** commonly known as the **First Mate,** heads up the Exterior/Deck Department and oversees the Bosun and the Deckhand(s).

→→ The **Chief Engineer** is in charge of the Engineering Department and oversees the other members of this department: the Assistant or 2nd Engineer(s).

→→ The **Executive Chef** heads up the Galley Department. On larger vessels, the Executive Chef will be assisted by the Assistant or Sous Chef(s), and possibly even a Crew Chef.

→→ The **Chief Steward/ess** heads up the Interior/Hospitality Department and oversees the lesser-ranked Stews, often known as the 2nd and 3rd Stews (or Senior and Junior Stews), the number of which depends on the size requirements for the crew. Note: I have seen instances where a yacht will refer to the stew working directly under the Chief Stew as a 1st Stew, rather than a 2nd Stew.

Table 3-1 demonstrates how the onboard hierarchy is typically organized for a crew of 12:

Onboard Hierarchy of Crew

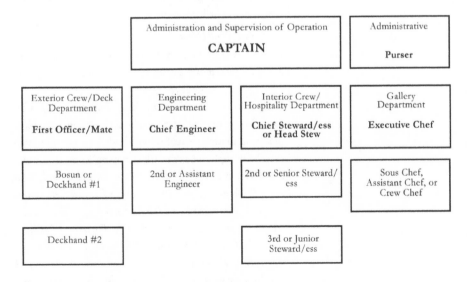

Table 3-1

A 12-crewmember make-up is typically the largest you will find until you get up to the vessels carrying 18 guests or more, and there are a limited number of those in existence. If a yacht requires more than 12 crew, Stews, Deckhands, Assistant Engineers, and maybe an additional Chef would be added to the bottom tiers.

Crew Numbers and Examples

The size of a yacht is going to determine the number of full-time crew required for her successful operation. **Table 3-2** lists some example scenarios of the crewmember numbers you will find on various-sized vessels:

Crew Numbers for Various-Sized Vessels	
YACHT SIZE	**NUMBER OF CREW**
<100 ft. (30m)	**1-4 Full-time Crew** **1–2 Crew:** A *Captain*, who doubles as the *Engineer*, with a temporary *Stew, Deck/Stew* or *Chef/Stew* hired when the owner and/or guests are onboard. **3–4 Crew:** A *Captain, Engineer,* who may double as a *Mate* or *Deckhand, Chef* or *Chef/Stew,* and a *Stew* or *Deck/Stew,* with additional temporary crew hired as needed.
<140 ft. (43m)	**4–6 Full-time Crew** **4 Crew:** A *Captain, Mate/Engineer, Chef,* and a *Deck/Stew,* with additional temporary crew hired as needed. **5–6 Crew:** A *Captain, First Mate, Engineer, Chef,* and a *Stew, Deckhand,* and/or a *Deck/Stew,* with additional temporary crew hired as needed.
<180 ft. (55m)	**6–12 Full-time Crew** **6 Crew:** A *Captain, First Mate, Engineer, Chef, Chief Stew,* and a *Deckhand* or a *Deck/Stew,* with additional temporary crew hired as needed. **7–8 Crew:** A *Captain, First Mate, Engineer, Chef, Chief Stew, Deckhand, 2nd Stew,* and/or an additional *Deckhand* or a combination thereof *(Deck/Stew).* A *Stew/Purser* might even be brought on as the 8th crewmember on this team. **9–10 Crew:** A *Captain, First Mate, Engineer, Chef, Chief Stew, Deckhand 1, 2nd Stew, Deckhand 2, 3rd Stew,* and/or a combination *Deckhand/2nd Engineer.* **11–12 Crew:** A *Captain, First Mate, Engineer, Chef, Chief Stew, Deckhand 1, 2nd Stew, Deckhand 2, 3rd Stew, 2nd Engineer,* and possibly an additional *Stew* or *Stew/Deck.* An *Assistant Chef* and/or *Purser* are also likely additions on larger vessels.

>180 ft. (55m)	12+ Full-Time Crew
	There are a limited number of yachts currently able to carry between 18 and 36+ guests. Based on the examples above, one can assume that supplements to a 12-person crew would be made by adding more Deckhands, Stews, Assistant Engineers, and Assistant Chefs, as is required for a particular vessel.

Table 3-2

Positions and Responsibilities

Now let's examine each position so you know where stews fit within the hierarchy, and how the various jobs onboard a yacht are broken down. I know, it seems easy enough to figure out: The captain drives the boat, the engineer takes care of the engines, the mate and deck crew clean the outside, the chef cooks for the guests and crew, and the stewardesses clean, serve, and keep the guests happy. Well, yes... all that is true. But there's a little more to it than that. This section breaks the crew down by department and position so you can see what each job is all about.

While annual salary guidelines are given in the following list of positions, the ranges for each crew position are wide because salaries will depend on a variety of factors, including the size of the yacht, the use of the yacht (private or charter), the style of boat (power or sail), and what other benefits are available to the crew, such as insurance packages or education reimbursement. Salaries may also vary depending on the specific qualifications of a crewmember, the amount of time the owner and guests use the vessel, and what itinerary will be traveled. Furthermore, the compensation ranges listed are base salaries and do not reflect tips, if those are applicable.

And without further ado, allow me to introduce to you the other members of your team, which like brother, sister, father, and mother, are the various roles that make up your future crew family:

Administrative Department

CAPTAIN (Annual Salary Range: $65,000–$200,000+)
Whether we're talking about Navy ships, commercial freighters, submarines, or private yachts, there's a reason we refer to marine vessels as being run by "a captain and his crew." This expression does not mean that the captain is not part of the crew, but rather, it certainly indicates who's in charge! The captain is the ultimate authority onboard any yacht, and he or she commands the utmost respect.

Becoming a professionally licensed captain requires extensive maritime training, not only in a classroom setting, but also out at sea. Captains therefore typically begin their careers as deckhands, or possibly stews, and move up through the ranks—next becoming bosuns, first officers, or engineers—while they accumulate enough logged hours of practical training, known as "sea time."

A captain's job description is dynamic and complex, and it entails far more responsibility than simply piloting the boat. Due to all of the required onboard experience they must have behind them, captains are usually awesome storytellers, too!

Job Function—The captain is responsible for the overall safe and efficient operation of the yacht and the management of the crew. As the owner's agent onboard, the captain is also to ensure that the yacht is in compliance with international regulations for the safe conduct of vessels similar to that yacht's size and type. The captain performs under the direction of the owner, and sometimes works in conjunction with a land-based yacht management company.

Responsibilities
- Overall vessel administration, leadership, and crew hiring and management
- Safety and emergency response management
- Vessel navigation
- Planning for voyages
- Representation of the owner regarding crew employment and general decision-making
- Accounting, budgets, and inventories
- Overall maintenance and repair strategy
- Public relations—with brokers, agents, contract laborers, and guests

Qualifications—A professional captain must possess the required licensing and documentation for the size and type of yacht in his or her command. This will be determined by vessel tonnage, waters cruised, and insurance required. A captain must also meet advanced fire fighting and STCW requirements. Extensive boating experience, preferably within the yachting industry, is without a doubt necessary.

PURSER (Annual Salary Range: $55,000–$94,000+)*
*Pursers are usually only found on larger yachts, over 160 feet in length.

A purser serves as an administrative assistant for the captain. This position is typically only found on the larger yachts and requires a strong background in everything from service to accounting and crew management. The pay can be outstanding. A purser position is not that easy to come by, though, and one reason is that married captains will often have their spouses fill this role so they can have them onboard. (Hey, captains are usually in this for the long-term, and it's only reasonable that they have the opportunity to lead a "normal life.")

Job Function—The purser carries out his or her duties and responsibilities under the direction and authority of the captain. As the executive clerical assistant to the captain and each of the department heads, the purser is responsible for all correspondence, record-keeping, and accounting onboard.

Responsibilities
- Accounting
- Administration
- Assistance with port and customs procedures
- Coordination of contractors and deliveries
- Human resources and crew management, especially with regard to the interior department
- Assumes full responsibility for certain onboard safety tasks (as assigned by the first mate) in an emergency
- Occasionally, inventory management

Qualifications—Previous yachting experience is usually always necessary, and most pursers will typically have previous chief stew experience. It also helps to have an administrative or accounting background. Computer skills are a must, especially Microsoft Word and Excel. Additional language knowledge is a plus. STCW Basic Safety Training (BST) certification is also now required to work onboard, and an ENG1 Seafarer Medical Certificate or its equivalent is also recommended (both will be covered in Chapter 7).

Engineering Department

CHIEF ENGINEER (Annual Salary Range: $52,000–$156,000+ and growing!)

The heart of any yacht is the engine room; and it also represents the most costly area of the vessel, with its powerfully priced engines and state-of-the-art mechanical equipment. It is vital that the person hired to control this department be highly qualified and knowledgeable.

Job Function—The chief engineer will carry out his or her duties and responsibilities under the direction and authority of the captain. The engineer is responsible for all engines and mechanical equipment onboard, and this includes electrical, refrigeration, and plumbing systems as well. This person will implement a preventive-maintenance program and adhere to it for all yacht machinery to meet or exceed vessel code regulations.

Responsibilities

- Systems and inventory monitoring
- Safety of the yacht and preventative maintenance
- Engine room appearance
- Crew safety training in all aspects of the engineering department
- Thorough knowledge, understanding, and proficiency with regard to the maintenance and repair of all machinery onboard: electrical, refrigeration, plumbing and sanitation, hydraulics, diesel mechanics, tender and toy (Jet Skis, WaveRunners) engines, electronics, and interior and exterior hardware
- Watchkeeping within the engine room when the vessel is underway
- Responsible for managing, motivating, and training the assistant engineer, if that position is required onboard
- Assumes full responsibility for certain onboard safety tasks (as assigned by the first mate) in an emergency
- Oh yeah, and chief engineers must emerge from the engine room (a.k.a. their lair) and interact with the owner and guests from time to time.

Qualifications—A professional engineer must possess the required licensing and documentation for the size and type of vessel on which he or she seeks employment; this will be determined by vessel tonnage, waters cruised, and machinery onboard. Previous mechanical experience is necessary, preferably in the yachting or cruise ship industry. Basic STCW requirements must be met, while Advanced Fire Fighting, Advanced/Medical First Aid, and Advanced Sea Survival certifications prove a major advantage (and are often mandatory on larger vessels). An ENG1 Seafarer Medical Certificate or its equivalent is also recommended (learn more at the end of Chapter 7).

ASSISTANT or 2nd ENGINEER (Annual Salary Range: $42,000–$90,000+)*

*Assistant engineers are usually only found on larger yachts, over 140 feet in length.

Assistant engineers, also known as 2nd engineers, are employed on the larger megayachts where the task of overseeing the engine and mechanical systems is too much for the chief engineer alone. Gigayachts may even employ several of them. On smaller yachts, there is sometimes a hybrid position of deckhand-engineer, whereby the person filling this role assists in whichever of the two departments needs him or her. Either way, the position of assistant engineer is an excellent starting point for those looking to later become chief engineers or captains, as an individual can gain sea time and further qualifications while working under someone more experienced (as in an apprenticeship).

Job Function—The assistant engineer will carry out his duties and responsibilities under the direction and authority of the chief engineer and the captain. As a member of the engineering department, this person is responsible for all engines and mechanical systems onboard.

Responsibilities

- Assumes full responsibility for certain onboard safety tasks (as assigned by the first mate) in an emergency
- Assisting the chief engineer (see responsibilities under the chief engineer listing)

Qualifications—On larger yachts, a professional assistant engineer must possess the required licensing and documentation for the size and type of vessel on which he or she seeks employment—this will be a different class of license than what is required of a chief engineer and will be determined by a vessel's tonnage, waters cruised, and machinery onboard. Smaller yachts may not require such a license. While this is an entry-level position, previous boating or mechanical experience is a plus, and preferably in the yachting industry. STCW BST certification is required and an Advanced Fire Fighting Certificate proves an advantage. An ENG1 Seafarer Medical Certificate or its equivalent is also recommended (learn more at the end of Chapter 7).

Exterior Department (A.K.A. Deck Crew)

FIRST OFFICER/MATE (Annual Salary Range: $46,000–$105,000)

While the stews handle everything going on inside the yacht, the exterior department, headed up by the first mate, takes care of the outside. It's all about keeping the owner's property looking spectacular for the parades of onlookers, and the task of keeping up outward appearances is never-ending. The deck department is constantly washing the boat down, removing all saltwater build-up, varnishing the wood handrails and teak decks, and polishing all the metal rails and fixtures until they glisten. The first mate oversees the deck department in this effort. A first mate's responsibilities also include navigational support, assisting the captain with docking procedures, and standing watch when the boat is at sea.

But don't think that just because the exterior team handles so much of this behind-the-scenes activity that they are excused from the service aspect of yacht work; the entire deck department interacts with the guests on a daily basis. The first mate and deckhands usually spend their afternoons overseeing the guests' water-sports activities—taking them skiing, fishing, scuba diving or snorkeling, and making sure the water toys are fueled up and ready for action. They are also in charge of driving the smaller tender boats, which means shuttling the guests to and from shore whenever the yacht is anchored off land.

Most first mates are captains-in-training. They've worked their way up from entry-level deckhand positions, and they fit in further course work when they can while continuing to accumulate enough sea time hours to eventually captain a vessel of their own one day.

Job Function—The first mate, sometimes called a first officer, will carry out his or her duties and responsibilities under the direction and authority of the captain. As the head of the exterior department, the first mate is responsible for the supervision and training of the deck crew and any junior officers who may be onboard. The first mate is also the captain's representative when the captain is absent or incapable through injury or illness. This person will make sure all safety requirements are met or exceeded onboard, and adhered to by guests and crew. He or she will also understand and implement all navigational laws.

Responsibilities

- Responsible for managing, motivating, and training the exterior crewmembers (the bosun and/or deckhands), if any are onboard
- Overall vessel maintenance and repair strategy, along with preventative maintenance
- Auxiliary watercraft (the tender boats and yacht toys) maintenance
- Safety of the yacht and guests—assigns certain onboard safety tasks to all other crewmembers, for use in emergencies
- Inventory monitoring and provisioning for the exterior department
- Accounting and budgeting for exterior department's needs
- Navigational support
- Watchkeeping management
- Knowing and following international protocol with regard to flags and anchors
- Guest services

Qualifications—A professional first mate will possess appropriate licensing as required by a vessel's tonnage. Extensive boating experience is a must, preferably within the yachting industry and on vessels of similar size to the one on which he or she seeks employment. STCW BST certification is mandatory. An ENG1 Seafarer Medical Certificate or its equivalent is also recommended (learn more at the end of Chapter 7). First mates should complete Advanced Fire Fighting, Advanced/ Medical First Aid, and Advanced Sea Survival courses. An Officer of the Watch (OOW) Certificate of Competency and an applicable VHF Radio Operator Certificate are almost always mandatory. A Powerboat Level II (RIB) Certificate—also known as a Tender Operator Certificate— is also a major bonus, if not absolutely necessary at this stage. (Note: This could be any type of small powerboat certification or may be referred to as Dinghy License Certificate. Regardless of what it is called, it is now mandatory to have this equivalent certificate or license in order to operate a tender/dinghy boat in the Mediterranean Sea, as well as in other waters around the world.)

BOSUN or 2nd MATE (Annual Salary Range: $36,000–$66,000)

The bosun's position is similar to the first mate's. The person holding this position will be training to move up to a mate's position. Essentially, he or she will be more experienced than a deckhand, but lacking enough skills or qualifications to become a mate. The role encompasses a variety of deck duties and responsibilities slightly above those of a deckhand.

Job Function—The bosun will carry out his or her duties and responsibilities under the direction and authority of the first mate and the captain. Along with the first mate, the bosun will participate in directing, motivating, and training the deckhand(s).

Responsibilities

- Assumes full responsibility for certain onboard safety tasks (as assigned by the first mate) in an emergency
- Assisting the first mate (see responsibilities under the listing for first mate)

Qualifications—Previous deckhand experience a bonus, preferably in the yachting industry. STCW BST certification is mandatory. An ENG1 Seafarer Medical Certificate or its equivalent is also recommended (learn more at the end of Chapter 7). Navigational watch certification (an OOW Certificate of Competency) will also likely be required, while an Advanced Fire Fighting Certificate, a Powerboat Level II (RIB) Certificate (or its equivalent), and a VHF Radio Operator Certificate are preferred, if not mandatory, at this stage.

DECKHAND(S) (Annual Salary Range: $30,000–$55,000)

The position of deckhand is the exterior department's equivalent to the junior stew, as it is also an entry-level position; many captains and first mates began their yachting careers in this role. The number of deckhands required onboard depends upon the size of the vessel.

Job Function—The deckhand will carry out his or her duties and responsibilities under the direction and authority of the captain via the first officer and/or bosun. A deckhand is responsible for keeping the yacht's exterior clean and exquisitely maintained, including all deck equipment, while also assisting in watchkeeping and docking procedures.

Responsibilities

- Exterior maintenance
- Watchkeeping
- Navigational support
- Guest services
- Assumes full responsibility for certain onboard safety tasks (as assigned by the first mate) in an emergency
- Assisting the first mate (see responsibilities under the listing for first mate)

Qualifications—This is an entry-level position; while previous yachting experience is not required, it does bring added salary benefits. STCW BST certification is mandatory, and an OOW Certificate of Competency is preferred. An ENG1 Seafarer Medical Certificate or its equivalent is also recommended (learn more at the end of Chapter 7). A Powerboat Level II (RIB) Certificate (also known as a Tender Operator Certificate) is a major advantage, as it's becoming necessary to have such a certification while operating tender boats in certain waters. The same holds true for a VHF Radio Operator Certificate—while not required, it's a huge bonus. Of course, Advanced Firefighting and additional medical certifications can only increase one's chances for employment. Entry-level deckhands will do well with these additional experiences and/or certificates: Rescue Diver, Dive Instructor, PWC Instructor License.

Galley Department

EXECUTIVE CHEF (Annual Salary Range: $42,000–$100,000+)

The job of the executive chef is to prepare well-presented culinary delights for the guests, while also making sure that the crew stays fed. On larger yachts, the executive chef may have an assistant chef working under him or her to accomplish both tasks, but in many cases, it's up to just one person. As you can imagine, it's an incredibly tough job to plan, prepare, and cook two to three meals a day, for both guests and crew (while also ensuring they maintain a balanced and varied diet). Most all executive chefs on the higher-end megayachts are culinary-trained professionals.

Job Function—The executive chef will carry out his or her duties and responsibilities under the direction and authority of the captain. The executive chef heads up the entire galley department, and he or she works in unison with the chief stewardess, who will relay guests' requests and dietary needs for meals and menus. The chef also handles menu planning and preparation and is responsible for stocking the vessel with the appropriate ingredients and cooking items. The chef must always keep the yacht's travel itinerary in mind with respect to provisioning.

Responsibilities
- Menu planning and food preparation for both guests and crew
- Inventory monitoring and provisioning
- Galley appearance and maintenance
- Accounting and budgeting for galley department needs
- Exterior crew support when needed
- Assumes full responsibility for certain onboard safety tasks (as assigned by the first mate) in an emergency
- Responsible for managing, motivating, and training the assistant chef(s), if any are onboard

Qualifications—A professional yacht chef should possess a certificate or formal degree in Culinary Arts, to include courses in food preparation, diet and nutrition, food presentation, and culinary hygiene. In some cases, it is recognized when an individual applying for an executive chef's position has been self-taught through an apprenticeship (working his or her way up from an assistant or sous chef position), but additional training courses should be taken to supplement such experiences. STCW BST certification is now required, and previous yachting experience is almost always mandatory. An ENG1 Seafarer Medical Certificate or its equivalent is also recommended (learn more at the end of Chapter 7).

ASSISTANT CHEF (SOUS CHEF) (Annual Salary Range: $30,000–$62,000)*

*Assistant chefs are usually only found on larger yachts, over 160 feet in length

Job Function—Assistant chefs, also known as sous chefs, are employed on the larger mega- and gigayachts where the task of overseeing all food preparation for both the guests and crew is too much for a sole executive chef. The assistant chef will carry out his or her duties and responsibilities under the direction and authority of the executive chef and the captain. It is an assistant chef's job to collaborate with the executive chef and chief stew to coordinate and execute all meal service for the guests and crew. This person will handle a lot of the prep cooking, galley cleaning, storage tasks, and most likely, the preparation of crew meals.

Responsibilities

➤➤ Prep cooking and crew meal preparation

➤➤ Galley appearance and maintenance

➤➤ Inventory monitoring

➤➤ Assumes full responsibility for certain onboard safety tasks (as assigned by the first mate) in an emergency

➤➤ Assisting the executive chef (see responsibilities under the listing for executive chef)

Qualifications—On larger yachts, an assistant chef may need to possess some sort of culinary training. However, often times, proof of previous professional cooking experience of some kind will suffice. STCW BST certification is now a requirement to work onboard. An ENG1 Seafarer Medical Certificate or its equivalent is also recommended (learn more at the end of Chapter 7). Assistant/sous chef and crew cook roles are an entry-level position, but previous yachting experience is also a bonus.

Interior Department

As the main subject of this book, the nuts and bolts of what goes on in the interior department—and what exactly a yacht stew's job entails—deserves two chapters unto itself (that's Chapters 4 and 5). To get you started, the following job descriptions for stewardess positions cover the basics.

CHIEF STEWAR/DESS (Annual Salary Range: $39,000–$96,000+)*

*For an explanation of chief stew salaries, please refer back to Chapter 2.

Job Function—The chief stewardess will carry out his or her duties and responsibilities under the direction and authority of the captain. As the person ultimately responsible for the interior of the vessel and for providing superior hospitality service to meet the owner's and guests' expectations, the chief stew will also train and manage any lower-ranking stews under his or her supervision. Excellent service, host/ess, and managerial skills are a necessity, as is having a good degree of creative flair.

Responsibilities

➤➤ Responsible for the everyday smooth operation of the boat's interior department, which means being adept in the arts of housekeeping services, laundry procedures and wardrobe management, food and beverage service and cleanup, and entertaining (while maintaining proper etiquette and a high-energy, can-do attitude at all times)

- Responsible for directing, motivating, and training the lower-ranked stews (2nd, 3rd, and so on)—if any are onboard—which includes the assignment and scheduling of rotational duties and implementing Human Resources (HR) procedures and guidelines
- Providing valet services and overall guest care. Note: In the hospitality industry, "valet" refers to any employee who performs personal services for guests (and refers to more than just parking cars, which is what we normally associate it with). With regard to yacht stews, valet services include tasks such as packing and unpacking guests' luggage, caring for their personal items and specialty garments, and even making daily activity arrangements for them.
- Protecting, maintaining, and caring for valuable interior items and surfaces, such as artwork, silks, china, crystal, linens, fine woodwork, and marbles
- Creating, implementing, and monitoring a financial planning system that includes accounting and budgeting for interior department needs
- Creating, implementing, and maintaining an informational management system of interior inventories and maintenance procedures
- Provisioning to maintain inventory supplies and cover guest usage
- Collaborating with the executive chef regarding meal service for the guests
- Creative planning and quality service of theme dinners and occasional guest parties
- Keeping all interior storage areas organized, orderly, and maintained
- Crew uniform purchasing
- Writing and updating all interior manuals and guest-information documents
- Maintaining and displaying knowledge of international etiquette and protocol
- Watchkeeping in accordance with the list of responsibilities in the crew mess
- Exterior-crew support as needed (requiring proficiency with exterior lines and fenders)
- Selecting, purchasing, and serving fine wines, specialty teas, and cigars, which may require advanced training
- Planning and managing destination experiences proficiently
- Assuming full responsibility for certain onboard safety tasks (as assigned by the first mate) in an emergency

Qualifications—A chief stewardess should possess some type of training and experience in the areas of bartending, silver service, cigar service, and wine presentation and service. (The more extensive a stew's wine knowledge, the better.) STCW BST certification is now mandatory for a chief-stew position, and previous yachting experience on either charter or private vessels is most always required. It is also recommended that you obtain an ENG1 Seafarer Medical Certificate (learn more at the end of Chapter 7), or its equivalent. Floral arranging and table decorating skills prove to be an advantage, while an Advanced/Medical First Aid Certificate or a higher degree of medical training is also a major bonus. In fact, many chief stews are now taking courses to become certified as a yacht's Medical Person-in-Charge. This requires a seven-day course that will satisfy the standards set forth by the STCW Code A-VI/4, 4.4-4.6, offered at many of the marine training schools mentioned in Chapter 7. While the new PYA Interior-Crew G.U.E.S.T certification is not mandatory (as of

July 2013), it is wise to follow the courses outlined and seek out equivalent intermediate and/or advanced interior-crew training classes, if not sign up for the full PYA G.U.E.S.T course modules. You can also read more about this in Chapter 7.

STEWARDESS—2nd and 3rd Stews; sometimes referred to as Senior and Junior Stews (Annual Salary Range: $30,000–$54,000+)*

*For an explanation of stew salaries, please refer back to Chapter 2.

Job Function—A 2nd or 3rd stew will carry out his or her duties and responsibilities under the direction and authority of the chief stew and the captain. Individuals holding these positions are responsible for assisting with the maintenance of the interior of the vessel and providing superior hospitable service, in line with the owner's and guest's expectations. Hostess skills should be well developed to fully accommodate the owners and their guests while onboard.

Responsibilities

- ⊷ Maintaining interior housekeeping during a trip (detail cleaning) while also being held largely responsible for guest-cabin care
- ⊷ Laundry, ironing, and other wardrobe maintenance tasks for guests and sometimes crew (when guests are onboard)
- ⊷ Applying excellent guest service (including silver service) and expert bartending skills when called upon
- ⊷ Guest care and valet services
- ⊷ Assisting in the creative planning and quality service of theme dinners
- ⊷ Assisting with physical product inventories, provisioning, writing and updating checklists, and all other applicable tasks within interior
- ⊷ Maintaining and displaying knowledge of international etiquette and protocol
- ⊷ Watchkeeping in accordance with the list of responsibilities in the crew mess
- ⊷ Exterior-crew support as needed
- ⊷ Assuming full responsibility for certain onboard safety tasks (as assigned by the first mate) in an emergency

Qualifications—This is an entry-level position; while previous yachting experience is not required, it does bring added salary benefits. STCW BST certification is now mandatory for obtaining even entry-level work on a megayacht. It is also recommended that you obtain an ENG1 Seafarer Medical Certificate (learn more at the end of Chapter 7) or its equivalent. Table service, bartending, and cocktail-service experience or equivalent qualification are crucial to landing a job— training and certification recommendations for these can also be found in Chapter 7. While the new PYA Interior-Crew G.U.E.S.T certification is not mandatory (as of July 2013), it is wise to follow the courses outlined and seek out equivalent introductory interior-crew training classes, if not sign up for the full PYA G.U.E.S.T introduction modules. You can also read more about this in Chapter 7.

- ❖ **INSIDER TIP:** Learn your nautical knots! For entry-level deckhands, this is imperative, as rope work is an everyday part of the job. For entry-level stews, it is not necessary...

but, if you want to impress a captain or other hiring party, being able to say you know how to tie a "bowline knot," and any of the other more common knots used when tying lines during docking maneuvers, will certainly impress your interviewer! And certainly put it on your résumé/CV if you learn this handy skill. (Instead of "know-how," we'll call it "knot-how.") I can recall being taught to tie several types of nautical knots while living in my crew house. Consider asking a deck crewmember in your own crew house. Otherwise, I recommend www.animatedknots.com for visual instruction.

Dual Positions

On smaller and midsize vessels, where not as many crewmembers are needed (nor is there room for them), the core crew positions listed in the last section are often fused into what I call "dual positions." An individual hired into such a position will assume a dual role and be expected to wear more than one "hat" during the course of a day.

Here are some examples:

- Deckhand-Stew
- 2nd Engineer-Deckhand
- Captain-Engineer
- Stew-Chef
- Stew-Purser

I Must Confess...
I chose to use the more formal,
British pronunciation for my new job title of "Stewardess."

This one is for my female, American readers.

Stewardess: Yes, this is the job title that was banished from airline-industry terminology during the political-correctness movement back in the '90s (a move toward "equality vocabulary" is, I believe, what they termed it). Stewardesses, as we once called them, became known by the more gender-neutral, and for some, more professional-sounding title of: Flight Attendants.

Knowing this, many of my American friends, when I told them I was a stewardess on a yacht, would come back at me with comments such as, "Do they really call you a stewardess?" or "Wow, that's an outdated term. Shouldn't it be something more P.C., like 'yacht attendant,' instead?"

I would then have to point out to my interrogators: "Did you not hear how I pronounced it? I did not say 'STOO-ar-diss,' but rather, 'stoo-ar-DESS' (with emphasis on the FINAL, not the first syllable, and also pronouncing it "ess"—rhyming with "dress"—not "iss")…'ar-DESS'…'DESS'…like a British person would say it."

You'll quickly learn that many of the terms in yachting are dictated by British standards, as is the maritime industry on the whole. Beyond nautical terms, the more regal and formal-sounding (at least in my opinion) British vocabulary is even favored in a yacht's interior department.

Some other examples are the words "rubbish" to mean "trash," and therefore, "rubbish bin" for "trashcan," "biscuit" instead of "cookie," "petrol" and not "gasoline," "wardrobe" over "closet," "serviettes" as opposed to "napkins," "tea towel" and not "dish towel," "whilst" instead of "while," and my all-time favorite: "knickers" for what Americans refer to as "underwear."

So there you go: Once you land your first job in this industry, if you are an American (and female), you tell your friends back home that you are a "stoo-ar-DESS," whose job it is to "empty rubbish bins, serve biscuits, tidy wardrobes, iron serviettes, fold tea towels, and hand-wash expensive knickers whilst working aboard a luxury megayacht, which is fueled by petrol," and which, "no, is NOT a cruise ship!"

Now, tell me **that** doesn't sound prestigious?

4

AROUND THE WORLD
WITH A SILVER TRAY
—WHAT BECOMING A
YACHT STEW ENTAILS—

"The steward/ess role encompasses many duties and attributes. [Stews] are responsible for housekeeping & interior maintenance, guest service including table setting & silver service and laundry. You need to be flexible and highly organized with an impeccable eye for detail. The level of service is second to none and the super stew needs to be able to think ahead and anticipate the guests' needs whilst providing the utmost luxury treatment with a wow factor!"

—**Peter Vogel**, Interior Yacht Services UK and
Warsash Superyacht Academy, Southampton, England

The above quote from Peter Vogel offers a great basic definition of a yacht stew's responsibilities. Sounds nice and simple when you put it like that, huh? Now, hold on to your life preservers while I take that short and sweet definition and apply a technique that yacht stews are best known for: It's called DETAILING (or thoroughly attacking every teensy-weensy aspect of it).

Endless Chores Earn You Distant Shores

This chapter outlines what can most appropriately be described as the plethora of tasks a yacht stew is expected to perform, as well as what skills he or she should possess. The good news is that you probably already have many of these skills. The bad news is, while you might *think* you know how to clean a room, vacuum a carpet, serve food, or make a bed, you don't yet realize to what degree you are expected to carry out these otherwise "common" tasks when working aboard a luxury yacht.

I am also dedicating what you might perceive to be an unbalanced amount of space to this chapter. The reason? Well, while the first few chapters of this book covered the amazing benefits and once-in-a-lifetime experiences awaiting you in this line of work, I now need to drive home that the great salary and accompanying perks do come at a price.

In other words, I'm not going to lie to you. **It's work!** There will be no sugar coating as I describe what a stew is expected to do in exchange for those aforementioned rewards. *But*, I know you can do it!

I Must Confess...

Before I became a yacht stewardess, I was the least domesticated of any person I knew.

No lie. Growing up, I was one of those kids with a mother who, when I let my bed go unmade for more than a day or two, made it for me. I never took notice of dust or accumulating dirt piles on a floor, nor did I pay heed to dishes piling up in a sink. When I went off to college, I was fortunate, or one might say "spoiled," enough that I attended a university located only an hour away from my parents. Believe it or not, I was sometimes able to avoid doing laundry for weeks until I could make it home to see my folks and, sadly, leave my dirty garments at the door. I only bought clothes that did not require ironing; if they did, well, then I usually wore them once.

Housekeeping, laundry, ironing, cooking: Yup, I was clueless in every domestic department. I don't think anyone could have made a case for me being a neat and tidy person, either. Even today, I work at a cluttered desk.

So trust me, if a non-bed-making, non-iron-using, hardly-ever-cleaned-her-room-during-adolescence, scatterbrain from landlocked Indiana can become a yacht stew, ANYONE can!

And I'll tell you another thing: While I may not adhere to the same stringent standards of cleanliness in my post-yachting days, there are some skills I learned as a stewardess that are forever part of me now. Today, I can't miss dust when I walk into a room, and while I've managed to avoid being obsessive about it, I have breaking points where it must be attacked. (Note to self: Stop doing it at parties—it insults the hostess.) I change my sheets once or twice a week, I can iron a pair of pants to perfection, and when I do clean my own home, I do it relentlessly, detailing every inch of it.

Yes, that trained yacht stewardess inside of me decides to rise to the surface every now and again, and I can be a domestic diva whenever I choose…. But, when I started, I was most definitely a fish out of water.

"At some level, anyone can do this. You give me any girl or any guy, from anywhere, who has the right attitude and some sort of retention for 'do it this way'—and who can follow the rules—and I can make that person a great stew. It just takes a little bit of dedication and some pride in your work. Well, it takes a LOT of dedication…. You have to put your time in, and that's sometimes what people don't get."

—**Tish Owen George**, a chief stewardess and
yachting professional for over 15 years

If You Get Overwhelmed, Don't Jump Ship

Do not let it scare you when you come across something in this chapter that you don't know how to do (or don't think you can do). It all sounded intimidating to me at first, so I understand if you feel the same way. Rest assured that there are *plenty* of resources and specialized training courses available to help you gain the knowledge and know-how you'll need to become a beginner yacht stew…and quickly.

Please notice the adjective I just used: beginner. That's what I'm pushing you to become. As you'll recall from the last chapter, within the hierarchy of the yacht's interior department, there is a chief stewardess who trains, instructs, and manages the other stews onboard. An entry-level yacht stew—distinguished from the chief stew by being termed a 1st, 2nd, or 3rd stew—is thereby afforded an ample learning curve. So no, you will not be expected to be a world-class sommelier, a highly skilled floral arranger, and a flawless silver-service provider all rolled into one when you first enter as a 2nd or 3rd yacht stew. (But you *will* be expected to want to learn.)

On a related note: If you're entertaining any thoughts of starting in the industry at the chief stew level, think again. There may be the rare case now and then, but essentially, reaching chief stew status takes a lot of onboard experience. Just because someone has an extensive job history as a server at a five-star restaurant or as a hotel manager for a top-ranking resort doesn't mean he or she can waltz into this position. Working on a yacht is unique within the hospitality industry, and it takes at least a couple of years to gain the skills required of chief stews. Sorry, folks, you gotta start at the bottom.

❖   **INSIDER TIP:** You will want to review the skills listed in this chapter in order to include them on your résumé/CV when applying for your first yacht job. As you read, think back over your previous jobs and life experiences. You might be pleasantly surprised at what you are already qualified to do. For example, while you may lack service skills, previous jobs in other areas of hospitality, tourism, customer service, childcare, fitness, nursing, and many other fields can score you some major points. We'll go over these examples more in Chapter 6.

Julie From *The Love Boat* Ain't Got Nothin' on a Yacht Stew

To begin with, yacht stews are not like Julie from *The Love Boat* (being named Julie, you can only imagine how many times I heard that comparison), nor are they there to simply clean and serve. A yacht stew does perform those functions, but for a more appropriate comparison, think of the interior department's role on one of these glamour vessels as equivalent to both managing *and* carrying out all of the tasks that go into running a five-star hotel—that floats.

For example, first consider all of the various functions performed in the daily operation of a hotel, and who is responsible for them. There are employees to clean rooms; employees to do laundry; employees to give information and to arrange for transportation; employees to assist guests at any time of the day or night; employees to serve food and employees to prepare drinks in the restaurants, at the pool, and for room service.

Next, take that same hotel and toss it out in the middle of the ocean as though it were a cruise ship, cut off from the conveniences of being on land and having a lot of outside resources at your disposal. You must now add in employees to entertain; employees to perform in medical emergencies; employees to handle safety issues; and employees to coordinate activities, both onboard and ashore.

Now, condense all of the employees from these previous examples down to two to four individuals who share all of those tasks and perform them for 12 or fewer high-maintenance guests. On luxury yachts, the ratio of crew-to-guests is a lot smaller, and therefore there is a lot more one-on-one attention that must be paid. And, mind you, at the end of what would be considered a normal "shift," you cannot very well escape the guests you are there to serve.

When offering the ultimate in personal service, hard work and long hours are par for the course. The crew is there to fulfill the guest's every whim. And the yacht stews—from the chief on down to the most entry-level—are expected to pull off everything I just described, along with the occasional help of the chef(s), perhaps a purser, and/or the exterior crewmembers.

Just for fun, let's consider what different functions this means a stew *could*, quite possibly, be asked to perform in a day…

As a Yacht Stew, You Might Be Expected to Be a:

Housekeeper (an umbrella role for a variety of different functions—among them Duster, Vacuumer, Smudge Remover, Silver Polisher, Toilet Cleaner, and Chambermaid, which is just a more formal way of saying Bedmaker); Bartender; Cocktail Server; Meal Server or Waitress/Waiter (who can handle anything from setting up buffets to providing silver service, who knows the difference between tea service and coffee service, who is familiar with most rules of etiquette, and who can balance plates up his or her arm on a rocking boat while running up and down tiny staircases); Table Setter and Decorator; Napkin Folder; Gourmet-Food Expert; Hors d'oeuvres Preparer; Prep Cook; Food Garnisher; Plate Runner; Wine Expert/Sommelier (who can decant wine in rough seas without spilling a drop); Barista; Provisioner/Purchaser (of beverages, toiletries, linens, decorations, décor items, games, and other amenities, sometimes even the glassware, crockery, cutlery, and other items used for serving meals); Dish Washer; Flower Arranger; In-Cabin Service Attendant; Shoe Polisher; Jewelry Care Provider; D.J.; Concierge; Tour Director; Laundry Person; Wardrobe Manager; Expert Stain Remover; Clothing and Linens Ironer; Social Director; Event and Party Planner; Interior Decorator; Nanny; Public Relations Specialist; Personal Assistant/Shopper; Errand Runner; Stylist; Hotel Manager and Customer

Service Representative; Porter or Bell Hop; Inventory Taker; Nurse; Accountant; Psychologist; Marriage Counselor; Butler; Negotiator; Diplomat; occasional Deckhand; Office Assistant; Crew "Parent"; and Fill-in Monopoly Player. Some stews even have their masseuse licenses and can offer massages to the guests (or reflexology, or yoga instruction, or manicures)... Heck, why not even come prepared with a set of tarot cards?

That's a lot of hats you must be prepared to wear, accompanied by a smile on your face, a bounce in your step, and a "Can Do!" attitude. (How appropriate that stew—as in the kind we eat—is a "*combination* of ingredients thrown together.")

In fact, the entire crew, as a whole, is expected to be ready for anything and to handle all requests, no matter how demanding or off-the-wall. A popular crew reminder given by one of my former captains just before the guests arrived: "Remember, there are no problems, only solutions."

Guests Onboard vs. No Guests Onboard

There is a big difference in a stew's daily routine when there are guests onboard vs. when there are no guests onboard. With guests, the crew is in service mode. This is when the workload is toughest on the interior staff. The hours can be grueling, and a stewardess must be available at all times, from dawn until the wee hours of the morning (depending on when the guests retire). Members of the stew department must be organized and prepared to provide effortless service throughout the trip, no matter what mishaps occur behind the scenes. But remember, this is a team effort. (No stew is an island, unless he or she is working on a small yacht, under 100 feet!)

The daily responsibilities are much different when there are no guests onboard. Then, the job is more about maintaining the yacht and cleaning and preparing for the next group of guests. The hours during these guest-free periods will more closely resemble those of a regular land job: 8 a.m. to 5 p.m., with either a half-day on Saturday, or the entire weekend off. The exception to those work hours would be if the crew is pressed for time between trips. Heavily booked charter yachts are known for having only a two- or three-day turn-around between sets of guests, which requires longer days (hence, the big tips you get on charter boats). On the other hand, some private yachts and chartered vessels can go weeks or months with no guests.

Other scenarios with no guests onboard are when the yacht goes into the shipyard for repairs or undertakes a long journey to relocate, such as a transatlantic crossing. Then, the lion's share of the work falls onto the exterior and engineering departments, giving the stews a bit of a break (and the deckhands a reason to complain).

The Big Three: Service, Housekeeping, and Laundry

"The best way to find yourself is to lose yourself in the service of others."
—**Mahatma Gandhi**, Indian political and spiritual leader

When you ask industry professionals to give you a brief summary of a yacht stew's duties and responsibilities, the answer they usually throw out is what I call The Big Three: "serving, cleaning, and doing laundry." Of course, they will then typically add that these tasks are performed "while being responsible for overall guest care at all times."

Be careful of this "overall guest care," for it is a topic with many tentacles, extending out into a variety of diverse categories. I will get into these less-thought-of—yet no less important—functions in Chapter 5. But first, The Big Three: Service, Housekeeping, and Laundry.

It is good to mention here that on megayachts with two or more stews (a chief plus one, two, three or more others), you will work in a rotation system, called a rota. The chief stew draws up this schedule and rotates the lower-ranking stews around so that one day, one of them is responsible for the cleaning; the next day, the laundry; the third day, the service; and so on, repeating every few days. I have included a sample rotation schedule at the end of this chapter.

Service

Service is considered the main function of a yacht stewardess when guests are onboard. More often than not, the chief stew bears the brunt of this responsibility, and this will be his or her greatest area of expertise. This does not mean that entry-level and lower-ranked stews do not serve the guests; on the contrary, they are involved in this process. Specifically, the chief stew oversees the coordination and execution of service full time, calling upon the other stews to assist in a particular manner (which is why, as a beginner, you aren't held responsible when a meal goes awry or the owner finds a hair in his soup). The chief stew has the most direct communication with the guests and is also the one to collaborate with the executive chef in the planning of menus and meal times.

Outside of main meal service, an eye must constantly be kept on guests (this is often referred to as Guest Watch) for when they might desire a snack, a cocktail, or simply a bottle of water. Even in the middle of the night, it's not unheard of for a guest to ring up the chief stew or the chef and request a sandwich.

Guests will make themselves at home on a yacht—especially when it comes to the owners, for whom it is home. But even charter guests should feel comfortable enough to just waltz into the galley and ask for a snack or to open up the refrigerator on the sundeck to grab themselves a soda. Yet, you do not want any of your guests to feel as though they had no other choice but to self-serve because you were not around. There's a fine line between giving the guests their privacy and allowing them free rein of the yacht while making sure they don't have to lift a finger.

You will quickly learn that owners and guests traveling on megayachts tend to be picky, and also quite demanding. Service is expected to be prompt and flawless, and it is key that you become skilled at anticipating your guests' needs. For this, a little bit of clairvoyance would go a long way. (Okay, so those tarot cards might just come in handy after all.)

The types of service that a yacht stew can be asked to perform run the gamut. (Did you know there's a six-step formal process for serving Irish coffee?) Furthermore, all food and beverage service—be it of a cheese plate, a seven-course epicurean feast, or a bottle of Perrier "poured slowly" into a rocks glass with two medium-sized ice cubes, a half a slice of lemon, three (not four!) drops of Bitters, two cocktail straws "with a cherry poked onto one," and a dash of salt on the cocktail napkin—needs to be as unobtrusive as possible. (And yes, that's an actual guest request I once received.) The bottom line when it comes to service: For the owner who is paying your salary, and for the charter guest who might possibly be paying more than your yearly earnings just to enjoy a single DAY on a luxury megayacht, no request is too much to ask.

Main Meal Service

Meals are held at the owner's or guest's request and are often discussed in advance with the chief stew or chef, and relayed on to the rest of the crew. Beware, though: Plans can change at a moment's notice. ("We've decided not to dine at a restaurant ashore this evening. Instead, we'd like Beef Wellington, served in the formal dining room, in, say, 30 minutes?")

While it can vary from yacht to yacht, in most cases the chief stew will be present for the service of all the main meals while being assisted by one or possibly two other stews. The one exception might be breakfast, when the service is a bit less formal and can be managed by one or two of the secondary stews.

It is typically also up to the chief stew to advise and discuss with the guests where each meal will be served, and it is imperative to take the boat's travel agenda into consideration when making this decision. The captain will try to relay to crewmembers the cruising plans for the day so all personnel can plan accordingly. For example, if the yacht is moving from one location to another and will be getting underway during the breakfast hour, it is not wise to set up an entire table on an outside deck, for it could become too rocky or windy once the boat begins moving. (And having a guest get knocked out by a flying cereal bowl never helps your tip.)

With one or two dining areas inside, and one or more on the various decks, you can count on a lot of running up and down stairs during meal service. (Choreography skills are required for maneuvering up spiral staircases with stacked, flaming desserts in tow.) The good news is that most all megayachts are equipped with dumbwaiters (small elevators, sometimes called food lifts by Europeans) for conveying food and other items quickly from deck to deck. And trust me, when you're expected to deliver hot, plated food up two whole flights of stairs, and get it there in appetizing condition, that dumbwaiter is a smart choice.

Breakfast—Rarely is a breakfast hour pre-planned as a group, sit-down meal, set for a specific time. Instead, the morning meal usually begins the moment the first guest shows up at the table, and the interior staff must be prepared for the earliest of risers. For the stew on breakfast duty, this means being up at the crack of dawn to allow time for setting the table and getting the coffee running before the initial body appears.

Due to the less formalized structure of the day's first meal, breakfast is often served on a "made-to-order" basis, where the chef is on standby in the galley to prepare whatever each person fancies. These dishes are then plated and served to the seated guest at the table.

It is also standard to have a small breakfast buffet arranged on or near the table for self-service. Items that appear here include cereals, fruits, juices, ham, cheese, yogurts, continental pastries, preserves, margarines, toast, and a selection of fine teas. Most every megayacht has a high-tech espresso machine for making Starbucks-style cappuccinos and the like. However, wise stews keep the percolated coffee always available—and always hot—for whomever might surface from slumber "needing it" ASAP. (From my experience, there's nothing quite like the wrath of yacht owners/guests who can't find coffee the instant they want it!)

Lunch—Lunch tends to be the most laid-back of all the meals. By the time midday rolls around, guests are often scattered about—exploring the port ashore, sunbathing, or gallivanting around on water toys—and taking time out to dine is a nuisance for them. Therefore, swifter and less-formal modes of service are employed. Buffet-style service, where guests select their food from a nearby display or off of passed trays, is the most common.

Having said that, some guests request formal service straight down the line: lunch, dinner, and even breakfast. Russian or European guests are known for this more than Americans. The guests will inform the chief stew of their preferred mode of meal service ahead of time. Your British guests will almost invariably request afternoon tea service shortly after you've finished cleaning up lunch, so be prepared to stick around.

You can also get lucky and have guests who prefer to dine at restaurants in port. On the other end of the spectrum, though, you have the dreaded beach barbeque. These always end up fun, but the work involved to set up and take down such a privileged picnic (often done on remote beaches) can be exhausting. The deckhands must use the dinghies to shuttle everyone back and forth, along with all the food, service items, condiments, and the hardest one, the ice. Just keep your fingers crossed that the guests don't also want stereo equipment set up. (I once worked for an owner who made us haul a karaoke machine.)

Dinner—Usually the most elaborate meal of the day, dinners tend to require more grandiose styles of service. In stewardess training classes, and when you start signing up with crew recruiters, you will hear a lot of talk about silver service—two examples being French and Russian style—and that you must know how to perform it.

Sounds intimidating, doesn't it? Actually, there's good news: Silver service is not all that common anymore. Instead, a majority of owners and guests opt for the easier-to-deliver, pre-plated dinner service. You can thank the advent of nouvelle cuisine for that, for in this trendy technique of food preparation, it is all about visual appeal and presentation. Chefs want to be in control of how the food looks when it comes out, and quite honestly, guests like to oooh and ahhh over the arrangement or the choice of garnishes (edible flowers, anyone?). That would not be possible with more formal silver service styles. Here are the definitions of the various types to help you understand the difference:

Styles of Service

American—Food is plated in the kitchen and placed before guests. This pre-plated style is used most often. A variation to this is a more "family-style American" service, where the main course (such as carved turkey or ham) comes out of the galley plated while the vegetables and other side dishes are placed on the table for people to help themselves. Sauces are then offered to each guest by the serving stews.

Silver Service—The general definition is that the server will present and serve the food to the guest from a food flat or dish: see French, Russian, and Guéridon.

French—This style of silver service is quite formal and elegant. The food is taken from the kitchen on heavy silver platters or chargers that are presented by the servers at the side of each guest. The guests then help themselves by using the serving pieces to lift the food onto their plates. French service is impressive but requires ample space between guests and takes more time to complete. (Sneezing is best avoided while performing this style of service.)

Russian—Russian service is similar to French in many ways, as it is also quite labor intensive, and each guest receives a great deal of one-on-one time with the server. Like French service, the food is prepared and arranged on formal serving platters in the kitchen. The main difference is that when the platter of food is presented to the side of each guest, it is the server who serves the desired portion directly onto the guest's plate, using a large serving spoon and fork pair, held in the right hand to form a sort of "tong," while the platter is held in the left. As you can imagine, this technique requires a good deal of dexterity and skill.

Guéridon—This type of service is where a dish comes either unprepared or more often than not partially prepared, from the galley to be completed tableside. The chief stew or chef plays a prominent part, as he or she is required to fillet, carve, flambé, or prepare the food with showmanship. Some familiar items served in this manner are steak au poivre, steak tartare, Caesar salad, and Crêpes Suzette.

English—With English service, the food is arranged on platters in the galley, brought to the table, and placed in front of the host. The host then carves the meat or entrée, dishes out the vegetables, and hands the plate to the server (standing at his or her left), who then serves the guests, beginning with the hostess, the guest of honor, and finally all other guests. All sauces and side dishes are placed on the table and are passed by the guests themselves.

A quick reminder: DO NOT let the discussion of these majestic styles of service scare you. You can learn the basics in a stewardess training course (covered in Chapter 7). I think it's worth repeating: Chief stews are the ones needing to know the ins and outs; you, on the other hand, are to be trained. As an entry-level stew, the likelihood of you having to perform advanced silver service methods out of the gates is slim to none. Also, service is not always so formal. I had plenty of guests come aboard who were quite content having a casual, no-hype dinner. In the case of one wealthy family I had onboard, the kids ate macaroni and cheese and hot dogs every night. Another group of incredibly well-off media moguls requested to have Jimmy Buffet-style cheeseburgers grilled out on the sun deck most evenings.

Finally, I have found that descriptions of these types of service, and what is entailed in each, can vary from guidebook to guidebook (and training school to training school), so it is rather likely yacht guests have their own interpretation as well. If a lead guest on a trip requests one of these types of service by name, it is wise to politely describe to them what that means to you, so that person isn't surprised or upset when your team of stews comes out serving in a manner he or she didn't expect. It's better to have such a conversation one-on-one and in private than to have to mend an embarrassing service mistake (which could just be a misunderstanding) when you're there to "put on your show."

Menus

Ah, on to one of my favorite subjects: the food!

When we talk about serving meals onboard a yacht, we are not referring to the type of service you find in a restaurant. There is no introducing oneself at the table, handing over a menu for the clientele to peruse, and then taking an order that will later be served. Service onboard a yacht is meant to feel like it would in a yacht owner's or guest's own home, and for the main meals, the menus are pre-discussed and arranged.

The chef plans the menus and discusses them with the guests early in the day. Once a menu is set, the stews need to become familiar with it and make sure they have sufficient knowledge of all the items being served. This is especially important for planning how to set the table and knowing the types of cutlery and crockery (known more commonly in North America as silverware and china) and serving trays to pull out for a particular meal's service. The chief stew will hold the most responsibility in this area, and he or she will know how to serve each dish correctly, including what types of wine should accompany the courses.

It is not unusual to have seven courses on a dinner menu: appetizer, soup, salad, fish, main entrée, dessert (also referred to as sweets), and a cheese board. Guests who go all out might even request a more abundant and lavish parade, such as eight to 10 courses. I know that sounds like a lot of food, but the portions are much smaller than what you find in American-style restaurants.

Following is the classic menu sequence, or order of dishes, in a formal meal service. No, you should not expect to find every one of these courses as part of a dinner; this would just be the most extreme scenario:

- **Hors d'oeuvres**—Also known as appetizers, or starters, this course could include a variety of salads, or items such as foie gras (goose liver) or other pâtés; anchovies; lobster; mousses; fruit, and charcuterie (sausages, ham, and other cooked or processed meat foods); or smoked fish, such as eel. Also common are canapés, which are slices of bread with crusts removed, cut into various shapes, then toasted or fried and garnished with salmon, prawns, capers, egg, tomato, asparagus tips, gherkins, or types of meat such as those listed above. Alternatively, you may serve caviar on blini, which are mini buckwheat pancakes.
- **Soups (hot or cold)**—This includes broths, bisques (shellfish soups), consommés (also a good cure for hangovers), and purées, to name but a few.
- **Egg dish, pasta, or rice dishes**—On occasion, this course may be included. You might present an omelet dish or a warm poached egg, served on mushrooms and glazed with Hollandaise sauce. Pasta or rice dishes are also common at this stage of a multi-course meal.
- **Fish** (Poisson; pronounced "Pwa-SAWN" and not to be confused with Liquid Draino, or *poison*)—If the meal includes a fish *and* a main meat dish, the fish comes first. This covers everything from grilled herring to mussels to cold lobster.
- **Entrée**—A meat course. If preceding another meat course, this is a small, well-garnished portion, served on its own. If not followed by an additional main entrée, then this course is accompanied by potatoes and vegetables.

- **Sorbet**—These are lightly frozen fruit ices, sometimes served as a pause within a meal sequence, so that the palate can be refreshed.
- **Main entrée**—This course could be a relevé or rôti dish. The relevé is a main roast or larger joint of meat, while a roast, or rôti, refers to game or poultry dishes. This could be furred or feathered game, and is usually accompanied by vegetables.
- **Vegetables (Légumes)**—This could be served as a separate course instead of with the main entrée, as described above. Examples would be asparagus and artichokes.
- **Salad**—If served this late in the meal, this is a small portion, usually a green salad, and used to refresh the palate.
- **Sweets**—Any type of dessert, such as puddings, custards, cobblers, mousses, tortes, sorbets, or more. The list is endless.
- **Cheese (Fromage)**—A cheese course can be as simple as one great cheese for guests to nibble on at their leisure after dinner, or it can be a carefully considered platter of selected cheeses, showcasing a variety of textures and flavors. Examples include a soft cheese like Brie, a semisoft cheese like chèvre or Gruyère, and a bleu cheese like Gorgonzola or Roquefort.
- **Fruit**—In addition to a sweet dessert and/or a cheese plate, it is common to have fruit served after a meal. You'll find pears, dessert apples, mandarins, tangerines, red and white grapes, pineapple, assorted nuts, and perhaps dried or candied fruits.
- **Beverages**—Traditionally this meant coffee, but nowadays it includes a variety, such as coffee, specialty teas, milk drinks, or after-dinner drinks, sometimes served with petits fours (tiny cakes that are served after a meal).

A stew should be able to describe all of the food items being served from memory and know about the accompanying wines. It is also wise to learn the culinary terms for various types of food. The chef will likely provide these to you, but knowing these terms, or at least having a resource around that contains them, will prove advantageous. Even if you don't know how to come up with them on your own, know how to pronounce them. The guests may turn to you to ask the name of a certain dish, and mispronouncing it would be embarrassing.

For a glossary of handy culinary terms, along with their pronunciations, turn to Appendix C.

Lending Help in the Galley

Stews should be prepared to assist the chef. Larger yachts, say 200 feet+, have room enough on the crew to hire full-time assistant chefs; however, more often than not, there is only one executive chef behind all guest meal preparations. (That person must also fix one or two meals for the hard-working crew at some point in the day.) As you can imagine, this is an awful lot of work for one person. When it comes to getting a meal prepared and served in a timely manner, teamwork becomes the name of the game; the entire interior staff usually pulls together to complete the mission.

Cutting up and dicing vegetables, garnishing plates, and holding a tray of steamed prawns while the chef douses them with herbs and oil—these are some of the duties you may be asked to perform. If the chef was running behind, I was often found feverishly putting together a second plate of pre-dinner canapés all by myself in order to delay the start of a meal by another half hour. I also became skilled at preparing a pretty impressive cheese board, decorated with fresh figs, grapes, and nuts, all placed "just so."

One of the perks in helping the chef is getting to taste some of the concoctions as he or she is whipping them up. I always looked forward to mopping the saucepans with chunks of bread and shoveling random bits of leftover crabmeat in my mouth when no one was watching. Another bonus is you can pick up a lot of culinary skills. I may not be a good cook, but I do have several treats I learned to prepare when working on yachts that make me the hit of every "pitch-in" party I attend.

I Must Confess...

I always made it a point to befriend the chef.

Not to say this was my main objective, but I did find that helping the chef whenever I had a spare moment, and really, becoming his or her pal in general, had its distinct advantages with regard to my own palate. You see, it is the chef's responsibility not only to purchase food for the guests, but also to shop and provision for the crew. I happen to be a picky eater, and when I was in yachting, I attempted to stay slim by adhering to a low-carbohydrate diet, which required a pretty specific shopping list. To make it through an entire transatlantic crossing eating egg-white omelets every morning meant needing a lot of eggs onboard when we set out. Thanks to the chef being my best buddy on that particular yacht, I had no worries: She stocked up on 10 cartons for me alone! In fact, I had no concerns as far as any of my dining preferences went during the entire time she and I worked together.

However, on another boat, where I did not get along so well with the chef, it was a different story. After expressing that I enjoyed eating fish, so long as they did not come served with their heads still intact, I probably counted at least three fish heads per week being served to me. And if I requested an egg-white omelet, she threw in double the yolks.

So, you've been warned: Befriend your chef (or warm up to the idea of cereal for dinner).

My two favorite books about what yachtie life is like, especially from the perspective of working onboard, are by megayacht chef and author, Victoria Allman. I highly recommend checking out either of her books: *SEAsoned: A Chef's Journey with Her Captain* (2011) and *SEA FARE: A Chef's Journey Across The Ocean* (2009). Talk about fun memoirs that give you an insightful account of crew life! I was so entertained by Victoria's stories in her books. And based on her illustration in *SEAsoned* about what it is like as a yacht chef working with both inexperienced and experienced crew, I asked her to contribute a comment to this section of my book.

Here is what Victoria Allman has to say with regard to the relationship between a yacht chef and a stew:

It's a delicate relationship between chef and steward/ess; one that can make or break at trip. When the bond between the two is strong, the guests get the best possible service, food goes out hot, pertinent information is passed to the appropriate people, service is smooth, and the whole crew is happy. This is not always the case. When the relationship between chef and stew has soured, the guests suffer, the rest of the crew are affected, and important information that could make the trip go so much easier is often left unsaid.…What is essential to me, as a chef, even more so than experience, is that we are all working on the same page; to deliver the best experience to the guests as possible.…My advice to every crewmember, in any position, is to work hard at building relationships with your crew mates, chef or not.

You'll definitely want to pick up a copy of Victoria's books. Meanwhile, she has contributed a post about what she calls "The Chef and Stewardess Dance" to my blog over at www.WorkOnAYacht. com. Look it up for an amusing read!

Table Setting and Napkin Folding

The *preparation* for meal service is a whole art unto itself. The traditional term is *mise en place*, but we Midwestern girls like to call it "settin' the table." Okay, it's a bit more cumbersome than simply remembering "fork on the left" and "knife on the right," but, those basics do apply. Though, just add on 35 other types of cutlery and flatware (eating utensils or silverware), a smorgasbord of crockery (chinaware or dishes), more types of glassware than you care to know when to use, some pretty fancy linen folding… and you're golden!

Joking aside, there is a lot that goes into pulling off a fancy dinner for yacht clientele. Keep in mind that you'll be handling the finest in everything: crystal, china, and sterling silver.

When setting—or laying, the slightly more formal word—a table in readiness for service, the "cover" is the place setting before each guest. There are a variety of covers that may be laid, the choice of which is based on the type of meal and service being offered.

In order to plan this, the stew must take into consideration factors such as:

- How many guests are coming to dinner, and is there a special layout needed?
- What is being served (which requires good communication with the chef), and in what order?
- What cutlery and plates, including serving trays, will need to be used to go along with each dish?
- Where is dinner being held—inside or out, and on which deck? (An outside meal when the yacht is in motion may mean using a different set of chinaware or glassware that is heavier and less likely to be bothered by turbulence.)
- What wines will you be serving, if any, and in what order if there are more than one? (Note: There will often be a different wine to accompany each course of a meal, and the glasses should be arranged in the order they are to be used, right to left.)
- Is there a special occasion or theme to the dinner that will require special table decorations, candles, napkins, or napkin rings?

Typically, a *table d'hôte* cover is used, where you follow the principle that the cutlery and flatware for the whole meal will be laid before the first course is served. Here are the basics of what this includes, and extras are added on according to the menu:

- a charger plate, which holds the space where the dinner plate will be set (a charger plate is slightly larger than a dinner plate)
- a side plate with bread and butter knife
- standard cutlery and flatware: a soup spoon, fish knife, fish fork, joint knife and joint fork (what you and I are accustomed to using every day), sweet spoon and sweet fork, and perhaps a salad knife and salad fork
- wine glass(es)
- a water glass
- salt and pepper (a cruet is often used, which holds salt and pepper, mustard, and a mustard spoon)
- extras you may find: ashtrays, butter pads, flower vases, and toothpick holders

Setting the table was a grand affair for me. I enjoyed it and often pretended I was setting up for a private dinner party of my own. *(Hmmm… tonight, let's use the crystal I received the day I became Mrs. Pitt.)* I'll admit, though, figuring out what tableware and flatware might be needed and how to arrange them was like working out a puzzle. Martha Stewart books made for great cheat sheets when it came to this.

It is key that every item be precisely placed—the bases of the flatware set approximately one inch from the edge of the table and everything aligned at exact distances from the center charger plate. In order to keep fingerprints off any of the utensils, stewardesses quite often wear white service gloves while laying the table. This also allows for last-minute polishing, including on the glassware (no smudges allowed!). One glove will usually do it, so if you haven't brushed up on your Michael Jackson moonwalk, you might want to; if you break out this dance while setting the table, you will totally look the part. (A guest caught me doing this once; thank goodness he had a sense of humor!)

When I mentioned earlier that the "extras" are added on from the standard cover setting, that encompasses a lot. Following is a list of the various types of cutlery, flatware, plates, dishes, and serving items you'll have to choose from:

- **Flatware**—In stewardess training school, I recall learning seven knives, 11 forks, 16 spoons, and 10+ types of serving utensils. I won't get into them all, but here are a few examples (where I was left thinking, *WHAT, there is a special utensil for this?*): oyster forks, a pastry slicer, lobster picks, fruit forks and fruit knives, ice cream spoons, the cheese knife, sugar tongs, nutcrackers, fish forks, fish knives, grape scissors, the preserve spoon, teaspoons and coffee spoons (yes, these two are different), snail forks, pastry forks, sauce ladles, and asparagus holders. Notice I haven't even gotten to your standard joint knife and joint fork.
- **Serving dishes**—These come in all shapes and sizes, some shallow, some deep; there are probably six varieties and several of each size.

- **Plates**—In a set, there are liner plates or chargers, dinner plates, salad plates, side plates, and dessert plates. And there's not just one set, either. Guests don't want to look at the same set of plates for every meal. You'll need at least three to four styles, one of which is fine china.
- **Bowls**—Say hello to pasta bowls, soup bowls, soup cups with and without handles, salad bowls, cereal bowls, and fruit bowls, plus saucers to go with all of these.
- **Cups and saucers**—There are tea cups and coffee cups; saucers for the teacups and coffee cups; milk jugs in all shapes and sizes; tea pots and coffee pots, also in all shapes and sizes; sugar bowls; sauce boats; and my favorite, the egg cup. (It doubles as a nice toothpick holder.)
- **Glassware**—You'll have quite an array to get to know, and note that a lot of these will also apply to serving cocktails and other beverages: wine goblets for white wines and red wines, champagne and rosé wine flutes, champagne coups, highball or "old fashioned" glasses, lager or Pilsner glasses, brandy snifters, liqueur glasses, tumblers, martini or cocktail glasses, beer mugs, glass coffee mugs, sherry or port glasses, slim Jims, "Collins" glasses, and more.
- **Napkins**—The more formal word is serviettes, and there is an art to folding them. I like to think of it as origami with starched linen. If you have a flair for this, here is a chance to exhibit your creativity and impress the guests. Lunches will usually entail just placemats and napkin rings, which can also be quite fun, as you get to pick out the décor and mix and match linen patterns and chinaware sets. The stews often get to shop for the linens and decorations, so if going into Williams-Sonoma or Pottery Barn to buy all the cool table dressings sounds like a day at the park, you're in for a treat.

I Must Confess...
I sucked at napkin folding.

I don't know what it was about it, but I had no retention for this craft. I could learn a particular fold one day and forget it the next.

I worked with a couple of Hungarian stews who could practically fold them in their sleep. They reminded me of the balloon man at the circus, who blows up a few simple balloons and then twists them and turns them and, in the blink of an eye, shuffles them around to reveal a dog or some type of flower.

These girls coached me on every well-known napkin fold there is: the peace lily, the rosebud, the Cardinal's hat, the cone, and the highly complicated bird of paradise. I can still hear them instructing me to "fold it in half, rotate it, pull up the corners, and make sure it tucks for a snug fit." Mine just turned into a wad of fabric. I felt like saying, "Yeah, well, have you seen this one? It's called the cootie catcher."

In the end, I always opted for the simple over the complex, which in my case meant grabbing napkin rings and just threading those puppies through them. After all, I'm sure the guests would appreciate that I hadn't just spent hours handling the linens they ultimately used to wipe their mouths. If you don't pick up on napkin folding quickly, you might try that excuse: hygiene concerns. (No pun intended on the cootie catcher bit.)

The final preparations for dinner service usually have stews scrambling about with checklists in hand: Is the coffee set up and ready to be turned on toward the end of the meal? Is the water on ice? Are the wine-bottle openers accessible? Are there extras of everything waiting in the wings: glasses, trays, silverware, ashtrays? Is the butter cut? Are the candles lit? Is there background music cued up to play? (And where's that darn Elton John CD?) All the while this is going on, you will be serving hors d'oeuvres, canapés, and pre-dinner cocktails to guests, who are not yet seated at the table.

Next, expect some scenarios like this to pop up: The main charter guest will have a last-minute change to make to the evening's wine selection. Another guest fesses up that he or she began a new diet that day and can no longer eat dairy products. And my favorite: After catching a glimpse of the elaborately decorated interior dining room with its intricately laid table, that "one guest," who is forever intent on terrorizing the crew, will casually inquire: "It's such a beautiful night for dining outdoors on the sun deck…. Do you think that could be arranged?" Yes, even the most perfectly laid plans—as well as tables—can go awry.

Once dinner is finally being served, there enters the task of clearing plates. This is another skill to master; not just the *how*, but the *when*. This process begins as soon as each course is finished—stews must sweep one course away to make room for the next. And on and on.

Washing Dishes and Polishing Silver

Finally, it's on to doing the dishes, and this party begins as soon as the first meal course is cleared. Breakfast and lunch service aren't so bad, but you can imagine, dinner-wise, if there are seven to 10 courses in a meal, that means seven to 10 rounds of plates and silverware to clean… and we can't forget the glassware. Thank goodness for dishwashers, one might say. Ah, but not for the crystal. Sorry, babe, the crystal glasses are done by hand!

And don't forget to check with the chef: He or she may need some help cleaning and drying all those pots and pans as well. The entire process of washing up after a multi-course meal can be daunting and typically requires help from as many bodies as are available. I was known for even grabbing the assistant engineer and bribing him to dry a few rounds of plates now and then. *("Yoo-hoo, we've got leftover chocolate gateau in the stew pantry!")*

Now here's the real kicker: While you may have one or two sets of stainless steel flatware onboard for casual dining or breakfasts, a majority of the time, you'll be using the really fine stuff. Yup, that's the sterling silverware. There are tricks to being able to use a dishwasher to wash sterling silver (special settings, and remove right away), and some chief stews may forbid it altogether; regardless, polishing the silver is a constant. Even without guests onboard, any and all sterling silver items must be routinely maintained. It's not just tableware, either; you'll have silver napkin rings, tea sets, coffee servers, serving platters, and even monstrous silver candelabras. Thus, if you are interested in becoming a stew, it's time to polish up on polishing.

Wine Service (Sommelier Skills)

You may know the term if you're used to dining out in nice restaurants: A sommelier is the person responsible for the service of wine during a meal. On yachts, it's usually the chief stew who handles this task and has thorough a grasp of all the wine choices available. The chef also helps in this department, for there is a definite art to choosing the best wines to go with certain foods.

Here is some advanced wine knowledge you should ultimately look to acquire:

- ➻ pairing complementary foods and wines: what goes best with fish, and how might the wine selection differ with red meat or game, or with cheese?
- ➻ when to serve Sherry, and at what temperature it should be served
- ➻ the various types of dessert wines, sparkling wines, and champagnes
- ➻ when and how to decant wine (transferring wine to a different container, leaving the sediment behind)
- ➻ the proper storage and handling techniques for various types of wine
- ➻ the standards used to evaluate wines, such as key grape varieties, styles, and climatic influence
- ➻ the characteristics of the world's top classic varieties and their food compatibilities—in particular Chardonnay, Sauvignon Blanc, Pinot Noir, Pinot Grigio, Gewürztraminer, Provence Rose, Riesling, Cabernet Sauvignon, Bordeaux, Burgundy, Malbec, Zinfandel, Merlot, Chianti, and Shiraz. (And that's a partial list.)

To learn about wines at a basic level, you can enroll in an introductory wine class. Such courses are usually offered at culinary colleges, through community-education programs, and even at your local specialty foods and wine markets. An introductory stewardess training course will also teach you the fundamentals of wines and the foods they complement. In recent years, many of the crew training schools have not only started offering introductory wine classes, but intermediate and advanced level as well. So once you're gainfully employed on a yacht, you can easily seek additional training if you're interested in advancing your career. It also wouldn't hurt to invest in a good "introduction to wine guide" to carry with you. Hey, if you can't have the wines of the world memorized and know exactly what foods they go best with off the top of your head, you can still be resourceful!

Bartending

Bartending skills are important. You will be serving alcoholic and non-alcoholic drinks before meals, at meals, after meals, sometimes throughout the day, and most obvious, well into the night. If you do not have a bartending background, do not fret. As a beginner stew, you are not expected to have a list of 100 drink recipes committed to memory that you can pull off to perfection. However, you should come in with a basic knowledge of the various spirits and liqueurs and know the difference between a martini and a margarita. You can pick this information up in any basic guidebook, plus many stewardess training programs will teach you the ropes. Advanced cocktail and spirit courses are now common offerings at crew training schools.

A chief stew will be on hand to walk you through the more common requests, such as various vodka, gin, and rum drinks. Beyond that, it will take practice to become well versed in the skills of shaking and stirring cocktails. The only time there's really pressure is if you have to make a drink in front of a guest, and it's one you've never heard of before. Easy solution: You can always say you left something on a different deck or at another bar and excuse yourself to duck back and check a bartender's book. We kept one at every bar, just in case that random drink request came out of left field.

A stew's bartending responsibility is not just about making and serving drinks. It's also about knowing how to stock the bars appropriately, and making sure you have all the mixing ingredients and spirits onboard that go into common cocktails, both traditional and fashionable. And what about supplies and tools such as strainers and stirrers, ice buckets and bottle openers, cocktail straws and cocktail napkins, and the all-important parasol umbrella picks to go with those frozen tropical drinks? Other important things to know are what types of glassware and garnishes are used with what beverages—even if it's a simple iced tea.

Beverage Provisioning

The interior department is not only responsible for serving the drinks, but also for buying them. All interior drink-making supplies—alcoholic and non-alcoholic beverages, for both the guests *and* the crew—are the interior team's responsibility. The stews must also organize, store, and keep the beverage items inventoried and up-to-date on a daily basis.

If this sounds like a piece of cake, consider this: Aside from all the varieties of soft drinks and sodas, beers, drink mixers, spirits, wines, liqueurs, coffees, teas, and juices there are to choose from, you then have countless choices of bottled water. I quickly learned that wealthy people are picky when it comes to their preferred brand of this simple substance of H2O. On one charter trip, we had to stock up on five different brands of bottled water, since no guest was willing to compromise: Evian, Volvic, Contrex, Acqua Panna, and Badoi. Oh, and add to that San Pellegrino for the sparkling-water fans. Now tell me, how tempted do you think I was to actually test them—to swap out one brand for another and serve it to a particular guest who swore he could tell the difference? The answer is very tempted. But, I never did (or maybe just once).

Serving Snacks and Hors d'oeuvres

Outside of main meal times, a request for food from a guest can pop up at any time throughout the day: while they are sunbathing, after a long day of water sports, during cocktail hour, prior to going ashore for dinner, when they return late at night, you name it. My advice here is to keep plenty of doilies (small ornamental mats, usually made of lace, cotton, or linen) on hand. You will use them to line every service tray or plate you serve a snack on (which can make even a PowerBar look elegant).

Other Types of Service

- ➥ **Cheese service**—After meals or as a snack, a stew will serve up lots of fromage. It's a good idea to learn how to put together a fancy cheese board on your own for when guests are requesting snacks and the chef is on break.
- ➥ **Champagne service**—Typically executed during celebrations, parties, and "welcome aboard" festivities, yacht stews end up serving a lot of champagne. This is a relatively

easy type of service, with the two tricks being a) to open the bottle with flair (while avoiding taking someone's eye out); and then b) to pour the bottle while holding it at the base, which takes a strong wrist. Serve it cold, with strawberries, and make sure you have enough glasses for the number of guests participating in a toast, and you've got that one down.

↦ **Traditional tea service**—By tea service, I do not mean simply serving a cup of tea for breakfast or after a meal. That's not to say there isn't a proper way to serve a cup of tea (or a cup of coffee), but this particular tea service is, in fact, more like a meal on its own. Here, tea service refers to the English tradition of sitting down for a formal afternoon tea break at 4 o'clock.

　　Any stew training course will cover the proper etiquette for serving afternoon tea. The thought of ever having to perform it always scared me to death, although I'm not sure why—when you break it down, it's not that difficult. In the end, I never had to call upon my training, mainly because we had more American guests than European. (For Americans, afternoon tea just "ain't our thang.")

↦ **Caviar service**—Serving caviar is a cinch. It might be served at a cocktail party or as a dinner appetizer. Most yachts have a silver caviar service set, and the chef usually prepares this for the stew to present. Caviar is served with various accompaniments including blini or hot breakfast toast, butter, lemon, chopped shallots, and chopped egg. Don't forget the caviar knife.

↦ **Cigar service**—I came to accept that the accumulation of vast amounts of wealth and the smoking of cigars just go hand in hand. When it comes to the finer things in life, cigars are savored like a rare wine. Stews should be skilled at not only presenting, cutting, and lighting cigars, but also storing them. They cover all this in stew training courses, but here's your first lesson: The best method for storing and presenting cigars is in a humidor, a polished box that is made of or lined with cedar, which allows cigars to breathe and keeps them at a constant level of humidity.

↦ **In-cabin service**—Simply put, this is room service. Stews must often prepare trays to deliver to guests' cabins. The things to remember here are attractive presentation and anticipating a guest's needs so that you include everything on the first visit, without having to be rung back for something that person needs *(and now!)*.

↦ **Fruit baskets**—This is not a type of service, but know that stews are in charge of fruit basket displays, which are to be set out in the main salon, other public areas, and, if requested, a guest's cabin. It's important to include a good variety of both colors and shapes in this assortment. We're going for visual appeal as much as anything here. The other key task is keeping it fresh, meaning changing the fruit every couple of days. The last thing you want is for a guest to be drawn to an attractive array of produce, only to pick up a pear and find flies stuck to the bottom of it. Also be aware that a guest may grab a piece of fruit and then want you to serve it to him or her properly. For this, you would do what is typically involved in serving dessert fruits at the end of a meal: take out a fruit plate, fruit knife and fork, napkin, and finger bowl right away.

Housekeeping

I always expect this topic to turn a few people off; I was turned off when I first started. I came into the yachting industry with a background in waiting tables and bartending, so serving extravagant meals and expensive wines to an elite clientele sounded like fun to me. As for the endless task of keeping the boat's interior looking spotless, on the other hand, well, that was not something I had counted on.

Cleaning, Dusting, and Vacuuming (Hoovering)

If you think you know what clean means, think again. When it comes to the interiors of these yachts, nothing is ever clean enough! Are you familiar with what it means to detail something, as when someone details a car? This process requires that even the hardest-to-reach places are washed, waxed, polished, and dusted, and that no spot is missed. That's exactly the type of cleaning that occurs throughout a megayacht, inside and out. Every detail, every inch, and to perfection.

All beginner stews hear the horror stories about picky guests who go to extremes. A popular one I remember was about an owner's wife who ran her fingertips along the tops of picture frames and then held up the accumulated dust to the chief stew's face as a warning that he or she had not cleaned thoroughly enough. Who knows if that really ever happened, or if it's just an old wives' tale (or mistresses' tale). No, most guests I encountered were not that attentive to detail. Once again, though, remember that these are people used to the finest of accommodations, whether it be their homes or one of the world's top resorts. Keeping things immaculate is imperative. (And I bet now you'll always remember to dust the tops of picture frames.)

One of the things that amazed me when I landed my first full-time job and stepped into a 2nd stew position on a 164-foot yacht was the *myriad* cleaning products I was shown for my use. The variety was astonishing, as was the range of different surfaces I was expected to clean. We're talking opulent surfaces, ones you may never have encountered before: gold sinks and gold-plated fixtures, marble floors, hand-crafted tiles, soft-finished woods, suede chairs, granite countertops, upholstered walls, and floor-to-ceiling mirrors, some of which twist around elaborate spiral staircases.

I Must Confess...

Those %#@&! GOLD SINKS... They were the bane of my existence!*

Ahhh, the gold-plated sink. The glint, the gleam, the sparkle... Such a symbol of decadence... and such a pain in the stewardess's arse!

We had one in the owner's cabin head (master bathroom) and one in the day head (main public bathroom). Now, I ask myself: What nitwit interior designer thought this was a good idea? Form dictating function? I think not. This type of opulence is impressive with regard to aesthetic appeal, but it certainly doesn't rank well in terms of practicality.

Consider what chemicals I had to battle: When people hover over sinks, they are using toothpastes, soaps, facial cleansing products, lotions, and all sorts of gobbledygook that drops and spills and can (and will) ruin that gold. Unsightly stains and scratches? You betchya.

It was critical that we stewardesses kept tabs on the gold sinks. The second a guest stepped out of one of those bathrooms, it was a **"Code Gold!"** We scurried straight in because those sinks *had* to be cleaned right away. But then there was the sink in the master cabin head: When that guest went to bed, you couldn't touch the sink until the next morning.

For the owners, this is the downside to chartering out their yachts—there's a lot of wear and tear to consider. Charter guests are going to be a lot less likely to think about what they are doing to a sink they rent, as opposed to own. The key words are PROTECT, PROTECT, PROTECT. A stew is in charge of protecting the owner's property. We stews therefore had to fight with all of our might to stave off the ultimate threat of gold lacquer deterioration.

And yet, no matter how valiant our efforts, by the end of each long charter season, the sinks were stained. Without fail, they needed to be re-plated.

Did I mention that our dining room chairs were suede? Don't even get me started…

Then there are the carpets—and not your average everyday carpets from Carpetland USA. We're talking custom inlay and hand-woven carpets. But don't worry, that doesn't mean you are going to have to pick them clean with your fingers or a pair of tweezers; the insanity to achieve perfect cleanliness does have some limits. You will, in fact, have access to a vacuum cleaner that you can use on most all carpeted surfaces. (Just don't expect that we're going to stop at carpet; the upholstered walls require vacuuming as well.)

As with the pronunciation of the job title stewardess, the British way of doing things tends to prevail in the yachting world. Therefore, vacuuming is most often referred to as hoovering. "Hoover," in the United Kingdom, is like using the brand name Kleenex for tissue, or Band-aid for bandage; they've adopted the manufacturer name of the most popular brand. In yachting, you'll hear stews, including the American ones, using this word all the time, as both a noun and a verb: "Have you seen the hoover?" or "I need to hoover the room."

Carpet is not the only type of floor surface you will encounter, either, for others such as wood and marble are pretty much a given. Every yacht is almost guaranteed to have fine marble flooring, if not in the main entrance and foyers, then in the heads. Here's a tip: Human vomit will stain marble. If a guest is about to get seasick, get him or her away from the marble! (If it can't be the toilet, even the carpet is a better target.)

Cleaning *Without* Guests Onboard

When guests are not onboard, all carpet and floor surfaces are protected by runners. These are cloth covers specifically cut to each room's floor size, and in some cases, to go around furniture. As soon as guests depart, the runners go down. That doesn't mean the hoovering stops, though; you simply hoover the runners.

Even without guests onboard to impress, the interior of a yacht is kept nitpickingly perfect and organized. The stews still clean, only not on such a strict daily routine. A lot of maintenance-type activities are performed during this "down time," such as clearing out the air conditioning vents and re-arranging storage areas. The crew area must also be detailed when no guests are onboard. Living in such incredibly tight living quarters, this is for health, as well as sanity, reasons.

The preparations for guests coming onboard can seem endless, and in the days leading up, the workload becomes heavier. All of the stews in the interior department will participate in detailing and setting up the yacht for a trip. This is when a stew might spend an entire day just cleaning one cabin or one specific area of the boat. But with the entire team working together, this process can be a lot of fun. For me, the key was just to play great music while I cleaned. Not to mention the fact that washing windows is great for the biceps!

Cleaning *With* Guests Onboard

With guests on the boat, one stew will be assigned to housekeeping duties for the entire day. This stew's job is to dust and hoover every room religiously—that is, every single day, and sometimes twice. Included here are all the common areas, such as the main salon, the dining room(s), the hallways and corridors, the stairways, the accessory rooms, such as media and fitness centers, and, then of course, the guest cabins (which we'll get to in a bit). The day head receives careful attention. Beyond that, there are the crew areas: the captain's office, the wheelhouse, the crew mess, and the laundry room. It is easy for the stews to neglect these spaces when the priority is the guest areas; however, you never know when you'll be pleasantly surprised by a guest who wants to come "hang out" with the captain and crew, or come into your laundry room to look for a shirt he's missing (and most likely never brought onboard in the first place).

Aside from dusting and vacuuming, the stew on housekeeping duty must worry about keeping the windows and mirrors fingerprint-free. Also on the general housekeeping list of duties: sprucing up cushions, straightening piles of magazines, watering plants, and just all-around picking up after people.

Ah yes, and then there's cleaning the guest cabins; this is next on our agenda.

Making Beds and Other Cabin Care

This area of responsibility held by a yacht's interior crew is more affectionately known throughout the industry as "heads and beds" (which translates as "cleaning bathrooms and cabins"). If you have your sights set on becoming a stew, get used to this expression, because as an entry-level crewmember, it's all you, baby!

The same attention to cleaning, dusting, and hoovering mentioned in the previous section applies to the staterooms as well. You will hoover each cabin every day with guests onboard. You will also dust everything from the window blinds (such a pain) to the bedside tables to the electronic equipment.

Sounds easy, huh? Well, it certainly isn't rocket science, but on the other hand, there's a little more to it than that.

Let me ask you this: How many times a week do you wash and replace your bed sheets at home? Well, on a luxury yacht, some guests will want their sheets changed every day! This varies, but the longest you should wait is three days. Depending on the size of the boat, there are typically five to 10 beds that require your attention. That equates to a lot of time and energy devoted to the maintenance of bed linens, especially when you consider that sheets not only have to be washed, but ironed, too. Regardless of a sheet change, the stews make up all guest beds each morning.

Making the perfect bed is another art form to be mastered. Stews are expected to know the mechanics of creating hospital bed corners, which involves a special folding and tucking of the top sheet snugly under the foot of the mattress so that the bed's surface is taut and flat. While hospital corner folds are not even seen, the result of using them is a bed that looks meticulously made. (Try bouncing a quarter on that puppy.) And, a luxurious-looking bed is essential to achieving the overall ambiance of a warm and welcoming cabin.

After bed-making, we've got the bed turndown, another cabin-cleaning ritual. While the guests are at dinner or off the yacht in the evening, the stews sneak in like little pixies to turn down the bedspread and dim the lights, thus making these overnight thrones look inviting for the guests when they come to bed. Mind you, during bed turndowns, the stew is also doing another light clean on the entire cabin, including drying out that shower if it was used before dinner.

A lot of stews like to get creative and add special touches to their bed turndowns, such as leaving gifts on the pillows or bedside stands: chocolates, a fresh flower in a vase, or even a postcard from the port they visited that day. I know one stew who tried leaving rose petals on one of her guests' pillows. Warning: Rose petals, unless they are freeze-dried, stain white sheets. And, if you opt for chocolates, make sure you place them where even an intoxicated guest is going to see them. The last thing you want is for someone to collapse into bed and end up rolling over melted chocolates all night. Believe me, it's happened. Not only does this result in an entire set of ruined sheets, but possibly even a chocolate-faced guest appearing at the breakfast table the next morning in a really foul (but yummy-smelling) mood.

In addition to all the cleaning, hoovering, bed-making, and bed turndowns, cabin care also involves other activities. You will straighten up shoes and tidy closets, remove soiled laundry and return clean laundry, remove trash (ah yes, rubbish), and make sure the fresh flowers are watered and kept looking nice. For yacht stews, beyond just the cleaning, "heads and beds" refers to all of these tasks, and more.

I Must Confess...
I tried on a pair of guest's shoes.

I only did it once. I couldn't help it. All the guests were at dinner, so barring any incident that would cause this particular guest to have to return to her cabin, I had a window of opportunity.

Besides, they were the same exact pair of teal blue, kitten-heeled, beaded Prada sandals I had seen in the previous month's *Harper's Bazaar.* I believe Kate Moss had modeled them. From what I could recall, they had been priced somewhere in the $800 range. And there they were, just staring up at me from the floor of this charter guest's closet—and in my size!

Temptation won out; I just couldn't resist. In Cinderella-like fashion, I slid my foot in—first the one, and then the other. A perfect fit! I pranced back and forth in the wardrobe, admiring my now-fancy feet in the mirror, heart pounding all the while. In less than 60 seconds, they were off and placed carefully back, exactly how I found them—their fortunate owner none the wiser.

I didn't make a habit of that; but hot damn, it was exhilarating while it lasted!

Guest Heads

Then there are the guest bathrooms, which you now know as heads. A stew spends an awful lot of time in these particular rooms. And there's something about wealthy individuals requiring that each time they enter a restroom, it's supposed to feel as if they are the first people to ever use it. Stews are expected to keep the heads spic-and-span, even throughout the day. This means getting into each one periodically to "wipe out" any evidence of an earlier use. If you've ever wondered why cleaning staff fold the front square of a toilet paper roll, well there's your answer: It sends a message to your client that you've been there and provided a service.

But it's not just the toilets that require attention. The guest showers and bathtubs need to be wiped down and dried after each use as well, even if they're used twice a day. You must also keep a fresh set of towels available.

You are constantly cleaning up around the sinks, too. The thing to keep your eye on here is watermarks on the mirrors, which occur from the splashing of water when a guest uses the sink. You know what these look like—we all cause them on mirrors over sinks. But unlike your own home, you must never let them sit long on a mirror onboard a yacht. That is the first sign that you have not done your job!

A Day in the Life of a Stew on Housekeeping Duty *With* Guests Onboard

So let's put it all together, shall we?

As a stew on housekeeping duty, you are up and ready to begin work at 7:00 or 7:30 a.m. Most likely, another stewardess has already been up for awhile handling breakfast preparations, such as setting the table, brewing coffee (grab some!), and getting service items ready.

You set out on your day armed with a well-stocked cleaning caddy.

Cleaning Caddy Essentials (a.k.a. Your Arsenal):
- a glass cleaner
- diaper rags (cloth out-cleans disposable paper products, hands down)
- a vinegar and water mix (the cheapest, most effective cleaning "product" out there)
- a non-abrasive cleaner or some type of bath scrub
- a scrub brush
- a sponge or two
- an all-purpose cleaner such as Formula 409 (used mainly in the crew areas)

- ↦ tons of cotton swabs (the key to hitting those hard-to-reach places)
- ↦ a toothbrush (the key to hitting those even harder-to-reach places)
- ↦ toilet bowl cleaner (let's stop talking about those hard-to-reach places)
- ↦ toilet bowl brush (do not use the ones in the guest cabins—you carry your own)
- ↦ diluted Murphy's Oil Soap or some other wood cleaner (no Pledge comes onboard a yacht, as it can strip varnish)
- ↦ a leather chamois (pronounced "shammy"), which is used for drying guest showers and tubs
- ↦ air freshener (the more neutral the better, as guests may have allergies or sensitive noses)
- ↦ a roll of mini trash bags
- ↦ a feather duster (these are useless, but they look good)
- ↦ latex or rubber gloves
- ↦ the Glove—as in the white glove (just in case you get asked to serve something as you breeze through a room, and you've just been cleaning toilets two minutes earlier)

You first head to the main guest area on the boat, the salon. If breakfast is being served indoors, you may want to clean the dining room first so as not to interfere with a potential early meal service, which may not have started yet.

You begin with dusting and polishing: All glass, wood, and marble surfaces get your attention. Straighten any furniture from the previous night's festivities. Fluff the cushions. Brush the suede. Dust the blinds, and check the windows for fingerprints. Water the plants. Organize the magazine stacks, and see if the deckhands have made it ashore to buy the day's newspapers yet (not always possible).

Once the main salon has been tackled, move on to performing the same duties in the dining room (or vice versa, depending on where you began). Vacuuming is next, but if some guests are still sleeping, you'll want to close off any doors to the guest areas first.

Move on to the day head. Get that toilet and sink looking spotless; disinfect the toilet seat, lid, bowl, pedestal, and floor. Replace the hand towels if needed. Polish the sink, fixtures, mirror, and cabinet fronts. Check the tissue dispenser. Empty the rubbish bin. Fold that front toilet paper square. (Just as with napkins, an origami of toilet paper folding also exists in this business. Oh yeah: "The Fan" actually uses up two entire squares! Quite frankly, it's all a waste of paper. But since you must do something to signal you've been there, stick with a simple V-fold.)

It's on to the sky lounge next, vacuuming the stairs, polishing the handrails, and cleaning the mirrors along the way. Dust and hoover the sky lounge before heading to the wheelhouse. (Also known as the bridge or pilothouse, the wheelhouse is the area where the captain steers the vessel and where exterior crew stand watch when the yacht is underway.) *Wait, did you get the windows and blinds in the sky lounge?* In the wheelhouse, it is important to dust the computer and navigational equipment, but without ruining anything electrical (or resetting any of the controls—yikes!). Next, you must clean the captain's cabin, and then vacuum your way out of there and back down to the main deck.

As the guests begin waking up and coming out for breakfast, it is safe to hoover the corridors and hallways leading to the cabins. If you have time to kill before this happens, head to the crew area to dust and hoover down there. See if the laundry or service stews need assistance. You can also visit the various bar and pantry refrigerators to restock drinks used the day before. Clean the bars that were used the night before as well.

Once guests are up, it's time to start cleaning the cabins. You will need about 30-45 minutes to complete each stateroom and its accompanying head. Here is what that will entail:

Open the drapes; raise the blinds (dust them first if necessary); check the windows for fingerprints; make the bed according to schedule, removing the dirty sheets if necessary; dust all flat surfaces; dust and wipe down the clock, phone, and TV/DVD and stereo equipment; hoover the entire cabin; brush the suede chairs; straighten the lamp shades; fold any guest clothes and place them at the foot of the bed; empty the rubbish bin; water and primp the floral display (if it's looking withered, it's time to order or make another); polish all door handles and light fixtures; fill the H2O jug; clean the drinking glasses; refresh the tissue bouquet; clean the mirrored doors in the wardrobe; straighten the clothes hangers; check the laundry bag, and take dirty items to the laundry room, being careful not to mix guests' garments; and straighten the guest's personal items (but don't snoop). If the boat is underway, check that all doors, drawers, and cabinets are latched closed.

Next, head into the cabin's bathroom (yeah, head to the head): clean and disinfect the shower or tub (or both if they're each present and both were used), and wipe them dry with a chamois; clean and disinfect the toilet and the bidet; clean around the sinks and faucets; polish the mirrors (leaving no watermarks!); wipe down the cabinets; tidy the soaps and guest personal items around the sink; check and replenish any guest toiletries supplied by the yacht; clean the drinking glass; detail the cabinet and door fixtures; wipe the floors; remove the used towels and get them to the laundry; hang fresh towels, including hand towels, washcloths, bath or shower mats, and bath towels—large and medium (fold them carefully, in threes, then in half; hang with folded edges facing out); check toilet paper supply (fold that front square); and empty the rubbish bin.

Remember that you'll most likely have up to six cabins on a megayacht, which altogether could contain nine beds (four to six twin beds that are doubled up in two or three cabins, and then three to four queen- or king-sized beds between the remaining rooms). Each of these cabins will have its own head, and while a few rooms may only have a shower in the head, the VIP and master cabins will likely have both a stand-up shower and a separate shower/tub. Thus, this cabin and head-cleaning saga can take up a good portion of the morning, and possibly even the early afternoon.

The good news is that this four-to six-hour cleaning frenzy is usually followed by a break. If you are on a yacht with three or more stews in total, there can be a stew on laundry duty full-time. If that is not the case, then a break may be delayed a bit longer for the housekeeping stew to assist either in the laundry or with lunch service. Either way, a break will happen somewhere in the afternoon, anywhere from one to three hours in duration.

Before going on break *and* immediately following: Check the day head for a "Code Gold" (refer back to my gold sinks confession if that confuses you); make sure all dirty linens have been taken to the laundry room and clean items taken back to the guest areas and put away; help dry the lunch dishes if needed; do a quick round of straightening in the salon and lounges; tidy up the guests' shoes in the basket perched outside the main entrance, making sure the shoehorn is accessible (score bonus points by sneaking shoes away for a good polish); re-stock any fridges if needed; and check that the laundry stew isn't in need of assistance. Most likely, he or she will, but in your effort to lend a hand, remember that your break is crucial to you being prepared to assist with dinner service and complete bed turndowns later that night. Go take a nap!

By the time you come off break, it should be around 4:00–5:00 p.m. Do your quick cleaning rounds, check that day head one more time, and then take over doing laundry or service while another stew takes his or her break.

Once all the stews are back from break, dinner preparations have begun. Keep doing your cleaning rounds, paying particular attention to where the guests will be dining that evening. While dinner is being served, clear hors d'oeuvre plates and cocktail glasses from the public areas, see if any last-minute help is needed by the chef, and then get into those cabins for bed turndowns: shut the blinds; dim the lighting; change the H2O in the bedside pitchers; turn down the bed(s); do a light clean through the room; clean the bathroom for the second time that day (the shower has got to be spotless and the towels fresh for morning); remove cabin and head rubbish; straighten the room; and finally, leave out the chocolates, flowers, postcards, or whatever you are doing for bed turndown.

After the cabins are all turned down, see if the service stew(s) need any help hand-washing dinner crystal or drying silverware. If not, then take over for the stew on laundry duty so he or she can retire for the day, and spend your last couple hours keeping the washers and dryers going, ironing sheets, and folding towels, while being able to catch a movie in the crew mess while you work.

Finally, the most important part of completing these tasks: Have fun! It may sound like a lot of work (it is), but it can actually be quite enjoyable. And while it isn't rocket science, you can usually go to bed each night feeling a tremendous sense of accomplishment. (I always hummed Donna Summer's "She Works Hard for the Money" as I brushed my teeth.)

I Must Confess…
I once cleaned a bit too thoroughly.

Up to now I have stressed getting everything as clean as possible, right down to the tiniest detail. However, you can go too far; I learned this the hard way.

I once over-cleaned a shower floor and caused a leak in the ceiling below it!

Here was my mistake: The tiles in cabin showers are smooth-surfaced, which makes them great receptacles for hardened soap scum. Also, the areas between them are filled with grout, a porous substance with plenty of nooks and crannies to hold dirt and mildew. Well, in preparation for guests to come onboard, I became so intent on clawing the soiled threads of grout from between the tiles in the master cabin shower that I actually loosened the grout between them, causing little leaks throughout!

On the day the guests arrived (and while I can't say who they were, just know they are famous), they enjoyed a fabulous champagne welcome before the main charter guest's wife decided she would retreat to her cabin for a shower.

It began as drips and drops. And I'm not talking about the shower water falling on her, but rather, on those of us beneath her. Down from her shower floor, through the ceiling in the main entrance foyer, and right onto the marble floor. The next thing we knew, there were actual **streams** of water falling.

Needless to say, it was slightly awkward having to send someone in to halt this woman mid-shower, requesting that she take her cleansing elsewhere (as in, to another cabin's bathroom downstairs). And because in order to mend my damage the engineer had to put silicone over the grout, which took a long time to dry, it would be another 48 hours before this guest or her husband could use their master shower. Meanwhile, in addition to being unsightly, the buckets we had to set out to catch dripping water were a nuisance to maneuver around.

I owned up to my mistake though, and once we were about three days into the trip, it became an ongoing joke among everyone, both the crew and the guests. So I did my job a little too well… Hey, at least it was the bottom of a shower, and not the bottom of the boat!

Laundry

Despite how little I did my laundry while growing up, when I entered yachting I at least had the basics down: separate lights from darks, empty all pockets, and beyond that, just read the labels. Okay, so I had a lot to learn. My first stewardess job was therefore a crash course in washing finer garments. The same holds true for ironing sheets, not to mention folding them.

What Gets Done (Can You Wash This?)

Handling all of the guest and crew laundry is a big part of the interior staff's role onboard. When I think back to doing laundry on yachts, what comes to mind is the theme song to the movie *The NeverEnding Story*. And yes, the title to that song was "The NeverEnding Story," which quite appropriately describes the amount of work a yacht stew faces in the laundry room.

I assumed doing laundry simply meant the guests' clothes, bed sheets, and bath towels. I soon found out there was a lot more to it than that.

Laundry *Without* Guests Onboard

The good news is that when guests are not onboard, the amount of laundry does lessen substantially. Unless linens are being prepared for an upcoming group of guests, cleaning rags and galley towels are about the only work-related items needing a stew's attention.

Otherwise, it's the crew laundry that makes up the bulk of the workload. Each crewmember is typically responsible for his or her own personal items, and the machines are made available during guest-free periods. However, crew uniforms, sheets, and towels will often still be done by the stews, and those will be run during the day.

With or without guests onboard, the dryers should be vacuumed out and the filters cleaned on a regular basis. As with the dryers in your own home, a buildup of lint in the air filters is a fire hazard.

Laundry *With* Guests Onboard

With guests onboard, the laundry runs all day, and there is usually one stew managing it at all times (and even someone to fill in when that stew is on break or grabbing a meal). The stew on laundry duty starts out in the morning by picking up right where things left off the night before, which usually means ironing guest clothing that is to be taken back to the respective cabins ASAP. There will also be the dinner napkins from the night before—now clean, but in need of ironing.

If you are the laundry stew, here is usually how it goes: The person on housekeeping duty comes in panicking that there are no diaper rags for cleaning. Then, it's the chef complaining that he or she is out of galley towels (since those had to be washed separately due to a smothering of cooking grease). Next, one of the deckhands can't find a pair of clean shorts and "just knows" there is one at the bottom of the nice, neat stack of crew shorts you have beside you (and over, topples the nice, neat stack of crew shorts).

As soon as you catch up and are on to ironing crew uniforms, the housekeeping stew, who has just gotten in to clean the first few cabins, begins delivering mounds of bed sheets, bath towels, and garment bags filled with guest laundry. To keep all of the guest garments straight—whose is whose and when it was received—you must write each item into a logbook. Then it's time to hunt for stains (guests won't always alert you to them), and thus, a hand-washing marathon begins. Yes, guest garments need to be carefully attended to, and most require hand-washing. If not done by hand, care should still be taken regarding fabric content, color, and cleaning instructions. There may be some items requiring dry cleaning instead, which yachts are not equipped to handle, so they must be sent out or simply refused. The stews should never feel coerced into cleaning an article that may inevitably create problems. When in doubt, ask the chief stew.

Before the sheets, towels, and guest items make their way through the washing and drying process, on come the soiled breakfast napkins (here again, it's a hunt for stains). Oh, wait, now the deckhands have changed from their morning to their afternoon uniforms—get ready for their sweaty T-shirts and shorts to come in. Next, more galley and cleaning towels are dropped off. And before long, guest beach towels damp with salt water are piled up outside the door. Now a guest is demanding a shirt he sent to the laundry a few hours before, and he wants to wear it *that instant*. You have it, but it's soaking in Woolite. A memo is delivered from the captain: He needs more starch on his collars. You pull out some king-sized bed sheets from the dryer, but there's no one around to help you fold them (it takes two for king sheets).

It keeps going like this all day long. No, there's never a dull moment in the laundry room.

Stains

Stews come across every type of stain under the sun. On clothing, furniture, bed linens, and table linens (tablecloths, placemats and napkins are laundered after each use, remember). The laundry rooms on yachts are therefore filled with a vast quantity of specialized stain sticks aimed at treating everything from blood to wine to human feces. Beyond that, every stew who comes along will claim to have the answer to getting out even the most difficult stains.

But again, if there's possibility of ruining the garment or other fabric, don't attempt it. Leave it to a professional dry cleaner.

❖   **INSIDER TIP:** Handling yacht linens and guest and crew laundry is a technically difficult part of a yacht stew's job, and it requires quite a bit of knowledge and skill. My biggest piece of advice is to always check the manufacturer's care tags and follow the directions. When it doubt, ask a senior stew or seek out answers in port dry-cleaning facilities. That's right, ask the experts. Ruining linens owned by the yacht is usually forgivable (unless it happens frequently). But, ruin an expensive piece of clothing owned by an owner's wife, and that could mean catastrophe.

Folding and Ironing

Everything, and I mean EVERYTHING, gets pressed by the iron—socks and underwear included. I even worked with a few stews who insisted on ironing the diaper rags we used for cleaning. (Yes, that is going a bit far.) Consistency is the key to a high-profile operation, and consequently, the interior team should maintain a manual of standards regarding folding, ironing, and which way to place items on a hanger.

Speaking of which: Do you know how to fold a pair of socks properly? They teach you all this in stew training courses, which is a good thing because before I was exposed to it, I just assumed you threw them aside and focused on shirts and pants. But yes, be prepared to learn a couple different ways to fold socks, and a special way to fold women's underwear as opposed to men's.

Ironing bed linens was always the most frustrating task for me. Those darn bottom sheets can be tricky. The good news is that most yachts come with a roller press onboard, which helps cut down the time it takes to iron sheets. (The king-sized category will still entail some linen-wrestling, but feeding them through a roller beats trying to tackle them on a flat board any day.)

Napkins and bed linens will require heavy starch, as will some of the crew uniforms. Men's dress shirts would also qualify to receive a little dose; however, as yachts are mostly in vacation mode, you won't see many of those.

With regard to crew uniforms, there are preferred ways to iron and fold T-shirts, polos, pleated shorts, stew skirts and skorts, and dress pants. The stews are in control of how the crew looks, and the idea is to have all the uniforms looking shipshape, even when there are no guests onboard. (You are always maintaining the overall image of the yacht, which is constantly under public scrutiny: No wrinkles!)

I Must Confess...

*I skimped on the laundry because I knew
bed sheets could be sent out to the dry cleaners.*

The good news on some yachts is that if the laundry is piling up and the stews fall too far behind, you can usually send a couple rounds of guest bed sheets off to a dry cleaner. It does take some careful planning, but if you can be sure you will be in a port on a specific date, and you feel 100 percent positive the guests aren't going to decide last minute that they want to depart that port early, you can get in touch with a local dry cleaner to have your sheets cleaned, and more importantly pressed, and back to you in under a day.

Secretly, I knew we could fall back on this; therefore, I always saved the sheets for last!

Rotation Schedule Example

Following is an example of a rotation schedule, or rota, that might be found on a yacht containing a staff of four stews—a chief and three others. If there are only three stews onboard, duties would be combined, still allowing for the big three areas of service, housekeeping, and laundry to be covered at all times.

Sample Stew Rotation Schedule				
	STEW #1 HOUSEKEEPING	**STEW #2** SERVICE	**STEW #3** LAUNDRY	**CHIEF STEW** SERVICE AND MANAGEMENT
06:30	Start cleaning main salon.	Set up breakfast. Start time may be earlier (5:30–6:00) if the guests onboard are early risers.	– Sleep Late – Wake time depends on how late up previous night assisting Chief Stew.	– Sleep Late – Wake time depends on how late up previous night.
07:00	Start cleaning cabins as soon as guests begin getting up.	Breakfast service as guests awaken.	–	–
07:30 – 08:30	Continue cleaning guest cabins and main areas.	Breakfast continues. Assist in the galley if things are slow.	Start laundry and clean in crew mess.	– Only if needed – (Otherwise, sleep in.)
09:00 – 09:30	Continue cleaning cabins.	Breakfast continues.	Continue with laundry. Help Stew #2 clean cabins as needed.	Join Stew #1 for breakfast duty. If no help required, work on menus, orders, and accounting projects.

10:00 – 10:30	Continue cleaning cabins and other main areas, including the pilothouse, bars, and the day head.	Begin clearing breakfast as it finishes. Do dishes, send linens to the laundry, and begin preparing for lunch.	Continue with laundry and helping Stew #2 on cabins.	Refresh fruit displays. Check floral arrangements. Assist with clearing breakfast. Guest watch.
11:00	Continue cleaning guest cabins and other main areas. Assist Stew #3 with ironing if needed.	Go on break when breakfast is finished.	Laundry & ironing.	Guest watch & service. Begin pulling service items for lunch.
11:30 – 13:00	Go on break once cabins are finished.	– On break – (Until needed for lunch service.)	Laundry & ironing.	Start setting the table for lunch.
13:30 – 14:30	– On break –	Help Chief Stew set and/or serve lunch. Do dishes.	Check cabins while guests are at lunch. Tidy them as needed.	Lunch service, accompanied by Stew #2.
15:00 – 15:30	Cover laundry for Stew #3.	Cover guest watch while Chief Stew is on break.	Go on break when Stew #1 comes back on.	Go on break.
16:00 – 17:00	Continue laundry & ironing.	Guest watch. Tidy main areas. Complete any projects assigned by Chief Stew.	– On break –	– On break –
18:00 – 18:30	Cleaning cabins, decks, and main areas.	Start pulling service items for dinner.	Back from break. Continue with laundry & ironing.	Back from break. Guest watch & service.
19:00	Change to evening wear. Cleaning continues.	Change to evening wear. Dinner preps continue.	Change to evening wear. Laundry & ironing continues.	Guest watch & service.
19:30	Assist with guest watch & service.	Set table for dinner. Guest watch.	Laundry & ironing continues.	Change to evening wear. Help set table.
20:00	Begin cabin turn-down as guests emerge for dinner.	Final dinner preparations. Serve cocktails.	Continue with laundry & ironing.	Final dinner preparations. Serve cocktails.

20:30 – 21:30	Cabin turn-down. Assist with dinner if needed. Clear main salon. Take over laundry when done.	Serve dinner with Chief Stew.	Help Stew #1 with cabin turn-down. Help clear main salon. Help clear dinner when it ends.	Serve dinner, accompanied by Stew #2, and Stew #1 as needed.
22:00 – 22:30	Finish when laundry & ironing is cleared (if it ever is—otherwise, go to bed at a reasonable time).	Clear dinner and do dishes. Finish once Chief Stew no longer needs assistance with guest watch & service.	Help clear dinner and do dishes. Finish when dinner is cleared.	Clear dinner & guest watch.
23:00 – Until Guests Retire	Finished.	Finished.	Finished.	Guests watch & service until they retire. Clear main salon. Stock pantry and fridges. Finished.

"When you work on a yacht, you are all about service, so consider this: The highest level of service is service within a private living environment, and the level of service performed on a yacht is often the highest level of all. This kind of service cannot be outsourced; the responsibility is all on us. The work yacht stews do in a private service environment adds value and enriches the lives of the owners and their guests. By agreeing to serve, we agree to follow someone else's agenda, and to do so with an open heart. As Gandhi said, 'The best way to find yourself is to lose yourself in service to others.'"

—**Alene Keenan**, author of *The Yacht Service Bible: The Service Manual for Every Yacht*

5

A STEW'S JOB IS NEVER DONE
—BEYOND THE BIG THREE—

"The stewardesses are the front line with guests. Typically most guests never meet the engineer, and because the captain is moving the yacht, they don't interact with him much. It is the stew who spends 24/7 with the guests, so if they do a great job, my job is a breeze. If they do not do a good job, I have very unhappy clients on my hands."
—**Debra Blackburn Boggio**, Yacht Charter Broker with Fraser Yachts Worldwide

"In my opinion, no one department influences the success of the guest or owner's experience more than the Interior Staff."
—**Julie Liberatore**, Regulatory Liaison Maritime Professional Training (MPT)

You should now have a strong grasp of what being a yacht stew is all about, at least with regard to "The Big Three" functions: Service, Housekeeping, and Laundry. However, as I mentioned in the last chapter, there are a variety of other responsibilities that go along with this position, and the most over-arching way to group them together is under the category of "overall guest care." This chapter covers such general duties, which unlike the duties described in Chapter 4, are ongoing and not really assigned to just one stew.

In addition, this chapter will also cover interior staff responsibilities that fall under the jurisdiction of the chief stew, or pertain mainly to the chief stew's role—the largest of which is household management. I include this information for several reasons:

1) For a beginner stew, it is advantageous to see the bigger picture of what goes on in the interior department. Just because a chief stew is not attending to "heads and beds" or assigned to laundry duties for an entire day does not mean that person isn't working his or her tail off. It is good for you to see just how grand and far-reaching a chief's responsibilities are.

2) As your manager, a chief stew may assign you tasks that fall under household management, such as taking inventories, putting together shopping lists, or updating the guest welcome book. You'll want to understand your boss's perspective as you take on these assignments.

3) I share with you these more advanced areas of responsibility overseen by the interior department since, after all, if you end up in this industry, you may aspire to be a chief stew yourself one day. (And remember from Chapter 3 that they can really rake in the dough!)

And finally, you will also find in this chapter some of a stew's responsibilities that come along with simply being a crewmember in any position onboard, stewardess or otherwise. These tasks relate to the overall "team player" aspect of working on a yacht crew, and they are crucial to securing the comfort of the guests and the safety of everyone onboard. All crewmembers are going to share these functions.

Host/Hostess (With the Most/Mostest)

The pampering begins the instant your guests enter a limousine at the closest airport (where there's a 99.9 percent chance they arrived by private jet) and begin heading to the embarkation port where the yacht and crew await them. It is often the captain, but sometimes the chief stew, who books the vehicles to pick up the guests, and this responsibility might also include transportation arrangements prior to that, such as making spur-of-the-moment helicopter reservations. Once the clients are onboard, it is the interior staff that is largely responsible for helping them settle in. Let the role of hostess roll!

A welcome reception is mandatory, and the chief stew will coordinate the festivities along with the chef. Be ready to spring into action to meet initial requests, because first impressions will set the pace for the entire trip. Even if the charter broker describes a group of guests as low key, be prepared to hype things up a bit. (Have that champagne and plate of hors d'oeuvres queued up in the galley, set to serve.)

It is primarily the chief stew's responsibility to put the guests at ease and make sure that their first requests for drinks are met quickly and accurately, and he or she will oversee the other stews (meaning you) in following suit. You will show guests to their cabins, learn to pronounce their names correctly (best to practice BEFORE they arrive, even memorizing the guest list), and make sure they are assisted with their luggage. While you may have a guest who leaves you a bit star-struck upon your initial introduction, don't worry, you'll usually get over it within the first 24 hours…after you've cleaned his or her room a couple of times.

Welcoming committee activities out of the way, the responsibility of playing host/ess remains ongoing throughout the trip, especially for the chief stew, who is established as the main point of contact for the guests. Yes, the chief stew is the go-to person, even before the captain, since he or she will be busy driving the vessel.

I Must Confess…

I was overwhelmingly star-struck by a guest once (and only once).

Wouldn't you know, with only one person on the planet (other than Madonna) who could have left me star-struck, it just so happened that he turned up as a guest of a guest one day for a two-night stay onboard.

I received word that this individual would be joining us only moments before his actual arrival. I'm not sure how I then missed the boisterous frenzy taking place on the dock as his brigade of vehicles turned up, drawing hordes of paparazzi and fans, but I did. Instead, I was down in the lower cabin he'd be staying in, sprucing up the pillows just one last time. Once I felt the room looked picture perfect, I vacated the cabin and went darting up the stairs to go perform one last celebration dance for my fellow crewmembers (which meant doing some victory-signifying arm motions while chanting "Sir X X is coming, Sir X X is coming" in an annoying, sing-songy voice).

But, as I reached the top of the stairs and made that final dash around a blind corner—BAM!—yeah, guess who I plowed right into? Sir X X. And yes, it was literally physical contact that I made with him—not quite a body slam, but definitely more impactful than a gentle "brush with fame." He was receiving a tour from the main charter guest, who took this opportunity to diffuse the awkwardness of the moment by giving us a more formal introduction: "Julie, I'd like for you to meet my distinguished guest, who will be staying onboard the next two nights, Sir X X."

Okay, it was my turn. I was supposed to say something. But I froze! Not only was I a bit shell-shocked from the collision, but th-th-this was my hero! My idol! The man whose framed photo sat on my desk back home. (This wasn't an infatuation based on physical attraction, but rather, admiration for accomplishments; to me, this person is the mogul of all moguls, and one of the greatest entrepreneurs of our time.) And oh my, was I screwing up my one shot to say, "Hello, I'm Julie. It's nice to meet you." That should have come easily.

But you see, in stewardess training school, one of the things they teach you is how to address various types of dignitaries, such as royalty and heads of state. "Sir X X," as you can tell by the title I write here, is a Knight of the British Empire. But, in that instant, all of those formal titles for individuals of distinction that I'd crammed into my brain for my stew-certification test came flashing at me. I knew that the proper way to address this individual, as one who was knighted, was **Sir** X X. And yes, duh, that was it. All I had to do was say, "It's an honor to meet you, **Sir.**" Sir. However, at that moment, the only words coming to me were ones like Duke, King, Lord… even Lady, Dame, and Your Royal Highness.

Blubbering helplessly, I came up with something along the lines of: "Nice to meet you, Sss…Um…Yes…Hi… Welcome aboard."

He smiled big, shook my sweaty hand, and said something quintessentially British and Knightly about it being a pleasure to meet me, too. Thank goodness over the course of the next two days I was able to redeem myself from that awkward introduction by engaging him in pleasant conversations on more than one occasion. I got to show him how to make an outside call from his cabin phone, I served him some killer cappuccinos on the aft deck two mornings in a row, and when I entered his room to help him carry his luggage out upon his departure, he emptied every last bit of change from his pockets, turned to me, and said, "I don't feel like carrying these coins around, so I'm leaving them. Please do not think this is meant to be a tip, for I will be leaving that with the captain."

Ha! A billionaire's pocket change. It amounted to nearly 100 U.S. dollars, but to me, it was even more valuable. To this day, I still have some of the coins.

A special note: It's quite scary when you meet one of your lifelong heroes—you fear that the person might not live up to your expectations. Believe it or not, this guest I just mentioned was the friendliest, classiest, and most down-to-earth guest I ever had onboard. Those two memorable days were among the best of my entire yachting career.

A Brief Word on Stew Panache

Being a good host goes beyond just pulling out chairs and making sure everyone has a drink in their hand. It's about creating relationships and interacting with people as well—and, in some cases, the boundaries are stricter than others. The interior crew should be friendly and outgoing at all times. As host, you want guests to feel comfortable and at ease, so socializing with them on occasion is good. Just don't overdo it! Remember, you are there to serve, not "hang out" with the guests. There is a balance you must master. It takes a certain maturity, a certain panache.

Since it is the chief stew who will have the most one-on-one interaction with the guests, he or she has the unfortunate job of also handling most of their complaints. Now, while the chief holds the brunt of this responsibility, the entire crew, including you, needs to be able to deal with the guests even if they're not particularly pleasant people (or are just not behaving like pleasant people at a particular moment).

Know that there will be some owners and charter guests who you will really connect with and enjoy. But on many of the larger, more prestigious yachts, the crewmembers might be resigned to more of a "servant" role. I don't mean that in a derogatory way. Yet, with European or Russian guests, there's a different relationship based on their cultural traditions. For example, you speak only when spoken to with certain clients. Because they speak a different language when they're not speaking directly to you, it's not like you're "in" on what's going on among the guests. Rather, you are an outsider. It can be tough to get in the groove with them because you are not interacting on a personal level. However, as I often found, for every group of guests in this category, there was another one where the people were relaxed and friendly with the crew.

Below is an excerpt from an interview I did with veteran chief stewardess Tish Owen George. Here is what Tish had to say about the types of guests you may encounter, and how best to deal with them (including your own attitude adjustment, if it's necessary):

> *I once had a five-week charter where the guests were incredibly tough when they came aboard. From Day 1, I thought,* **these people are going to kill us**. *After I cried, I said, 'Okay, we're going to turn them around. By the time they leave this boat, they are going to love us!'…And they did! You just have to fight through all those negative things and make it positive, because not every charter is a dream walk.*
>
> *You'll have those good charters that you tell people about: 'Oh, it was so fun, we became such good friends, we write all the time, blah blah blah'… But not all charters are like that. You will get these people—especially when the money gets REAL big—who are used to getting what they want, and some people handle that well and some people do not. You need to get over it. You are basically domestic help…only on a yacht. And this is something I used to have big talks about with the stews I managed. You need to leave that 'I'm too good for this' attitude behind when you work in this industry.*

Finally, a stew's role as host does not only pertain to the guests. The interior staff may also be called upon to give tours for the yacht agents and brokers to assess what is needed for upcoming trips and charters. At boat shows, the stews might also be showing around a potential buyer, who could turn out to be a future boss. The stews are the ones who know the interior of the boat the most intimately, and like a good host, they will enjoy showing it off as well. (Besides, it's your home, too!)

Concierge and Valet/Personal Assistant

This is where things get a little, well, personal. Providing concierge and valet services are a big part of the interior team's role. You are probably familiar with what a concierge does in a hotel. It is the same for stews on a yacht, and then some. Stews are called upon to handle such things as assisting guests with their offshore plans; researching proposed port-of-call destinations; making shore-excursion arrangements, restaurant reservations, or other travel plans; and even offering tour advice when the guests decide to go ashore for a day.

To function as a valet means to perform personal services for guests. Helping them pack and unpack is an example of a service you offer when wearing your valet hat. The deckhands will likely be the ones to carry heavy bags and suitcases to the staterooms when guests arrive, but interior crewmembers take over from there. This means hanging garments up, setting shoes out, placing toiletry items in the bathrooms, and taking clothes immediately to the laundry room that need washing or ironing (getting guest permission first, or course). You will also help them find ample storage space for their belongings. Guests don't always "get it" at first that the vessel will eventually be set into motion, so they should be encouraged to find a secure resting place for their fragile and valuable items. The stews then pass off the empty luggage back to the deckhands, who face the daunting task of finding a place to store it (and you just hope they are collapsible pieces).

Stews are also responsible for "small touches" like obtaining daily newspapers in the mornings and having them displayed when the guests awaken. When you are anchored out from port, this may entail sending the deckhands ashore early to buy whatever is available; in some of the more remote ports, the options will be limited. Making sure guests have an umbrella if they go ashore with rain in the forecast, handing them a map of the local port as they head out, and having pairs of slippers waiting for them upon their return (with no shoes allowed inside the boat, guests are always looking for slippers)—these are examples of the small tasks a stew should always be thinking of doing.

Sometimes the valet role might entail handling shopping requests for the guests. *Can you go ashore and pick out a black handbag for me to take to dinner this evening?* (Yeah, like that's not stressful.) Or you might be picking up bags from an already completed shopping spree. I once had a guest request that I accompany her on a shopping trip ashore so I could help carry her bags around. Don't expect it, but when you take on a job like that, the guest might even pick out something for you, such as a bottle of cologne or a pair of earrings.

You might also find yourself completing tasks normally handled by a personal assistant, like sending emails for a client or helping him decide what to wear for an evening ashore. And if it's a big-named star attending a big-named event, such as the Cannes Film Festival or the MTV Music Awards, you might get to meet a famous designer who comes onboard for a fitting. I know a stew this happened to, and I was jealous!

There really is no end to the responsibilities that fall under serving as a concierge and valet. At the end of the day though, this is what makes a yacht stew's job the most rewarding because you are making the guests happy and establishing good relationships. I think this point is best made through the following quote from my interview with veteran chief stewardess Tish Owen George:

> To me the cool part is that you get to know all of these people in such an intimate way— much more so than if you worked at a hotel and you were the concierge. A hotel concierge might learn what their favorite restaurant is or whether or not they like heavy starch on their shirts.... But as yacht crew, we get to know them in a totally different way that's hard to describe until you do it. Sure, I did a guest's laundry, but she'd also come back from shopping and say, 'Come in here and see what I just bought,' and we were in her cabin acting like little kids, pulling stuff out of her bags.
>
> After all, they're on a yacht, and most likely on vacation. That's liberating for anyone, no matter what kind of luxury or exciting places you're used to; being out at sea definitely has something to do with it. And they're much less guarded due to the privacy factor. People are just more relaxed and open in this environment. That's not with every charter guest, but you still have a certain relationship with them, where there's no one else in the world doing your kind of job who has that sort of rapport.

Entertainer and Activities Director/Party Planner

By far my favorite part about being a yacht stew was keeping things fun—for the guests, and even the crew. If you have a knack for entertaining, you will love this aspect of the job: having theme dinners and throwing parties! Remember, your guests are on vacation, and when the yacht is anchored away from land-based activities, it's up to the crew to keep things interesting. Not all guests will get into it, so you'll want to run it by them before going too all-out with a party idea.

Simply adding a theme to one of your dinners is something most any group will enjoy. For this, simply play up a menu theme with table decorations. Serving Thai? Scatter orchids around a light-pink tablecloth; hang white lights on the potted deck trees; use glimmery, gold napkins rolled up and tied with bamboo string; and even bust out the tiki torches.

Outside of the actual meal-centered themes, there are events you can coordinate such as beach parties and BBQs ashore, as well as afternoon picnics. Of course, you'll want to plan something unique for any birthdays or special occasions being celebrated while the guests are onboard—and believe me, they will make you aware of such events.

> *"The interior staff generally have more interaction with guests or owners on a daily basis than any other crew member. Very often a guest's overall experience onboard a yacht—good, bad, or indifferent—will be based on this interaction. A stewardess has the power to truly make the onboard experience exceptional."*
>
> —**Julie Liberatore**, Regulatory Liaison Maritime Professional Training (MPT)

Party-Planning Checklist

To pull off any type of party for the guests, you will need razor-sharp planning skills. Here's a good party-planning checklist:

- Plan the menu: Will this be a sit-down dinner, or do they wish to have a buffet, passed hors d'oeuvres, or a combination of all of these? Develop a menu that fits the theme or occasion, and brainstorm ways to decorate the table or room.
- Guest list: Will this only be for guests currently onboard, or will other guests be invited? Find out how many you can expect, since you will need to plan your provisioning and supplies list.
- Contact a florist if you need any floral arrangements or centerpieces to fit your theme.
- Will tables, linens, tableware, glassware, or other accessories need to be ordered? And how about wine, beer, and liquor?
- Do you need extra staff to help out, such as hiring a day worker? You might find that the basic interior staff cannot handle the entire event on their own, and even hiring a day worker to stand inside washing dishes and glassware all day will be enough to lighten the heavier-than-usual workload.
- Remember that regular stew responsibilities do not stop simply because there is a party going on. Guests may have invited 20 friends aboard to celebrate with them, but there are 12 original guests staying on the boat whose beds still need to be made and whose laundry still needs to be done.
- What about music: Should you hire live music, even if it's just a D.J.? If you have a piano onboard the yacht, can you find a professional pianist to come on for the evening?
- Is the party going to be held mainly indoors or out on deck? Options for weather changes need to be considered.

↔ Do you have a secure area set up for guests' possessions? If there will be a lot of partygoers roaming around the decks and interior, security could be an issue.

↔ You need to think about various theme dinners and parties you could throw way in advance so that you are prepared when different holidays or events spring up. For example, will you have Americans onboard over Fourth of July (when you are in Sardinia)? And always have birthday-party decorations in supply.

You might think planning parties and theme nights would be solely the chief stew's job, but that is not necessarily the case. In fact, on one yacht I worked on, the chief stew didn't get into the concept. The other stew and I loved it (perhaps a little too much, for each time we were sent ashore to pick up provisions for the yacht, we came back with some new decoration, costume, or item to be used for one of our theme nights). We were actually able to build up a small "library" of themes guests could choose from if they were interested in having a festive evening. On one particular charter, we had a theme dinner or party each night! Feel free to one day borrow from our list of guest favorites below:

Theme Night Suggestions

↔ **Casino Night**—Have Vegas-style decorations, mini blackjack tables, and a poker tournament.

↔ **Disco or '70s Night**—Hang that disco ball on deck, and get ready to see the guests pull their favorite John Travolta moves. (And if you're lucky, John Travolta could end up onboard; after all, he does charter yachts!)

↔ **Pirate Night**—You can find fun costumes for this occasion at any party store. Have the guests partake in some swashbuckling! To get people more into character, pass out a list of good pirate lingo everyone can use. Visit www.TalkLikeaPirate.com for ideas.

↔ **Hollywood Night or New York, New York Night**—This requires some advanced preparation, and decorations are key. We always combined it with a karaoke night or movie trivia. I don't recommend this one with big Hollywood stars, though—they are most likely trying to escape this world.

↔ **Beach/Caribbean/Luau Night**—Choose a secluded beach ashore and set up a BBQ. The menu choices are endless. Don't forget the limbo contest.

↔ **Pajama Party**—A good choice when there's bad weather. Tie this in with a movie night, popcorn all around. Another option would be to break out the board games, and every yacht has plenty of these. (As a stew, you're in charge of shopping for them.)

↔ **Toga Party**—This is a great one when you're cruising around Italy. Have sheets on hand that you buy especially for such an occasion. Otherwise, it's a great way to ruin those expensive guest sheets. (With this theme, there will typically be lots of red wine being served.)

Going out of your way to add these special touches could very well boost your tip! Get creative. The guests understand that you are going to have limited resources. This is your chance to make a huge impression on these people and to create an experience they will cherish. I've had guests be moved to tears over some of the evenings we made extra special for them.

I Must Confess...

*I had my fair share of party debacles... one of the most
disastrous being the "Academy Awards Night Gone Awry."*

We had some super-prominent charter guests onboard, and the moment they arrived, they told us the one big thing they were looking forward to that week was watching the Academy Awards on television, the third night of the trip. We began planning right away to throw an entire theme night based around the televised ceremony.

With only three days to prepare, I ran ashore and purchased a bunch of tabloid magazines to cut out images of the movies and stars who were up for awards that year. I went online to find the list of nominees for each award so I could make ballots to print out and have the guests cast their own votes before the ceremonies began, with a prize going to the one who got the most correct. We had the chef bake a cake in the image of a director's movie clapper board. I found fabric to make a fake red carpet. I bought tons of silver and gold stars and hung them from the ceiling with strands of ribbon. We used black and gold tablecloths with silver napkins and sprinkled star confetti and glitter everywhere. I even managed to find a bunch of costume bow ties and long white gloves for the guests to wear.

Lights, camera, action! On the night of the awards, they gathered in the main salon for the festivities. They were thrilled! Throughout the Joan Rivers pre-awards show, they raved about our frou-frou decor as they devoured the Oscar-themed nibbles we served. Then, the clock reached 8 p.m.—time to switch the channel to the major network that was airing the show. I punched the correct buttons on the remote, clicked enter, and: FUZZ! Unless they were experiencing a blizzard in downtown Hollywood, we weren't getting proper reception. Perhaps I entered it wrong. I tried again...and again...and again. You could have cut the tension in that room with a Q-tip from my cleaning caddy. I immediately radioed to our engineer, assuming there would be an easy fix. There was not.

Forty minutes later, the engineer delivered the bad news. Our satellite was not programmed to pick up that station, and it could not be programmed to pick it up for at least 24 hours.

With sullen looks on their faces, and huffs of disgust, the guests got up and began filing off the boat. Apparently, while we'd been scrambling to adjust the satellite reception, a member of their party had been making phone calls. It just so happened they had some friends chartering a yacht down the dock, and to make us look even worse, that yacht DID have reception (and now my crew couldn't just blame our technical problems on the fact we were on a remote island in the Caribbean). So, off they went to join their friends, and they watched the show from there. Meanwhile, my crew and I took down all of our hard work. Our blockbuster idea for a party was a bust.

Guest Care

Being a good host also means being able to handle awkward or even difficult situations. Following are some common situations where you'll need to lend support and stay professional—not always easy, but my tips will help you do your job the right way.

Tending to Seasickness

It is uncommon for a yacht owner or his immediate family to have a major problem with seasickness; since they own a yacht, they most likely do not get it, or they've learned to prevent or deal with it. (And yes, rest assured, there are ways to prevent and deal with it.)

However, it never fails that when a guest comes aboard who is new to yachting—be it a charter guest or someone the owner has invited onboard—he or she will suddenly do that dance of cupping his or her hand to mouth and running to the nearest head for relief. Of course, this most often occurs after a period of fighting seasickness where they whine and complain and seek their nearest stew to offer relief. And understandably so. If you've ever suffered from the queasy sensation of having your equilibrium confused by turbulent waves of movement, you know how absolutely miserable it can be.

The good news is that the body will adapt after time, so you hopefully won't have to be helping your guests ward off the illness for an entire trip. But when they do come running to you for assistance, there are many remedies you can offer: seasickness medications, which usually come in pill form (and will make them drowsy, put them to sleep, and get them out of your hair); acupressure elastic wristbands; and skin patches they stick behind their ear. These options all provide effective control of seasickness, motion sickness, and all forms of nausea.

The other thing to suggest is that they stay above the lower decks. Get them to go outside and look out at the distant horizon, rather than objects or the water nearest them. Have them take deep breaths while they are doing this. Gingersnap cookies are another common antidote for nausea, as is any form of ginger, including ginger ale or using ginger root to make tea. If they just can't knock the ill feeling, get them to lie on their back and close their eyes. Ultimately, if you can get them to take a seasickness pill, they will either "do the deed" or fall asleep.

Psychiatrist

This is self-explanatory: Be it a guest or a fellow crewmember, someone will inevitably pour his or her soul out to you (possibly under the influence of alcohol), and you will feel obligated to don your hat as the resident psychiatrist. Don't do it. Okay, for your fellow crew, you want to be supportive, but it's a different story with the guests. Keep it professional. As I mentioned earlier, friendly chats with your guests are fine, but while it might be tempting to let a person of fame and power cry on your shoulder as you strive to be the great advice-giver who will leave them indebted to you for life, you really need to resist that temptation.

Draw a line at how personal you get with these people, because being let in on their most intimate life details could come back to haunt you. There are problems you are meant to be solving for your guest—like getting the red-wine stain out of someone's Versace white-linen pants—and then there are the personal problems, which need to be left alone. The best things to do in these situations are avoid saying too much, nod politely, and stay positive. And whatever you do, don't share your own troubles with them.

Childcare

When yacht owners or guests bring their children onboard, they will in most cases bring along a professional nanny to look after them. In other words, the full-time interior crew should not be expected to provide babysitting services unless it has been requested of them and agreed to beforehand in the employment or charter contract. Out-of-the-blue requests for the stews to serve as babysitters are discouraged by charter brokers, and again, unless it's something the owner has written into your job description, you should never be asked to fulfill this function. Stews just do not have those spare moments in a day to allot to nannying.

HOWEVER, I warn you now: At some point in your career, you will no doubt find yourself taking up the slack for a lazy nanny who has been brought onboard by guests. I found it amusing how some of these "professionals" like to think of their employer's vacation as being their own vacation as well. Alternatively, you may find yourself changing a diaper or two out of just plain feeling sorry for some poor nanny who is left to care for four rambunctious kids at once.

Either way, kids will be coming onboard these yachts, and this is why it is important that you are prepared to lay down the rules: As a yacht stewardesses, you are not required to babysit! (The only trouble there is, if something has to get done, you are responsible for making it happen, one way or another.) If you have past nanny or babysitting experience, however, by all means, include that on your résumé/CV—it's a plus when it comes to getting hired, for it shows that you're an experienced caregiver. You may come across a yacht where the owner is actually looking to hire a combination stew-nanny, and you can actually get paid accordingly to perform that role.

Please also note that having children onboard raises some extra safety concerns with regard to water sports, staircases, and man-overboard emergency procedures, to name a few. Make sure that all special precautions are taken to ensure the security of the children, such as not leaving sharp objects around, putting gates in front of staircases, and keeping your cleaning caddy (with all those yummy chemicals) way out of their reach. And even though you aren't the nanny, keep a constant eye on them when they're near the edges of the boat!

I Must Confess...

I told the kids too much. (I'm not good with kids.)

We had a family charter with four sweet little girls onboard. They loved to sit and chat with me while I cleaned the staterooms in the mornings. *Remember that line I told you not to cross when talking to your guests?* Well, I didn't think I had to be so attentive when it came to 6-, 8-, 10-, and 12-year-old girls. I learned the hard way.

One morning, all four of them sat in the wardrobe area just off of a guest bathroom asking me a hundred questions while I covered my usual bases: the tub, the sink, the toilet. When I got to the toilet, the 8-year-old commented, "Ewww... you have to put your hands in there?" I do not recall my specific answer, but I certainly didn't put a lot of thought into it.

Later that night at dinner, as I was circling the table, removing plates from in front of each guest in the most unobtrusive manner possible, the little girl shouted out, "Hey, Julie told us today that the part she hates most about her job is cleaning our toilets!"… Um, okay…so maybe that is what I answered.

I learned a big lesson that day: That line you mustn't cross with your guests extends to all of them. Oh, and another thing I learned: When young children ask uncomfortable questions, lie to them!

Nurse

You never know what emergency could occur onboard when you are away from land and professional medical services. It is imperative that you be familiar with the fundamentals of first aid, which is the care given before regular medical aid can be obtained, and the step-by-step protocol for handling medical emergencies with skills that can save a life. All crewmembers should be trained and prepared to respond to situations such as soft-tissue wounds, broken bones, poisoning, choking, burns—from mild sunburn to third-degree—and, of course, urgent needs like bee stings and anaphylactic shock.

A standard first-aid course will teach you how to assess an emergency and how to approach the situation to rectify it, such as administering CPR or the Heimlich maneuver, immobilizing an injured body part, or properly caring for an open wound. You will learn about the basic safety-training requirements for yacht crew, including how and where you obtain this education, when I cover the STCW Basic Safety Training Course in Chapter 7.

These days, more and more yacht stews, especially chief stews or those aspiring to become chief stews, are taking Proficiency in Medical First Aid courses, which are three- day classes and are offered at most crew-training centers. Some are even going a step further and enrolling in what's called Proficiency in Medical Care course work. This goes beyond basic first aid and teaches skills such as suturing, IV therapy, medication administration and injections, pain management, and what to do in the case of behavioral, respiratory, and cardiovascular emergencies. Essentially, you are able to serve as the eyes and ears of a doctor at the other end of a radio. Having this more advanced skill set increases an individual's value as a crewmember and can quite often lead to a higher salary. It's a great qualification to have and will make a candidate stand out from the competition when vying for a chief stew job on a big-time charter yacht.

Privacy Protection

Consider for a moment the name of Tiger Woods' yacht: M/Y Privacy. All jokes aside about how a multi-million-dollar yacht is going to attract attention, the name about sums it up, I think. Luxury yachts are one of the last bastions of privacy for the elite of the world, and while guests are onboard, the crew is expected to give 110-percent effort to keeping it that way. This means practicing discretion by not leaking out to others who you have aboard on a particular trip. It's one thing if the guests walk off the gangway and allow themselves to be seen by a crowd, but you should not be the one to tip off the onlookers.

Nor should you post anything to Facebook, Twitter, or any other social media site, or so much as send an email to family and friends, regarding who's onboard. And while you're at it, don't even think that posting "just" a photo of yourself onboard and mentioning the yacht's name and where you are or where you're heading to is acceptable. You can—and likely will—get fired for doing so.

Your employment contract no doubt includes a section that states you're prohibited from divulging these details. One such contract reads, "You will keep confidential all information of a confidential, private, or personal nature regarding the Yacht, the Company, guests, and passengers, whether or not the same shall be common knowledge amongst fellow crewmembers."

Depending on the status of the guests, a professional bodyguard may accompany them on the trip to handle the more advanced security measures. But as crew, you still deal with issues such as fan control, security, and public relations when it comes to handling the paparazzi or other spectators on the dock. They may see you on deck and begin shouting a barrage of questions, such as asking who is onboard, who owns the yacht, how much does it cost? You are to keep quiet about all of this. In fact, besides it being common sense (and common dignity), as noted above, your employment contract will require you to do so. The same contract I quoted from there also states, "All communication with dock walkers is to be polite but brief…. Owner's name, guests on board, value and costs, specific cruising schedules, etc. are not to be discussed." In addition, there are some occasions when the guests aboard wish to remain so private that the crew will not even be told who is arriving or where they are headed, and once guests are on the yacht, there is no outbound communication. That's rare and is likely only the case with royalty or government officials, but still, you are going to hold key information that a lot of people want their hands on, and you need to keep it confidential.

Take this all into consideration when fulfilling tasks for the guests, such as booking dinner reservations (do it under a false name so as not to tip off the media). Also, be careful of where you take trash that has been removed from the yacht, for people will go to any length to collect something used or worn by a star. The deckhands will be the ones to keep strict guard over the entrance to the yacht at the foot of the passerelle, making sure no one steps onboard, but the stews need to keep a watchful eye over this, too. Security awareness is vital to the protection of the vessel, her owner, all crewmembers, and guests onboard. Never let anyone step foot on the vessel who is not a current guest, unless you have been authorized first. If possible, the guest or crewmember should come to the passerelle to meet visitors.

Safety

Beyond simply being a service professional, a stew is a safety professional as well. I've talked a lot about what it takes to keep guests comfortable and happy, but even more important than that is making certain they are safe. That's right: Safety first, always. By this, I mean the safety of everybody onboard. We've covered the responsibility of administering basic first aid for medical situations. Then there are other emergencies that we hope a crew never has to face, but for which they must be prepared, such as a fire, a sinking ship, or a person falling overboard. All crewmembers must know how to prevent and respond to these types of emergencies and should possess the necessary training related to fire prevention, basic fire fighting, emergency evacuation, personal lifesaving skills, operating safety equipment, and sea-survival tactics.

All new crewmembers should be familiar with a yacht's systems and her abandon-ship, man-overboard, and firefighting emergency procedures and equipment within their first week onboard. It is the captain, the first mate, and the chief engineer's responsibility to impart this information and to reiterate safety procedures to all crew at frequent intervals, but it is an individual's responsibility to make sure he or she is confident with how to respond if a real emergency should occur.

Emergency billet assignments for each crewmember are posted on what is often referred to as a "Station Bill," posted in convenient places throughout the vessel. Following are the chief, 2nd, and 3rd stews' designated duties and responsibilities from an actual yacht's fire-station bill:

- **Chief Steward/ess**—Assigned to the aft deck: Establish and maintain radio contact with the wheelhouse, gather the guests, and maintain an accurate head count and location of all guests and crewmembers onboard. Make certain that life jackets are on all persons and that any other necessary safety gear is obtained by the 2nd steward/ess. Prepare to launch tenders and life rafts if directed.

- **1st or 2nd Steward/ess**—Runner/Communicator: Deliver spare flashlights and personal communicators to all crewmembers, to the wheelhouse, and to the scene of the emergency, as directed by the captain. Assist the chief steward/ess in organizing and protecting the guests. After all the guests are gathered, return to the bridge to gather passports, logs, and ships papers.

- **2nd or 3rd Steward/ess**—Assist with dressing the fire team. Collect first-aid box, water supply, and oxygen set from the wheelhouse emergency locker. Report to your station and administer first aid if necessary.

As crew, it is your responsibility to learn all you can about how to perform your emergency duties so that carrying them out becomes second nature. All crewmembers are expected to take charge of their own lives, the owner's and guests' lives, and the lives of their fellow crewmembers with appropriate actions: call for help, sound alarms, report what has happened, and adhere to the yacht's various response plans. With regard to prevention, always be an inquiring mind. For example, if you smell smoke, follow through with proper detective work and alert the captain and crew of your suspicions.

The basic skills required in the type of emergencies I've mentioned are taught in the five-day STCW Basic Safety Training Certification Course, which again, I cover in Chapter 7. It is crucial for all individuals seeking employment on yachts to have this basic training.

Household Management

The interior team is expected to ensure that the "household" onboard the yacht runs smoothly, and the bulk of this responsibility resides with the chief stew, who then delegates tasks on down the chain of command.

In order to grasp this role, let's turn to the hotel example again. When you stay in a hotel, you are aware that it is the housekeeping staff who makes your bed, vacuums, removes your dirty room-service tray, rinses out (and dries) your shower, puts out new towels, and straightens up all the toiletry items surrounding the sink.

But...do you ever stop to consider who ordered the room stationery, picked out the pen, made sure the batteries in the remote controls are operational (and who bought the batteries in the first place), set the alarm clock to the correct time (and don't you hate it when it's wrong!), purchased and stocked the toiletry items, alerted the maintenance staff to the leak in your bathroom sink, made sure the hair dryer was there, and wrote and typed up those guest-welcome letters and information sheets?

Such tasks should not be overlooked when we discuss the stew's role. The stew department is responsible for keeping detailed inventories of all interior items as well as shopping for and purchasing what is needed, keeping purchase records, and updating maintenance logs so that the yacht never loses her continuity of care.

The chief stew oversees all of this, and when it comes to this more managerial role, many of the duties resemble those of a traditional office job. Whereas a 2nd or 3rd stew can get away without them, a chief must possess basic computer and accounting skills, such as knowing how to use Microsoft Word and Excel or, in some cases, Quicken. A lot of purchasing tasks will require sending emails or shopping online.

Let's take a look at what managing the "household" onboard a luxury yacht entails.

Inventories and Maintenance Logs

Interior items (you will find examples of what I mean by this below) should be organized, inventoried, and updated on a daily basis. All of this is documented to ease the eventual task of getting the boat ready for guests. There are the hard copies, and then there are the files on the computer used to create them.

The interior team is also expected to keep track of and log all needed repairs on each level of the boat so that these can be made in a timely manner; a routine maintenance log should also be kept. The chief stew is usually responsible for submitting weekly reports to the captain that will contain all of this information.

When it comes to household management, here are some examples of what the interior department must consider:

- ➡ How much do we have of: bed-linen sets, mattress pads, towels (bath, beach, galley, and tea), guest stationery, board games, service items, candles, cutlery and flatware, napkins, placemats, party supplies, batteries, guest toiletries, crew toiletries, DVDs (and the list goes on)?
- ➡ What cleaning products are in stock, and what needs to be ordered? (It is wise to have an inventory-control system in place to manage this.)
- ➡ What items are stored under what guest beds, such as extra crew linens and crew uniforms, extra crockery, candelabras, pillows and blankets, flower vases, and guest bathrobes and slippers?
- ➡ Do we have all the necessary cabin items, are they in good operating condition, and does anything need to be replaced? Things to consider are the number and condition of guest alarm clocks, telephones, remote controls, lint brushes, lampshades, light bulbs, pens, stationery folders (and did we get the new set back from being monogrammed?), and bedside water pitchers, trays, and glasses.
- ➡ When were the ice makers and air filters last cleaned and the light bulbs and the batteries changed?
- ➡ When were the irons last cleaned and the kettles last descaled?
- ➡ Who can fix the broken espresso machine? Can the engineer handle this task, or do we need to hire a contractor?

➤ Do we need to order any additional entertainment equipment, party supplies, theme-night costumes, or table decorations for upcoming trips?

➤ Have we re-labeled the guest telephones since we changed the onboard communications system?

A majority of the interior repairs are done when your yacht goes into a shipyard, especially since a boat will often be under a warranty with the builder. Since these yard periods can be few and far between, the stews must keep an ongoing list of all things that need to be fixed. Here is a brief list of those types of noteworthy troubles you may have on your "wish list" when going into a shipyard:

➤ There is a stain on the suede bureau chair in the starboard VIP cabin and a leak in the VIP port cabin shower.

➤ The dresser drawers in the master cabin keep coming off the tracks.

➤ The Corian countertop material in the starboard VIP cabin is cracked, as is the marble on the port forward lower cabin's bathroom floor.

➤ The TV cupboards rattle in the forward lower cabins when underway.

➤ There are carpet stains from saltwater leaks along the port side of the dining room.

➤ The cupboard doors in the pantry and galley need new sea latches.

➤ The marble tables in the main salon have stains that need to be buffed out. (By the way, drink servers beware: this happens when condensation on wine-glass bottoms bleeds through cocktail napkins and stains the "oh so porous" marble.)

➤ The sliding doors in the dining room "catch" on the carpet from time to time.

And as usual, the list goes on. Keeping close contact with the yacht's interior-design team and/or decorator is key, for these people will know how to care for and replace a lot of the décor items, such as furniture pieces, throw pillows, and even the artwork.

Hiring Contractors and Staff

The chief stew handles this area of responsibility, and it might entail interviewing and hiring the other stews onto the crew (with final approval from the captain) or simply hiring contractors, such as repair technicians. The interior department should maintain a card file of carpet cleaners, insect exterminators, carpenters, and all other services that might be necessary for efficient interior maintenance. Since the yacht is always on the move, a filing system categorized by destination works the best. When enlisting the aid of outside workers, the chief must make sure the work is done on time and at a fair price, so using a rating system is another great idea.

The chief stew takes care of hiring temporary crew, also known as day workers, to help on the interior when the full-time staff is in need of an extra hand. Candidates must be carefully screened, and for this, a chief will often employ the services of the crew placement agencies, which will provide employment backgrounds.

Stowing for Sea

Each time the yacht prepares to move—be it from a dock or from anchor—it is the stew department's responsibility to safeguard all interior spaces. This includes making certain all doors and port holes in both the guest and crew cabins are closed, all toilet seats and lids are in the down position, all fragile items and free-standing objects such as flower arrangements, picture frames, and dining room chairs are secured, and that all guests and crew are onboard. Once everything is checked, the chief stew will report to the captain that the interior is ready for getting underway.

If the vessel is departing late in the evening or early morning, it would be prudent for the stews to secure the cabins before the guests retire for the evening. I recommend leaving a typed note on their beds alerting them to the departure time and reminding them to make sure all breakable items are stowed properly.

On a major crossing, such as a transatlantic journey, stews will go to great measures to protect interior items from damage during rough seas. This entails wrapping breakables in bubble wrap, tying down furniture, and storing other free-standing objects in safe places, such as under beds or in containers that can be weighted down. That's right, you really "batten down the hatches" when preparing for an overseas voyage. (And batten down those expensive bottles of wine while you're at it!)

Stowing for an "Out of Water" Experience (the Shipyard)

It's not always about just stowing for sea, however. Many of these same measures used to protect objects on the yacht's interior before an overseas trip will also be taken when a vessel enters into a shipyard once or twice a year for maintenance.

For example, if a yacht is going to have any major work done, such as a paint job or a complete refit, the boat comes out of the water and goes into what is known as "dry dock." Typically, the crew will move off the boat to land-based accommodations during such a time, although, if not a major job, it is sometimes feasible for the crew to remain living onboard. Either way, the interior team has their work cut out for them in prepping the inside of the vessel to have the outside work done. This is usually the time that a lot of the interior repairs will also be made.

The big concern for the stews when a yacht goes into a shipyard is DUST, DUST, DUST. It gets in through every vent, crack, and filter there is, and it will wreak havoc on a yacht's meticulous inner sanctum. To safeguard against this, stews will go to extremes, covering every inch of the yacht's interior in plastic tarps, while oftentimes even removing a lot of the items from the boat and keeping them temporarily in a storage container.

On one yacht I worked on, we spent four months in the Azimut-Benetti shipyard in Viareggio, Italy having all kinds of work done on the exterior. To prepare, we stewardesses bubble-wrapped and foam-packed most every item from the interior; placed what we could in cardboard boxes, trash bags, and plastic crates; sealed, labeled, logged, carried, and loaded it all into a storage container; and then covered every square inch of the yacht's interior, floor to ceiling (and with mirrored ceilings, those too), in plastic tarps.

We removed nearly everything: chairs from the dining room and salon (25 total); all the china, sheets, vases, candles, towels, trash bins, pillows; every item from under the beds; thousands of dollars worth of wine and liquor; and all the bar equipment, coffee machines, plants, and books. And while the guest mattresses stayed behind, they were wrapped airtight in plastic!

Alas, when the yard period was over, and the scaffolding all came down from around the outside, guess who got to put Humpy Dumpty back together again? It wasn't so bad, though. During that entire four months of "yard time," our crew got to live ashore in Italy. We were given our own apartments, rental cars, and a food allowance. During this time, we worked a consistent 8 a.m. to 6 p.m. each day and got most weekends off, so in many ways, we were able to live like locals and get to know what it's like to live and work in Italy. (At one stage, I thought I'd stay forever if I could've.) Oh, and the Italian shipyard workers who congregated onboard the yacht each day didn't make for such bad scenery, either.

Interior Manuals

Not every chief stew does it (but he or she should), and that is to create and continually update interior manuals, to maintain continuity of care for the vessel. The idea here is that whoever might come along down the line will know exactly where to find things and how an owner or particular group of repeat charter guests prefers things when they're onboard. The owners should feel that they have never left and that their yacht is their home. Pictures of all stateroom set-ups and contents of cabinets are usually found in such a manual.

This information should also include helpful cleaning tips, daily stew routines, a preparation-for-sea checklist, and a list of things to do before a charter. All records and inventories should also be kept as part of this data. Of most importance is to note where various items are stored throughout the yacht. Again, this makes for a smooth transition when there is a crew changeover and a new chief stew takes over. Believe it or not it will also help your existing crew when guests are onboard and you can't remember under which bed you've stored something that's been requested and is needed right away.

The interior staff also prepares and updates a guest-welcome booklet. This should contain a welcome letter, personalized for each trip (adding an elegantly drawn-up itinerary is a nice touch), and a current crew-profile list, which will contain crew-background information and impart a sense of professional peace of mind for guests. A welcome booklet might also include telephone dialing sequences; instructions on how to use the controllers (either Crestron units or iPads) for the lighting, temperature, and entertainment systems; and an updated version of the DVD, CD, and satellite TV channel lists. Emergency-exit, flashlight, life jacket, and fire-extinguisher locations and use, as well as familiarization with the emergency-rallying location, should also be presented as a reminder to the captain's personal welcome-aboard safety speech given during the welcome reception.

Shopping

Part of managing the interior of a yacht is guaranteeing that everything a guest would need is onboard—from manicure sets to shoe horns to Pepto Bismol. The good news is the stews get to shop for it all. The bad news is this responsibility is a bit more stressful than you might think. After all, if the guests want to play poker, and you don't have a deck of cards, it's your fault. No hair rollers onboard? *Well, what terrible service!* When shopping for a yacht, you have to think of **everything.**

The chief stew handles the accounting of expenditures, and any items bought for the boat need to be thoroughly documented with such information as the date of purchase and the cost. Major purchases (which are usually cleared with the captain first) often entail even more documentation than that, such as the commercial name of the item; the name, address and phone number of the retailer; and any other information that might save time if an item needs to be replaced later.

Aside from trying to imagine the types of requests guests might make when onboard, the stews must also think about all of the day-to-day items that they will need to have on hand. Here are some examples from one of my old shopping lists. *Now, would you have thought of some of these things?*

- guest writing pens
- baking soda for fridges
- cereal containers
- laminating supplies for guest manuals
- ice buckets
- icemaker scoops
- presentation trays and lighters for cigarettes
- books and cruising guides
- magazines from France, U.K., America, and Italy
- candlestick drip protectors
- 10 pairs of tweezers and 10 pairs of cuticle scissors for guest toiletry baskets
- sink plugs for the stew pantry
- shakers for chili flakes
- citrus press
- insulated cooler bags
- ironing-board cover
- laundry bags
- laundry drying frame
- swizzle sticks
- watering cans
- wine vacu-seal with stoppers

I Must Confess...
I loved shopping for the boat.

We (my chief stew at the time and I) managed to spend $18,000 in one day buying new items for the yacht's interior: new crystal glassware, chinaware breakfast sets with napkins and table linens to match, 100 new DVDs, 50 new CDs, new serving plates, two new vacuums (Dyson!), and an assortment of fine liquor—top-shelf everything! We got to wear our interior-decorator hats, too, as we picked out candles galore, flower vases, breakfast napkins, and decorative throw pillows. Talk about a spree; we got to buy so much crap, it was awesome! And believe it or not, we came out *under* budget.

Another time, when our yacht was on the island of Malta in the Mediterranean, we didn't have a crew car, so I had to be taxied around all day by a local yacht agent in search of last-minute items for an upcoming charter. This guy thought I was a nut. Here I was with this shopping list of quite specific, yet not so common, things I needed to find on this tiny island: 10 tissue-box covers (four long, six short), a flower pot with a 7.5-inch diameter, a CD case to match our old one, poster board, seasickness bands, bath salts in sachets, picture books on Greece and Turkey, and tons of stuff for theme parties (we were planning on doing a '70s night, a beach party, and a Broadway musical night on the upcoming trip). Our shopping excursion was like being on a scavenger hunt.

I read to him from my list: "Okay, now we're on the search for Christmas lights—the all-white kind." (It was the middle of June.) He told me there was no way we'd find them. But darn it, I needed them to pull off this Broadway theme party; the guests were bringing a professional pianist onboard, and we were told they loved show tunes. I begged him to try. Every stop we made, I'd leave him in the car with his cell phone, as he called upon his list of contacts.

It wasn't until the very last hour of our time together that he got the call: Someone had white Christmas lights in a storage unit! Even better, when we got there, I discovered he had a lot more than that. I climbed back onboard the boat that evening carrying a life-sized, stand-up cut-out of Marilyn Monroe in Times Square, a poster of the Statue of Liberty, and a mini replica of the Empire State Building. Yep, Broadway night turned into New York, New York night, and the guests who joined us the following week could not have been more pleased with the results of my day shopping in Malta!

(But my chief stew was not pleased; I never did find the tissue-box covers.)

Guest Profiles

It is the interior staff's responsibility to write up a guest profile either about the owner and his or her regular guests, or for each separate charter. The purpose of these profiles is to record in detail all pertinent information about the yacht owner's and guests' needs, likes, dislikes, and idiosyncrasies: information such as what foods and beverages they prefer and how they like them served, how they like their cabins set up, what their favorite music choices are, and whether or not they go ashore to dine a lot. Anything that can improve guest service on a return trip goes into these profile write-ups.

While the entire crew should make contributions to this project, the stews keep it updated. At the end of a trip, the interior team compiles the raw data into a charter review form. This form should consist of dates of the voyage, the cruising profile, an overview of the guests, plus an individual profile on each separate guest. Even with charter guests, recording this information is important in case they should ever charter the vessel a second time. An example of a comprehensive guest-profile charter review, compiled once a trip is complete, can be found in Appendix E.

During the trip, you will find that noting and recording guests' personal preferences early and sharing that information with other crew will pay off greatly by even the second day of the charter. For example, at breakfast, if the guest takes a second cup of coffee, you note it. If they use cream, write that down for the next person who may be serving breakfast. As you can imagine, when it comes to impressing the guests and "anticipating their needs" (those clairvoyant abilities I spoke of in Chapter 4), keeping track of such small service details can prove tremendously advantageous.

Sample Breakfast Notes

Here's a sample of just how detailed it got:

1) MR. G.:

- He always wants his breakfast served on the owner's deck, alone. The other guests will eat either in the inside dining room or on the sundeck, except Mrs. G., who eats in the owner's cabin. He takes nearly two hours for dining.
- Drinks TONS of coffee (had three pots on the first day, so always go with the biggest size we have). Have it ready as soon as he's out there. He wants it piping hot.
- Begin with one bowl of yogurt, served alone. Do not add any fruit, even as a decoration.
- Next, he wants a fried egg with ham and bacon (well done) every morning. Ketchup on the side.
- Cream, not milk, with coffee. Uses cubed brown sugar only.
- Wants water served alongside—NO ICE or lemon. (Never ice or lemon with any beverage for Mr. G.!)
- Serve him one glass of orange juice, and one separate cup of coffee with two packets of Sweet'N Low on the side, and a coffee spoon, which he will take into his wife, who eats in the cabin.
- Be ready to change his ashtray frequently. He chain smokes.

2) MRS. G.:

- Eats in the owner's cabin every morning. Mr. G. will order for her and take to her.
- One glass of OJ and coffee in a cup (do not make a pot for her) that you will take up to Mr. G. as soon as he's up. She takes her coffee black and uses two packets of Splenda.
- Has buttered toast (six pieces) with strawberry jam and honey on the side. Mr. G. will request it when she's ready.
- Only use smallest plates (dessert plates) with one doily.

3) MRS. B.:

- Set out a wide variety of muffins in a basket AND have every flavor of jam on display. (She just wants to see variety, but she'll still go for the croissants every time and rarely touches the jam.) LOTS of butter.
- Takes a three-minute egg, in an egg cup. Serve with a teaspoon. Have an empty bowl for the shell.
- Serve egg with a lime wedge (just one!), a peeled and sliced tomato, and always put out the hot-sauce jar, on a liner, with a spoon—even if she doesn't ask.
- Do NOT pour her coffee for her, unless she asks.
- Put out only Splenda sugar substitute. She doesn't even want to see the Sweet'N Low or Equal.
- Takes skim milk ONLY with her coffee. (And she can tell the difference.)

Back-Up Deck Crew

If you think that understanding basic seamanship skills is something you can skip because you are applying to be a stewardess—not a deckhand—think again. To be a good team player on a yacht crew, you should be willing to jump in to assist the exterior crew if it means getting a job done in a timely manner. In fact, each crewmember needs to be vigilant that everything is in order and operational in all departments. (It takes a village, people!) It doesn't happen frequently, but when it does, you will be shown exactly what you need to do. In the meantime, always be willing to learn. If you have nothing to do on a particular day, wander out on deck and ask one of the deckhands if they could use some help. After all, deck work does equate to time in the sun!

Docking and Handling Lines and Fenders if Needed

One of the most common instances of the stews being asked to assist the exterior crew is when the yacht is departing or coming in to port. It is usually the case that all crewmembers are on deck in proper uniform to assist in maneuvers. Especially upon an arrival, the interior crewmembers need to be out there to give a hand with docking procedures, such as holding fenders (air-filled cushions) along the sides of the vessel to protect it from bumping up against neighboring boats or the pier. It's a major help if the stews are familiar with how to handle lines, adjust fender saddles, and even tie nautical knots. This is the type of stuff that you will pick up over time working on a yacht, and as I mentioned earlier, the deckhands will be happy to instruct you on what to do. The introduction to yachting courses I mention in Chapter 7 will also teach some of these basics, so you aren't completely clueless when you first begin working on a boat.

The Decks

For the most part, taking care of the yacht's exterior is the job of the first mate and deck department. The deckhands are responsible for washing, waxing, polishing, varnishing, buffing, and even painting the boat. However, because the interior crew are responsible for serving the guests, and because the guests like to lounge about the decks during the day, the stews do end up playing a role in the appearance and upkeep of the outside decks.

The number of decks varies from yacht to yacht. Here is a selection of what you might find onboard, listed by location:

- **Top Deck or Sun Deck**—There is typically a sunbathing area on this deck, complete with lounge chairs, cushions, a killer sound system, and a hot tub. Larger yachts will also have room for a dining area, an outdoor grill, and a wet bar. If the yacht has a helicopter, the helipad will be located here as well.
- **Mid-Deck**—On a multi-level yacht, you will have a mid-deck, or possibly more than one. Mid-decks in the aft, or rear portion, of the vessel tend to have more shelter from wind, so you will typically find a formal alfresco-dining area here.
- **Aft Deck**—This is the back deck of a yacht, on the ground level, or main deck, from where passengers—guests and crew—enter and exit the yacht (via a passerelle/gangway). It is common to find a U-shaped seating area here.
- **Forward Deck**—Also referred to as the "bow" (pronounced like bow, as in curtsy) of the boat. Remember in *Titanic* when Leonardo stood Kate on the front tip of the ship? That was the bow. On a majority of yachts, this deck is designated as the crew area. Not that guests cannot enter the space, but if crew want to sit outside and read, sunbathe, or smoke a cigarette (if it's allowed) on their breaks, this is where they typically head.

Separate from the actual bow (which is technically the forward main deck), there may also be a forward mid-deck where guest seating areas or benches are found.

⇢ **Bathing or Swim Platform**—This will be found below the main deck on the aft portion of the vessel. It's either a fixed platform or formed when a hydraulically powered transom door (the very back of the vessel, a.k.a. stern, where the yacht's name appears) folds down. There's also typically a swim ladder.

The deck areas most utilized by the interior staff are the outside bars, of which there are usually two or three, and the outdoor storage lockers, where the stews keep their service items. The stews are responsible for keeping these areas clean, neat, and organized. This includes stocking the bar fridges and cleaning out the ice makers, for guests will inevitably try and help themselves by getting into these machines, and you don't want them finding an unsanitary workspace. The same holds true for the deck lockers assigned to the interior crew. It won't take long for guests to pick up on the fact that the stews open these units to retrieve items such as cup holders, spray bottles, ashtrays, beach towels, and even serving glasses and plates. Before you know it, they'll be going into these spaces on their own. Many meals are served outside, so the stews must also watch out for the areas around the dining tables. (You don't want greasy food items dropping on and staining the teak.)

Another aspect of a yacht's exterior that sometimes falls under the interior department's jurisdiction is the outdoor ambiance, such as the décor. The stews are the ones to order, pot (or replant), and water the outdoor plants and deck trees. They also watch over the throw pillows in the exterior seating areas. When it comes to the sunbathing spaces on deck, the interior staff is in charge of setting out baskets of suntan lotion, perfectly folded beach towels, bottled water, magazines, and any other items that will enhance the sun-worshipping experience. You'll also need to remember to return to remove empty glassware, bottles, or other service items that you delivered to outdoor guests earlier. From my experience, yacht guests hate looking at food and beverage service items once they've consumed what was on or in them. It's up to you to clear the decks of evidence.

And by all means, don't forget to monitor that guest shoe basket on the aft deck; it sits just off the passerelle at the entrance to the vessel. Stews need to check this receptacle periodically to keep it looking tidy. You'll have some pretty fancy footwear being placed in there, and you can't let one person's Gucci sandals dirty up another's Manolo Blahniks. (Keep some shoe-shining tools behind one of the outdoor bars, just in case.)

Crew Care

Along with managing the guest areas of a yacht's interior, the stewardesses are also expected to take a majority of the responsibility for the crew areas of a vessel. Notice I did not say *full* responsibility, as exterior crew members also have a part to play in cleaning and maintaining not only their respective work areas, but their own personal space as well. To understand this, it is helpful to first get to know what crew areas typically exist on a luxury yacht:

Crew Areas

There is an entire separate list of rooms and areas of a vessel designated for the crew. Let's take a look at these before we discuss how the interior staff keeps tabs on them:

- **Wheelhouse, Bridge, or Pilothouse**—It may be called any one of these things, but essentially, this is the area where the captain steers the vessel and where exterior crew stand watch when the yacht is underway.

- **Navigation Room, Control or Switchboard Room**—An extension of the wheelhouse/bridge (and usually contained within), this is where the navigational instruments and control switches to operate the vessel are found. When stews clean this area, they must be delicate and careful not to alter or damage any expensive equipment.

- **Engine Room/Generator Room**—Consider this the engineer department's "office." As the names suggest, this is where the engines and the power generators are located—the "heart" of the vessel, so to speak.

- **Galley**—This is the yacht's kitchen, plain and simple, and it is the executive chef's workspace. This is not to be confused with the kitchenette area found in the crew quarters. On some yachts, the galley will be off limits to the rest of the crew, unless it's the chef's day off and everyone is to fend for him- or herself for meals.

- **Walk-in Refrigerators and Freezers**—With the amount of food provisions needed for both guests and crew, the chef's fridges and freezers might be like big rooms unto themselves. Crew food will be kept in these larger units, but the everyday items crewmembers are grabbing will reside in a smaller fridge in the crew mess.

- **Dry-Storage Area**—There will typically be a walk-in storage closet for non-perishable goods. The chef and stews may share this space, since the stews need access to items such as condiments, cereals, and coffee beans.

- **Wine Cooler and Wine Closet**—These are the wine-storage areas for the stews—wines served chilled and those served room temperature are separated.

- **Vehicle and Tender Bay**—This is the area from which the tender boats or dinghies, and other personal-watercraft vehicles, such as Jet Skis and WaveRunners, are launched.

- **Bosun's Locker**—This storage compartment, or locker, is where the exterior department stores most of their tools and equipment for maintaining the yacht's deck.

- **Lazarette**—This is a watertight storage compartment at the stern, or aft portion, of the vessel, mostly reserved for the exterior and engineering departments. Fishing, diving, and other boat gear are often stored here.

- **Stew Pantry**—This "room" is for the stews to carry out their "behind the scenes" service duties; there may even be more than one. This is where the dishes get done, the silverware is polished, and coffee is prepared. The area may come with nifty floor pedals or electric eyes to open the doors to the guest areas automatically (which is convenient unless you have children onboard and they figure out the button on the other side).

- **Captain's Quarters**—This is the captain's living space—much more spacious and private than the rest of the crew cabins, which are often shared by two people.

- **Laundry and Ironing Room**—This is stew territory. How many washing machines and dryers are contained within depends on the size of the vessel (and a stew's luck). This area could always be just a little bit bigger. It is most likely located within the crew quarters.

- **Crew Quarters**—This is where the crew lives. In most cases, it is located below deck, and then either far forward (beneath the bow) or in the mid-ship part of the vessel. The entire space is made up of the crew cabins and the crew mess, which is the common area shared by the crew.

Crew Mess

Crewmembers have cabins to call their own (although typically shared with one other person), but the crew mess is the common living area for everyone. The entire crew area is expected to be presentable at all times for the occasional owner, guest, or broker visit.

Every boat is different in terms of how this area is managed. On some yachts, the stews alone look after this common space, while for many boats, every crewmember is asked to participate in the process, in which case the task is often assigned to the person on watch duty for the day (when no guests are onboard, which is explained in the following section). The exterior crew like to moan and groan about this, arguing that they cannot be bothered to set and clear the table for crew meals, help to stock the food cabinets and crew fridge, and load and empty the crew dishwasher—so while they do lend a hand at times, the overall duties of caring for the crew mess typically fall on the stews.

Watch Duty

When guests are not onboard, all crewmembers share the responsibility of performing daily watch duty on a rotating basis. The idea here is that someone is always in charge of the vessel and must stay on the boat the entire day, even if the rest of the crew has been given the day off. The person assigned this responsibility must monitor the yacht's systems and make certain that the vessel is secure. The first mate is typically in charge of outlining the work that should be accomplished by the duty person and for putting together the rotation schedule (and every crewmember will be a part of this rota).

Here are some examples of daily watch-duty responsibilities:

- ↔ Watch runs for 24 hours (0800 hours to 0800 hours the following day). The crewmember must be in crew uniform 0800 hours to 2200 hours.
- ↔ The yacht's flag is to be raised at 0800 hours and lowered at sunset or 2000 hours, whichever comes first. On days when exterior crew are off duty, chamois the main deck caprails, stainless steel, and passerelle immediately after hoisting the flag.
- ↔ Unlock needed exterior doors at 0800 hours, and lock all doors after lowering flag. The boarding gate is to be closed and crew door is to be locked at 2200 hours.
- ↔ Turn the deck and prescribed exterior lights on at sunset, and check that all overhead and deck courtesy lights are working. Turn off interior lights that are not needed. If the duty watch crewmember is the only person onboard and feels that it is in the best interest of the vessel and her crewmembers, all doors may be locked at all times.
- ↔ Periodically check the interior, decks, and the engine room to ensure that everything is in order. A checklist will be provided by the chief engineer. (Make one final walk-through before crew door is locked.)
- ↔ Frequently inspect dock lines for chafing, check fenders for placement and damage, and check the passerelle for position.
- ↔ Answer the telephone. Post messages on the message board.

↠ Keep the crew mess clean and shipshape. Remove crew trash throughout the day, and leave the garbage empty. Replace any videos and CDs used. Be mindful of other crewmembers who may be sleeping in if they are off work for the day.

↠ Set table for evening meal by 1800 hours. Assist in taking food from galley to crew mess. After the evening meal, clear and clean the table and sink, start the dishwasher, and empty it when the cycle is finished.

—from an actual yacht crew manual, contributed by Captain Carl Sputh

Crew Cabins

While the stews do end up doing more of the crew-mess chores than the exterior crew, each crewmember is responsible for the condition of his or her own cabin, which includes the bathrooms. Bed linens should be changed and the cabins themselves vacuumed once a week. The exception to the "every man to clean his cabin" rule is the captain. The interior staff will clean the captain's cabin on most yachts.

It's still a good idea for the interior staff to check on whether or not crew are staying on top of this task. I recall an instance where we had a male crewmember moving off the yacht, and when we went in to clean his bathroom for the new guy to come on, we found the departing individual must not have cleaned the areas around his sink and shower in months (if ever). The stains left behind were revolting!

The stews need to make sure they check every crewmember's cabin and head several times a month for cleanliness (with advanced warning given for privacy's sake) because these rooms still count as interior-staff territory. Stews protect the inside of the boat, and that means every inch of it.

Crew Uniform

The interior team will attend to all crew uniforms, washing and ironing them, both with and without guests onboard. This does not mean, however, that the stews also wash the crew's personal laundry. As noted in Chapter 4, it's every person for himself or herself when it comes to underwear, linens and towels, and personal (a.k.a. "street") clothes.

More important than just cleaning and ironing them, the stews are responsible for ordering the crew uniforms as well. The chief stew is usually the one to handle this job, but the other stews may be called upon to help take inventory of existing uniforms and find out what items need to be purchased by surveying the other crewmembers. Every time a new member joins the crew, the stews have to make sure they have the proper sizes of uniform pieces to fit that person. Last-minute orders are always taking place.

It sounds easy, but consider for a moment the types of things you must keep tabs on:

↠ Does the chef have enough aprons, or does he or she need a chef's hat to put on when greeting the guests?

↠ Does the engineer have enough presentable overalls/dungarees—ones without permanent oil stains streaked all over them?

↠ Did that deckhand you hired three months ago outgrow his current selection of khaki shorts after partaking in too many second helpings of the chef's blueberry ricotta cheese streusel coffeecake?

➧ How about epaulettes (those shoulder ornament stripes that crew wear to show their rank and status)? Did the first mate lose his *again?*

➧ And did you notice that the evening skirts worn by the female stews are a little too susceptible to wind gusts on those spiral staircases? Perhaps it's time to switch to skorts.

Keeping track of and taking care of crew uniforms is an ongoing battle, but it's an important one. As representatives of the yacht, the crew's appearance is important. In addition, keeping the uniforms inventoried and taking proper laundering care of them will help save the yacht money in the long run (which pleases the boss!).

Special Skills

There are a variety of extra skill sets that are not necessarily required of a yacht stew; however, having expertise in these areas can not only set an individual apart from the competition for stellar job opportunities, but also mean a higher salary (or even larger tips on charter trips). Three of the special talents most frequently sought after by owners and captains searching to hire new stews are massage training, floral arranging know-how, and cooking abilities.

> *"Having a wide skill set is without a doubt an advantage: massage, beauty, and also certification as a trained nurse/medical are all seen as a real benefit. The more you, as a crewmember/candidate, can offer to the yacht the better."*
>
> —**Paul Rutterford**, Marine Recruitment Manager at Viking Recruitment

Massage, Beauty, and Fitness Training

Being trained as a masseuse or having any type of skill giving massages is a big bonus when working on yachts, as is beauty school training (hair, nails, and makeup). Think about it: Spa vacations are trendy. The type of clientele you are catering to are people who are used to vacationing at spas or in fancy hotels where the masseuse comes to the room or there's a hair and nail salon on the premises. While only the super-large yachts and gigayachts have full-service spa facilities and/or beauty salons onboard, many owners and guests want to receive massages as part of the amenities offered on any vessel. And many female guests would be thrilled to have a resident hair/nail/make-up person there to assist their primping. (That is, if they don't bring their own stylist onboard; yes, that happens a lot.)

In fact, there are actually freelance masseuses who make a living just traveling back and forth between the Caribbean and the Mediterranean all year, going where the yachts go, and hanging around the busy marinas offering their services. They come aboard for only a few hours and give massages to all the guests. I talked to one of these individuals once who told me she makes nearly $100,000 a year just hanging out around these chic ports, freelancing her way onboard.

However, since freelancers are not always readily available, especially when a vessel is at sea, stews with massage or beauty school training are in demand. The same holds true for any background in being certified to lead yoga, aerobics, weight-training (many larger yachts have full gyms), or any type of fitness activity, which becomes very appealing to image-conscious yacht vacationers out at sea for so many days. Most guests would be thrilled to learn there is a crewmember onboard who can help them get a little exercise. For this, you might even consider water-based activities. Get certified to teach paddleboarding—the latest water fitness craze—and you might even find yourself getting off the boat to enjoy yourself a little more by taking the guests on a paddleboarding expedition around a marina! A yoga break might not be too shabby either, especially if you're leading.

Many chief stews like to acquire these additional skills because it makes them much more marketable when competing for jobs. For an entry-level stew, the same holds true. If you already have a background in massage, beauty, or fitness coaching of any kind, highlight it on your résumé/CV.

Floral Arranging Know-How

When the owner or guests arrive, they will expect fresh flowers to be placed throughout the yacht. And here, I'm not just talking a few stems in a vase, but rather elaborate floral displays that preferably match the color scheme of their designated room. There should be at least one display per guest cabins, several displays placed in the master stateroom, and a minimum of two displays each in the main salon and dining room. Then come the displays for the outside decks. I had a few trips where we went so far as to order flowers for the guest bathrooms and the day head.

For yachts with massive budgets, these floral arrangements typically come straight from a floral shop. About a week before the guests are to arrive, the chief stew has a florist come onboard and size up what's needed. However, if the yacht is only arriving in port a few days before a trip starts, there might not be enough time for that. In this case, the stews can either send pictures of previously used arrangements to a local florist ahead of time (which, thanks to email or text, can be done quite easily) and have them mimic the colors and styles, or make them "in-house." This is when floral-arranging skills are a major plus.

It helps to have a knack for assembling flowers if you are on a yacht where the owner only allows a small budget for floral displays. When you have limited funds, doing your own floral arrangements is a great way to save money. These skills also come in handy when flowers from original displays begin to die off. Stews blessed with "green thumbs" will have a knack for preserving the display longer and for salvaging portions of various arrangements and combining them into new displays. Otherwise, in the middle of a trip, you may find it necessary to reorder a complete new round of flowers.

Cooking Abilities

Knowing how to cook is in no way a skill you are expected to have as a stew; however, if you do have cooking experience, you want to highlight it on your résumé/CV. Here's why: Executive chefs are always overworked. Keeping up with meal preparations for both the guests and the crew is incredibly taxing for just one person. Most yachts do not have room on the crew (as in, space in the crew quarters) to carry an extra staff member to assist the chef. Without an assistant cook onboard, a stew with some cooking skills is a tremendous asset.

Whether it's assisting in the galley as a part-time prep cook, helping out by preparing the crew meals every now and then, or simply being on hand to garnish plates, clean some pots and pans, or make a snack for the guests while the full-time chef is taking his or her only, short-lived break of the day, such heroic acts truly can save the day on many occasions (like when guests make a last-minute menu change). Some yachts even hire stew-chefs, a dual position, whereby that one person holds responsibilities in both departments and operates on an "as needed" basis.

"She works hard for the money..."
—Donna Summer

PART
II

GETTING HIRED

THE QUICK START GUIDE:
THE A TO Z OF HOW TO
BECOME A YACHT STEW

I realize that a lot of people reading this book might be thinking, "*Fine*, you've sold me… I want to do it! Get to the 'how-to' part already!"

If that's you, well, lo and behold, you've made it to the nitty-gritty group of chapters. If you are eager and ready to become a part of this exclusive industry, then Part II is where you'll learn the step-by-step process for acquiring a yacht stew position. I think you'll be shocked to discover just how easy it is to land one of these dream jobs.

To get off to a quick start, I am going to throw at you, in an "a, b, c" fashion, what I consider to be the main action steps to get you from where you sit now to your first stewardess position on a luxury yacht. The order of these steps might vary, but what I want you to glean from looking down the list is just how uncomplicated the process really is. And not to worry, I will expand upon every step throughout Chapters 6–11, along with delivering practical insider advice on how to get hired in a short period of time.

Use **The Quick Start Guide** as a checklist reference as you prepare to take your own leap into what I hope will be a well-lit path.

Are you ready? Here goes:

a) Assess your skills and determine whether or not this opportunity is for you. (Chapter 6)
b) Find storage for your major belongings and plan to pack up what you'll need because you're going away for a while! (Chapter 8)

c)   Select the hiring port where you will conduct your job search, which you will determine based on convenience to your set of circumstances, as well as on the time of year. (Chapter 8)

d)   If you do not already have a passport, apply now! (Chapter 8)

e)   If you are a non-U.S. citizen, you need to apply for a B1/B2 visa before leaving your home country. (Chapter 8)

f)   Prepare a preliminary résumé/CV highlighting your applicable skills and work experience, along with your special abilities, talents, and interests. (Note: I'll explain what a CV is in Chapter 10.) A cover letter is optional, but it is a nice touch. And make sure your social media profiles project you as a reliable person to hire. (Chapters 6 and 10)

g)   Compile a list of preliminary work references to include with your résumé/CV submissions. (Chapter 10)

h)   Have a headshot photo taken of yourself (or use an existing one) to include with your résumé/CV submissions. (Chapter 10)

i)   Research the yacht-crew training schools in your chosen hiring port, and find out their respective STCW Basic Safety Training (BST) Course schedules ahead of time. You should plan to arrive in town when courses are being offered and can accommodate you. The same holds true with any optional preparatory classes you plan on taking, such as a specialized stew training course. (Chapter 7)

j)   Research yacht-crew housing options in your chosen hiring port, and call ahead to check availability for the date you plan to arrive. Consider booking your initial accommodations once you've determined your STCW Basic Safety Training course dates and made your travel arrangements. (Chapter 8)

k)   Send preliminary e-mails to the yacht-crew placement agencies that you hope to register with *before* you make your move. Simply introduce yourself, let them know you will be coming in to meet them soon, and tell them your planned arrival date. Consider sending along your résumé/CV in advance, with expected course-completion dates listed. If possible, go ahead and schedule your personal interview. (Chapters 9 and 10)

l)   Book that airplane ticket, and move to a hiring port. (Chapter 8)

m)   Once you are physically in a hiring port, go meet with the agencies. I recommend registering with a minimum of two crew placement agencies to get started. The crew agents will want to interview you when you arrive, so dress the part, and be ready to sell yourself as a serious job candidate. If you haven't already e-mailed it in advance, hand them your résumé/CV and get their feedback. Make any necessary updates or adjustments that the crew agents suggest. (Chapters 9 and 10)

n)   If you have not already done so, enroll in, take, and complete a five-day STCW Basic Safety Training Course from an accredited training school. (Chapter 7)

o)   Let the crew placement agencies know when you've completed your STCW training, and update your résumé/CV accordingly. (Chapter 10)

p)   Consider enrolling in a specialized interior-crew training course (highly recommended!) to increase your chances of getting hired fast. Completing this training really can be the deciding factor on whether or not you are offered a position as an entry-level stew. (Chapter 7)

q) Set aside 1-2 hours to go and get your ENG1 Seafarer Medical Exam or its equivalent from an approved physician so you may obtain your ENG1 certificate… just in case you might need it.

r) Look for day work at local marinas and shipyards in your hiring port. Going boat to boat letting captains and current crew know you are available for work could even lead to a full-time position. This is referred to in the industry as "dockwalking." Much more on this later. (Chapter 9)

s) Seek out alternative job-finding methods such as classified "crew wanted" ads in the yachting newspapers and trade publications as well as on their websites, public bulletin boards in well-known yachting establishments, and by networking with people in your crew house and at local yachtie hot spots, such as bars and restaurants. Not to worry, I'll supply that list, too. (Chapter 9)

t) Update your résumé/CV and referral list with all the new training and day-work experiences you accumulate. This includes acquiring and passing along to the crew agents reference letters from captains or supervisors from any yacht that hires you to do day work for a period of three or more days. (Chapters 9 and 10)

u) Keep checking in with the crew agencies as often as possible (which you can do online via their websites and/or their social-media presences), to remind them of your availability and update them on your own efforts to find a job. (Chapter 9)

v) NETWORK, NETWORK, NETWORK! (Chapters 7–10)

w) Take advantage of all interview opportunities that initially come through from the agencies or by other means listed above. It may not be the case for everyone, but if you're able to interview with several yachts before accepting a position, be selective! (Chapter 10)

x) Think overnight before accepting a position. If you are not interested, let the hiring party know as quickly as possible.

y) Accept your first job, and get ready for an extraordinary, life-altering experience! (Chapters 10 and 11)

z) (Because I needed a "z"): Send me an email at Info@WorkOnAYacht.com and let me live vicariously through your adventures at sea!

6

THE RECIPE FOR A GREAT STEW
—THE SKILLS AND TRAITS
REQUIRED TO GET HIRED—

"These changes in latitudes, changes in attitudes,
nothing remains quite the same.
Through all of the islands and all of the highlands,
If we couldn't laugh, we would all go insane."
—**Jimmy Buffet**, American singer, songwriter, yacht owner; from the song
"Changes in Latitudes, Changes in Attitudes"

You should now have a comprehensive understanding of what the daily duties and responsibilities are for a luxury yacht stew. In this chapter, we are going to assess your current skills to find out if you are cut out for the job. To do this, I will lay out the necessary character traits and technical skills that this position requires, as well as what background experiences serve as the best foundation for pursuing this line of work. I call my resulting formula "the recipe for a great stew."

Recipe for a Yacht Stew: The Prime Ingredients

We will look at two different types of qualifications (or, shall I say, "ingredients") for becoming a luxury yacht stew:

1) Before we even begin to talk about technical know-how, we need to examine the requisite character attributes and interpersonal skills required of someone applying for this role. I am going to ask you to take a long, serious look at yourself and honestly consider whether or not you are a viable candidate for this job. If you are merely drawn to the idea of the exotic travel and rubbing elbows with celebrities, then perhaps you need to reconsider this path.

2) Next, we will address the more technical qualifications. If you've read Chapters 4 and 5 thoroughly, you now know the types of tasks you will be expected to perform and therefore should easily be able to figure out what vocational skills you need to have or acquire to land a job in this industry. Rather than rehash what those talents and abilities are, we will instead examine the type of background experiences—whether it be former jobs or just life experiences—that will lend themselves to your becoming a great yacht stew.

In other words, without a specific background in yachting, what have you done up until now that demonstrates you either have the necessary qualifications already, or at least have the capacity to learn them? To stick with my recipe analogy: Are there any transferable ingredients from your previous recipes for achievement that pertain to what is expected of a stew? We'll take inventory of those applicable experiences.

After we've determined whether or not you are fit for a yacht stew position, and by that I mean that you stand a chance of getting hired based upon both your personal qualities as well as your background, I will then move on to the training you will need to further develop those skills in Chapter 7.

❖ **INSIDER TIP:** As you read this chapter, I want you to highlight or take notes on the skills you currently have that make you marketable for this line of work. In Chapter 10, when we put together your résumé/CV, you need to return to this list when I ask you not only to identify your key talents and abilities, but also to provide evidence that you've developed and used these skills previously.

Personal Attributes Assessment

As a yacht stewardess, your role as part of the crew is paramount to the experience that each of the guests has onboard. You will be expected to personally interact with some of the world's wealthiest and most distinguished people. To handle this, all the experts I interviewed agreed: More than actual skills, you need key personality traits.

Certain personality "ingredients" are **required** to be well-suited for this job: people skills, a positive attitude, the ability to be a team player, proper etiquette, a pleasant appearance, discretion, observational and listening skills, problem-solving skills, organizational skills, and the ability to be flexible.

People Skills

Are you what many would consider a "people person"? Do you like, or generally get along with, most people? I hope so, because if you ultimately land a position on a yacht, you will be surrounded by them—and that means your guests and your fellow crew. At the end of the day, no matter how good you are at service, ironing, or making beds, if you can't get along with people, you do not belong on a yacht crew. Excellent communication skills are crucial to your success at this job.

It seems the experts would agree:

"I think the most important qualification is to be a people person. You have to want to meet new people, be able to interact with them and make them feel welcome in your 'home' while working long hours, sometimes for long stretches at a time."
— **Debra Blackburn-Boggio**, yacht charter broker with Fraser Yachts Worldwide

"Good people skills! That's the most important thing. You need to have an even-keeled temperament—no knee-jerk reactions...Learn how to diffuse anger and keep the bigger goal in mind. A good crewmember remembers there's no 'I' in "Team."'
— **Kristen Cavallini-Soothill**, owner and operator of American Yacht Institute

"The A-#1, most important thing is being able to get along with other people. You live, sleep, breathe, and work with so many different people. It takes a lot of flexibility. You have to actually enjoy making other people happy and taking care of others' needs. This is a service industry, and you are making sure the guests have everything they need at any time, and all the time."
— **Ami Ira**, owner and operator of Crew Unlimited

Furthermore, you will also be expected to move comfortably within the world of wealth and fame. Are you the type to get flustered around celebrities? (I hope not.) Can you handle stress without flying off the handle or taking it out on those closest to you? Having a small ego helps in this business, since the guests' needs must always come first. You should also not have a problem being subservient to others. For a yacht stew, it's the name of the game.

Are you guilty of being ethnocentric? Are you put off by people who are "different" from you? If you are, you won't make it long in this industry. Working on a yacht crew, you will be mixing with an international crowd—whether it's your guests, your fellow crewmembers, or representatives and service agents from the yachting community. You will be traveling to other countries and dealing with wide varieties of people from other races, cultures, and creeds. You therefore need to have an open mind and be tolerant of others, despite any cultural differences. If that's going to be a problem for you, stay away from yachting.

Positive Attitude

It goes without saying that all crewmembers must project positive, cheerful, and caring attitudes toward the owner, the guests, and other crewmembers, not to mention the yacht, herself. But never expect that showering anyone with kindness will be duly reciprocated. You need to be prepared for the fact that as much as you'd like to retaliate against someone who makes an insulting or demanding comment to you, or forgets to say "please" or "thank you" when appropriate, you must just learn to grin and bear it. Remain positive, don't show emotion, and whatever you do, do *not* pick a fight with a guest.

If a guest yells or is condescending to you, you must conduct yourself in a diplomatic way. Sure, that might mean ducking into the privacy of the crew quarters and throwing a stack of just-ironed serviettes against the wall (or worse, the iron itself); but in the presence of guests, you cannot show that type of emotion. If you do react, it should be in such a way as to diffuse the situation; you have to remain focused and address them on a professional level. (And if you're going to complain about it later to fellow crewmembers, please make sure you're not standing near a vent that carries sound into the guest cabins.)

My best advice in dealing with not-so-nice guests: Be resilient, and just tuck that little story away for relaying back to all your friends and family back home. They'll listen in awe.

◆——————◆

I Must Confess...
I had to bite my sassy tongue at times.

For someone who has never felt shy about voicing her opinions, and who has been referred to by her friends as a bit of a smart aleck (especially when it comes to altercations with people in unworthy positions of authority), I was surprisingly able to exercise a tremendous amount of self-restraint and made it through my time as a stewardess without incident. Ahhh, but that's not to say there weren't some close calls.

Take the Playboy Bunny girlfriend of a charter guest's multi-millionaire son. (My example of an "unworthy position of authority.") This girl practiced yoga every day she was onboard, demanding that we first clear the entire sundeck for her to remain undisturbed while she got in touch with her "inner being" for hours on end. What a hassle for our deck crew to be banished from a primary workspace for most of an afternoon!

On one particular day, she approached me in the main foyer as I was pulling the dead blooms off a quickly fading floral display: "Judy" (Day 4, and she still couldn't get my name right), "I am heading up to the sundeck for my daily meditation. Could you alert the boys that I mustn't be disturbed?"

"Certainly," I replied through my teeth.

"You know, Judy," she continued *(it's Julie, you nitwit),* "you really should try some relaxation techniques, yourself... you seem awfully uptight." She went on to explain to me about how, through her daily routines, she was nurturing that part of her soul that is free of earthly possessions and physical reality.

Now, take note: These comments are coming from a girl who, at breakfast the previous morning, complained to the entire table about how disappointed she was with her recent breast implants and how downright distraught she was that she needed a second surgery to have them repositioned. Unlike two of our lingering deckhands, I managed to escape the scene before she reportedly removed her blouse to get everyone's opinion on the matter, causing the 80-year-old main charter guest to nearly choke on his oatmeal.

And here she was, now standing before me, coaching me on ways to achieve a similar level of "spiritual enlightenment." How I made it through that moment without a) laughing in her face or b) handing her one of those dead flower blooms as I pointed out that her negative aura was having a destructive effect on other life forms in the vicinity, I'll never know.

Make no mistake about it, the intellectually ill-equipped, trophy girlfriends are the toughest guests to deal with when it comes to not telling them what you *really* think.

Team Player

Remember that your team's primary goal is to create the best experience for your guests—these are dream vacations you are providing. The work ethic has to be that you do whatever it takes to get the job done, and that you must function as part of a team. You should always be willing to jump in to help another crewmember, even if it's not your direct responsibility or under the jurisdiction of your own department onboard. Be open to learning new processes and skills that will contribute to this overall team mission.

This job may challenge your own limits and beliefs about what it means to work with other people. In fact, imagine for a moment what it would be like to live with the people you work with at your current job. (Crazy thought, huh?)

It takes a lot of selfless qualities to work effectively as a team with individuals who you will almost feel married to after a period of living and working together in tight quarters, and at times under tremendous amounts of stress. If you get a well-functioning team where everyone cooperates and respects one another, then it can be a magical experience; but it has to be on the basis of the boat, guests, and crew first, and you second. Again, leave your ego at home.

Proper Etiquette

Becoming a yacht stew entails being propelled into a world most people never see—an exclusive world of money and glamour where formal styles of behavior are expected. In this environment, it is essential to have a thorough knowledge of etiquette. Remember, you are going to be paid as a professional, and you will need to act the part and "fit in" as best you can.

Formality is not only about displaying professionalism, it's about giving the owner and guests the respect they deserve. The basic "dos and don'ts" are just common sense: no chewing gum while on duty; guests should be addressed by Mr., Mrs., or Miss, accompanied by their surnames (unless they ask to be called by their first name); when asked a question, crewmembers should reply with "yes or no," "Ma'am," "Madam," or "Sir"; do not interrupt guests when they are speaking to you, nor challenge anything they might say.

However, rules of etiquette go beyond just being polite and using proper forms of address. When it comes to table manners, the stews will of course need to know the proper standards for setting the table and for serving a meal. But it doesn't stop there: As a professional yacht stew, you should also have a grasp of the table manners exhibited by your guests.

Think about it: Many of these people will have been raised with silver spoons in their mouths, and if they weren't, then they will likely have attended a finishing school or read books on how to behave in an acceptable manner among their elite peers. You need to know what they know, such as how they've been taught to communicate to you that they have finished with their plate, or what signals they use to indicate wanting you to pour (or not pour) more wine. To read these cues, you need to familiarize yourself with the more advanced rules of etiquette. Once you know these rules, you may even catch your own guests breaking them. (The Playboy Bunny trophy girlfriend, mentioned in my last confession, didn't know which fork to use with her salad.)

I suggest you pick up a book on the subject of etiquette. Take it with you to use as an onboard resource. I also recommend enrolling in one of introductory interior-crew training courses, which will teach you all about the decorum of high society, including awareness of cultural differences and guidelines and the protocol for interacting with guests at all levels of society. For more of the specific table manners etiquette, enroll in a yacht interior basic food service course. This knowledge is great not only to have for this job, but also as you move on through life.

Appearance and Personal Hygiene

During my many interviews of crew placement experts, this was often a tough subject to handle with honesty and tact. Some chose to broach it with diplomacy, others opted to be blunt and straightforward. I will summarize for you here what I found is difficult for many to admit about the reality of first impressions: Appearance has *a lot* to do with landing a job in this industry. No one is proud of that fact, and it is even uncomfortable for me to write these words. Therefore, let me explain this from a perspective that will perhaps allow you to see why image matters:

As a yacht stew, you are a representative. How you look and the image you project are more often than not seen as a reflection of the quality of service to come. You will be expected to reflect the prestige that these magnificent and admired vessels possess—not only when interacting with guests, but when being viewed by onlookers.

Your appearance, then, is critical. I'm not saying you must have supermodel or Miss Universe potential... but what you do need to have is a neat and classy appearance and good personal hygiene. Pay attention to aspects of your grooming. While on duty, keep your hair pulled back and if it's long, consider wearing it up. Shower and wear deodorant, but leave the strong-scented perfumes for your times off the vessel. Use light amounts of makeup when guests are onboard, but also don't look like you just rolled out of bed. Avoid gaudy and bright-colored manicures, as your hands will be on display a lot when serving, and that can be distracting for guests. Heavy jewelry is also a no-no, with the exception of a watch for keeping track of time. Male stews should remain clean and shaven (no beards). Mustaches and goatees may be allowed, but only if they are kept neat and trimmed frequently. I recommend hiding any obvious tattoos as best you can.

To work in this industry, it is important that you are fit, healthy, and energetic, for you will be running up and down tiny staircases and doing a lot of physically challenging work. You need to be able to move fast and to keep on going for long stretches at a time. Having any major health problems or being out of shape is also not going to cut it. This is an energy-driven job.

Stews need to focus on their physical demeanor as well. One of the fastest ways to present a more polished appearance is through your posture. Stand or sit up straight, keep your shoulders back, and carry yourself with aplomb. Try this where you are sitting right now, and I guarantee you will instantly feel more sophisticated.

On the opposite end of the spectrum, however, stews want to avoid oozing sexiness or going to great lengths to exude attractiveness. Occasionally, for a formal dinner, you may wear nicer earrings or dressier uniforms to complement the atmosphere, but otherwise, you should avoid being showy. While you might be tempted to doll up or look your best when in the presence of important or famous people, remember that they probably don't notice you for more than the job you are doing—and there will most always be a significant other lurking about, so if they feel threatened, jealous, or as though they're losing attention to you, it could lead to a disaster!

Discretion

Part of what high-profile people like about being on a yacht is the privacy it offers. Stews become privy to intimate details about their guests' lives, which is why the importance of keeping secrets and not disclosing information to people who should not know it is one of the most valued of traits. Guests do not want their private lives being exposed on the docks by members of the crew or publicized via social media. Discretion is a key part of working on a superyacht. And, as pointed out in Chapter 5, all the scoop on who and what is onboard, or who owns the vessel and how much it costs must remain as confidential as if the crew were members of the CIA on a top-secret mission. Keep it under wraps.

The following comes from an actual yacht crew manual:

> The yacht's owner and guests have entrusted crewmembers with personal information that should not be repeated. This yacht has an exceptional collection of art, multimedia equipment, and expensive objects onboard. Specific objects and/or the prices of any items onboard should never be discussed. All crewmembers would suffer deep remorse if the safety and security of this yacht and its passengers were compromised by a slip of a tongue. If asked questions regarding the vessel, her owner, or her guests, inform curious people courteously of her size and the fact that she is 'company owned' and available for charter without getting into other aspects of the boat's history.
>
> **—contributed by Captain Carl Sputh**

It bears repeating: Crewmembers should never divulge information or discuss the owners or the guests traveling onboard their yacht, or even give hints to outsiders as to who might be coming on at some point in the future. Start practicing this phrase now: "I am not at liberty to disclose that information." That's called job security. (Pun intended.) And for goodness' sake, keep it off Facebook!

I Must Confess…
I watched Naomi Campbell watch TV.

I don't like to mention names of my former guests because I'm all about protecting their privacy. However, I will admit to having been on a yacht that was docked *next door* to a yacht carrying Naomi Campbell. (And actually, we wound up three boats down from her on another occasion, too—just six months later, and in a port halfway around the world from the first.)

On this particular occasion that we were directly adjacent to her, Ms. Campbell was on a yacht chartered for a high-profile photo shoot on the island of St. Barts. One night, having slipped out from the galley for a moment to catch some fresh air before serving dinner, I was standing just outside our side-door entrance, and, well, I couldn't help it…I had no choice. Her porthole (window) was right there in front of me, in direct line with my view. She was simply lying on her bed in one of the lower cabins next door, watching TV, fully clothed, and doing absolutely nothing but gazing at the set before her.

It was pretty uneventful, really. Not that I wish I had more to report. (Although, the deckhands on my yacht, who I called on the radio to come marvel at my discovery… I think they were a tad bit disappointed.)

Observational and Listening Skills

If you've ever worked in a service or hospitality industry, most specifically as something equivalent to a restaurant server or bartender, then you know how important it is to have keen observational and listening skills. If you've never held a position like that before, well, then listen (and observe) up:

The power of observation is about reading people. To offer quality service, you must be able to anticipate the needs of your clients. Observe and listen more than you talk. Try to pick up on their habits and preferences right away so that you can be prepared to meet their needs before they have to ask or remind you to do something again in the future. In other words, be proactive—not reactive.

Along with your eyes, keep your ears open! Quite often, you can pick up a lot about what a person might ask of you next simply by paying attention to what's going on in a room. At breakfast, if you hear one guest tell another that he didn't sleep well the night before, ask him later if you can provide him with extra pillows or layer a duvet onto his mattress for that upcoming night. The reason he didn't sleep well may have nothing to do with comfort, but hey, at least you tried.

Listening skills are also critical for understanding exactly what your guests want. Stews multi-task all day long, but when one of your guests addresses you, take time to focus on what he or she is saying and be an effective listener. Don't botch something because you weren't paying attention to what a guest said or asked you to do.

Problem-Solving Skills

As a stew, you are expected to be prepared for anything at any time. Guests on yachts don't care how you get something done, so long as you get it done. You must be able to think quickly on your feet and control your emotions in crisis situations. The big rule is to get the mission accomplished, but never let them see you sweat (even if it's a 90-degree day in Capri, and you're serving lunch on the sundeck).

Stews must come up with creative solutions to household management dilemmas as well. Lack of adequate storage space for provisions and items used by the interior department is a constant problem on yachts. I worked under one chief stew who was incredibly skilled at solving such space issues. She filled our laundry room walls with hooks and random shelving units and was constantly hiring carpenters to come aboard and redo the insides of cabinets and closets in an attempt to maximize storage space.

Furthermore, in order to meet a demanding or eccentric guest's requests, you have to be willing to go that extra mile. It helps to have good persuasive speaking skills when it comes to obtaining things from the outside world. If you've ever worked in sales, this is most likely a talent you developed along the way. Sweet-talking local service people or yacht agents to help you get what you need never hurts. (Nor does flat-out begging.) Just whatever you do, don't break the law; it's not worth it to go that far.

I Must Confess...
I once bribed some customs officials.

We were preparing to leave Palma de Mallorca, Spain to pick up the owner in Venice, Italy, but we were still waiting on a shipment of $10,000 worth of crystal glassware, crew uniforms, and 250 DVDs to arrive. Two hours before departure, I learned that the items were stuck in customs. Our customs agent didn't seem too concerned, and just kept telling me he was "doing his best" to get me my packages. Frustrated, I told him "his best" wasn't good enough, grabbed two bottles of Johnnie Walker scotch and three bottles of Jack Daniels whiskey, marched off the boat, and hopped a cab to the cargo delivery area at the airport. Once there, I bribed two customs workers, a guy from the shipping agent's office (oh yeah, and a Mallorcan police agent) into letting me have the stuff. One of them even escorted me to the police station, helped me get the last bit of paperwork signed, and then came back to the boat with me to assist in loading everything onboard.

We completed the mission with only 10 minutes to spare before our scheduled departure time. Talk about an adrenaline rush!

Now wait a minute, didn't I warn you against breaking the law right before I confessed to you that I once did? Well, sorta. Note that I was working *with* the authorities—it's just that in some countries, you have to work with law enforcement a bit differently. I don't recommend you necessarily follow in my footsteps, nor can I promise you doing so won't backfire.

Organizational Skills

The best yacht stews tend to be assertive people with strong organizational skills. You must have an innate ability to get things done, often while tracking several projects simultaneously. For this, exceptional project-management and prioritization skills are key. Let's also not forget being detail-oriented; the ability to focus on minute details is an essential part of this job.

Being organized is an especially vital attribute for the chief stew, since he or she is the one managing the interior department and the rest of the stews. I cannot stress enough the importance of having systems in place to keep the everyday management of the yacht under tight control. The rotation schedule discussed and presented in Chapter 4 is one example of a system, as are filing systems for contacts, inventories, and shopping receipts. A chief stew will usually be meticulously organized and will assign a place for everything on the boat.

As an entry-level stew, it is your job to then make sure that everything is in its assigned place. In other words: Follow the systems. Get comfortable with your daily routines so that they become automatic. You will be juggling a lot of various responsibilities at one time, and the chance of being interrupted at frequent intervals is high. It helps to make a habit out of writing things down on scraps of paper—things that you'll need to remember to do or go back to doing later.

Flexibility

Once you've got your routines and operating systems down pat, the next step is learning how to be flexible with them. I think this is one of the biggest challenges for stews: being organized and flexible at the same time, since the two traits don't necessarily go hand-in-hand. But when guests are onboard, you can never fully predict what's going to be requested next, so if certain aspects of the day can run like clockwork (the organized part), then the more clear-headed you will be when it comes to handling a sudden crisis (the being flexible part). Have contingency plans set up in case there's a mishap beyond your control.

Flexibility is also important with regard to crew life in general. For example: You thought you were going to have the day off tomorrow, but now there are guests coming onboard. In this line of work, there are a lot of times when you won't know what the long-term schedule is, or even where you are going to be the following week. Not being able to plan your free time is a down side to this job. Sure, you are given some advance notice, but it's nearly impossible to plan vacations a long time out. (Although the upside there is that when you do get to go, the boat often pays to send you home.)

On the whole, things rarely go as planned in this industry, and it's also not unusual for things to change suddenly. Owners and guests of megayachts are typically eccentric people, and they are used to getting what they want, when they want, and they make decisions and requests on a whim. You never know what to expect. That lack of control and of living on somebody else's schedule is a definite challenge for yacht crew. This is why you need to be a flexible person.

I Must Confess...
No matter how hard I tried to be prepared
for anything, I was caught off guard a lot.

This next tale demonstrates the importance of remaining organized enough in your daily routine that when emergencies arise, your problem-solving skills kick in on autopilot.

We had a charter on for the Monaco Grand Prix, and it was the morning of the race. When breakfast began, we were prepared to serve the 12 individuals who had slept onboard the night before their morning meal—these were the guests we knew of. However, the main charter guest owned a home just around the corner from where we were docked, and little did we know, but he had instructed our deckhands to take one of our dinghy boats there to shuttle over an entire slew of additional guests, who would be arriving in time for the race. And arrive they did… just as we were wrapping up breakfast.

The next thing we knew, we were taking requests for omelets and cappuccinos from 20 of the newly arrived. (Fortunately, we were on the dock, so one of our deckhands was able to run to a nearby grocery store for more eggs.)

If that wasn't bad enough, by the end of the day, the number of guests had swelled to over 50, and wouldn't you know it, but it was champagne all around at the finish of the race. Ah, but wait! Champagne must be served in champagne glasses!

You'll be hard pressed to find any yacht carrying 50 or more of any one type of glassware. Normally, you would order extras for a special occasion, but remember, we were not forewarned about these additional guests. We had to think fast!

I leaned over the side of our boat and got the attention of the chef on the yacht next to us. I asked if they had any extra champagne glasses we could borrow. "Sure, I'll walk them over," she replied. "No, wait," I shot back, "the guests will see." At that point, a stewardess on her boat joined in, and they began handing glasses overboard to us, one at a time. We were able to rack up another 25 glasses and pulled off the champagne toast with success. (Whew.)

Transferable "Ingredients" From Your Previous Recipes

If you're at all like I was in my pre-yachting days, then your knowledge of boats is pretty limited. This doesn't mean you won't make a perfect addition to a yacht crew, though. There is more than enough work to go around on a luxury yacht, so really, the more "Jack (or Jill!)-of-All-Trades" you prove to be, the better. While you might not already have the exact makings of a yacht stew, you may have plenty of other skills from experiences in your background to make you beneficial and worth bringing onboard to train.

You will want to review the applicable background experiences listed in this chapter in order to include them on your résumé/CV when applying to work on your first yacht. To get started, create a work autobiography beginning with your first full-time job, or your graduation (whichever came first) and continuing through your present position. The eventual compilation of this work history will serve as the goldmine from which you will be able to extract those talents or skills you have used throughout your life to date. We will work on skills identification again in Chapter 10, at which time I will have you look back at this section that follows.

The Excavation of Your Work History

As you go excavating through your life's experiences up to now, here are some specific experiences to pull up:

The Obvious

- ➡ **Hotel/hospitality experience:** Any type of background working in hotels, motels, or welcome centers, be it as a member of the housekeeping staff or as a concierge or front desk clerk, is excellent experience. Don't overlook that summer working the kiddy rides at the state fair or the ticket booth gig at your local concert venue, either. Ah, and remember the political golf fundraiser when you volunteered to drive the beverage cart? That was hospitality service.

↦ **Restaurant or catering experience:** It's beneficial if you've had actual food-serving experience, but host/essing and cocktail waiter or waitress jobs are good, too. If you've had experience serving wine, that can win you even more points. The higher the caliber of establishments you've worked in, the better; but I still wouldn't rule out having been a waiter at your local country kitchen restaurant as good preparation for becoming a stew. It still counts as table service.

↦ **Bartending/barista experience:** A former job mixing and serving drinks is a great foundation to have. Chief stews love managing staff they can rely on to handle the more advanced tasks of preparing complicated cocktail orders. Aside from serving beer, wine, and liquor, if you have worked as a barista at your local coffee shop or have any training in the intricacies of espresso or other hot-beverage preparation, this is great experience as well.

↦ **Culinary training or cooking background:** That's wonderful if you have some cooking know-how, but it's not necessary. Prep or line cook jobs in restaurants, or any food preparation you've done for large groups of people at one time (as with catering or cafeteria jobs), are all worthy of being noted. These experiences show you are well-rounded and capable of assisting in the galley if necessary. If you've had any exposure to food-hygiene management, that is also a plus.

↦ **Nanny or babysitting experience:** If you are thinking about counting babysitting for neighborhood families where you grew up, only list these jobs as experience if you held them in the last four years, and on a consistent basis. Nanny and au pair jobs held for extended periods with one family at a time are much more applicable (and impressive), especially if you traveled with your employer. And hey, camp counselor experience counts, too.

↦ **Cruise ship job experience:** I know this is obvious, but the point I want to make here is that any stew or non-stew jobs for a cruise line are notable because at least you've had some exposure to the marine industry. For example, after the first edition of this book came out, I received an enquiry from a former baggage handler for one of the major cruise lines wanting to know about becoming a deckhand on yachts. Although he'd never worked on the ship itself, he'd had exposure to the staff who did and knew all about what is expected of a deckhand. He still had a lot to learn, but I assured him he had the perfect foundation for yachting.

↦ **Professional housekeeping experience:** I had friends in college who made extra cash working part-time for Merry Maids, the national housekeeper franchise. Maybe you've done something similar? If you've served on the housekeeping staff at hotels or on cruise ships, this is even more directly related to yacht stew work. Ah, and wait: Have you ever worked for a car-detailing business or a professional carpet-cleaning service? These jobs demonstrate good housekeeping skills, too.

- **Professional garment-care experience:** If you've ever worked in a laundromat or a drycleaners, you have more garment-care experience than most people. Brag confidently about it when you apply to be a stew. What about sewing? Most yachts will have a sewing machine, and finding a stew who can actually use it is rare. If you know how to sew on buttons, fix zippers, or repair uniforms or other garments, any yacht would love to have your talent onboard.
- **Medical knowledge/Nursing experience:** If you have first-aid training or a background in a medical field of any kind, even if it's as a pharmaceutical rep, this is good. You will still be required to take the First Aid Module of the STCW '95 Basic Safety Training course, but at least you can point to the fact that you have been exposed to all of this before. Nursing is another fantastic background to have when entering yachting, as is any position where other individuals were under your direct care.
- **Diving certifications:** If you are certified by the Professional Association of Diving Instructors (PADI) as a scuba diver, you just earned triple bonus points. It's certainly not something you have to have (although, there are some yachts that only hire certified divers because the owners are avid divers), but it will make you an asset to any crew. I never dove; in fact, I didn't even enjoy snorkeling. For me, it was all about the Jet Skis and water skiing.
- **Water-sports proficiencies:** While you are not expected to know the ins and outs of boating when you come into this industry, it is recommended that you aren't afraid of being out in the middle of the ocean on a boat and that you at least know how to swim. In fact, strong swimming abilities are something you want to highlight. If you know anything about other water sports, such as how to drive Jet Skis, WaveRunners, or speedboats, that's another bonus, as are fishing, rafting, and canoeing competencies. It's not necessary for a stew to have these qualifications, but they do demonstrate your affinity for the water.
- **Lifeguarding experience:** Previous lifeguarding work is wonderful experience to point to, especially if it was on a beach. The local country club pool counts, too, so long as you were certified (that CPR training is another attention-getter).
- **Domestic-arts background:** Training or experience in any type of domestic art is extremely pertinent. This includes floral arranging and/or plant care; sewing and tailoring; caring for art, silver, jewelry or antiques; furniture restoration; and interior decorating.
- **Massage certification:** This is a highly sought-after skill these days. If you have massage therapy and bodywork training, great. Please note that this is not a skill you are expected to have; I only list it as a way to make yourself more marketable or to beat out competition for stew jobs.

The Not-So-Obvious

- **Cruising or sailing experience:** It may just consist of recreational boating from your years growing up, perhaps confined to large lakes or reservoirs (the fresh-water experiences), but this is still a pertinent background. Whether it was travel on a houseboat, sailboat, ski boat, paddleboat, or even just a canoe, it counts. Even more applicable are any trips taken at sea, such as commercial cruises. Or perhaps I'm underestimating your marine aptitude: If you were the captain of your college sailing team, a state champion competitive water skier, or a dolphin trainer for the last five years at Sea World, you will definitely fare well in terms of proving your ability to work at sea.

↠ **Event-planning experience:** Have you ever served as an event planner or organizer for professional parties, dinners, fundraising events, networking or breakfast clubs, or even grand openings of a store or business? If you have, that is evidence that you have the makings of a yacht stew.

↠ **Work- or study-abroad experiences or an extensive leisure-travel background:** A broad and varied travel background demonstrates a willingness and ability to live onboard and travel with a yacht. If you have extensive travel experience, especially if it was an overseas trip or a work- or study-abroad opportunity, you are definitely primed for a job in this industry.

↠ **Language proficiencies:** Whether you studied a language in college and only know the basics, or you immersed yourself in another culture to learn it, any and all knowledge of other languages is an asset in the yachting industry. Be sure to make note of whether your skill level is basic, intermediate, or advanced, or if you only speak, read, or understand particular languages. But most certainly, noting every language you have some basic knowledge of is a must.

↠ **Administrative or personal assistant job experience:** Any job where your responsibilities entailed managing or organizing someone else's day is a great prerequisite. If you've been a celebrity personal assistant or handled administrative duties for a business executive or CEO, this is an even bigger plus. Professional errand runners will also do well.

↠ **Tour director or travel agent experience:** If you've escorted groups of people on tours, provided onsite destination management, or coordinated group or individual travelers' daily activities, including any logistical elements of their trips such as flights, hotels, day tours, transportation, or daily communications, this is a superb foundation for stewarding on a yacht. If you've been a travel agent, providing assistance in any aspects of pre-trip preparation or post-trip evaluation for other people, this makes you a valuable asset.

↠ **Customer service job experience:** If you've ever held a position where you provided customer service support, then you are used to handling complaints and communicating with people. Your interpersonal skills are likely sharp. This is a perfect background.

↠ **Patient-care experience:** Any previous positions (even non-medical or volunteer positions) held in hospitals or nursing homes, whether as a candy striper, patient care liaisons, or a hospice volunteer to name but a few, are great preparation for offering guest care.

↠ **Sales experience:** If you've ever worked in a sales job, whether as a sales representative for a product or service or as a retail-store clerk, you have experience in the art of persuasion and dealing with people. If your experience involved selling luxury goods or dealing with a more elite clientele, you are even more primed for dealing with guests traveling aboard yachts.

- **Computer skills:** In no way are computer skills required for an entry-level stew, although chief stews should definitely have them. Either way, office-job backgrounds and work involving computers can still be looked upon favorably (especially if the captain is not so handy at it and requires assistance). Make note of all Microsoft Office software programs you are proficient in, with Word and Excel being the most important.

- **Carpentry or mechanical experience:** They are more important for entry-level deckhands or 2nd engineers, but if you have carpentry or mechanical skills, these are transferable to yachting. In fact, if you have these abilities, an exterior or engineering crew position may suit you even better. Perhaps you would want to look into the dual position of a stew-deckhand (covered back in Chapter 3). If you're interested in interior work only, having these skills is still beneficial because you will make a great team player.

- **Volunteer work:** Participation in civic, fraternal, sports, or any other after-hours activity or interest (artistic, handicraft, gardening, theatrical) may very well serve as noteworthy training grounds for becoming a stew. As far as what skills you gained from such experiences, ask yourself this: In what ways would any organizations you have served have been poorer in resources, profits, or values if you had not been there? Whether for family, school, church, your community, a business, or your own enterprise, volunteer work typically provides you with lots of great qualifications.

- **Accounting/bookkeeping knowledge:** While it is the chief stew or purser's responsibility to handle accounting and bookkeeping tasks for the interior department, that doesn't mean that such skills aren't important for entry-level stews to have. Again, either the captain will see it as a positive that you can assist him or her in administrative duties (I did this on one yacht), or these skills might just demonstrate to a potential boss that you are detail-oriented and budget-conscious. And if it isn't obvious, bring it up during interviews.

- **Experience living with a large number of people:** Don't laugh. This takes skill. If you've ever lived in a sorority or fraternity house, you know what I'm talking about. I even mentioned on my résumé/CV how I'd lived with nine people in a three-bedroom flat in London for four months. So, if you grew up in a family of 10 children, all living under the same roof, please realize that you are well on your way to making a good yacht stew.

Now that wasn't so bad, was it? Hopefully, after reviewing this list, you are feeling a bit more confident about your already-existing skills and qualifications and are encouraged to know you will shine in this line of work. If that's not the case, then take comfort in knowing that there are plenty of ways to learn the ropes. Onward we go into what essential training you must add to your recipe for success at becoming a luxury yacht stew.

7

LEARNING THE ROPES
—ESSENTIAL TRAINING
FOR ENTRY-LEVEL STEWS—

"While most people will readily accept the advantages of senior officers such as the Captain, Mate, and Engineer participating in formal training, it's also important for interior crew."
—**Amy Morley Beavers**, VP Regulatory Compliance and Academic Principal of Maritime Professional Training (MPT) in Fort Lauderdale, Florida.

No matter what kind of previous work experiences you've had, and no matter how perfectly groomed you feel you are to enter into this industry, there's still some work to do. Training is essential. Training to get on a boat, and more than anything, to stay on it.

There are two types of training that I strongly recommend you get under your belt before beginning your job search (or simultaneous to it, and I will explain how to do that later).

The two essentials for entry-level interior crew are:

1) An STCW five-day Basic Safety Training (BST) Course in order to obtain an STCW Basic Safety Training Certificate for International Compliance. While it used to be that an entry-level stew or a chef might be able to get away without having this certification, you won't find those scenarios anymore. To work on a yacht in any capacity, consider STCW BST mandatory.

2) An Interior Crew Training course that covers, at the very least, yachting etiquette and service. Official certification is not mandatory yet, but it may be in the future. Meanwhile, you are doing yourself (and your job hunt) a big favor by at least getting a couple introductory classes under your belt.

I will tell you all about both of these training options in the pages to come. Finally, I will round out this chapter with guidance on how you can acquire some other types of education and experiences to prepare you for the functions you will be expected to perform as a luxury yacht stew.

STCW Basic Safety Training (BST)

All crewmembers working aboard commercial vessels (which means all charter yachts) are required to have what is called an STCW Basic Safety Training International Certificate of Competency (referred to generally as basic safety training). When crew recruiters and captains ask entry-level crew, "Have you got your STCW?" or "Do you have your basic safety training?"—this is what they are talking about.

(Note that you will occasionally see this course written with reference to "STCW '95" or "STCW '95, as amended" or possibly even "STCW '78, as amended." Due to the confusion with dates, the coast guard offices are now simply referring to it as STCW, as amended. I will address why that is in the next section. Please know that I am referring to the same thing.)

The five-day STCW Basic Safety Training (BST) Course is aimed mostly at those going to sea for the first time. It teaches essential safety information that every seafarer should know, such as how to deal with onboard emergencies (which hopefully won't ever happen, but at least if you have training, you stand a much better chance of coming out okay). Specifically, the four important skills it covers are sea survival, first aid, personal safety, and firefighting.

A Quick Background on the STCW Code

In 1978, the International Maritime Organization (IMO), which is a division of the United Nations (UN), held a conference in order to discuss improving the worldwide standards for safety and training of professional mariners. Basically, at this event, all of the signatories to the IMO (today there are 185 countries) sat down and said, "Okay, we've got to set 'rules of the sea,'" so to speak. They wanted to establish a code of internationally agreed-upon regulations, which set minimum training requirements to be met at various levels during the course of a career at sea. Then, the signatories could go back and get those rules made into law in each individual country.

The result of this initial meeting was the Seafarers Training, Certification, & Watch-keeping Code (STCW '78). Subsequent meetings were held to update and revise this code, so that by July 1995, the process was finalized with the adoption of a package of amendments to the STCW '78 Convention. The amended code, STCW '95, was named for the year that it was accepted by the

IMO and its signatory countries. From the mid-1990s onward, training schools around the world have been offering classes in compliance with STCW '95.

Another major revision of the STCW code took place at a meeting in Manila in the Philippines in 2010, resulting in the aptly named Manila Amendments. These went into effect in January 2012, with a five-year transition period allowing for full phasing in of the requirements. While many crew companies still refer to this code and accompanying training courses as "STCW '95," and while the significant changes within the 2010 Manila Amendments didn't impact the basic training classes, technically it is not necessary to refer to them as the STCW '95 courses anymore. Although, since the official amendments don't actually take effect until 2017, you will likely still see it written as "STCW '95" in course manuals. The proper way to refer to it now is actually "STCW '95, as amended" (or "STCW '78, as amended," which is how it appears on most captain's licenses); but to save you from text clutter, I will refer to it as simply STCW BST throughout the remainder of this chapter. Again, this is the same set of modules and the same BST certificate that training schools refer to as "STCW '95" or "STCW '95, as amended." *Boring stuff, I know.*

Note: The description above was written based on information largely supplied by the IMO. Visit www.imo.org for more specifics regarding STCW Conventions, Codes, and Amendments.

STCW Basic Safety Training Standards

We've established that the STCW code requires every level of crewmember to have some sort of minimum training. The level of certification that crew must receive is based on the capacity in which they serve onboard (their crew position), and on what type of vessel. The STCW '95 Conventions set codes for the basic training one must have as an engineer, a first officer, or a captain. As one goes up the career ladder, the training requirements increase. The idea here is that if someone is a first mate on a boat in France, and another is a first mate on a similar-sized vessel in Australia, these two individuals should both have had the same sort of training. The schooling and the institutions where it was received may be different, but it will be based on, and in compliance with, the same broad outline of the STCW code.

For entry-level crew, the IMO set down regulations for the most basic level of safety training. For example, what to do in the event someone injures himself (**first aid**), and what happens if you have to abandon ship and get into a life raft (**sea survival**). Then, there's **firefighting**. If you don't treat a fire quickly and correctly, you're going to have to get off the boat, so seafarers need to know how to deal with a fire. With regard to **personal safety and social responsibility**: how to conduct yourself onboard, how not to injure yourself, and how to look after yourself and the rest of your crew (what you do and don't do). These are the things the IMO wants all mariners to know when they come into the industry.

As complicated as I know it all sounds, here's the bottom line: Starting out as an entry-level crewmember, you just need the basics. That means taking an STCW-approved Basic Safety Training course. And moving forward, it must be compliant with the Manila Amendments of 2010 that went into effect January 2012.

Note: The STCW is not a certificate in and of itself. Rather, you will be earning a certificate, known as an STCW Certificate for International Compliance for having completed a Basic Safety Training course that is in compliance with the minimum safety training requirements, as dictated by the STCW code. (And yes, that's a mouthful.) The following section goes more in depth about what you can expect this course to entail.

The STCW Basic Safety Training Course

STCW Basic Safety Training is a five-day training course made up of four separate modules. The order that the modules are written into the STCW requirements is not necessarily the order in which they will be taken during a BST five-day course, and the number of days devoted to each module may also vary depending on the institution offering the training. For example, there are some schools around the world that may take five to seven days to complete this same training, such as by offering three days of fire school as opposed to only two. The most common structure, however, is four modules over a period of five days. While some schools refer to their modules by different titles, the course names given below are essentially what you will find. Regardless of title, however, the information in parenthesis refers exactly to the corresponding STCW '95 code sections:

- **Personal Survival Techniques (Ref A-VI/1-1):** 1½ days of basic sea survival; this course includes a practical session in a swimming pool. Some schools will take two full days for this module.
- **Fire Prevention and Basic Firefighting (Ref A-VI/1-2):** This two-day course includes both theory and live fire scenarios.
- **Elementary First Aid and CPR (Ref A-VI/1-3):** 1 day of CPR and first aid training. Some schools will take two full days for this module.
- **Personal Safety and Social Responsibility (Ref A-VI/1-4):** A half day of learning effective communication, use of safety equipment, using appropriate escape routes, and more. This 4-hour module is usually taught on the same day as the second day of Personal Survival.

With the exception of Personal Safety and Social Responsibility (PSSR), which is classroom instruction only, the modules are made up of both theory and practical learning. This means there's a lot of hands-on training where you will be required to perform certain skills. And please note that, based on the Manila Amendments, there could be a new module required as of January 2014. This will be in maritime security awareness for all crew that do not have specific security duties and more training for crew that do have security responsibilities. Please keep updated via the various training school sites.

Here is what you can expect of the four modules currently required:

Personal Survival Techniques

Instructed in compliance with STCW Code A—VI/1-1. 1½ to 2 days.

This course module consists of 1½ to 2 days. The first day is spent in the classroom covering subjects such as emergency situations, abandonment and survival at sea, survival craft and rescue boats, personal lifesaving appliances carried on ships, emergency radio equipment, and helicopter assistance.

How important is this? Well, did you see the movie *Titanic*? You will learn such things as delegating responsibilities during an emergency and making sure that everybody has something to do to prevent them from panicking. For example, if you're in the water and there is no means of egress (way to escape), get everybody together as quickly as possible into one group, and pacify them by explaining that the reason you are all in one group is because a) body heat will keep them warmer longer, b) you are a bigger target for visibility by potential rescuers above because you're a giant orange circle now, c) it's a morale booster, and d) you are now less appealing to sharks. (Sharks are predators, so if you're in a big group, you don't look like a pool of tiny feet, but rather a large object that sharks won't want to mess with.)

The remainder of the class is spent in a swimming pool with life jackets, survival suits, and life rafts, performing the simulation of abandon-ship procedures. You learn how to jump off a 40-foot deck with either a life jacket or immersion suit on (which is like wearing your parents' pajamas) and how to get into, out of, and even flip over a life raft. You learn how to work together as a team in the water. You will also be asked to swim laps in order to determine your competency. No one's expecting you to be of Olympic caliber, but if you can't swim (and by that, I mean at least having the doggy paddle down), you need to learn. The theory and practical are both followed by a written examination.

> *"The information that you'll learn in the class is amazing and important to know. And, it's fun! One thing I hadn't realized is that you don't jump into the water with your clothes on; if you do, you can't lift yourself onto the life boat."*
> —**Ami Ira,** owner and operator of Crew Unlimited, a crew placement agency

Fire Prevention and Basic Firefighting
Instructed in compliance with STCW Code A—VI/1-2. 2 full days.

The classroom portion of this module includes shipboard firefighting organization, the elements of fire and explosion, types of ignition, and fire and smoke detection. You will learn about what chemicals or agents combat which types of fire, and how to determine what the causes of a fire might be and to dissect the issue. Breathing-apparatus use and automatic-alarm-system familiarization are also covered.

The second day of basic fire training is the practical application: how to operate a fire extinguisher and how to do a search and rescue in a smoke-filled room, which includes how to navigate through the dark (the blind maze and right-hand search). Trainees will don fire suits and use a Self-Contained Breathing Apparatus (SCBA) as they fight and extinguish actual fires using personal equipment. This practical instruction is taught by licensed and certified firefighting professionals. The two-day fire-school module is followed by a written examination.

First Aid and CPR
Instructed in compliance with STCW Code A—VI/1-3. 1 to 1½ days.

This module consists of theory and practical, covering basic first aid and CPR (cardiopulmonary resuscitation) in marine situations. An EMT or fire paramedic will teach you the step-by-step protocol for various emergency scenarios. Find out how to assess emergency situations, draw likely conclusions, and to rectify them. You will learn to administer CPR and the Heimlich Maneuver and will practice these techniques on mannequins. This course also teaches you about injury maintenance, suppressing bleeding, and creating splints. The course is followed by a written examination.

Personal Safety and Social Responsibility
Instructed in compliance with STCW Code A—VI/1-4. 1/2 day.

In this module, you will learn about conducting yourself professionally. This industry is based on protocol, prevention, and propriety, and you have to behave accordingly. The course covers such topics as working relationships onboard, health and hygiene, drugs and alcohol, shipboard-management structure and responsibilities, and safe working practices. It's really common-sense stuff. This theory-only course is followed by a written exam.

I Must Confess...
I sorta freaked out during a fire-school drill.

I admit it: I'm a girly girl. It was therefore surprising to me how much I enjoyed fire school. I was so into it. That is, until it came time for the final drill.

When I took the STCW fire-training module, I was already working on a yacht, and my entire crew took it together. (I was already in the industry when STCW requirements were first required of crew aboard charter yachts. These days, crew-training schools and placement agencies strongly advise you taking the classes before you apply for a job. In fact, few boats will even bother to interview you if you don't have it.) We had completed our final test, entering a burning building and extinguished the fire, and I passed. The problem was, I had an "eager beaver" captain. He asked the head trainer of the school if his crew could stay an extra half hour to attempt putting out a more daunting fire. The orders were, "Give 'em the works, and let's see how they do."

I'd been such a good sport all day up until then: relentless with the fire extinguisher, able to crawl through smoke-filled rooms with ease, and unafraid to attack oncoming flames with a hose. But, to pull off this final stunt (not required for my STCW basic training, by the way), I had to put on the entire fire suit: turnout pants, the anti-flash hood (like a ski mask), the turnout coat, an SCBA (self-contained breathing apparatus), an SCBA mask, thick pigskin gloves, massive rubber boots, and to top it all off, the hard, leather-lined helmet. It was layer upon layer of protection that probably weighed close to 70 pounds altogether. And mind you, it was 90 degrees in South Florida that afternoon. In that get-up, it now felt like 190.

Once I was all suited up, something awful happened: I got an *itch* on top of my head. Instinctively, I raised my hand to go and scratch it, and POW! (That was the helmet, so I took that off.) Ugh, the glove on my hand, the facemask, the anti-flash hood—it was all in my way! I couldn't get to the itch...and it was getting more and more uncomfortably, agonizingly, and unbearably, well... *itchy!*

Okay, so maybe what I was experiencing was a slight tinge of claustrophobia, which was leading to an even greater bit of panic. But yes, I was losing it.

Thankfully, the first officer from my crew came running over to assist me in pulling the stubborn masks off over my head. And, ahhh *(scratch, scratch, scratch)*—excruciating discomfort gave way to immense relief. I must say, getting to scratch that itch was one of the greatest senses of euphoria I've ever experienced in my life. The captain let me sit out that final mission, given I'd already performed the minimum skills I needed to become certified. (And let's face it, he assumed I needed to chill out for a few.)

As I sat there on a nearby park bench, watching the rest of my crew rush in to attack that burning building, I paused to reflect a moment. That day, I had gained a completely new respect for firemen and rescue workers. (As well as a newfound respect for my fingernails, and their ability to make contact with my head.)

Cost of STCW Basic Safety Training Courses

The full five-day STCW Basic Safety Training modular course, consisting of the four independent modules, costs approximately US$900–$1,000 if taken in the United States, and anywhere from US$900–$1,880 if taken in Europe or Australia. These figures will also vary depending on what school you attend. Most institutions offer each separate STCW module à la carte, so you can take them one at a time if you'd like, rather than the five (or in some cases six) straight days in a row.

I will not cover what day working is all about until Chapter 9, but know that essentially this is day-to-day, freelance work that you can do to earn income while you search for a full-time position. If you have budgetary constraints, you can therefore always fit your STCW BST modules between day working gigs in order to cover your expenses while you earn your certificate of compliance. (Note: You do not necessarily need your STCW certificate to day work, as day work positions usually do not entail the vessel going out to sea.)

On the other hand, while breaking the STCW training up over the course of several weeks may be less of a burden on your wallet, also remember that the sooner you get this training out of the way, the closer you are to earning a consistent salary. It may be wiser just to take the hit up front, and then let your first month's salary on a luxury yacht (with no expenses) earn that money right back. The exception to this advice is if you are interested in simply signing up for one module to test out this industry and see what it's about before committing to finding a job within it. In that case, just sign up and pay for one module out of the gates.

❖ **INSIDER TIP:** Rather than an STCW BST module, the better option for testing things out would be an introduction to yachting course offered at one of the training schools. Maritime Professional Training in Fort Lauderdale, for example, offers an Introduction to Yachting #807 Yacht Etiquette & Service Arts class, which is a one-day course covering yacht roles and definitions, etiquette and personal graces, individual and interpersonal relationships, and more. International Crew Training and many of the crew-training schools in Australia and Antibes, France also offer similar introduction courses that provide a wonderful foundation for entering yachting.

If finances have you concerned, be sure to check out the various training schools' websites I list for you to consider. They will all run price specials at some point during the year. When calling to enroll, be sure to ask about any current or upcoming specials that you might qualify for. A few even have packages that can include interior-crew training at a discounted rate.

Also with regard to budgeting for your STCW BST training, be aware that beyond the basic enrollment tuition, parts of the training may take place off-premises from the school itself, and quite often, you are left to find your own transportation. Examples of this are when you attend the practical portions of sea survival and fire training. You can hire a taxi or take a bus, but I suggest carpooling. My advice is to make friends on your first day of class (and preferably, friends with cars).

As a final note on the subject of training costs, because I am sure you may hear talk of this once you've established yourself in a hiring port: There are cases where entry-level job candidates avoid having to pay for their STCW BST training because they find a yacht that wants to hire them badly enough that the captain or owner agree to pay their course tuition for them. *Do not expect this to happen.* This was a much more common occurrence years ago when the industry first started cracking down on requiring STCW for all charter-yacht crew. Nowadays, though, captains expect that if you are truly serious about finding a job in this industry, you will undertake the STCW training on your own, before you even begin interviewing for jobs.

Note: The STCW Basic Safety Training courses will prepare you to begin your yachting career, but they have to be retaken every five years. Under some situations, showing that you have at least a year of service on a vessel of more than 200 gross tons will suffice to take the place of the basic safety training renewal for your STCW certification. If you stay in this industry longer than five years though, you will likely have to take all four modules again. If you are employed on a vessel at that point, it might be a situation where a yacht is likely to take on the cost. Otherwise, look at the cost of taking the STCW BST courses as an investment.

STCW Basic Safety Training Schools

There are a number of schools around the world offering Basic Safety Training courses that meet the requirements of STCW. When choosing a training provider, make sure that it is a British Maritime and Coastguard Agency (MCA) and/or U.S. Coast Guard (USCG)-approved facility for both training and testing. The following list is a selection of institutions offering STCW-compliant courses.

STCW Basic Safety Training in Fort Lauderdale, Florida

❧ **International Crew Training (ICT)**
> 910 SE 17th St., Ste. 200 (In the Coldwell Banker Building, 2nd Floor)
> Fort Lauderdale, FL 33316
> Tel: 1-954-779-7764
> Website: www.yachtmaster.com, Email: info@yachtmaster.com
> Facebook: www.facebook.com/IntlCrew
>
> International Crew Training (ICT) is the new name for a longstanding school previously known as International Yachtmaster Training. ICT certificates are recognized by the MCA, USCG, and PYA G.U.E.S.T, and they are further approved by the UK's Royal Yachting Association as well as a few countries' yacht registries. All of this means

ICT's certificates allow you to find employment on megayachts around the world. Courses fulfill the requirements of STCW and are offered year-round. You can check the website for schedule information.

ICT also has a crew placement division, called CREW.ICT (www.crew-ict.com), which promises to help you perfect interviewing techniques, find networking events, and of course get a job.

➡ **Maritime Professional Training (MPT)**

1915 South Andrews Ave., Fort Lauderdale, FL 33316

Contact: Julie Liberatore—julie@MPTusa.com

Tel: 1-954-525-1014, Toll Free: 1-888-839-5025, Fax: 1-954-764-0431

Website: www.MPTusa.com, Email: info@MPTusa.com

Facebook: www.facebook.com/mptusa

MPT offers programs to meet all levels of certification and training requirements. MPT offers over 100 different courses, including STCW, that are approved by the MCA and USCG, the RYA, the PYA G.U.E.S.T, and many other organizations and maritime administrations around the world for yachting professionals and commercial mariners. MPT has been offering practical and classroom training for over 30 years.

MPT offers many programs for new crew called STCW "PLUS" which discounts packages of classes taken together. MPT also offers a course called the Career Seminar which teaches new crew how to write a resume and how to get into the industry and how get a job, and more useful tips everyone wishes someone had told them when they started. This course is free with your STCW class and includes dinner.

MPT's Student Services Staff and Career Counselors will help you every step of the way until you are trained and on a boat! Check MPT's website for schedule information; STCW offered almost every week year-round.

➡ **STAR Center**

2 West Dixie Hwy., Dania Beach, FL 33004

Tel: 1-954-921-7254, Toll Free: 1-800-445-4522, Fax: 1-954-920-4268

Website: www.star-center.com, Email: email@star-center.com

STAR Center is a not-for-profit maritime training school. Opened in 1983 in Toledo, Ohio, STAR expanded to its current location in Dania Beach, Florida (just south of Fort Lauderdale) in 1986, consolidating all training there in October 2008. STAR Center's courses meet USCG, STCW, and IMO Model requirements.

➡ **SeaSchool**

SeaSchool Headquarters

8440 4th St. N., St. Petersburg, FL 33702

Tel—Toll Free: 1-800-237-8663

Website: www.seaschool.com, Email: hqstaff@seaschool.com

SeaSchool Fort Lauderdale

2323 South Federal Highway, Ft Lauderdale, FL 33316

Tel—Toll Free: 1-800-542-4551

Website: www.seaschool.com, Email: ftlauderdalestaff@seaschool.com

Facebook: www.facebook.com/seaschool

In operation since 1977, SeaSchool offers U.S. Coast Guard approved STCW BST courses in several Florida locations, including its headquarters in St. Petersburg, with STCW BST courses offered year-round in Fort Lauderdale and Jacksonville. At various periods throughout the year, SeaSchool also offers STCW BST in South Carolina and Alabama, as well as some other locations in the U.S. and Caribbean. Please check the website for times of year and U.S. locations.

STCW Basic Safety Training in Other Parts of the U.S. and Canada

↔ **Confident Captain/Ocean Pros**
250 Thames St., Newport, RI 02840
Tel: 1-401-849-1257
Website: www.confidentcaptain.com, Email: captain@confidentcaptain.com
Facebook: www.facebook.com/pages/Confident-CaptainOcean-Pros/23986867111

↔ **Maritime Institute, Inc.**
1310 Rosecrans St., Ste. G, San Diego, CA 92106
Toll Free Tel: 1-888-262-8020, Fax: 1-619-225-1783
Website: www.maritimeinstitute.com, Email: info@maritimeinstitute.com
Facebook: www.facebook.com/MaritimeInstitute

↔ **In Canada:** For a list of marine schools throughout Canada that offer the STCW BST course, please visit Transport Canada's website: www.tc.gc.ca

STCW Basic Safety Training in Antibes, France and Palma de Mallorca, Spain

↔ **Bluewater Yachting**
Locations: Antibes, France and Palma de Mallorca, Spain
Website: www.bluewateryachting.com & www.bluewatercrew.com
Facebook: www.facebook.com/pages/Blue-Water-Yachting/81710752968
• **In Antibes:** 7 Boulevard d'Aguillon, 06600 Antibes, France
• Tel: 33 (0)493 34 47 73, Fax: 33 (0)493 34 77 74
• Email: training@bluewateryachting.com
• **In Palma:** Calle San Juan 4, La Lonja, 07012 Palma, Spain
• Tel: 34 (0)971 67 71 54
• Email: palma@bluewateryachting.com

Bluewater Yachting's MCA/RYA-approved crew training division, operating out of both Antibes, France and Palma de Mallorca, Spain, is the largest in Europe. They are also one of the first schools to offer PYA Interior Crew Certification courses, which you'll learn more about later in this chapter.

Bluewater Yachting also offers a crew placement division, Bluewater Crew, which is located in in both offices. Learn more about that in Chapter 9.

↔ **D and B Services**
3 Boulevard d'Aguillon
06600 Antibes, France
Tel: 33 (0)4 93 34 09 67, Mobile: +33 (0)6 07 57 28 30

Website: www.dandbservices.com, Email: info@dandbservices.com
Facebook: www.facebook.com/DandBServices

Since 1999, D and B Services has specialized in crew training, yacht management, crew placement, and also crew declaration, in the capacity of ship manager. They offer STCW Basic Safety Training, MCA Deck Officer Modules, tender driving licenses, and a wide range of RYA training, including Dayskipper, Yachtmaster Offshore and Ocean. MLC 2006 compliance. Situated in the center of yachting, you can find D and B Services within a two-minute walk from the Riviera's largest yacht harbor: Port Vauban.

- **Zephyr Yachting**
  11 Rue Fontvieille, 06600 Antibes, France
  Tel: 33 (0)493 33 34 04
  Mob: 33 (0)621 92 76 12
  Website: www.zephyr-yachting.com, Email: info@zephyr-yachting.com
  Facebook: www.facebook.com/pages/Zephyr-Yachting/116300905146004

  Zephyr Yachting's STCW courses are available in Antibes, French Riviera. Check their website for more information.

STCW Basic Safety Training in the United Kingdom

While ports in the UK are not necessarily recommended for hunting down entry-level jobs, if you are a British citizen or someone coming over from countries like Australia, New Zealand, or South Africa, there are schools located throughout the UK that offer superb STCW-compliant Basic Safety Training. You can take these courses prior to heading down to ports where you will have much better luck with your official job search, such as either Antibes or Palma in the Mediterranean, or Fort Lauderdale in the United States.

- **UKSA, United Kingdom Sailing Academy**
  Location: West Cowes, Isle of Wight, UK PO31 7PQ
  Tel: 44 (0)19 83 29 49 41, Fax: 44 (0)19 83 29 59 38
  Website: www.uksa.org, Email: info@uksa.org
  Facebook: www.facebook.com/uksasailing

  The UKSA is a registered charity and non-profit organization set up with the specific aim of providing top quality seamanship training. Courses are MCA-and RYA-approved and meet the requirements of STCW.

- **Lairdside Maritime Centre**
  Location: Wirral, UK
  Liverpool John Moores University, 3 Vanguard Way
  Campbeltown Road, Birkenhead, Wirral CH41 9HX
  Tel: 44 (0)151 647 0494/6, Fax: 44 (0)151 647 0498
  Website: www.lairdside-maritime.com and www.ljmu.ac.uk/lairdsidemaritimecentre
  Email: lairdside@ljmu.ac.uk

  Lairdside Maritime Centre offers MCA-approved courses that meet the requirements of STCW.

- **Warsash Maritime Centre**
  Location: Southampton, UK

Newtown Road, Warsash, Southampton, Hampshire SO31 9ZL

Tel: 44 (0)1489 576 161, Fax: 44 (0)1489 573 988

Website: www.warsashcentre.co.uk and www.warsashsuperyachtacademy.co.uk

Email: wmc@solent.ac.uk

Facebook: www.facebook.com/warsashacademy

Owned by Southampton Solent University, Warsash Maritime Centre has provided first class training, consultancy, and research to the international shipping and offshore oil industries for over 50 years. The school offers courses that fulfill the requirements of STCW and are approved by the MCA.

STCW Basic Safety Training in Australia

Note that if taking the STCW training in Australia, you have a choice to enroll in an AMSA-endorsed or an MCA-endorsed BST course. An AMSA-endorsed STCW certificate is internationally recognized on both Australian and foreign-flagged yachts. Those holding an MCA-endorsed ticket can only obtain work on a foreign-flagged yacht, so this could decrease an individual's chances of employment, because the schools and placement agents cannot put these candidates forward for jobs on superyachts within Australia. Please be sure to do your own research into this when choosing a school for STCW Basic Safety Training in Australia.

➡ **Club Sail & Superyacht Crew Academy**

Location: Sydney, Australia

Newport Anchorage Marina, 79-81 Beaconsfield St., Newport, NSW 2106, Australia

Phone: 61 (0)2 9979 9669, Fax: 61 (0)2 9979-3463

Websites: www.superyacht-crew-academy.com and www.clubsail.com.au

Email: Fill out contact form on website

Facebook: www.facebook.com/superyacht

The Superyacht Crew Academy, a division of Club Sail, is a Maritime Institute offering International Yacht Training (IYT) for both professional and recreational yachtsmen and women. Through Club Sail, the academy offers professional sail and motor vessel training courses, including the MCA-recognized STCW BST course. The Superyacht Crew Academy also offers introduction to yachting classes, as well as deck crew, steward/ess, and chef certifications for entry-level crew and up. Please check their website for more information.

➡ **Crew Pacific**

Location: Cairns, Australia, 22 Minnie Street Cairns QLD 4870

Phone: 61 (0)7 4041 7243, Fax: 61 (0)7 4041 3163

Website: www.crewpacific.com.au, Email: training@crewpacific.com.au

Facebook: www.facebook.com/crewpacific

Please note Crew Pacific does not officially offer STCW courses at their school, but you can check their website or the various maritime schools they are affiliated with around Australia that conduct the AMSA (Australian Maritime Safety Authority)-endorsed STCW BST course. Meanwhile, I include Crew Pacific on this list due to its strong connection to the megayacht industry. Crew Pacific has been in business since 2001 and provides crew to yachts throughout the world, both motor and sail.

The school often has captains come in to teach components of its five- and eight-day deckhand and stew/deck courses. Crew Pacific also offers free career nights throughout Australia. Visit Crew Pacific's website and click on the Crew Information tab, then select the Free Career Nights tab to learn more.

For other schools offering STCW Basic Safety Training courses around the world, please check my website at www.WorkOnAYacht.com. Remember, this is mandatory for you to have this training. Expect to invest in this course at the start of your job hunt.

❖   **INSDIER TIP:** Once you have earned your certificate of compliance, update your résumé right away and let all the crew agencies you are registered with know that you have your official STCW Basic Safety Training completed.

Specialized Stew Training

Is specialized stew training *mandatory?* No…at least not yet. But I cannot recommend it highly enough!

One of the main reasons I advocate this training is because it will help you to land a job much faster. Of course, you also have to look at it this way: You want to be as prepared as possible so that you are as comfortable as possible when you accept your first position. You wouldn't take on a job working at a computer all day if you had no idea how to type, would you? Having specialized stew training prior to taking employment on a yacht will give you confidence that you know what you are doing, and that will be reflected in your attitude and demeanor with your fellow crew and guests.

A stew training course, more formally referred to as "interior-crew training" (sounds more professional, no?) can be taken before or after completing your STCW Basic Safety Training; it does not matter. Going back to our discussion of your budget for the preliminary training you need, I suggest taking your STCW training *first*, since it's mandatory. However, as most specialized, interior-crew training courses can be broken down into separate classes taken sporadically, you might consider taking the first day or two of a longer, more comprehensive course. These beginning classes will usually entail an introduction to the yachting industry, so you can feel out how well you take to "this yachting stuff" before you go investing your money in the full five-day+ courses.

I Must Confess…
Stew training was mind-boggling.

When I signed up for stewardess training, I was under the impression that this was simply a course on serving food and being a hostess to the guests. To my surprise, they spent an entire day teaching us nautical terms and familiarizing us with the layout of a yacht. For someone who didn't have much recreational-boating experience outside of water skiing on lakes in northern Indiana, it was exactly what I needed. (Perhaps it's news to you, as it was to me, that the various sides of a boat are referred to as port, starboard, aft, and forward.) We also learned how to tie knots and handle lines because, they forewarned us (as I have you), oftentimes the stew is called out on deck to help the deckhands when the yacht is docking. I took full advantage of the opportunity to become versed in these basic and introductory yachting terms, and the effort wound up saving me from some otherwise embarrassing moments when I took my first job.

In the remaining days, they taught everything from how to serve caviar to how to iron a shirt properly. But it didn't stop there. In fact, they spent half a day going over cleaning products and which ones to use on which surfaces. We spent time on how to get out each kind of stain—be it on laundry or interior fabrics. We learned how to fold sheets, make beds, and polish silver. And of most benefit, we learned all about the types and methods of silver service and were even expected to perform our newly acquired skills in the practical portion of the class.

It was a week of heavy learning, but less than a week after earning my certificate, I got my first job. I am confident that had I not completed the course, I would not have been hired for the position. If you want to know the truth, I think the chief stew on that boat (who, by the way, had not taken the course) pushed to get me hired so she could pick my brain on what I'd learned. And yes, once onboard, I often wondered how any entry-level stew could get away without having this training.

❖ **INSIDER TIP:** If you are 100 percent confident that you want a job in this industry, then plan on taking your STCW Basic Safety Training Course all at once during one week, and a comprehensive three- to five-day yacht stew training course the following week. Once those two weeks are up, your chances of being hired as an entry-level stew are vastly improved…as is your confidence. Check the various training schools' websites to see if any are offering package deals where you can sign up for both at a discount. Remember, you'll make this money back in the first month of full-time employment. Consider it an investment.

Interior Crew Training and G.U.E.S.T. Certification

"The introductory interior and exterior courses, even though these are not mandatory courses, have been developed to give you the skills, knowledge, and confidence to understand what your job entitles as a professional stewardless aboard or deckhand aboard a superyacht."
—**Joy Weston**, owner and operator of Crew Pacific (Australia) since 2001

While a number of schools in the United States, Europe, and Australia have been offering programs for interior crew for many years, the course work has never been regulated or mandated the way safety training is. Therefore, there have been variances in the classes given and the way they're taught. Now, this is not to say that overall, schools have been doing a sub-par job in preparing stews for work. Rather, there simply was no set standard for hospitality aboard megayachts. The good news is, the yachting industry has tried to come together in recent years to develop a formal set of standards, albeit voluntary, to ensure that the high quality of service needed aboard megayachts not only continues, but advances and exceeds expectations.

The Professional Yachting Association (PYA), which represents the interests of captains and crew worldwide and champions their interests, played a key role in developing the Interior Crew Training and Certification courses that many of the training schools are now offering. Many more schools are preparing to offer these courses in the latter part of 2013 and beyond.

In fact, PYA collaborated with more than 40 industry professionals, ranging from captains and stews to yacht-training instructors, to develop the Guidelines for Unified Excellence Service Training, a.k.a. G.U.E.S.T., which I will refer to in the remaining of this section as GUEST (no periods). The GUEST initiative, as its name states, attempts to unify the varying approaches in different levels of qualification. From the Introduction Level to Operational Level and even Management Level, classroom instruction is combined with onboard interaction with guests.

Since you won't have had any experience working aboard a yacht yet, you will need to sign up for the Introduction course modules, a total of five (four courses, plus STCW), with each building upon the lessons learned in the one prior. No sea time is necessary for this program, so you will be receiving instruction alongside plenty of other people in the same situation as you. You will also need to obtain your ENG1 Medical Exam, or its equivalent (see the end of this chapter for more on this). Successfully completing all of these requirements will qualify you to receive a PYA-endorsed Yacht Junior Stewardess Certificate of Competence.

Here's a breakdown of each PYA introduction-course module and what you will learn:

1) **Interior Introduction Course.** This is given as a full-time course over a minimum of three days. You'll learn many different things, including the demographics of the yachting industry; what each department aboard a yacht does and who reports to whom; the standards of personal presentation; the etiquette of interacting with guests of different countries and cultures; the proper presentation and detailing of cabins, bathrooms, and all other guest areas; health and safety issues; and more.

2) **Interior Basic Food Service Course.** This one-day class teaches the basics of guest service; different food service techniques; prepping foods for the chef in the service area; and menus.

3) **Wine & Cocktail Introduction Course.** Another one-day course, you'll gain an overview of the world of wine; learn about the regions where wine grapes are grown as well as the grapes themselves; learn the basics of proper wine service and wine storage; gain an overview of spirits (a.k.a. hard liquors); and learn about the tools and methods of cocktail making.

4) **Food Hygiene Course/Catering.** This class is similar to ones given for people entering the restaurant and catering businesses. You'll learn about things such as the importance of keeping your hands and food-prep stations clean and sanitized; how to prevent food-borne illness; and the importance of carefully and properly storing food (whether "dry," like in boxes and cans, or in need of refrigeration or freezing).

5) **Four (4) Elements STCW Basic Safety Training.** Recall that STCW Basic Safety Training is outlined earlier in this chapter. Even though a stew's job mostly entails taking care of the interior and guests, you may be called upon in an emergency to assist deck crew. And it's crucial overall to be prepared for any situation. STCW BST certification is mandatory, regardless of any additional interior training you obtain on top of it.

In addition to the above courses, you will also need to obtain an ENG1 Seafarer Medical Exam Certificate to qualify to receive the PYA's Yacht Junior Stewardess Certificate of Competence. Also known as a seafarer's medical exam, the ENG1 or its equivalent is often mandatory for working aboard charter yachts (mainly by request of yacht-insurance companies, although upcoming new regulations in the industry may start calling for a medical fitness exam of some kind), so it's worth getting anyway to increase your employment opportunities. Learn more on this at the end of the chapter.

Since the GUEST program is just getting off the ground in 2013, the PYA has a provision to assess experienced and current interior crew for direct entry to the GUEST program. Further to this (and probably of more importance to those just coming into the industry), you can apply to have certificates of academic achievement from previous training or employment recognized for credit toward a PYA-endorsed certificate by downloading and filling out a form from www.pya.org; you must then submit either certificates from previous courses attended or a declaration from employers stating your relevant experience.

According to its website, beyond 2014, all PYA interior-training modules, including the assessment and examinations, will need to be taken at a PYA-accredited training establishment to be recognized by the organization. A list of training providers accredited to run the PYA modules is included later in this chapter, but because it is still in development, you will want to check an updated list available on the PYA website.

❖ **INSIDER TIP:** Please be aware that, as of July 2013, the yachting industry is in a transitional stage of adopting the PYA GUEST standards. It could be a few more years before these training guidelines become recognized and accepted industry-wide. On the other hand, it could be much sooner than that as more and more schools become authorized to teach the modules and issue certifications. You will want to keep tabs on what is happening by researching online. Check the training schools' websites and www.pya.org, as well as my website at www.WorkOnAYacht.com, to follow progress of this initiative.

It's a time of great change in professional training standards for the yacht-crew industry, especially with regard to interior crew. I personally believe it's overdue and will be a very positive thing in the long run. In the meantime, just getting any type of entry-level, interior-crew training is your goal.

PYA G.U.E.S.T. Career Path for Stews

"The PYA has done an extraordinary job of putting together guidelines for interior training at all levels; this for the purpose of someday becoming mandatory, just like certifications for exterior positions on superyachts are. High standards must be maintained, and with all interior crew having this training, it will help ensure that level of service. In addition, if this training becomes required for specific positions, it will make the hiring process a little less painful knowing the crew has these certifications."

—**Heather Adams**, Crew Placement Specialist at Crew Unlimited

One of the biggest benefits of the PYA GUEST initiative is that it provides a formal structure for interior crew who see working on yachts as a long-term career path. This is the part that really excites me, as I think it's encouraging when embarking upon a journey like this that you have a clear idea of how you might advance in the future… It allows you to set goals for yourself and keep looking to expand your knowledge and skill set.

Below are PYA interior-crew courses for experienced stews looking to move up quickly through advanced training and certifications. While it's premature for entry-level stews to consider getting this training from the start, I include this to give you an idea of how a future educational track might look—whether the courses you take are PYA-endorsed or simply teach similar topics. And know the PYA has said it is not necessary to complete all modules in any one level before starting to undertake modules in the next level(s). Please visit training school websites and www.pya.org for more information about the structure and content of these courses:

- PYA Yacht Interior Intermediate Course
- PYA Wine Intermediate Course
- PYA Cocktail and Spirit Intermediate Course
- PYA Barista Course
- PYA Yacht Interior Management Course
- PYA Wine Advanced Course
- PYA Cocktail and Spirit Advanced Course

On the next page is how the these intermediate and advanced courses are to be taken along the developmental route of earning a PYA Yacht Senior Steward/ess Certificate of Competence, and ultimately a PYA Yacht Chief Steward/ess Certificate of Competence (Head of Department, both under and above 500gt), in the future:

Interior Crew/Stew Training Centers

There are a number of schools and training centers in Fort Lauderdale, Europe, Australia, and South Africa that offer interior-crew training courses; some are aligned with the GUEST program, while others are on their way to being. Please know that since this program is not yet mandatory, nor agreed upon industry-wide, getting any type of introductory stew training is what matters. (Yes, I know I keep saying that.) A little piece of my quirky advice: Trust me, you don't know what you don't know—and as a yacht stew, there's a lot to know!

In other words, don't be too concerned just yet if certain courses aren't marked "GUEST-approved," as since these are introductory classes, it is not going to make a huge difference. There are still programs offered by other schools and trainers that are worth exploring. In fact, there are stand-alone classes offered by multiple training centers. If it is within your budget to enroll in them, they will not only make you more marketable when breaking into the industry, but will also give you more confidence as you waltz into your first yacht job with some extra applicable skills. Furthermore, you can count on the fact that most any introductory course will cover a similar list of topics, and you will likely be able to receive some form of credit toward getting an official GUEST certificate in the future.

PYA G.U.E.S.T. Interior-Crew Training & Certification Development Route

GUEST I	GUEST II	GUEST III	GUEST IV
Junior Steward/ess	Senior Steward/ess	Chief Steward/ess (under 500gt)	Chief Steward/ess (over 500gt)
No Seatime Required	12-month yacht service. Plus 60-days guest service time.	12-months yacht service, plus 60-days guest service time, whilst holding Senior Steward/ess Certificate	Half the required management entry-level yacht service will be on vessels over 500gt for those wanting to apply for management level above 500gt
PYA Interior Introduction	Interior Intermediate	Interior Management	
PYA Interior Basic Food Service	Wine Intermediate	Cocktail & Spirit Advanced	MCA Human Element and Leadership Management
PYA Wine and Cocktail Introduction	Cocktail & Spirit Intermediate	Management of Food Safety in Catering	Yacht Accounting & Budget
Food Hygiene	Barista & Tea Master	MCA Medical Care	Introduction to International Safety Management (ISM)
STCW BST	Powerboat Level II	MCA Advanced Fire Fighting	PYA Written & Oral Exam
	MCA Medical First Aid	MCA Sea Survival	
Yacht Junior Steward/ess Certificate	Yacht Senior Steward/ess Certificate	Yacht Chief Steward/ess Under 500gt Certificate	Yacht Senior Steward/ess Over 500gt Certificate

Following is a list of all interior-crew training schools. I note which schools are currently GUEST-approved, as well as which ones offer advanced courses for your future training. To find out if any schools have become GUEST-accredited since the publishing of this book, you can do so by checking the PYA website, www.pya.org.

Interior Crew/Stew Training Schools in Fort Lauderdale

➼ **American Yacht Institute Classes (also offers Advanced Courses)**
Fort Lauderdale, FL
For information on where and when AYI classes are being provided, visit the website or Facebook page, email, or call the numbers below.
Tel: 1-954-522-1044, Mobile: 1-954-540-9503
Website: www.americanyachtinstitute.com, Email info@americanyachtinstitute.com
Facebook: www.facebook.com/pages/American-Yacht-Institute/42484781109

American Yacht Institute (AYI) holds classes at various locations in Fort Lauderdale, Florida, but primarily at Roscioli Yachting Center and Bradford Marine. AYI further holds custom and private classes aboard yachts and at estates.

AYI has a few popular programs. There's a five-day Super Yacht Crew Course, a three-day Silver Service Course, and a two-day class, aptly named the Two-Day Stew. The latter is particularly ideal for newcomers to the industry, to see if you're truly up to making it your career. As owner Kristen Cavallini-Soothill puts it, "If they find out they don't like living and working aboard, they haven't spent a small fortune on days and days of schooling…and they can still use their skills elsewhere."

The Two-Day Stew Course covers one day of Silver Service (Russian, French, and Plate) and one day of Interior (Fine Detailing, Valet, Laundry & Guest Services). The three-day course covers the same but also includes a day of Basic Bar, Champagne & Wine Service, and Flowers. The five-day Super Yacht Crew Course includes the following modules: Introduction to Yachts, Crewing & Etiquette; Basic Seamanship; Silver Service; Interior (Fine Detailing, Guest Services & Laundry); and Basic Bar, Champagne & Wine Service, Flowers. Finally, AYI also offers a Professional Deckhand Course for exterior crew (or those interested in deck-stew positions), as well as Chief Stewardess MGT I and MGT II ADV Certifications (by appointment with a professional butler).

➼ **International Crew Training (PYA GUEST & Advanced Courses)**
910 SE 17th St., Ste. 200 (In the Coldwell Banker Building, 2nd Floor)
Fort Lauderdale, FL 33316
Tel: 1-954-779-7764 (Contact Claire French)
Website: www.yachtmaster.com, Email: info@yachtmaster.com
Facebook: www.facebook.com/IntlCrew

International Crew Training (ICT)—also listed in the previous STCW training schools section—offers a number of interior crew training classes. Their ICT Yachting 101 is a fantastic basic introduction to anyone wishing to enter the yachting industry. Gain special skills with interior course offerings such as ICT Floral Design and Care; ICT Food Service, Safety, and Hygiene; and ICT Introductory Barista Training.

ICT offers all of the courses required for the PYA GUEST Introduction level certificate, including: PYA Yacht Interior Introduction, PYA Wine & Cocktail Introduction, and PYA Yacht Interior Basic Food Service (Silver Service). Combine those with the ICT Food Service, Safety, and Hygiene course, your STCW BST course, and an ENG1 Medical Exam, and you will qualify to earn your PYA Yacht Junior Steward/ess Certificate of Competence.

At various times in the year, ICT offers specials where you can save money by completing all of these courses in combination with the STCW modules. They refer to this package as the STCW PLUS Interior Operations 5-Day. Other course packages are also available, so be sure to check www.yachtmaster.com to find out what's coming up.

➥ **Maritime Professional Training (PYA GUEST & Advanced Courses)**
1915 South Andrews Ave., Fort Lauderdale, FL 33316
Contact: Julie Liberatore—julie@MPTusa.com
Tel: 1-954-525-1014, Toll Free: 1-888-839-5025, Fax: 1-954-764-0431
Website: www.mptusa.com, Email: info@mptusa.com
Facebook: www.facebook.com/mptusa

Maritime Professional Training (MPT)—also listed in the previous STCW schools training listing—offers programs to meet all levels of certification and training requirements, including the PYA GUEST Classes for Introductory Interior Certification, as well as Intermediate and Advanced Chief Steward(ess) Upgrade Courses, Wine, Bartending, Intro to Yachting/Yacht Etiquette, Barista, Flowers, Silver Service/Food/Table Service, Advanced Medical Training, Vessel Security, Tender Operator Licensing, Firefighting, and many other interesting courses from as short as one day to five days or entire programs. MPT offers many options for new crew called STCW "PLUS" which discounts packages of classes taken together.

MPT also offers a course called the Career Seminar which teaches new crew how to write a résumé/CV and how to get into the industry and how get a job, and more useful tips everyone wishes someone had told them when they started. This course is FREE with your STCW class and includes dinner. MPT's Student Services Staff and Career Counselors will help you every step of the way until you are trained and on a boat! Check MPT's website for schedule information, STCW offered almost every week year-round.

Interior Crew/Stew Training Schools in Europe
➥ **Bluewater Yachting Antibes (PYA GUEST)**
7 Boulevard d'Aguillon, 06600 Antibes, France
Tel: 33 (0)493 34 47 73, Fax: 33 (0)493 34 77 74
Website: www.bluewateryachting.com, Email: training@bluewateryachting.com
Facebook: www.facebook.com/pages/Blue-Water-Yachting/81710752968

Bluewater Yachting—also listed in the previous STCW training schools section—offers all of the courses required for the PYA GUEST Introduction level certificate, including: PYA Yacht Interior Introduction, PYA Wine & Cocktail Introduction, and PYA Yacht Interior Basic Food Service (Silver Service). Combine those with the

ICT Food Service, Safety, and Hygiene course, your STCW BST course, and an ENG1 Medical Exam, and you will qualify to earn your PYA Yacht Junior Steward/ess Certificate of Competence. Bluewater also offers the full program of intermediate- and advanced-level GUEST training (GUEST II and III).

↦ **Fine Wine Works (PYA GUEST-approved wine courses)**
Cote D'Azur, near Nice
Tel: 33 (0)6 42 15 51 21
Website: www.finewineworks.com, Email: info@finewineworks.com
Facebook: www.facebook.com/pages/Fine-Wine-Works/303936072996766

Based on the Cote D'Azur, husband and wife team Nigel & Helen Brotherton, set up Fine Wine Works in 2008. Helen holds the WSET (Wine and Spirit Education Trust) Diploma with Honors and is a WSET Certified Educator. FWW offers wine training to all levels, ranging from the WSET Level 1 Award in Wines (Foundation) up to the comprehensive and challenging WSET Level 3 Award in Wines and Spirits (Advanced). They run courses either at their Villa in the hills behind Nice (Vence) as well as onboard yachts. They are a part of the PYA GUEST program for wine training.

↦ **Warsash Superyacht Academy (PYA GUEST & Advanced Courses)**
Location: Southampton, UK
Newtown Road, Warsash, Southampton, Hampshire SO31 9ZL
Tel: 44 (0)1489 576 161, Fax: 44 (0)1489 573 988
Website: www.warsashcentre.co.uk and www.warsashsuperyachtacademy.co.uk
Email: wmc@solent.ac.uk
Facebook: www.facebook.com/warsashacademy

While the school offers STCW training from its Southampton location, the PYA-accredited stewardess training courses are focused mainly on onboard training for interior teams as a whole. Warsash's experienced team, led by industry veterans Peter Vogel and Danella Lamb, train stews and stew teams not only on yachts, but on cruise liners, in private residences, and in hotels and resorts. Some of their trainers even have experience working for the Dutch Royal Family and Queen Elizabeth II.

Beyond 2013, Warsash will likely be establishing shore-side facilities to accommodate individuals looking to develop their career in yachting. In fact, they are currently scoping out a location in Barcelona, which is quickly becoming a hub of superyacht activity due to the number of vessels coming to Marina Port Vell for refits and long yard periods. So do keep an eye on their website for more information about when their new facilities and individual courses become available.

Interior Crew/Stew Training Schools in Australia and South Africa

↦ **Crew Pacific (also offers Advanced Courses)**
Location: Cairns, Australia, 22 Minnie Street Cairns QLD 4870
Phone: 61 (0)7 4041 7243, Fax: 61 (0)7 4041 3163
Website: www.crewpacific.com.au, Email: training@crewpacific.com.au
Facebook: www.facebook.com/crewpacific

Crew Pacific has been in business since 2001. Owned and operated by industry veteran Joy Weston, this long-established training school provides crew to yachts throughout the world, both motor and sail. It often has captains come in to teach components of its five- and eight-day deckhand and stew/deck courses.

Crew Pacific offers both a five- and eight-day Superyacht Stewardess Training Course designed for steward/esses looking to advance their careers in the maritime industry. This well-known course provides training in the necessary skills required to carry out your duties within the shipboard environment. Topics covered include: specifics regarding the yachting industry; professional decorum and social skills; practices of storing and stowing a yacht; International customs and procedures; silver service, table settings, and bartending (food hygiene); exterior and interior detailing; laundry formalities; floral arrangements and care; wine appreciation; and basic seamanship terminology. For experienced stews looking to bring their skills ashore, Crew Pacific is in partnership with the Australian Butler School to deliver a three-week Superyacht Steward/ess training to Luxury Estate Service Course.

Crew Pacific also offers free career nights throughout Australia. Visit the website and click on the Crew Information tab, then select the Free Career Nights tab to learn more. The school also offers placement services and is very active on Twitter, so keep an eye out there for job notices: @CrewPacific.

➪ **Australian Superyacht Crew (PYA GUEST)**
James Craig Road, Rozelle, Sydney, Australia 2038
Tel: 61 (0)2 9818 2024
Website: www.superyachtcrew.com.au, Email: crew@superyachtcrew.com.au
Facebook: www.facebook.com/superyachtcrew

Australian Superyacht Crew Recruitment & Training are professional Sydney-based yacht-crew recruiters placing quality crew on superyachts and megayachts worldwide. The school enjoys recognition and full accreditation through the PYA GUEST program to offer its steward/ess training courses. Please see their website for more information.

Also offering crew placement services, Superyacht Crew Academy is another training school to watch on Twitter: @AuYachtCrew.

➪ **Superyacht Crew Academy (also offers Advanced Courses)**
Location: Sydney, Australia
Newport Anchorage Marina, 79-81 Beaconsfield St., Newport, NSW 2106, Australia
Phone: 61 (0)2 9979 9669, Fax: 61 (0)2 9979-3463
Websites: www.superyacht-crew-academy.com and www.clubsail.com.au
Email: Fill out contact form on website
Facebook: www.facebook.com/superyacht

The Superyacht Crew Academy, a division of Club Sail and also listed back in the STCW training school listing, is a Maritime Institute offering International Yacht Training (IYT) for both professional and recreational yachtsmen and women. The Superyacht Crew Academy offers introduction to yachting classes, as well as deck crew, steward/ess, and chief certifications for entry-level crew and up.

The Superyacht Academy's five-day Steward/ess Superyacht Interior Crew Training Course is an orientation for students new to the industry of yachting teaching interior and seamanship skills. The course is five days of very hands-on, practical ,and theory classes. At Superyacht Crew Academy, crew train in their roles in a "simulated superyacht environment" interacting with each other onboard during the seamanship and RIB small power boat portions. Days 3-5 of the stew training includes Silver Service, Interior detailing, laundry/valet, napkin-folding ,decorating tables, and floral arrangements. Day 5 includes other services, such as wine appreciation, bartending, and cocktails.

↔ **Super Yachting South Africa (PYA GUEST & Advanced Courses)**
Pier House, 10th Floor, Ste. 1001, 13–17 Heerengracht Street, Cape Town 8000
Tel: Isobel Odendaal: 27 82 558 9400, Main enquires: 27 72 419 5457
Website: www.stewardessonthego.co.za and www.sysa.co.za/pya-stew-course
Email: enquiries@sysa.co.za and isobel@sysa.co.za
Facebook: www.facebook.com/superyachtingsouthafrica

Super Yachting South Africa is one of two South African training facilities to enjoy full international accreditation from the PYA or Professional Yachting Association. Their courses follow PYA guidelines and certificates are recognized. They also offer other types of introductory-level training as well as advanced courses for stews.

↔ **SuperCrew Training (PYA GUEST)**
11 Bay Avenue, Gordons Bay
7140 Cape Town, Western Cape
Tel: 27 79 591 5314
Website: www.supercrew.co.za, Email: oceanpotions@hotmail.com
Facebook: www.facebook.com/SuperCrewGordonsBay

Super Crew is one of two South African training facilities to enjoy full international accreditation from the PYA or Professional Yachting Association. Their courses follow PYA guidelines and certificates are recognized. And if you book your STCW BST course through their partner school, Maritime Medicine, you receive a R200 discount.

Suggested Classes for Quick Training

Additionally, there are a number of other ways to get training in key areas of working as interior crew, and these are classes you can pursue on your own, before even heading to a hiring port. Remember, when you are initially interviewing, you want to be able to prove to the hiring agent— whether that's a captain, chief stew, owner, or even a crew placement specialist—that you have experience. Showing them a certificate from your local bartending school will certainly be better than saying you've never had formal training. The same goes with floral arranging, wine courses, and certainly for massage or yoga training.

In the following sections I present some alternative ways for getting your introduction to yachting training, both broadly and in specific skill areas. These are merely suggestions for giving you that special edge over the competition; by no means are you required to take them.

Bartending

If you can manage a quick bartending course where you currently live, this is excellent knowledge to have under your belt when you set out for a career as a yacht stew. You might check out the website for ABC Bartending, a chain of nationwide bartending schools in the U.S. (www.ABCBartending.com) to see if they offer a course in your area.

Floral Arranging

The skills you'll need to be able to create your own floral displays onboard a yacht go beyond simply knowing how to use floral foam, stem wires, glue guns, anchor pins, and even what flowers will look the prettiest (and please, no silk flowers; only the fresh will do). You will also want to be aware of what flowers are expensive and what are least expensive; what last the longest; what sheds and what doesn't shed; what looks good outside vs. inside; and how you can fill in dying displays quickly and cheaply mid-trip.

There's a lot to know, but if you can master the art, this can end up being one of the more enjoyable parts of your job. I had one former chief stewardess even tell me she chose to do her own flower arrangements because, for her, it was relaxing.

If the ability to create your own floral displays is a talent you'd like to have, or to improve upon, check with a local florist or look into community education programs—such sources will usually always offer workshops and mini-courses on this domestic art.

Massage

If you already have massage training in your background, get it on that résumé/CV. And if you don't, consider that one cool way you can land a job quicker and easier than you might otherwise (and probably make some extra tips from the guests).

Note: Like floral arranging, cooking skills, and extensive wine knowledge, massage training is simply a way to stand out from the competition when vying for stew jobs, and even then, we are talking about chief stews and those looking to advance in the industry and pursue stewing as a long-term career. Among entry-level stews, none of these special skills are common. Only seek out this extra training to either make up for a lack of other qualifications, such as a background in food or beverage service, or because you have a genuine interest in pursuing such crafts.

Bottom line: Taking any type of interior-crew training—whether endorsed by the PYA GUEST program or not—along with completing your STCW Basic Safety Training Course, is the best way to prepare for an entry-level stew position on a yacht.

ENG1 Seafarer Medical Certificates

The ENG1 Seafarer Medial Certificate is an MCA (Maritime & Coastguard Agency) document issued by registered ENG1 doctors. Having an ENG1 Seafarer Medical Exam Certificate (or its equivalent) is not as widely mandatory, but it is starting to be required for employment consideration on many charter-yachts, mainly for yacht-insurance purposes, and especially if the yacht is a U.K.-flagged vessel. I recommend obtaining this to increase your chances of getting a job. But, the test takes less than an hour and is something you can wait to get if a yacht requires it. In other words, don't stress it until you are actively interviewing.

For a young, fit person, it is usually a formality; although people who are color blind or have a medical condition may have problems. You will need to visit a doctor that is approved by the MCA—and you will find them on both sides of the Atlantic, including in Fort Lauderdale. Learn where to get this done in your country by visiting www.mcga.gov.uk.

Now, here's the scoop on this (and as with most things in the yacht-training world, it's not altogether straightforward as to what's required and what's not):

Yes, the ENG1 is required by British-flagged vessels. However, they will also accept equivalent certificates; for instance, most European medicals are acceptable. If you are based in Europe, or are heading there, you will have no problem obtaining this exam—and rather cheaply for that matter.

For Americans, however, the basic problem is that the MCA doesn't accept the U.S. seafarer medical certificates, issued by the U.S. Coast Guard. (I know, can't we just all get along?) The only reason it is an issue is because, as of July 2013, there are only two doctors in the U.S. who are approved to issue ENG1 certificates and this, in turn, means that they are rather more expensive than the U.S.-equivalent, which is available all over the U.S. They cost about $150.00 versus about $50.00 for a U.S. equivalent. (The cost of this exam in Europe is approximately 100 euros.) That said, the ENG1 is valid for two years, not one, so it's not three times the price as many say, but about 50% more in price than the U.S. equivalent.

To be honest with you, while some crew agencies are telling you to have this before they'll submit you for jobs, if you are conducting your search through other means, this is not a make or break factor for getting hired. And again, since the test takes less than an hour, it is something you can obtain at the last minute if it required for any job. In some cases, the USCG medical examination will work for certain vessels. And finally, if you are taking your STCW in Europe or the U.K., it is recommended that you are already in possession of a medical fitness certificate (ENG1) before the swimming and fire-training portions of the STCW modules.

Also note that drug tests are now frequently carried out in the industry, so it is advisable to "keep clean" for at least four months prior to looking for your first job. The most common test apart from urine sample is a hair follicle test that will pick up most drugs consumed in the previous three months.

❖   **INSIDER TIP:** The yachting industry as a whole is not good at understanding
     equivalent certificates, so the bottom line is that if you do your training in the U.S.,
     you are wise to get an ENG1, not because it's any better or any different to any other
     medical, but because it is recognized and understood. The last thing a newbie needs is
     a reason not to hire them! Find an approved doctor in your country by visiting www.
     mcga.gov.uk.

8

PICKING UP ANCHOR
—CHOOSING AND MOVING
TO A HIRING PORT—

*"A person needs at intervals to separate from family and companions and go to new places.
One must go without familiars in order to be open to influences, to change."*
—Katherine Butler Hathaway, American writer

Now that you know what a yacht stew does and the skills and training you need in order to start at the entry level, it's time to lay the foundation for your job hunt. If the question running through your mind right now is, "Yeah, but where do I begin?" then you're about to receive your answer.

In this chapter, the focus is on some of the key yacht-industry hubs. I will advise you on how to strategically select and move to a hiring port, including how and where to obtain "crew house" accommodations once you arrive at your chosen destination. I will also go over passport and visa considerations, which are especially important for non-U.S. and non-Canadian citizens and should be dealt with before picking up and moving anywhere.

Not to be left out of the mix is some important packing advice. Pack rats, beware—you're about to face a challenge. Can you fit your entire life into one or two collapsible luggage pieces? If not, hopefully my advice at the end of this chapter will give you some ideas, because traveling light is going to be in your best interest.

The goal in this chapter is to set you in motion toward relocating, moving, and settling into a hiring port that fits your set of circumstances, as well as your budget. The sooner we get you to where the action happens, the sooner you can get all your necessary training out of the way and kick off your job quest.

So let's get movin'!

The First Big "To Do"—Choose a Hiring Port

❖ **INSIDER TIP:** Before you do anything, choose which hiring port you will target, and prepare to move there.

There are several key destinations around the world that qualify as major yachting centers due to the large number of yachts passing through or nearby them frequently, and often for extended periods of time throughout the year. Think of these locations as "hubs," similar to what we find in the commercial-airline industry, where an airline's hub airport serves as its base of operations as well as from where most of its flights originate (or connect).

The yachting equivalent—hub seaports—are where you will find the highest concentration of marinas, shipyards, and yacht-related businesses. Consequently, these locations are where yacht crew, *especially* novice job seekers (that means you), need to base themselves in order to be available for job openings. I refer to these yachting hubs as "hiring ports," and I urge you to select which one you will target before taking any further steps.

The reasons are simple: Your choice of a hiring port affects the entire job-finding process. And once you've made a decision, you can get started right away—as in today. For example, where you begin your quest will determine what crew-placement agencies you can register with and help you figure out what STCW-accredited training schools you can attend (both of which you can do online, in advance of arriving), and what type of accommodations are available to you (which again, you can research, and even reserve, before arriving).

Looking at this decision-making process from another angle, you also want to make sure your timing is right. Which hiring ports have the most job opportunities available will fluctuate throughout the year. You need to take into consideration what season it is and what your citizenship is (and visa status for non-U.S. citizens only), because these two factors determine how many potential jobs you'll have to choose from. Before selecting a destination and planning to shove off somewhere, you therefore need to understand all you can expect out of the various yachting locales. I will help you do that in the next section of this chapter.

Whether you relocate yourself there in the beginning or after completing some of the other job-hunting tasks, it is wise to first decide what port you will ultimately target. This will help you determine your timeline and plan of attack.

To Move or Not to Move? There Is Little Question. (MOVE!)

"Go where the boats are. For higher-echelon job seekers with tons of experience—say, a captain, a chef, or a chief stew with a really good reputation—they can be anywhere and get hired. But for the rest of them, especially novices, they've got to be where the boats are.... Let me stress that again: They are not going to get hired unless they go where the boats are. Most all the clients I have are not going to hire somebody sight unseen."

—**Lynne Cottone**, Crew Placement Specialist with Luxury Yacht Group

I get this question all the time: "But do I have to actually pick up and MOVE there—as in, not plan on coming back to my home?"

Let's get one thing straight right now: Pursuing a job as a yacht crewmember means opting for a life away from home, period. If you want to work in this industry, you will be leaving your current place of residence, no matter what. Enough said there.

The next line of business: When I talk about "moving" to a hiring port, I only mean temporarily. The hiring port you choose to "inhabit" is simply where you go to complete your STCW safety training, meet face to face with recruitment agencies, remain on-hand to interview with captains, and subsequently, get hired as a yacht stew. You are not going to be apartment hunting, signing a lease, registering for a driver's license, or any of the other tasks that typically accompany a move to a new city.

If you play your cards right, you may only need to be "on location" in a hiring port for one, possibly two, months—and far less, depending on the season and location. So, while packing up and changing cities is normally a major ordeal, in this case, look at it as simply making a pit stop on the way to your final destination: your new job aboard a luxury yacht.

There are certainly ways around doing an all-out move right at the beginning. If you want to "test the waters" a bit (a horrible pun!), take a mini-trip or vacation to one of the hiring ports I list in the next section, and check out the scene. One- or two-day "Introduction to Yachting" courses or the first modular of the STCW Basic Safety Training Course (which can be taken à la carte) should give you a clear indication of whether or not you dig this kind of work. Plus, there are a number of schools around the world that offer STCW training, so if a course is offered near where you live now, you could get that knocked out before making any final decisions on a long-distance move.

Otherwise, once you are indisputably ready to commence your job search, you need to make yourself physically available in a main hiring port. This is a fast-paced industry, and quick crew turnover between seasons often requires that jobs be filled in a hurry. Once a job offer is accepted, it can often be a "can you start tomorrow?" situation, with little preparation time on your part.

Moreover, as soon as your STCW training is complete, you can start interviewing for jobs. In fact, some job seekers start interviewing even while they are taking this required course. We know from the previous chapter that the preferred schools for obtaining your STCW certification and other stewardess-specific training courses are in these main hiring ports, so if you want those courses to have immediate payoff—and given the amount of money you invest in taking them, I would think you'd want to recoup that—then, in my opinion, why not go at this wholeheartedly?

And while crew recruiters can meet you on an exploratory pre-move trip, every captain or chief stew looking to hire you will want to interview you in person, if not take you to meet his or her entire crew to see if you're a good fit. For an entry-level position, do not expect anyone to fly you in for an interview—that happens with experienced crew, but as a novice, your chances are slim to none. It is to your advantage to *be in port*. Captains want you to be available immediately.

Once we cover day working (Chapter 9) and how this can benefit not only your job search, but also your wallet, I think you might be more willing to accept my suggestion to move right away as the best option. You can always move back home if you do not find a job in a sufficient time period for your circumstances. But what I wouldn't do is count on having one month between the time you are hired and the time you start work to return home and "get ready" to go. If you manage to negotiate any time to "return home" before starting a job—wherever home may be—it might only be a weekend.

The main point I am trying to make is that, if you have the financial and personal wherewithal to do so, head to one of these locations, and do it all at once. It bears repeating: You are not going to find your first job in the yachting industry without physically getting yourself to a main hiring port.

Here's how you make that leap of commitment: Start planning to leave your current living space, store those major belongings with family or in a rental space, pack your bags (don't worry, I'll tell you everything you need), and buy that one-way plane ticket. Get to where it all happens, and make it happen.

❖ **INSIDER TIP:** Choose one of the four recommended hiring port destinations for the easiest and fastest means of breaking into the yachting industry.

Hiring Port Options

Here are the four best choices for your landing spot:

➼ Fort Lauderdale, Florida
➼ Antibes, France
➼ Palma de Mallorca, Spain
➼ Newport, Rhode Island

Now, notice I am talking about your "best" options. That's not to say that there aren't other places in the world where you could find a job in yachting. However, these four locations are the hiring hotspots and will offer far greater access to quality job opportunities for individuals just entering the industry.

The following is a list of what I'll term "secondary" options for worthwhile hiring ports. Megayachts pass through these destinations, but just not in vast numbers or as frequently as with the list above. These are places that have STCW-recognized training schools, or at least some crew-recruitment agencies in the area, so you can get take your STCW certification and register with a placement service before heading to where more boats are located.

Here are some of these additional choices where it is certainly not unheard of to find work:

➼ St. Martin/St. Maarten in the Caribbean
➼ Dubai, United Arab Emirates
➼ Sydney, Australia

- Auckland, New Zealand
- Antigua in the Caribbean
- San Diego, California
- Viareggio, Italy

And while they may not be the key spots for finding an actual position, the destinations below can be considered a third tier. Experienced crew tend to do okay basing themselves in these locations, but I do not recommend them for entry-level job hunters. For some individuals, however, these locations may be the only option due to proximity and the inability to travel far:

- U.K.—London, Southampton, and Dover
- The Netherlands
- Sweden
- The Bahamas
- Singapore
- Croatia
- Brazil

Please visit my website, www.WorkOnAYacht.com for yachting businesses and other resources in the lists of second- and third-tier destinations above.

What Criteria Do I Use to Choose a Hiring Port?

Aside from your proximity to the destination and what restraints, if any, your travel budget may pose, the two main factors to consider when choosing a hiring port are a) what yachting season coincides with your job-hunting schedule (and you are better off planning your job hunt according to the yachting seasons, rather than just heading wherever is most convenient when you feel like it), and b) what visa requirements you face, which for U.S. citizens is a non-issue.

Seasonal Decisions

When referring to the industry's main seasons, we look at what times of the year a MAJORITY of yachts converge upon the same geographic cruising areas. While it is true that luxury yachts are constantly on the move and can end up in ports all over the world (this is why I say it's not impossible to find work outside of the main hiring ports), consider seasonal trends to increase your chances of getting hired. The question to ask is, "What do *most* yachts do, and *when* do they do it?"

Chapter 1 highlighted where yachts travel. To reiterate, there are two actual cruising seasons you will hear discussed in this industry: summer and winter. The months on either side of the summer and winter seasons—what in layman's terms are known as spring and fall—are most often referred to by yachting professionals as the time when yachts are "getting ready for the summer season" (April–mid-June) and "getting ready for the winter season" (September–mid-December).

The two off-shoulder seasons, also referred to as "down time" for yachts, serve as transition periods when yachts are changing locations, heading into shipyards for repair or maintenance, and provisioning for the next cruising season's big string of charters. This is usually the time when current crew take their vacations. **And pay attention here:** These transition months are also the peak time periods for finding jobs, as this is when crew changes will most likely occur.

So where do the yachts end up during these transition periods? Well, naturally, the industry's cruising seasons are dictated by when and where the weather is warm and pleasant. In the South of France, the port of Nice (pronounced like "niece") is nice, but not necessarily in late November.

A couple main events that coincide with these time periods are Antigua Race Week in late April (after which time most yachts head back to Fort Lauderdale for transitioning over to summer season plans) and the Fort Lauderdale International Boat Show at the end of October, when you can be guaranteed there are tons of yachts in town. Other big superyacht industry events during such transitional periods are the Monaco Yacht Show in late September, which could offer a last chance to hop on a yacht in the Mediterranean that is heading back across the Atlantic for Caribbean winter cruising, and then two Caribbean-based yacht shows that tend to kick off the winter season there, the Antigua and St. Martin/St. Maarten yacht shows in early December.

Summer Season

During the summer months (May to early September), most yachts either travel across the Atlantic Ocean to cruise around the Mediterranean Sea, or they head up the northeast coast of the United States to areas such as Newport, Rhode Island, Martha's Vineyard and Cape Cod in Massachusetts, and New York City and Sag Harbor in New York. Some also venture up the West Coast of the United States to visit Alaska, though typically only in June, July, and August, given that the temperatures are best those months.

Between Summer and Winter

As the summer draws to a close, usually in mid-September to early October, many yachts will finish up their cruising season and head into transitional phase. Yachts already located in the Mediterranean may opt to go into a shipyard somewhere in Europe. Unless they have a good reason to be there, though, most boats pretty much clear out of that area and head back across the Atlantic. Yachts that were in the U.S. Northeast for the summer will also migrate back down south, nearly always stopping off somewhere in South Florida before departing again for the winter season, usually to the Caribbean. And, yachts that ventured to Alaska will do one of a few things: head down the West Coast to winter in Mexico, head elsewhere across the Pacific Ocean, or transition over to South Florida, in preparation for Caribbean cruising.

Winter Season

During the winter months (late November through March), most yachts cruise to the islands of the Bahamas and the Caribbean, including St. Martin/St. Maarten, Antigua, the Virgin Islands, and St. Barts. Those that do not head there are based in Florida during these months, are in a shipyard elsewhere (such as Europe), or follow an atypical itinerary and are located in parts of the world such as Australia or the islands of the South Pacific. If you are seeking employment for the Caribbean season and have not found anything out of the Lauderdale-based agencies by early December, it is recommended that you look into heading to the Caribbean to find work.

Experienced crew report that St. Martin/St. Maarten and Antigua make great bases for finding work at the start of the holiday season in mid- to late-December, through February; however, I encourage you to exercise caution if heading to these areas alone. Connect with crew agencies ahead of time for an honest assessment of the job market. I also recommend traveling with another person and not making your intentions for job-hunting known when you speak to immigration officials at the airport. Go with a return flight booked (that you can always cancel), and make sure you've arranged your accommodation in advance. Do your research.

Current yacht stewardess, Kate Chastain (who also assisted with research for the 2nd edition of this book) says this about job hunting in St. Martin/St. Maarten:

It is not a port I would necessarily recommend to a green stew. It is "illegal" to dock walk (although I've done it many times after learning some tricks), and passengers with one-way tickets into the island are often stopped at customs, questioned, and not released until a departing flight (which you can cancel later) is purchased. I wish I had known to be careful on the island when I went there during my first year in the industry and found myself in customs, passport being held. I was then horrified when I realized how DIFFERENT it was from looking for work in Fort Lauderdale. Now that I know what to expect, I have returned looking for work two years in a row with no problems. For someone new to the industry though, it is not advised.

❖   **INSIDER TIP:** The chart in **Table 8-1** summarizes the peak times to find yacht crew jobs according to location:

Peak Times to Find Yacht Crew Jobs				
	FT. LAUDERDALE, FLORIDA, USA	ANTIBES, FRANCE	PALMA DE MALLORCA, SPAIN	NEWPORT, RHODE ISLAND, USA
January	Good	No	No	No
February	Good	No	No	No
March	Great	Good	No	No
April	Outstanding	Good	Good	No
May	Outstanding	Great	Great	Good
June	Good	Outstanding	Outstanding	Outstanding
July	No	Outstanding	Outstanding	Outstanding
August	No	Outstanding	Outstanding	Outstanding
September	Good	Great	Great	Great
October	Great	Good	Good	Good
November	Outstanding	No	No	No
December	Outstanding	No	No	No

Table 8-1

- ↦ **No** = As an entry-level job seeker, don't try it.
- ↦ **Good** = A decent chance, but you may find yourself either a bit too early, or too late, for prime hiring season. In the case of Fort Lauderdale, many of the agencies will be hiring to send crew down to the Caribbean during January-February (that's how it happened for me: hired in Lauderdale to join a boat in San Juan, Puerto Rico), so this is why they have received the rating of "Good." Otherwise, the yachts hanging around Florida during these months are more than likely having repairs done and are not hiring.
- ↦ **Great** = Your odds are increasing. In fact, for months and locations where I have noted the hiring possibilities as "Great," if these months are followed by a month rated "Outstanding," you may actually choose this "Great" month to arrive in town. This will give you time to complete your STCW training, an interior training course, and to get some day-work experience under your belt so that you can be networked and poised to grab the jobs that become available during the months marked as "Outstanding" times to find permanent positions.
- ↦ **Outstanding** = Be here during this time for the best chance to find a job.

Passport and Visa Considerations

A passport provides proof of citizenship, and you need it to gain entry into all other countries. Make sure you have a passport (and a valid one at that) before taking off for any hiring port. If you don't, start the application process immediately. If you are a U.S. citizen, visit the U.S. Department of State's website for more details: www.state.gov. If you are a non-U.S. citizen, you should consult the equivalent government agency in your country.

Passports for U.S. Citizens

For U.S. citizens, an adult passport is good for 10 years, but you will need to renew eight to nine months before it expires, since many countries require at least six months validity for entry.

If you are applying for a passport for the first time, or your previous passport was issued when you were under the age of 16, you must apply in person at one of the thousands of U.S. passport-acceptance facilities with two photographs of yourself, proof of U.S. citizenship, and a valid form of photo identification such as a driver's license. Visit www.state.gov for details.

Time Required: 4 to 6 weeks

Here's how it works:

1) Fill out a passport application form, called Form DS-11. You can download one at http://travel.state.gov/passport/forms/ds11/ds11_842.html. You'll need to hand it in at the passport-acceptance facility. Do NOT sign the DS-11 application form until the Passport Acceptance Agent instructs you to do so.
2) Have proof of U.S. citizenship. You must submit a document that proves you're a U.S. citizen when you hand in Form DS-11, and that document will be returned to you either when your newly issued U.S. passport is mailed, or in a separate mailing. Acceptable forms of proof are: a previously issued, undamaged U.S. passport; a certified birth certificate issued by the city, county, or state where you were born ("certified" means it has a registrar's raised, embossed, impressed, or multicolored seal, a registrar's

signature, and the date the certificate was filed with the registrar's office, which must be within one year of your birth); a Consular Report of Birth Abroad or Certification of Birth; a naturalization certificate; or a certificate of citizenship. See the U.S. Department of State's website for special circumstances, such as if you were born abroad and do not have a Consular Report of Birth Abroad or Certification of Birth on file.

3) Have additional identification. Acceptable secondary proof of identification includes a previously issued, undamaged U.S. passport, a naturalization certificate, a valid driver's license, a current government ID (city, state, or federal), or a current military ID (military and dependents). If you don't have any of these, or if you are applying at an Acceptance Facility and submit out-of-state primary identification, visit the U.S. Department of State's website for a list of acceptable secondary identification.

4) Make a photocopy of the front and back of each identification document you select in #4, and take it with you when you apply in person. The photocopy must be on plain, white, 8½ x 11" standard paper. It must have the images on only one side of each page submitted; if you can't make copies of the image on the same side of one page, you can present two separate pages, one with the front of the ID, and the other with the back of the ID. The paper shouldn't have any other images or markings. You're permitted to enlarge the image of your ID on the paper, but you can't decrease it, nor can you submit larger or smaller paper, even if the larger paper can fold down to the 8½ x 11" size. See the U.S. Department of State's website for additional information on special situations.

5) Provide one passport photo. Visit the U.S. Department of State's website for information on acceptable digitized photos. Note: Vending machine photos are generally not acceptable.

6) Visit a passport acceptance facility to submit the application form and payment. Acceptable forms of payment vary among locations but usually include check or credit/debit card. The cost of a U.S. passport depends on the type you request and how quickly you need it. Under normal circumstances, though, an adult passport book costs $110, plus an additional $25 execution fee, which is paid separately. Check the U.S. Department of State's website for payment instructions, as they can vary according to facilities.

7) If you need the passport faster than the normal 4- to 6-week waiting period, you will need to pay an expedition fee and overnight delivery costs, in addition to the above-outlined fees. The expedition fee is $60. You'll also need to schedule an appointment at one of the regional passport agencies listed on the U.S. Department of State's website.

Visas

A visa is an authorized permission issued by the embassy or consulate of a country that permits a traveler to visit that country. Your need for a visa depends not only on the country where you are headed to look for work, but also on all the countries where any vessel that may hire you might be traveling.

If you are an American or Canadian citizen, you do not need to apply for a visa of any kind to work on yachts, unless you are accepting a position on a vessel that will be traveling to a country that requires it. Regulations vary from country to country, though thankfully the majority of places that yachts frequent do not mandate them. If you end up getting hired by a vessel that will be visiting such a port (and there is that possibility), your new captain or chief stew will help you sort out details of necessary visas and paperwork before your start date. For now, American and Canadian citizens do not need to worry about applying for any visas.

If you are *not* an American or Canadian citizen, you should apply for a B1/B2 Visa, in addition to having a valid passport. According to the U.S. Superyacht Association, which serves as the industry voice within the United States and assists yachts visiting its waters, embassies generally do not like to issue visas to applicants who aren't residents of the country where the embassy is located. It's therefore best to apply for the B1/B2 visa in your home country. Find out where to do that at www.usembassy.gov.

Note: A Visa Waiver *will not* allow a non-U.S. citizen or Legal resident entry into the United States except by commercial carrier (airline). Most yachts inevitably pass through U.S. waters at some point, so even if you are beginning your job search in Europe, you will eventually need a B1/ B2 Visa if a vessel you gain employment on ever heads to the United States.

It may take several months for this visa to be processed, so act now.

More on the B1/B2 Visa

Category "B" temporary visas cover individuals coming to the U.S. for short-term business (B1) or pleasure (B2) purposes. The type of visa you need to obtain is a combination of these, known as a B1/B2 Visa. Again, this is so that you do not shut yourself out of jobs on yachts that will ultimately make their way to U.S. waters. Instead, most yachts want non-American crew to have their B1/B2 multiple-entry visa, which allows free entry and exit from the U.S. from between 6 months to 10 years, depending on which country an individual is from.

I stated it above, but to be clear: you must apply for your B1/B2 Visa from outside of the U.S. As mentioned, it is advised you do this *before* you leave for your first hiring port, even if your current circumstances do not require it (such as if you are heading to Europe first). To apply, you must go into your home country's U.S. embassy for an interview. You will need to have proper documentation, fill out a visa application and an anti-terrorism checklist, and provide proof of a residence in your home country (they want to be sure you have no intentions of abandoning your home). Unless you have already secured employment on a yacht—and have a letter to prove it—do not tell them that you are wishing to enter the U.S. to look for a job, because you may get denied. (This is going to become tougher and tougher with the changes being made by Homeland Security.)

Foreign-flagged boats in the U.S. can fly crew in from various parts of the world as long as the crewmember holds a B1/B2 visa. If you are coming into the U.S. to join a yacht that has already hired you, you will also need to obtain a letter of employment to gain entry, and you will arrive in the U.S. in B1 status, able to work.

Please note that the B1/B2 Visa does not guarantee entry into the United States. Furthermore, a B1/B2 Visa only allows an individual to enter and exit the U.S.; it does not legally permit foreign nationals to work on U.S.-registered yachts (more on this in the next section). Also, a C1/D Visa, required for cruise ship and airline employees, is not a valid visa for working on yachts.

For more information on applying for your B1/B2 Visa, please visit the U.S. Department of State's special website on U.S. visa policy and procedures: http://travel.state.gov/visa/ visa_1750.html.

"So many foreign crew come to Fort Lauderdale without their B1/B2 Visa, hoping they can get a job and the boat will write them a letter. And a lot of them think we as crew agents can write them a letter. Wrong! It's something they need to do before they get here."

—**Lynne Cottone**, Crew Placement Specialist at Luxury Yacht Group

European Visas

South African readers note: Some nationalities are required to carry Schengen Visas to work on foreign-flagged boats while they are cruising Europe. The Schengen Visa allows travelers to enter and travel freely throughout 15 of the 25 Schengen member countries. You are allowed to travel freely within these countries for a maximum stay of up to 90 days in a 6-month period.

While South Africa is one such country where citizens need to obtain a Schengen Visa, the U.S., U.K., Australia, Canada, and New Zealand are not. For others, please be sure to look this up online. For more information and to download the Schengen Visa Application, visit www.schengenvisa.cc.

Important Information for Non-U.S. Job Seekers

Here is the rule you must be aware of if you are a non-U.S. citizen looking for work on yachts: Only persons holding a Resident Alien Card ("green card") and American citizens are legally allowed to work on U.S.-registered vessels, unless the vessel is outside U.S. waters and will remain outside U.S. waters for at least the next 6 months. Foreign-registered vessels, about 75% of the world's yachts, can hire any nationality they choose.

—**from Crew Unlimited's website (www.crewunlimited.com)**

The discussion as to why this is the case is a complicated one, but I will do my best to simplify it: Every yacht has to be registered in an internationally recognized jurisdiction to provide proof of nationality and ownership. A yacht then assumes the nationality of the flag/jurisdiction where it is registered and is therefore subject to the regulations laid down by the governing register. Of the approximately 90 different flags under which a yacht can be registered, the two most common are 1) the British MCA red ensign (also known as red-flagged vessels, who follow the Maritime and Coastguard Agency code of practice) and 2) the American U.S. Coast Guard blue ensign (also known as blue-flagged vessels, who follow the U.S. Coast Guard code of practice).

If you are a non-U.S. citizen looking for work in the yachting industry, you cannot be employed on a U.S.-flagged vessel. However, as I mentioned in Chapter 2, the good news is that many of the world's yachts are registered elsewhere, such as in the Cayman Islands, which is classified as the red ensign. Most of these vessels are owned by U.S. nationals, but just because the yacht has a U.S. owner does not mean the vessel has to be registered in the United States. As long as a vessel is foreign-registered—which means either it flies a red ensign (flag) or it belongs to one of the nearly 80 other countries where yachts are registered—it can legally hire any nationality it chooses. But again, if you are not a U.S. citizen or do not hold a U.S. Green Card, there is no use looking for work on U.S.-registered vessels because they are not legally allowed to employ you.

Non-U.S. Job Seekers Seeking Employment in the U.S.

In a November 2009 post titled, "Unmasking the Truth: What's the deal with B1B2 Visas?" on Dockwalk.com, yacht-crew journalist, Janine Ketterer, interviewed Elliot Norman, a crew immigration lawyer with Williams Mullen Immigration Practice Group. Janine asked Elliot about the ability for non-Americans with a B1/B2 visa to look for work while the United States.

Question: Can a non-American with a B1/B2 visa look for work while in the States?

Answer on Dockwalk.com, with quote from Elliot Norman: "Yes is the simple answer. Interestingly, it's legal for crew to look for work while they are on holiday in the U.S., 'provided your primary reason for entering [the U.S.] was other than looking for work,' according to Norman. So crew lawfully in the U.S. in tourist status, whether carrying a 90-day visa waiver or a B1/B2 visa with an I-94 embarkation card stamped B2, can indeed register at an agency and look for work. But, it's the I-94 embarkation card that dictates one's right to work, not the B1/B2. So if a crewmember arrived in the U.S. and received an I-94 entry card stamped B2 (pleasure/tourism), they can't accept work. They would have to leave the country and return with the yacht's papers in order to be stamped in B1 (business) status."

This same post also called attention to the fact that it is **not legally permissible for non-American yacht crew to day work in the U.S.** This is something to keep in mind for non-U.S. crew who may leave a vessel once making it to U.S. waters. You can look for a full-time crew position, but it is illegal to accept day work (covered in Chapter 9) while doing so. That's not to say there aren't ways around this; however, know that you do so at your own risk, and it could result in fines or deportation.

The Skinny on Hiring Ports

Fort Lauderdale, Florida USA

I'm a bit biased here, because not only is this where I first got started in yachting, but it's where I lived while I was writing the first edition of this book, and where I resided for three wonderful years in my post-yachting life. Fort Lauderdale is undeniably the world's center for the megayacht industry. In fact, it has been dubbed "The Yachting Capital of the World"—an apropos moniker not only due to its world-class facilities and high concentration of yacht-industry businesses, but also because it has a double season. Yachts come through Fort Lauderdale in the spring on their way north or before they head to the Mediterranean, and then again in the fall on their way south for the warmer weather in the Caribbean. Consequently, yachts tend to hire most of their crew when they are in Florida, between the two main cruising seasons.

If you are a U.S. citizen, Fort Lauderdale is the obvious choice for beginning your job search. The one exception might be during the summer months, when the vast majority of megayachts have cleared out of Florida. Anytime between the months of June and August are rather silly for conducting a job search there. If the boats stay in the United States, they head up to the Northeast and stay based around Newport, Rhode Island.

Most of the crew-placement agencies are based in Fort Lauderdale. Some of them do have offices in other locations, but their headquarters are there. Many yachts will also still use the Fort Lauderdale-based agencies no matter where they are located when they need crew, simply because they know these Florida agencies will have some of the largest databases of crew and will have most likely met all of their registered crew in person at some stage (meaning, they can vouch for the person's character when the captain and crew cannot take the time to meet an individual before hiring him or her). This is why it's wise to come to Fort Lauderdale first: You will have had face-to-face contact with the crew recruiters, who may continue to find you jobs in any port for the remainder of your career in the industry.

Another perk to beginning your job hunt in Fort Lauderdale is that the area harbors the largest amount of marinas and shipyards where captains will hire day workers to help out during shipyard and maintenance periods. This is a chance to get temporary work experience onboard to better prepare you and to help keep money rolling in while you search for a permanent position. Crew housing is also more plentiful in Fort Lauderdale than in any of the other ports.

Getting Around Fort Lauderdale

Fort Lauderdale is an easy place to get around, which will no doubt facilitate your job search. The area of the city where all the crew agencies, training schools, crew houses, and yachtie hangouts are located spans about a 10-block radius. This epicenter of Fort Lauderdale's bustling yachting community is located right around U.S. Highway 1 (Federal Highway) and SE 17th Street. The Embassy Suites Fort Lauderdale-17th Street Hotel is a good point of reference for this area (just before the 17th Street Causeway leads over the bridge to the beach).

There is literally a yachting subculture that exists in this part of town. ("Where it all happens," you might say.) Maritime Professional Training, International Crew Training, and all the major crew agencies and crew houses in Fort Lauderdale are located within walking distance. The main shipyards and marinas (where you go to look for day work) are no more than a 10-minute drive from this spot and can usually be reached by a bike. Crew uniform shops, yacht provisioning specialists, and crew services providers abound. Hang around here for one week, and you can bet you'll start running into yachties all over the place that you've either met or seen before. The beach is also a short bicycle, bus, or taxi ride away, as are the hotspots on trendy Las Olas Boulevard and the Riverwalk, on the edge of downtown Fort Lauderdale.

To get around, you can rely on taxis, which are super easy to come by in South Florida due to the tourism factor. It is also easy to find cheap bikes for purchase or rent while you're in town. I would recommend buying or renting a bike or scooter (see my Insider Tip below) once you get to Fort Lauderdale, or in any of the hiring ports, for that matter. Check www.craigslist.org or in one of the yachting-trade or crew publications or websites for classified ads on bikes for sale. Crew are always trying to get rid of their bikes at the last minute because they're taking off on a job. I got by without a bike while in Fort Lauderdale because there were plenty of them at my crew house to borrow. Otherwise, most every place I needed to be was a short walk away—even the grocery stores. There is also a good bus system in Fort Lauderdale. Pitching in with other people in your crew house to rent cars for mini trips down to Miami or Key West on the weekends is an affordable way to have a fun weekend.

❖ **INSIDER TIP:** Scooter rentals are also a great way to get around Fort Lauderdale. They are easy to park when you want to stop at restaurants and beaches, and they go all day on a dollar in fuel. The scenic A1A route starts in Fort Lauderdale and runs over 40 miles north along the ocean all the way to Palm Beach. It's one of the most scenic coastal roads in the U.S. and is a great ride on a scooter. Check out Yachty Rentals at www.yachtyrentals.com or on Facebook: www.facebook.com/YachtyRentals. Note that Yachty Rentals also rents cars (and even airboats if you're feeling adventurous).

Getting to Where It All Happens in Fort Lauderdale

This "yachting central" portion of the city is a short taxi ride from both the Fort Lauderdale-Hollywood International Airport, and the Tri-Rail Commuter Station (if you are coming from Miami International or West Palm Beach International Airports). Following are directions for landing you right at this U.S. Highway 1 and 17th Street intersection (the bull's eye):

Public Transport In and Around Fort Lauderdale

↠ **Arriving by Air:** Approximate cab fare from the airport to the area around U.S. Hwy 1 and 17th Street will run from $10 to upwards of $30, depending on traffic. Free shuttle bus stops are located on the lower level. Safe, reliable, and efficient mass transit to and from the Airport is available through Route 1 of the Broward County Transit (BCT) buses. BCT operates daily schedules and the bus stop is located at the Rental Car Center, Stop 7. For more information, visit Broward County Transit (www.broward.org/BCT) or call the Rider Info Line at 954-357-8400.

↠ **Amtrak/Tri-Rail Station:** Approximate cab fare from the Amtrak station is $12. Dedicated shuttle buses provide free and convenient service to and from select Tri-Rail stations and connect to all that South Florida has to offer is easier with. For additional information call 1-800-TRI-RAIL, from anywhere in the state of Florida, or visit www.tri-rail.com.

Public Transport from Miami to Fort Lauderdale

↠ **Arriving by Air:** Take the free Tri-Rail Shuttle bus from Terminal E to the Tri-Rail Station. Take the Tri-Rail north to the Fort Lauderdale Station. For additional information call 1-800-TRI-RAIL, from anywhere in the state of Florida, or visit www.tri-rail.com.

↠ **Driving Directions from Miami to Lauderdale:** Exit Interstate 95N at Davie Boulevard, exit 26. Go East to U.S. Highway 1 (Federal Highway). Turn right, and you will now be going south toward the intersection at 17th Street and U.S. 1.

Antibes, France

Many yachts spend their summers in the Mediterranean operating charters. If you are a non-U.S. citizen, you may wish to target your search in the South of France, namely Antibes, which is the next biggest yacht-industry hub after Fort Lauderdale. Antibes will welcome job-seeking crewmembers, and yachts traveling all over the Med will typically conduct their candidate searches through the crew-placement agencies based there.

This fascinating medieval village is situated along the French Riviera about halfway between Nice and Monte Carlo and less than 10 kilometers from either city. Antibes' main port, Port Vauban, is the largest yachting port in the Mediterranean and its harbor can accommodate over 2,400 boats—from small fishing vessels to some of the largest megayachts in existence. You can guarantee that at any given time during the summer, there will be a row of well-known and celebrated boats lined up along the large quay at Port Vauban Marina. Many more anchor out along the coast. Antibes is the undisputed mecca for yachting activity in the Western Mediterranean, with many of the same yacht-services businesses you find in Fort Lauderdale based here (including most all crew-placement agencies). Antibes is also well connected to the other Cote D'Azur hotspots such as Cannes, Monaco, St. Jean-Cap-Ferrat, and St. Tropez.

Antibes is a chic but quaint town, worthy of being explored if you go there (and once you get a job on a yacht, the chances of making your way to this port one day are high). Within its "Vieille Ville," or Old Town, you will find mazes of narrow streets, many of them cobblestoned and lined with bistros, bars, and cafés of all types and price ranges, and lots of shops. Be sure to also check out the Picasso Museum, the Absinthe Museum, and the Provencal Market (located on cours Masséna), which is open every day except Monday from 6 a.m. to 1 p.m. Juan-les-Pins, a seaside resort and nightlife area just down the way from Antibes' Old Town, is another great place to visit for its sandy beaches, boutiques, nightclubs, and casinos.

There are some downsides to job hunting in Antibes, and one is that there are so many people looking for work there at one time, and only during the small window of the summer months. A captain once told me he had 30 people knock on his hull looking for work in one day. And there are a limited number of crew houses to choose from. Being that Antibes is a trendy Côte d'Azur resort town, living here while job hunting can also be quite expensive. Furthermore, I do not really recommend Antibes as a place to look for work anytime between October and March.

One final warning in regard to Antibes is that because it is a popular stop on the Europe circuit for backpackers, many of these more vagabond-type travelers will show up in town because they "heard about this yachting thing and thought it sounded like a cool summer job." While such people don't stand much of a chance of getting hired—especially since they won't be as prepared as you are going to be—they will still be competing with you for crew-house beds, day work, and maybe even interviews. This is why it is even more important that you have your training and are set to go if you decide to look in Antibes for your first job.

Otherwise, if you are trying to get that first job when it's peak season in the Med, and your travel budget can handle it, positioning yourself in Antibes is not a bad idea. I recommend getting there in April, and no later than June. Definitely take advantage of the many crew agencies located there. Just know that there will be a lot of competition and that experienced crew will do better at getting the jobs that become available (which is where networking becomes important).

Getting Around in Antibes

If you do decide to look for work in Antibes, do not restrict your search to just the Port Vauban Marina. The regional express train system, known as the TRE, operates between the main towns on the Côte d'Azur, from Cannes to Vintimiglia. It is user-friendly, and you are just a 5–20 minute ride away from other nearby ports and marinas where you can look for day work or dockwalk for a job. I highly recommend checking out Port Golfe Juan and Camille Rayon (7–

10 minute train ride from Antibes), the Old Port and Port Canto in Cannes (15–18 minutes), the Port of Nice (approximately 30 minutes), or Port Hercules in Monaco (approximately 45 minutes) for the same types of opportunities. If you don't travel to these towns to look for work, at least visit them to network. You will find swarms of currently employed crew (and captains) hanging out in the marina bars and restaurants, and a tip on a job lead could easily come about this way.

And finally, there is no need to worry about not being able to speak French when heading to Antibes to job hunt. You can get by without speaking a word of it, because a majority of the yachting businesses based there are run by English-speaking individuals (mostly British citizens). Having said that, in order to communicate with the locals, you should learn at least a few phrases before arriving—the French are known for appreciating the effort.

Getting to Where It All Happens in Antibes

➼ **Arriving by Air**—Nice International Airport (www.nice.aeroport.fr) is just 20 km east of Antibes, which is a 20-minute drive by car or taxi. Sixty airlines fly to Nice from around the world. To get to town from there, be cautious of the cab services; they will charge you an arm and a leg. Instead, there's a frequent and reasonably fast (about 40 minutes) bus service from the airport to Place de Charles de Gaulle, which is an ideally centralized drop-off spot in Antibes. The bus costs around 9 euros and departs from immediately outside the airport at Terminal 1.

➼ **Arriving by Train**—Antibes is on the main Paris-Nice line of the French high-speed trains (TGVs), with local trains serving most of the coastal towns. Prices vary by day and season.

Palma de Mallorca (Majorca), Spain

Another option (especially for non-U.S. citizens, for whom travel to Europe is more convenient) is Palma de Mallorca, which has really come onto the scene in recent years as a sophisticated hiring port. By that, I mean they have a decent amount of crew housing options popping up all the time, there are STCW training opportunities and several reputable crew-placement agencies, and a lot of yachts are now coming here for both maintenance and provisioning while in the Med. It forms an important holiday resort and commercial port, while its bay is often clogged with luxury yachts (and like Antibes, several of Palma's marinas can accommodate the largest of megayachts). This is also a convenient port to get around in, which makes networking a cinch.

Lying in the Mediterranean about 60 miles off the coast of Spain, Mallorca is the largest of the Balearic Islands—the others being Menorca, Ibiza (the island made famous on the E! and Travel Channels for its wild nightlife), Formentera, and Cabrera. The traditional spelling of the island is Mallorca, but sometimes it is spelled Majorca. Either way, it is pronounced My-YOR-ka, or as you'll find most English speakers calling it, May-YOR-ka. The island is mountainous but also has beautiful beaches and a mild climate, which has made it a popular vacation destination for Europeans. Michael Douglas and Katherine Zeta Jones, Boris Becker, Richard Branson, and Claudia Schiffer all have homes on the island.

Mallorca's capital city, Palma (referred to as Palma de Mallorca), is a cosmopolitan and vibrant city with tons of shops, restaurants, and other activities for visitors. The Old Town of Palma, which has managed to retain much of its ancient charm, is also quite enchanting and offers a lot of sightseeing opportunities.

While it is a Spanish island, there are many British and German expatriates who have settled here in recent years. So, as with Antibes, English speakers should not encounter many language barrier issues.

Getting Around in Palma

In Palma, you can navigate the Old Town on foot. There are also pedestrian and cyclist sidewalks that run along the Paseo Marítimo (the sea front), which make getting around a breeze. I did well with roller blades. Otherwise, you can make limited use of taxis or use one of the buses that cut across the city. To venture outside of Palma and explore the rest of the island, you can rely on buses, rental cars, or two railways. Ferry services are available to take you to the neighboring islands of the Balearics, such as Ibiza (a must!).

Be forewarned that Palma is an extremely nocturnal city. It seems no one goes to dinner before 10:00 p.m., and many bars do not get going until midnight–1:00 a.m. (and even that is considered "showing up early"). Yes, the nightlife is fantastic.

Getting to Where It All Happens in Palma

↦ **Arriving by Air**—Palma Airport is located just 8 km east of the city. For a brief period over the busy summer months, it actually becomes the busiest airport in Spain; normally, it is the third busiest. Transfers from the airport to Palma can be made by taxi, bus, or shuttle. You will want to research your options more thoroughly online.

Newport, Rhode Island, USA

Newport, Rhode Island is a quintessentially New England city, with a rich history. Though dating well back to the 1600s, it's perhaps best known for being where the Vanderbilts and other fabulously wealthy people built stately mansions around the early 20th century. It's also where the famous America's Cup resided from the 1930s straight through to 1983, an unprecedented string of success. Newport is the hub of the Northeastern U.S. yachting circuit, where you will find a lot of boats cruising during the summer. This is the destination to choose if you absolutely *must* begin your job search during the months of June, July, and August. Otherwise, Newport is a better hiring port for experienced crew who already know the ropes and are "turnkey," ready to jump onboard. Green job candidates do not do as well.

Here's why: Crew housing is not as readily available (and what is there is expensive), and there are fewer crew agencies. Having said that, the agencies that are there also have offices in Fort Lauderdale, and therefore your placement could just as easily come out of the Florida-based headquarters. If you decide to try Newport, I recommend first heading to Fort Lauderdale for training, as well as to meet with the more well-known crew agencies, and then simply relocate up to Newport for the summer months so you can interview one on one with the vessels traveling there at that time. A good time to aim to be in Newport is mid- to late-June, during the Newport Charter Show. It's the only American-based show of its type, an industry-only event that better informs charter brokers and megayacht crew alike of the opportunities in the region. It includes seminars and various crew competitions.

Overall though, as a newbie to the industry, if you can't be in the Mediterranean region, I would avoid job hunting during the summer months altogether. Save Newport for once you have experience.

Getting Around in Newport

Newport is a bustling town come summertime, with sailing events, music festivals, and more all occurring along the waterfront. Much of the yachting hubbub takes place along America's Cup Avenue and Thames Street, which each run parallel to the water. Given that a number of marinas and wharves (fitted with shops, restaurants, and bars) jut out into the water off America's Cup Avenue, one right after another, the port is easy to get around on foot or by bicycle. There is also the option of using the Rhode Island Public Transit Authority (RIPTA), which offers authentic-looking trolleys that travel around Newport. There are a few local taxicab companies you can use, as well.

Getting to Where It All Happens in Newport

The Newport State Airport does not offer commercial flights. Therefore, the best option for getting there is to fly into T.F. Green Providence Airport (PVD), which is located in Warwick, Rhode Island—only 40 minutes from Newport. From the airport, you can choose to make your transfer to the port by shuttle, taxi, public bus, limousine, or even a ferry.

Travel times will vary between 45 minutes and 1 hour, with the exception of the ferry, which takes about 1½ hours. I advise you to search online to determine your best option. Be sure to check that your flight times coincide with when your chosen means of transportation is operating.

You can also reach Newport by a combination of train and car/van service. Amtrak has a station in Kingston, Rhode Island, which is 18 miles from Newport, or about 30 minutes. You can take a car/van service from the station into Newport. The schedule for the car/van service varies, and reservations are required, so call (401) 295-1100 for information.

Note: For information on other hiring port options, such as San Diego; islands in the Caribbean; Sydney, Australia; and Auckland, New Zealand, please visit www.WorkOnAYacht.com.

Finding a Crew House in Your Hiring Port

❖ **INSIDER TIP:** Look into crew housing before you book your plane ticket!

I explained earlier that temporarily relocating to a hiring port on your way to finding your first yacht job is so highly recommended that it might as well be considered mandatory. I stress again, though, that this is not the same cumbersome process we are familiar with when we think about moving somewhere new. Special crew accommodations, known as **crew houses,** can be found in every major hiring port and are available to crew throughout the industry for the purpose of giving them somewhere to stay when they are either looking for work or going through training.

Basically, a crew house is a facility that is privately owned, most of the time by fellow or former yacht crew who do not live in the home, but manage it on their own or through a local agency. The size and type of home can vary. Many have been renovated or upgraded over the years, and while they aren't exactly luxury accommodations, they are certainly clean and livable. Some of the larger crew-housing businesses manage a number of properties—entire homes, apartments, studios, and efficiencies—that are typically only available to yacht-industry professionals.

Crew houses will also be used by entire crews; if a yacht must come out of the water or have its power shut off, a captain and crew will move into a house all to themselves while they wait for the work to be completed. These homes differ from the ones you will look for as an individual, which are those catering specifically to crew who come into town and stay temporarily while they look for work. Such crew houses operate similarly to hostel-style lodging, where you receive a bed in a room with one or two other people.

And here's the beauty of crew houses: You don't sign a lease; you usually don't pay a deposit; the furniture, bed, linens, phones, and TVs are all there; and the kitchens come stocked with pots, pans, and utensils. Most all homes offer Internet access nowadays, but make sure to ask when you contact them.

There are many reasons why crew house accommodations are your best bet for a place to stay in any hiring port, especially over backpacker hostels, motels, and hotels:

- ➡ They are economical like hostels, but in most cases, everyone there will have some connection to the yachting industry.
- ➡ They are ideal places for networking.
- ➡ They will typically be located near the yachting action in town. Rides places will typically be plentiful.
- ➡ Day working opportunities may just come to you if you are staying in a crew house (rather than you having to chase them down).

Crew Houses and Your Budget

Prices will tend to change depending on the season, but the standard range is $150 to $200 a week, all inclusive except food. Some of the crew houses actually operate as hostels, where you can pay by the night. Please be aware that this pricing entails sharing a room. For example, if it's a two-bedroom home, they'll normally have two twin beds in each room, or even two bunk beds, so you can expect to have as many as four to eight people staying there. (And not to worry: Most all crew houses I know of would never mix genders in these shared rooms.)

Private bedrooms may be available in some homes, but the price will be much higher (more like $250 to $350 a week). You can pay a premium for some very nice private apartments, or private homes if you have a group and can afford it. Weekly rates may also edge a bit higher in Europe than in the United States.

Crew Houses and Networking

Crew from all around the world will be staying in these accommodations. Because most of the houses are focused exclusively on the yachting community, the people staying in them not only find opportunities for new and lasting friendships, but also make many valuable career contacts. A person in your same crew house could come home one day with news of a job opportunity that fits what you're looking for, including day work. You may find your roommate is also looking for work, and you can swap stories.

I once had a job lead come to me from a guy I'd lived with in a crew house, two years after the fact! We'd kept in touch by email, and when I wrote to say I was leaving a position, the boat he was on was looking for someone with my exact qualifications. He recommended me to his captain, and that held a lot of value; after all, he'd lived with me before.

Crew Houses and Convenience

Unlike other types of accommodations in the hiring ports (like hotels and campsites), most all crew houses will be within close proximity to the yachting hot spots in town, including where all your job search activities will be focused. While it may require a short walk, a bike ride, or a cab, you can rest assured that you will be conveniently located near the crew agencies, training schools, marinas, and yachtie hang-outs.

Crew Houses and Day Working Leads

There are many ways to find day-work job opportunities, but one of the easiest is by staying in a popular crew house. Quite often, yachts requiring temporary workers will call around to the more well-known crew accommodations because they know that eager-to-work crew are there in abundance. When you first move in, find out how word gets out when these calls come through. Some of the busier crew houses handle the day work offers that come in via a lottery system.

Other times, when yachts are really desperate for extra help, they won't even call first; they will just send crew cars around to pick up anyone willing to work that day. You can guarantee that when staying in a crew house during a busy season or just before a big boat show, there will be a crew car sent over by several boats in the mornings to gather up day workers. I encourage you to jump on such opportunities.

Finally, even though you are looking for interior work, if the request comes in for someone to help wash down a yacht's deck, and you have no other offers for the day, volunteer to take it. Be sure to let them know your background experience working on a yacht's exterior (which is likely none), but since the skills required for such a task do not take long to pick up, if they are willing to take you on, go for it. This opportunity will still get you on a yacht for the day and will provide you a great chance to network with current crew. (And look at it this way: You'll be getting paid to work on your tan!)

Booking Crew Accommodations

While a business, this is also a privately owned house, not the Marriott. The one drawback to crew houses is that, unless you are somehow willing to put down a deposit, they cannot always guarantee rooms will be available when you are coming to town—especially if it is during peak hiring season in that particular port. To score a good deal on a plane ticket, you of course want to purchase that as far in advance as possible. Therefore, do your research in advance.

I advise you to call around to several houses before booking your air ticket to find out what your options are. If you can pay a deposit to guarantee your spot, do so. Know, too, that there are back-up options that you can probably find once you arrive, even if you have to splurge on a hotel room for your first couple nights in town. This would most likely only happen during a peak hiring time or when a boat show is being held. Therefore, my suggestion is that you aim to be in your chosen hiring port just prior to the start of those peak hiring seasons, which will allow you several weeks to fit your training in, and then be primed for your job hunt when things pick up.

I Must Confess...
My own crew-house experience was tough to leave.

This one's straight from my journal:

"I arrived in Fort Lauderdale on February 3rd, and here I am a month later getting ready to leave for my first yacht job. I have failed to write at all these last four weeks because, well, a LOT has been going on. The Fort Lauderdale experience has been a blast. I never would have thought job hunting could be this much fun! I have been living in a crew house since the day I got to town. It is filled with individuals looking for work. There is only one other 'newbie' here, while everyone else is between jobs, having left their previous gig for one reason or another.

"The house sleeps eight people: three in one room, three in another, and two in another. I've been in a three-person room since I arrived; although, only two of us are in it. There's me, and a girl named Jenny, who's from Manchester, England. She's hysterical and has been my 'partner in crime' for the last three weeks. The accommodation is really a great deal. It's a good-size house with two living rooms, a kitchen, two bathrooms, a huge front porch, cable TV, a nice stereo system, and a fenced-in backyard complete with a BBQ and sun chairs—all for $140 a week (oh, and free laundry facilities)… Despite an occasional cockroach (welcome to Florida; they call them "palmetto bugs" here) and having to be exterminated once for fleas, it's been real comfortable!

"When I first moved into the house, there was an almost entirely different make-up of inhabitants from who is here now, as I get ready to depart myself (although, the first two people I met when I arrived have been with me to the end). In the beginning, there was a British guy, my roommate Jenny, one American guy, a South African guy, an Aussie, and a girl from Grenada (the house wasn't full). Many people came and went over the course of four weeks, but in the end, there are two Americans, two Australians, one Kiwi (from New Zealand), one British, one French, and one South African. I swear it has been like being on MTV's Real World, as we were all just randomly thrown together into one house to live so closely together. Despite our different backgrounds and our different nationalities—because we were all doing the same thing: looking for yacht jobs—it's been easy to grow close quickly. (I supposed you could say we are all 'in the same boat!')

"Honestly, though, support, advice, and even job leads and recommendations were always readily available. It's been a great experience, and I made some fantastic, lifelong friends (and threw some kick-ass parties in the meantime). We even had a little family ritual: Sunday brunches at the Bimini Boatyard Bar & Grill with mimosas out the wazoo. Needless to say, this was often family bonding time (although few could ever recall the final hour of the four-hour meal), and it made for some good footage on the new video camera. Then there was going for steak dinners at Chuck's Steakhouse, playing pool at the Quarterdeck, hanging out at Waxy's on Saturday nights, and many at-home BBQs.

"And somehow, through all of this socializing, I also managed to get in good with the crew agencies, take a 5-day stewardess training course, and get some day work on several different yachts (which kept the money coming in and was a great learning experience). One month and three interviews later, I have been hired! Leaving these new friends, though—it's bittersweet."

Crew Housing Lists

Following are lists of crew houses to check out in the main hiring ports, but it is by no means exhaustive! Crew houses tend to go come and go quite frequently, so be sure to call and email any establishment you find here or online. I will do our best to keep an updated list on my website at www.WorkOnAYacht.com.

❖ **INSIDER TIP:** You should be aware that many crew-housing websites advertise their low-season rates and do not show the taxes that are included. Always email or call prospective crew houses for current rates before making a final decision.

Fort Lauderdale Crew Housing

Most all of the crew houses in Fort Lauderdale are safe. There are some, though, that I don't recommend because they also advertise themselves as hostels and therefore tend to attract people on the backpacking circuit. The following are recommended based on either my experience or referrals from current crew as of spring 2013.

➡ **The Neptune Group**
417 SE 16th St., Fort Lauderdale, FL 33316 Tel: 1-954-763-1050
Website: www.theneptunegroup.com, Email: info@theneptunegroup.com
Owners: D.J. Parker and Captain Dwight Ledbetter

Type of Accommodations Offered: two-, three-, and four-bedroom homes; and two-bedroom/two-bath and one-bedroom/one-bath apartments.

The Neptune Group gets my strong recommendation among crew house options in Fort Lauderdale. The properties are owned and managed by Captain Dwight Ledbetter, a former yacht captain with many years in the industry, and D.J. Parker, a well-known charter and yacht broker as well as past successful charter captain.

Each property has been completely renovated, newly decorated, and extensively landscaped. Each house or apartment includes free Wi-Fi and DSL Broadband Internet, free cable TV/DVD, safes, all basic supplies, and professional cleaning services. All homes also come with BBQ/patio/private backyards. The Neptune Group places two or less people in a room, and they have lots of fully private apartments with queen-size beds available for couples.

Due to the high demand for the Neptune Group's properties, especially during peak season, they do operate from a registration system. You are wise to register early, which you can do by contacting them directly or filling out a form on their website.

In order to get on Neptune Group's waiting list without a prior history in the industry, you will have to go through an intensive screening process. Once you've submitted a registration form online, you will most likely be called and interviewed by Captain Dwight or his assistant manager, who will ask a lot of questions to confirm that you are career minded and that your heart is in the right place. He does reserve the right to turn you down if he feels that's not the case. The Neptune Group also conducts interviews to best match you up with fellow residents who share your same goals or interests.

It is well worth going through this screening process because both Captain Dwight and DJ Parker have the ability to help you with your job search, as both are very well connected throughout the industry and hear of job leads all the time. They recommend tenants whom they feel will make good crew. The Neptune Group also offers a first-class crew placement service known as Neptune Crew, part of an online service to match crew staying in their houses with day work opportunities and full-time positions. You can check this out by visiting their website at www.theneptunegroup.com.

➥ **Crew Castle**

Call for address, Fort Lauderdale, FL 33316

Tel: 1-954-931-8945

Website: www.americancrewhouses.webs.com, Email: guiltfree@earthlink.net

Contact Person: Samantha (Chef Sam)

Type of Accommodations Offered: The Crew Castle is a million-dollar crew house with double occupancy bedrooms; one bathroom for every two bedrooms.

Another strong recommendation based on both my experience and the experience of many readers of my first edition: Crew Castle is run by Chef Sam, a former yachtie herself. Located close to U.S. 1 and 17th Street, Crew Castle is a top-notch facility, referred to by some as "the Hilton of crew houses." Accommodations are clean, quiet, safe, and close to everything.

The home features a huge kitchen, big screen TV in the den, individual TVs in each bedroom, wireless DSL Internet connections throughout the house, three decks, patio, outdoor BBQ, free airport pick-up with advance notice, and even a ladies' library. This is not a party house; Chef Sam runs a tight ship, and she is looking for serious-minded job hunters. She is very selective.

Chef Sam has put up a website with a lot of valuable resource information for crew. While not the easiest to navigate, the site contains a wealth of curated content on everything from job-hunting tips to the latest word on visas. If you're considering staying here, she also lists some glowing testimonials from former tenants. Find it at www.americancrewhouses.webs.com.

➥ **Mary's Crew Houses**

816 SE 12th St., Fort Lauderdale, FL 33316

Tel: 1-954-242-1109 (Mary's cell and 24-hour office), Fax: 1-954-321-8406

Website: www.maryscrewhouse.com, Email: maryscrewhouse@yahoo.com
Contact Person: Mary E. Gaudette

Type of Accommodations Offered: Three houses with shared accommodation, as well as private rooms, located right off 17th Street in Fort Lauderdale.

Mary's crew houses are fully functional crew houses, which opened in September 2003. They provide accommodation to crewmembers both new and old to the yachting industry. Captains call Mary's Crew House when they need day workers/crew, as they know she will send them reliable, hard-working individuals.

Full free Internet and Wi-Fi access in all places, telephone for local United States calls, big screen cable TVs in every room, large community kitchen and living areas in both apartments, heated pool, BBQ, exercise equipment, free airport pick-up when you arrive in town, washing machine and dryer, personal lockers for valuables, and full bedrooms with plenty of personal space. Central air conditioning and many fans are provided.

↦ Palm Place Residences

1324 SW 31st St., Fort Lauderdale, FL 33315
Tel: 1-954-655-8526 or 1-954-566-7182
Website: www.palmplaceres.com, Email: lcooksey@bellsouth.net
Contact Person: Lisa

Type of Accommodations Offered: The main house features one shared and two private bedrooms, one with private bathroom. The property also has a separate cottage that is ideal for a couple that wants all the amenities in a quaint, quiet setting.

Newly renovated, tastefully decorated, and fully furnished in southern Florida motif, Palm Place Residence is a crew accommodation that features new appliances, cable TV with premium channels, DVD/VCR, complimentary local phone service, wireless internet access, and free laundry facilities. Both the house and the cottage are complimented with private gardens, decks, and lounging patios replete with BBQ.

↦ Crew Quarters

Call for address, Fort Lauderdale, FL 33316
Tel: 1-954-296-0457 Fax: 1-954-522-6139
Website: www.crewquarters.com, Email: beverly.crewquarters@gmail.com
Contact: Beverly Cronen and Louis Dupree

Type of Accommodations Offered: One fully furnished home offering semi-private accommodation (maximum two persons per room).

The Crew Quarters home is owned and actively managed by Louis Dupree, a captain of 28 years, and Beverly Cronen, a captain and stewardess of 15 years, who strive to provide a personalized, informative, and supportive haven for maritime students or those looking for maritime employment.

The home is fully furnished with a large living and dining area, a newly renovated and well-equipped kitchen, satellite TV with a diverse range of viewing options, wireless internet access, free laundry facilities, an outside sitting porch, BBQ, and a large, tree-shaded backyard. Located within a three-block walking distance to crew agencies and maritime schools. Rates fluctuate throughout the year. It's helpful to contact Crew

Quarters at least a week in advance. Last-minute bookings will be accepted on a space available basis.

➼ **Smart Move Crew Accommodations & Property Management**

716 SE 17th St., Fort Lauderdale, FL 33316

Tel: 1-954-525-9559, Fax: 1-954-527-0595

Website: www.smart-move.com, Email: info@smart-move.com

Type of Accommodations Offered: Crew houses. Two-, three-, and four-bedroom crew house-style homes (to accommodate larger crews); one-bedroom/one-bath apartments; and studio/efficiencies.

Smart Move has catered to the yachting industry since the business started over 20 years ago. Tenants of Smart Move tend to return year after year, from entry-level crew who seek crew house-style living quarters or efficiencies to captains and entire crews who rent three- or four- bedroom houses.

Smart Move's headquarters is located on 17th Street Causeway, in the heart of the Fort Lauderdale yachting scene. All properties are fully furnished and all inclusive (including Wi-Fi, Cable TV, BBQ's, laundry facilities) and are fully air-conditioned. Many have pools or Jacuzzis as well.

➼ **The Bridge at Cordova Boutique Hotel and Crew House**

1441 Cordova Rd., Fort Lauderdale, FL 33316

Tel: 1-954-525-2323, Fax: 1-954-523-4518

Website: www.bridgeatcordova.com, Email: thebridgebedandbreakfast@gmail.com

Type of Accommodations Offered: Nine "Captains Quarters" suites with kitchen and private patio; six "Junior Suites" around the pool; and four private rooms, with their own private bathroom, fridge, and microwave. Premier crew and hostel accommodations: dormitories for male or female, 3 people per room, en suite bathroom. Free breakfast bar. Free transportation for private rooms only. There is a fee for dorms.

The Bridge at Cordova has 22 units with varying configurations from efficiencies to suites. Every accommodation provides free local phone calls, free wireless high-speed Internet connection, and cable TV. There is a large pool with lounge chairs and a huge BBQ grill for use by all guests. They have their own Cordova Diving School with PADI certification. The international staff is friendly and congenial. Short-stay as well as longer-term accommodations are available in a relaxed, tropical setting. Rooms recently renovated in the summer of 2012. Assistance with job hunting and day work searches is also offered.

➼ **Sabra's Crew Accommodations**

SE 14th Ct., Fort Lauderdale, FL 33312

Tel: 1-954-294-0641

Website: www.sabrascrewhouse.com, Email: info@sabrascrewhouse.com

Type of Accommodations Offered: Each suite has two bedrooms, one bathroom, full kitchen, and a comfortable living room. Maximum two people per room. Private rooms are also available with queen size beds.

Sabra's Crew Accommodations offers quiet comfort in the center of Fort Lauderdale's yachting community. The rooms are clean, affordable, and never overcrowded. Amenities include satellite TV, wireless internet, laundry facilities, and a great patio area with barbecue grills and seating. Discounts are offered to students enrolled in local maritime schools.

Antibes Crew Housing

↦ **The Crew Grapevine**

16 Rue de la Baume & 25 Rue du Bas Castelet, Antibes, France 06600

Tel: 33(0)6 16 66 28 43 or 33(0)6 19 03 26 52

Website: www.crewgrapevine.com, Email: info@crewgrapevine.com

Type of Accommodation Offered: The Crew Grapevine has two large private townhouses providing accommodation for professional yacht crew in the heart of Old Antibes. The Crew Grapevine sleeps up to 15 guests in each house with three to four guests max in each room.

All bedrooms at The Crew Grapevine have air conditioning and heating. Each house has a fully equipped kitchen, lounge area with big screen television, and office equipped with computers, printer, and fax. Wi-Fi is available throughout the building. Laundry facilities on premises. Rates vary depending on season, and as of spring 2013, range between 144 and 222 euros per week.

↦ **The Glamorgan**

20 Avenue Thiers, Antibes, France 06600

Tel: 33 (0)4 93 34 42 71 or 33 (0)6 25 16 54 57 (only call between 10 a.m. and 6 p.m.—Standard Time = GMT+1, Summer Time = GMT+2)

Website: www.theglamorgan.com, Email: glamorgan@orange.fr

Contact: Chris Browne

Type of Accommodation Offered: The Glamorgan can accommodate up to 14 people. The rooms either have two or three beds inside as not to overcrowd. Each room is provided with an en-suite shower and toilet.

The Glamorgan has been a crew favorite since it opened in 2002. It is ideally situated near the crew agencies, training facilities, bars, restaurants, super markets, and post office. Only a two-minute walk from the bus and train stations. Port Vauban Marina is a five-minute walk.

All the rooms are fully air conditioned and heated. Sky satellite TV is currently available in all bedrooms. They have a large fully equipped kitchen perfect for cooking your own meals and also a large dining room with seating for up to 10. The Glamorgan has a communal crew lounge area.

The house is equipped with a Wi-Fi. They have two computers in house for your use, also a printer/copier/scanner with free printing. Free laundry facilities include two washing machines, three tumble dryers, and ironing boards. Hair driers are supplied in ladies rooms only. Shaded garden. Free mobile phone rental is also available (subject to availability).

↦ **Bel-Air Crew Accommodation**

10 Avenue Bel-Air, Antibes, France 06600

Tel: 33 (0)6 98 15 09 22

Website: www.frenchprimecrewaccomodation.com (notice "accommodation" is spelled incorrectly in the website URL; missing an "m."), Email: bel.air.crew.house@gmail.com
Contact: Carolyn

Type of Accommodation Offered: Shared room. Bel-Air is strictly for crew, which means it's smaller than a hostel, but offers plenty of outdoor space.

A 5-min walk to Port Vauban, the Bel-Air is close to crew agencies, local bars, restaurants, and the train station. It has Wi-Fi throughout the house, cooking facilities, free and onsite laundry facilities, and British TV. They also offer help and advice for those who are new to the industry and are available for translation from French to English.

➥ **Debbie's Crew House**

67 Blvd Beau Ridge Prolongé, Antibes, 06600 France

Tel: 33 (0)6 3238 7528 or 33 (0)4 9374 4140

Website: www.debbiescrewhouse.com, Email:debbie@debbiescrewhouse.com

Contact: Debbie and Franco

Types of Accommodation Offered: Three rooms with double beds (no more than two people per spacious room); and two self-contained studios for couples, at no extra cost.

Located five minutes by train from Antibes station and 20 minutes by train from Nice, Debbie's Crew House is a relaxed crew house with a pool, outdoor tables, BBQ, spacious lounge and kitchen, and a big-screen HD TV with full HD Sky satellite. You will have free Wi-Fi access, printing capabilities, and free laundry facilities.

Across the road you will find banking facilities, as well as a small supermarket, bakery, pharmacy, and tabac. The beach is only a five-minute walk away. Free transportation offered to Blue Water Training Centre. Note: this house has four rabbits and a dog.

Palma Crew Housing

➥ **Hostel Apuntadores**

Calle Apuntadores, 8, Palma de Mallorca, Spain 07012

Tel: 34 (0)971 71 34 91

Website: www.apuntadoreshostal.com, Email: hostalapuntadores@yahoo.es

Type of Accommodation Offered: Ensuite, budget, and dorm-style accommodation options. Some rooms have small balconies.

Hostal Apuntadores is in the heart of the old town and has a rooftop terrace with great views of the city. There is air conditioning and heating and the Wi-Fi is free. A café in the reception area serves breakfast and light snacks. The sightseeing buses and the airport and ferry transport pass nearby. Reportedly clean and friendly, but very basic.

➥ **Hostel Terramar**

Plaza Mediterraneo, 8, Palma de Mallorca, Spain 07014

Tel: 34 (0)971 73 99 31

Website: www.palma-hostales.com, Email: hostalterramar@yahoo.es

Type of Accommodation Offered: Fully equipped apartments, en-suite rooms, budget doubles and singles, and a dorm-style crew house.

The Terramar is set back 50 meters from the Paseo Maritimo and overlooks the yacht harbor with convenient location to marinas, shopping, and nightlife.

The Terramar offers a guest kitchen and dining area, a shady terrace with a cooling water feature, a large sunbathing terrace with panoramic views, and plenty of comfortable communal areas. Buses pass within 75 meters of the front door connecting you with the rest of the city and the beaches. Reportedly clean and friendly.

St. Martin/St. Maarten Crew Housing

→ **The Crew House**

130 Airport Rd , Simpson Bay, St. Maarten, Dutch Caribbean
Tel: 1-721-545-3300 (Reservations: 1-954-600-4577)
Website: www.thecrewhouse-sxm.com or www.l-mg.com, Email: thecrewhousesxm@gmail.com or info@l-mg.com
Facebook: Lighthouse-Marine-Group

Type of Accommodation Offered: Accommodations for up to 24 people. Dorm rooms with or without air conditioning are available and sleep maximum four persons each. Each dorm room has its own bathroom.

The Crew House St. Maarten is the newest crew house on the island of St. Maarten. It is conveniently located within five minutes from the island's international airport and is close to the yachting center of Simpson Bay and the hottest night clubs on the island, Bliss and Tantra. Because of the high demand in the yachting season The Crew House expanded in September 2012 to a second location in the Cole Bay area close to the marina at Port de Plaisance.

Amenities include: Free Wi-Fi, Cable TV, and flat screen TVs, coin-operated washing machine and vending machines, access to private dinghy dock, onsite bar and restaurant offering crew discounts, onsite ferries to Anguilla, daily shuttle to and from Simpson Bay. The Crew House is located on the airport road. The second location is in Almond Grove, Cole Bay. Properties managed by Lighthouse Marine Group.

→ **Smiley's Crew House**

1 Windmill Rd, Colebay
Tel: Smiley: 1-721-522-5651 / Elona: 1-721-522-9894
Website: www.sxmmarinetrading.com, Email: smilerelona@hotmail.com

Type of Accommodation Offered: Shared accommodation with two bunk beds per room or private studio apartments for couples.

Smiley's Crew House has been in operation since 2001. It is centrally located in Cole Bay and is convenient to reach all marinas. Amenities include large living rooms, kitchens, A/C in large bedrooms, hot water showers, Wireless internet, Cable TV, secure lockers, clean linen, and laundry facilities.

Smiley's crew house is reportedly a fantastic spot on the island. Run by the well-known Smiley and Elona, I've been told you can't go wrong staying here. They do fill up quick but are happy to offer further suggestions. The owners also do crew placement and can help with day work. You can register online at under the Crew Placement tab at www.sxmmarinetrading.com.

Newport, Rhode Island Crew Housing

- **Seamen's Church Institute**

  18 Market Square, Newport, RI 02840

  Tel: 1-401-847-4260, Fax: 1-401-847-4284

  Website: www.SeamensNewport.org, Email: seamensnewport@gmail.com

  Type of Accommodation Offered: Ten affordable European-style rooms for seafarers and others for overnight or brief stays are available with shared baths, seasonal A/C, and free Wi-Fi access.

  Founded in 1919 as a non-profit corporation to provide a "safe haven" to seafarers, Seamen's Church Institute moved into its own building in 1930 in the heart of the Newport waterfront. Seamen's offers newly renovated accommodations in the National Register Historic building, now fully accessible for all levels. The Aloha Cafe is open to the public with breakfast and lunch menus. Also available are public laundry facilities, the Mariners Lounge, Memorial Garden, Henry H. Anderson Jr. Library for Mariners, and the quaint Chapel of the Sea. Reservations can be made online at www.SeamensNewport.org. This is a non-smoking facility.

What to Pack

Travel light! For two reasons—both in preparation for your crew-house experience and your ultimate live-aboard experience. (We need to be thinking ahead, optimistically!)

First and foremost, make sure you use soft, collapsible luggage. This is not so much important for staying in a crew house, but rather, when you get a permanent job. Space onboard a yacht is tight, especially in regard to the crew living quarters. When you join a boat, you don't want to take up already-limited closet space or burden your new crew with finding a place for your suitcase or trunk. It wouldn't be a good first impression to be a hassle.

I always recommend carrying a large backpack, as you would use if vagabonding around Europe, for example. And you are not limited to just one. I actually carried a large backpack, a small backpack, and a small duffle bag. The key again is to make sure the pieces are collapsible and easy to store. Of course, that amount of luggage will limit you to what can fit. I'll get to some packing advice in a bit. Meanwhile, the important rule is that, however much you decide to take, it all must be able to be carried by you and you alone. You will be moving around a lot—don't weigh yourself down!

A Quick Word on Valuables

In regard to staying in crew-house accommodations, do not take a lot of valuables. Leave your expensive jewelry at home—especially family heirlooms and things of that nature. (But, definitely take a watch. Having a watch on at all times was the number-one rule when I was working on one yacht.)

Most all of the crew houses are safe, and most provide lockers or in-room safes, but there are also a lot of crew going in and out at these homes. If something gets taken, you will have an awfully difficult time tracking down the culprit. Also remember some crew houses qualify as hostels, meaning they take bookings from people outside the yachting industry. You just never know what type of people you are going to run across in these types of accommodations (which is one reason I recommend you stick with the more yachtie-oriented options). Regardless, consider taking some mini locks to put on your luggage in order to secure what valuables you do have; and that includes important documents, such as your passport.

Clothes

While searching for a job, adhering to something close to a crew uniform will win you bonus points. Quite simply, you want to look the part, thereby making it easier for crew agents or captains who interview you to envision you on a professional yacht crew. When you head off to your chosen hiring port, especially if you plan on taking the day-work route at some point (and everyone should), there are some key items you will want to have with you to wear. These are the staples of the ol' yachtie wardrobe:

- **Khaki shorts**—Okay, I say khaki, but navy or white will also work. Khaki is just the standard. And I'm talking Bermuda-style shorts here. Having pockets is really helpful. I suggest you pack two or three pairs. You can typically find appropriate styles at stores like Gap, Old Navy, J. Crew, Eddie Bauer, and American Eagle. Another suggestion is to wait until you arrive in a hiring port, and then go buy what you need at the same crew-uniform outfitters where current yacht crew shop, like Liquid Yacht Wear (Theresa carries some fashionable options), Big Blue Yachtwear, and Smallwood's in Fort Lauderdale; Sea Design and Dolphin Wear in Antibes; and Deckers Ocean Attire in Palma. This will also give you a good opportunity to network.
- **T-shirts**—Take plenty of basic, loose-fitting T-shirts. Logos, theme shirts, and designs are fine, but don't go overboard with attention-grabbing or vulgar shirts. Color doesn't matter, but you'll always do fine with white. Oftentimes, boats you accept day work on for a duration of three days or more will give you a crew T-shirt to wear, which will have a picture of the yacht on the back. Even though the boat might be in a shipyard or docked with no guests onboard, captains like to keep everyone looking professional and a part of the team for all the onlookers walking by. They just may be satisfied if you are wearing any yacht's shirt, so if you are ever given one to keep, you can wear it on any day-working job you get. So long as it has a picture of a yacht on the back, and some name across the front that has "M/Y" or "S/Y" before it, you will definitely fit in.
- **Polo shirt**—Take at least one short-sleeved, collared, three-button polo-style shirt— plain and simple. This is to wear to any interviews you may get with crew agents, captains, or chief stews. You should also show up to interviews dressed in the khaki or navy shorts I mentioned earlier. Once you've registered with the crew agencies, you could get a call at any time about a captain wishing to meet you, so having at least one polo and one pair of nice khaki shorts with you when you arrive in port will have you prepared for the best.
- **Deck shoes**—You should take at least one pair of comfortable work shoes, preferably deck shoes or docksiders (a handsewn, moccasin-style shoe with rubber, non-slip soles,

rawhide laces, and non-corrosive brass eyelets). Dockers and Sperry are commonly worn brands in the industry. You can always wait until you get to a yachting port to purchase these.

- **Bathing suit**—*Need I say more?*

- **INSIDER TIP:** If you're American and were ever a part of the Greek system in college, do not wear any of your old Greek T-shirts, even when you're just hanging out in the yachtie bars. You will be working alongside a lot of Aussies, Kiwis, Brits, Canadians, and South Africans, and many of them have a negative impression of the entire American frat-house stuff. Wear these shirts, and you'll get stereotyped quickly.

Other Clothes to Take

Of course, you should also take clothes that you normally wear. Your *whole* life won't be absorbed by yachting, and once you start traveling onboard a vessel, you will have time off in ports where you'll want to go away for a weekend or have a big night out. Take your "going-out clothes"—maybe one nice outfit if you ever head to a fancy restaurant or casino with the crew. (Remember that you might end up partying in Monte Carlo at some point.) I would pack several pairs of jeans or slacks, or whatever you normally wear. The weather is going to be nice most every place you visit, so warmer-weather clothing is the way to go. One light jacket and a sweatshirt or two are also wise. In regard to shoes, take one or two nice pairs, perhaps a pair of running or athletic shoes, and sandals or shoes for the beach.

For females, one other piece you may consider for interviewing purposes is a black or navy skirt. I do not recommend anything shorter than knee length or just above the knee.

Once you secure a permanent, live-aboard job, you will be provided with all the uniform pieces you need—right down to socks and shoes—so these items I'm telling you to come prepared with are not for your ultimate full-time job. In other words, don't go hog wild buying T-shirts and khaki shorts. Just take enough for day-working purposes (and to keep from having to do laundry daily), saving one polo and one nice pair of shorts or skirt for interviews only.

When you are packing to first head to a hiring port, don't start going over all of these "what ifs" and think you need to be prepared for any and every situation. Keep in mind that there will always be times and places to shop for things you need. After all, once your yachting career kicks off, you stand to have a lot of extra money on your hands. (Just don't blow it all on clothing!)

Laptop/Tablet PCs

Should you take your laptop or tablet? By all means, YES! You will be glad you did. You definitely want to have your computer with you if you plan to stay in touch with family and friends. Most yachts have Internet access of some kind; however, the use of the service can be restricted due to high costs (running Internet over satellite is far from cheap). What may end up happening is that you only get a certain amount of time a week to be online. Having your emails already composed and saved on your computer to quickly upload all in one go is a great idea. Internet connectivity can also be a problem in some ports and marinas, especially in older harbors. You may end up using a lot of Internet cafés in the various ports you visit, so being able to compose your messages prior to going ashore will be a big time (and money) saver.

You may also find that having your own computer onboard proves useful on the job. Most yachts will have several computers, one of which will likely go to the interior staff, and another one to the exterior staff. The captain will also have one. But the time may come when there is more work to do than the number of computers onboard will allow. You could end up saving the day by having an extra computer to use.

Mobile Phone & Plans

You probably never leave home without your phone as it is, so this may seem an obvious tip. But remember, things happen very quickly in the yachting industry, so you want to make sure you are able to be reached at all times, whether it be for day work, a request for an interview, or a permanent job offer.

Don't worry yet about what plan you'll need when you go out of the country—that's something you can explore once you get to a hiring port. Find out what the other yachties are using. The way the mobile calling and data plans are changing these days, there are plenty of options for obtaining good service that will work around the world. (And whatever I tell you today will likely have changed tomorrow anyway.)

❖ **INSIDER TIP:** Skype VoIP services and Google Hangouts are the cheapest and most convenient ways to stay in touch with family and friends far away. With Skype, video and voice calls to anyone are free, while calls to mobile and landline numbers worldwide, text messaging, and group video calls are available for a fee. Use Google Hangouts to video chat with up to nine friends with no extra cost. Bingo!

Miscellaneous Items to Consider

Your music—MP3 players are the obvious choice, but if you take CDs, it's a good idea to write your initials on them in permanent marker.

Books—as far as books go, definitely limit what you take (or go the electronic route), as they can really weigh you down. This was the toughest part for me because I'm a bookworm. If packing physical books, take your top five favorites with you (and put your name in these, too). Most crew houses, and even the yachts, have mini libraries that you'll have access to if you run out of reading material.

Toiletries—If you're tight on space when packing, just forgo packing a lot of the toiletry items. Once you are settled in a crew house, you can always pick this stuff up at nearby pharmacies and grocery stores. The one item I definitely recommend you invest in is sun block, but again, you can wait until you get to your destination to buy it.

Prescription medications—If you happen to take prescription medications of any kind, keep in mind that you will be seeking a job that takes you away from home for an extended period of time. I recommend having any necessary prescriptions filled on a long-term basis. Inquire about this with your doctor or pharmacist, for you will probably have to fill out some paperwork—and it may even require battling with your current health-insurance provider a bit. Start looking into this now if it's something that could be an issue. You want to be prepared in case you end up being hired by a boat that says, "Cool, we leave tomorrow!" Have your ducks (and your pills) in a row.

And that just about does it, aside from the various items you will need to take for your job search, such as your résumé/CV, photos, references, and any copies of licenses or professional certificates that you should present. I will go over these items in Chapter 10. Meanwhile, you are now free to start packing!

"Man cannot discover new oceans unless he has the courage to lose sight of the shore."
—**Andre Gide**, French author and winner of the 1947 Nobel Prize in literature

9

LET THE JOB HUNT BEGIN!
—CREW AGENCIES, DAY WORKING,
AND NETWORKING—

You now know how to choose a hiring port, book your initial crew accommodations, and even what you should pack to bring with you when you head out on your new adventure. With this foundation laid, it's time to get down to business. In this chapter, we will examine the major steps you must take to line up interviews for stew positions, including how to find and register with crew recruitment agencies, as well as how to seek out and land day working jobs (which may even help you find a permanent position faster). I also share with you some practical, insider advice on how to get hired quickly, easily, and with little investment.

While I do recommend relying heavily on crew placement agencies (of which there are many eager to assist), there are alternative avenues you can take to find jobs that might not otherwise be advertised. I will provide you guidance in pursuing such strategies as searching in online forums, "dockwalking" (explained later in this chapter), and posting/responding to either job postings in the online industry trade publications or public notice boards in the various yachtie hangouts. I will also give you some great ideas on how to network with members of the yachting community, which should be a priority on your job finding "to do" list.

Yes, there is definitely a lot to tell you about. So let's jump in!

Crew Agencies (Employment Agencies)

One of the best ways to break into the yachting industry is through the crew placement or recruitment agencies (referred to by most as simply "crew agencies"). These agencies are not the ones who do the actual hiring. Rather, they are the middlemen—the ones who match you up and arrange your job interviews with yachts who are looking for crew. They then act as a liaison throughout the interviewing and hiring process.

Ultimately, a yacht's captain, owner, or personnel manager will make the decision to hire you. If you are hired as a stew through an agency, the agency will charge the yacht a percentage of your first month's salary. (And no, that money is not taken out of the pay you are to receive.) Therefore, it is not the crewmember's responsibility to pay to be placed; employers pay the placement fees once they have hired you.

In fact, never, under any circumstances should you have to pay money to a recruitment agency in order to be placed in a crew position. According to the new requirements of the ILO Maritime Labour Convention, 2006 (MLC 2006), it has been established that seafarer recruitment and placement agencies are not allowed to charge crewmembers directly or indirectly, in whole or part, any fees or other charges for recruitment or placement services or for providing employment to crew members (excluding the cost of the crew obtaining a national statutory medical certificate and a passport or other similar personal travel documents). [Ref MLC 2006 A1.4.5b, B2.2.2.4i, B1.4.1.2e] You can learn more at www.mlc2006.com. In the meantime, know that registering with placement agencies will always be free to you. So beware of online scams.

The Advantages of Using Crew Agencies

Going through the crew placement agencies isn't the only way to find a job, but it is certainly one of the most reliable and productive. Since the agencies only get paid if you get hired, they are more often than not making a sincere attempt to find you a position (the "not" being the case only if you make a bad impression on them). Since you are required to interview with the crew agents first, and then to continually check back with them as you add training and experience to your résumé/CV, using crew agencies will help keep you on track with your job hunt. Most crew agents really take the time to get to know the individuals they are trying to place, and in doing so, they can even serve as cheerleaders, inspiring you to stay motivated throughout your job quest.

Crew agencies are in the business of providing a professional service, which entails assessing the needs and requirements of owners, captains, and crewmembers alike. For this reason, some yachts prefer to work exclusively with the agencies to find their crew. They like the fact that a lot of the dirty work, such as checking references and licenses, has been taken care of for them. From your perspective as a job seeker, you can therefore feel a certain degree of confidence that the vessels interviewing you via the agencies are dedicated to finding the right candidate and having the very best crew onboard.

However, not all yachts rely on the crew agencies. If a captain or chief stew can shortcut the process and find someone on his or her own—either through public or Internet-based job boards, taking on and testing out day workers, or just by word of mouth—then obviously, it saves the yacht money in not having to pay placement fees. This doesn't mean that vessels not using agencies are less professional. In fact, most yachts will use a combination of all these methods when they are searching to fill a position. This is why there are alternative job-seeking methods that you want to pursue simultaneously to relying on the agencies—to make sure you cover all the various bases for finding the right job.

To start out, I recommend registering with a few crew placement agencies. Test your initial selections and make a genuine effort to get to know them and to show them all you've got. If several weeks go by with little response, then you might consider signing up with an additional source. After all, the more people you have working on your behalf, the better. Just know that using too many agencies can be counter-productive because you will be diluting your efforts and may even upset the agents who have been out there working diligently to promote you from the start. (A lot of the agencies will receive the same job orders, and it can end up being a question of, *okay, which agency was the first to set me up with this captain who ended up hiring me?*…In other words, who gets paid?)

As an entry-level job seeker, using crew agencies also benefits you because, even though you have no previous experience onboard a yacht, the crew agents will have met you and can vouch for your character. According to most crew agents I interviewed, it is not likely that a vessel will hire a candidate sight unseen, but when it does happen, it is usually because of a recommendation on behalf of the crew agency who has met and screened that person.

Crew Agency Hiring Process

The crew agency's role is to match job candidates with the needs of owners and captains. To kick off a relationship with an agency, you need to register with them and submit a résumé/CV, a list of professional and/or personal references, copies of any licenses and certificates, and a digital photo. (Preparing these items is covered in Chapter 10.) They will then handle all of the preliminary screening, which will include a review of your résumé/CV, along with research and authentication of all your certifications and work references (and they *will* run your references). You will also be invited to go in for an interview with a crew agent. The placement agents need to get a feel for who you are and make a face-to-face assessment that will allow them to best advise the captains and stews who contact them with job openings to be filled.

> ❖ **INSIDER TIP:** For best results with the agencies, do not register with them until you have your confirmed plans for when you can be in a hiring port to come meet with them in person. Most agents will not even move forward with the bulk of the screening process until this interview takes place. (And registering with them prematurely will only make you a nuisance.)

What happens next on the agency's end is that they receive a call from yacht personnel (a captain, chief stew, or purser, for example) regarding the need for a new crewmember. The crew agent takes down all the specific details of the job order, such as what qualifications and experience are necessary, what type of yacht it is, where the vessel will be traveling, and what the salary or pay package will be. They may even get information regarding the owners, existing crew, and what type of personality traits a prospective applicant should have.

The crew agent then searches the agency database for suitable candidates. Most all agencies are computer-based, so the software programs they use will generate a list of available job candidates who match the objectives specified by the yacht's hiring party.

The smaller agencies may still handle this matching process manually, but that is not necessarily a bad thing. They will usually have a smaller pool of candidates to sort through and may also deal with you on a more personal level, thus making a more sincere attempt to focus on finding you a position (which works especially well if the crew agent has a lot of industry contacts and a great reputation). The downside here is that these smaller agencies may not get as many job orders, nor will they deal with as many high-profile vessels.

Whether they are computer-based or not, all agencies search on criteria such as certifications (including STCW and specialized stew training), previous yachting experience, availability, and even what hiring port candidates are located in at a particular moment—whatever information they can use to determine the most perfect match.

Just about all of the larger crew agencies are Internet-based now, whereby you can keep your résumé/CV updated and remain in touch with them via login access to their website. These agencies give you the broadest chances of getting hired. With some agencies, the captains and owners can even log in to search their online databases for prospective applicants. Note that once you register online and upload your information to these agencies' sites, you still need to participate in an in-person interview with the company's agents before they push you for any jobs. For entry-level crew, phone interviews aren't going to cut it.

❖ **INSIDER TIP:** Crew agencies that are also Internet-based are one of your best options to register with because you can upload your existing résumé/CV from anywhere and then keep them updated on your whereabouts simply by going online. These agencies are also better equipped to match candidates all around the world, so you will not be limiting yourself to just one hiring port.

Please note that when I refer to Internet-based crew agencies, I am not referring to those that are solely web-based, with no physical office or agents in any hiring port. These website-only sites are where anyone looking for yacht jobs can randomly post résumés/CVs to be hosted and viewed online. It's not that I don't recommend those types of services (in fact, I discuss some good ones later in this chapter), just know that these websites are far different from the ones operated and managed by traditional crew placement businesses, who, although they have become more Internet-based, still actually review, screen, and meet with the candidates they place.

At this stage of the hiring process, emails are sent out to all of the candidates who match what the job order is requesting. When the position is a perfect fit, the agent may even call a candidate, to bring his or her attention to the opportunity. (This is why you want to get to know the agents well.) Candidates can then log in to their online file or call the agent to learn more about how the job is pertinent to them. Some agencies even allow their registrants to log on at any time and see a full list of all job orders waiting to be filled. Candidates must let the agency know if they are interested in the position. (For Internet-based agencies, this is usually a matter of just "ticking the box"; no one even needs to pick up a phone.) Once a pool of candidates has confirmed interest in the particular job, a placement agent reviews and narrows the batch down to a selection of five to ten applicants to present to the hiring party for consideration.

An agency should never recommend a candidate for a job unless they make the individual aware that they have done so. It is rare for that not to be the case since the placement agent wants his or her applicants to know they have been submitted so they can be prepared. (Remember, they only make money if you get hired.) Typically, the moment a candidate's information has been forwarded to a potential employer, an email goes out saying, "You have been submitted to this job # X, and the contact information is as follows…"

Ami Ira at Crew Unlimited estimates that about 70 percent of the time, it is the captain who does the pre-screening of candidates, while the other 30 percent, it's the chief stew. Somewhere along the line, there may also be input from the owner, but this is not likely on the larger yachts.

The crew agent may be involved in setting up an interview, but oftentimes, the captain or chief stew will contact the individuals directly. They may schedule to meet at the crew agency's office first, since it's a neutral ground. A similar choice would be in a public place, such as a local restaurant or Internet café (which is typical in Europe). Then, if the captain or chief stew holding the interview finds someone they like, there's a chance they will invite him or her to the yacht to meet the rest of the crew. It's also possible that candidates may be invited to the boat for the very first interview. And quite often, there may even be two rounds of interviews (for example, first interview by a chief stew, and a final interview with the captain). I cover how to handle the interview process and determine what job you want to take in Chapter 10.

It is usually the captain who makes the final hiring decision. After all, the captain is ultimately responsible for each crewmember's life, so the job has to go to someone whom he or she can feel comfortable with.

If you are offered and accept a position on a vessel, it is your responsibility to update the agencies of your intentions to take the job. And here, I mean every agency with whom you are registered—not just the one responsible for setting up the interview that led to your job. Don't burn any bridges. If there are other agencies you've been dealing with, let them know to take you off their lists so they are not working in vain to find you a job. With the Internet-based agencies, this usually just means logging in and changing your online profile to inactive status. (Although, if you've been working closely with another agent, a personal call would be the more professional thing to do… Remember, you may need their help in finding a different job in the future.)

Once you have accepted an offer, any further arrangements for joining the vessel are handled between you and the captain or hiring party. Most boats have a 30-day trial period before they will give you an actual contract to sign. The agencies themselves typically offer a three-month trial where they provide a replacement to the vessel for free if the first hire does not work out. You need not concern yourself with that, though; your own personal trial period with the yacht will likely just be 30 days.

It's Not Easy Being Green…

You have probably heard the term "green" used to refer to novices or people who lack experience when they first enter a new field or industry. Yachting is no different. In this industry, being green means you have never worked on a yacht before, and you are searching for your first job. (That's right, it has nothing to do with the expectation that you'll become seasick your first time at sea.)

Before I get into the disadvantages of being a newcomer to yachting, I will point out one of the positives, which is that you don't have any "bad habits" you may have learned on another yacht to carry over to the next one. Each vessel has its own way of doing things, and the last thing a captain or chief stew wants to hear is, "Well, we did it another way on the my last boat." For that reason, sometimes novices can be refreshing—a chief stew can get you onboard and train you to do things the way he or she wants you to do them.

It is still the case, however, that crew agencies have much better luck placing individuals with prior onboard experience. Be prepared that when you first begin registering with the crew agencies, they most likely won't pay much attention to you. Do not be offended by this. You need to realize that crew agents have people calling on a regular basis to inquire about the industry—people who may register and submit résumés/CVs (especially if there is no registration fee), but who then never show up for an interview, disappearing as quickly as they came. This is why it is important to show the agencies your heartfelt intentions by not only registering and submitting your information, but then getting in front of the placement agents for a face-to-face interview.

As I mentioned earlier, do not register with agencies in advance of getting to a hiring port, or until you can give them your scheduled date of arrival. Even then, without experience, it may take awhile before the agents begin putting you forward for jobs (or even warming up to you, for that matter). This is because they want to make sure you are a sincere candidate.

Here again is why having STCW basic safety training *and* a specialized stew training course on your résumé/CV is going to increase your chances of getting hired. The agencies will obviously feel better about recommending you for a position than someone who does not have these qualifications. Completing this training also shows you are serious about your desire to work in the industry. Agencies want to make sure that the individuals they recommend are top-notch. If you make a good impression on their staff by going about your job hunt in the most professional way possible (you take your courses, make your résumé/CV sharp, and perform well in your interview), they will remember you when quality positions become available.

And while it might not be easy being green, try spinning it as something positive when you are interviewing: "I love a challenge, and I cannot wait to learn everything I can as quickly as possible!" This approach works well with agents, and especially well if you ever get to interview with a chief stew.

What follows are some techniques for impressing the crew agencies.

Be Persistent

Once you are registered and have undergone your preliminary interview, it is smart to check back with the agencies on a weekly basis, if not more frequently, once you've acquired additional credentials. Keep them in the loop by letting them know what progress you have made in the way of training and day work. Also tell them where you are if you suddenly change hiring ports. When using the Internet-based agencies, make sure your files stay up-to-date, which again, is simply a matter of logging on and making the changes online.

Show You Are Eager and Dedicated to Your Quest

Even though the agencies might not pay much attention to you at first, do NOT wait to register with them until after you have your STCW and stew training certifications out of the way. Get them some form of preliminary résumé/CV either before or just after arriving in a hiring port. This not only allows you to have your personal interview right away, but it then provides you many opportunities to wow them.

Think about it. If you log in to your file or visit an agency's office to simply "check in on your status," but with nothing new to report, then you don't make much of an impact. However, if a week or two after your initial interview, you log in to update your résumé/CV because you've completed your STCW training and done three days of day work on a 170-foot yacht—needless to say the agencies will be very impressed at your "go get 'em" attitude.

❖ **INSIDER TIP:** The Internet-based agencies know exactly the last time a candidate got into his or her file and what was done (e.g. uploaded or changed something), so they can see who's active and eager. When crew agents log into their computers each morning, it puts you right in front of their faces to consider for the various job orders of the day. In fact, if you can log in once or twice a day, while making updates at least once a week, you're really putting yourself at an advantage.

Be Patient

You never really know when opportunity can land. The hiring process can take as long as a month or two, but you could find a job in one week, or even one day. This all depends on the season, and whether your profile corresponds with the jobs being offered at the moment. But no matter what your nationality might be, it's more about just getting to one of the top four hiring ports, making connections, and showing that you work hard, are eager to learn, and can get along with fellow crew.

Do not let a crew agent "convince you" that a certain job is one you should take. You need to remain selective and draw that conclusion for yourself. Because there is a placement fee at stake, there is that small chance a crew agent won't tell you all the potential negatives of a position. For example, the agent may know that a particular vessel has had a poor history keeping crew onboard due to a problematic owner, and he or she may withhold this information from you in an effort to get the job order (and maybe even you) off the agency's plate. In other words, do not think that a crew agent is always telling you what is in your best interest. Interview for the jobs and base your decision on what you feel.

And do not be afraid to conduct a little research on your own if you can. (This is another advantage to networking. Let the more experienced crew staying at your crew house know the name of a yacht you are considering interviewing with—you might just learn some scoop that could save you from a bad experience.) Of course, you can always do a little Facebook sleuthing to learn about existing crew as well. Just remember, an interviewer might also be looking into you, so be sure to have those privacy settings turned up and put your best foot...er, face forward online.

Get Registered

To select the agencies you wish to register with, see my list of recommendations that follows. Visit their websites and scope them out. I also recommend checking out their respective Facebook pages, maybe even give 'em a "Like" so you can start following news about the industry and get an idea of what types of jobs are posted. Consider looking up the agencies' other social media profiles as well; some have taken to Twitter, although for many, they don't tweet much.

If you want, you could consider sending a few preliminary emails to get a better feel for the various agencies. Just remember that they probably won't jump through hoops to help you out until you can prove your intentions are sincere. To start, simply introduce yourself, tell them you are going to be registering (or that you just did), give them a date when you plan on arriving in their location—quick, to the point, and be done with it until you can provide them with a bit more substance. I recommend having your arrival date set in stone before sending any emails.

Once you've scheduled an arrival date, upload a preliminary résumé/CV a couple weeks in advance of getting to town—but no earlier than that. If the date is more than a month out, you are wasting their time (and yours). If it's within a month, this will allow you to go ahead and schedule a day for an interview. When going this route, I suggest you note in your file or in a separate email that your résumé/CV is still in a rough stage and that you will update it as you add your STCW BST, stew training certifications, and day working experiences over the coming weeks. In fact, try enrolling in your training classes before even getting to the hiring port so that you can list "enrolled" and dates of "expected completion." This tells them you know what you have to do next and demonstrates that you are a bona fide, serious candidate.

Don't be offended if some agencies either don't reply to you or respond to let you know they are not interested in entry-level crew until you have experience. (I know, talk about a chicken-egg dilemma: which comes first?) It might just be that they don't wish to correspond until you've actually made it to town. Once you're physically there, it will be harder for them to ignore you. And once you're physically there with course certificates in hand, they'll warm up.

The items you should be prepared to submit to any crew agency upon registration:

1) Résumé/CV (Most agencies allow you to fill out an online application/résumé builder or upload an existing Word document.)
2) Scanned reference letters or a list of contact information for professional references (only use personal references if you have no previous work experience).
3) Scanned copies of licenses and certificates applicable to employment.
4) A digital, head and shoulders photo is preferred by most employers.

Crew Agencies in Fort Lauderdale, Florida

Following is a list of some of the most popular crew placement agencies in Fort Lauderdale. This is by no means an exhaustive list. Once you arrive in town, you will likely begin uncovering independent agents who are able to assist you. For additional options, as well as any updates to this information, you may check my website at www.WorkOnAYacht.com.

⇥ **Crew Unlimited**

069 SE 17 St. Causeway, 17th Street Annex, Fort Lauderdale, Florida 33316

Tel: 1-954-462-4624, Fax: 1-954-523-6712

Website: www.crewunlimited.com, Email: info@crewunlimited.com

Facebook: www.facebook.com/CrewUnlimited

Crew Unlimited is one of the longest-running crew agencies in Fort Lauderdale, with 22 years in the business. The agency offers exposure to over 3,000 current and previous luxury yacht clients. Crew Unlimited is an Internet-based agency, and you can register online via their website. After your information has been submitted, one of Crew Unlimited's placement coordinators will contact you to set up an interview.

Once you complete the registration process, you will be allowed to view and edit any of your information, update your résumé/CV, photo, and references at any time, and check-in online to see the current job list, 24 hours a day, 7 days a week. Crew Unlimited also offers video conference interviewing capability and free Internet access in their office. Note that Crew Unlimited has a summer office in Antibes. Be sure to check under "Events to Attend" in Chapter 9 to learn about Crew Unlimited's Annual Fort Yachtie-Da International Film Festival, held a couple weeks after the Fort Lauderdale International Boat Show. It's a fun event with great networking opportunities.

➡ **Luxury Yacht Group**

1362 SE 17th St., Fort Lauderdale, FL 33316

The office is located right off of the 17th Street Causeway, in the South Harbor Plaza.

Tel: 1-954-525-9959, Fax: 1-954-525-9949

Website: www.luxyachts.com, Email: info@luxyachts.com

Luxury Yacht Group is a one-stop shop for yachts, offering them not only crew placement services, but also yacht management, charter management, security officer training, and brokerage services. As a yacht management company, they offer their yachting clients free crew placement.

Luxury Yacht Group is another Internet-based crew agency. Online registration can be conducted anywhere in the world via their website. Once you have registered and submitted all your information, you will be contacted by the Crew Placement Division to set up a personal interview at their Fort Lauderdale office. Use their Internet-based service to later update your résumé/CV information, add experience and certifications, and apply for available jobs.

➡ **The Crew Network Worldwide & Fraser Yachts Worldwide**

The Crew Network—Fort Lauderdale

1800 SE 10th Ave., Fort Lauderdale, FL 33316

Tel: 1-954-467-9777, Fax: 1-954-527-4083

Website: www.crewnetwork.com, Email: fortlauderdale@crewnetwork.com

Facebook: www.facebook.com/pages/The-Crew-Network/265864406827522

The Crew Network's office is located in the Fraser Yachts building. This is off SE 17th St., behind the Embassy Suites and across from Outback Steakhouse.

The Crew Network (TCN) has been providing crew to the yachting industry for over a decade. The agency is the recruiting arm of the well-known brokerage firm Fraser Yachts Worldwide, a company whose services include yacht sales, the representation of brokerage motor yachts, international yacht charters, charter marketing, luxury yacht management, private yacht construction, and yacht crew placement. The Crew Network's global crew placement agents specialize in matching service-oriented, entry-level yacht crew as well as experienced and seasoned crew on a worldwide basis. With so many yachts under Fraser's management, The Crew Network always has jobs available for all different levels of employment.

An Internet-based crew agency, The Crew Network maintains three offices located around the world (Fort Lauderdale, Antibes, and Viareggio), each linked by an international database of crewmembers. You can register and make updates to your profile online via the agency's website. Crew are encouraged to update their employment status online or at any of its office locations. Every candidate that The Crew Network represents is thoroughly screened and pre-qualified by an in-person interview.

➥ **Elite Crew International, Inc.**

714 SE 17th St., Fort Lauderdale, FL 33316

Tel: 1-954-522-4840, Fax: 1-954-522-4930

Website: www.elitecrewintl.com, Email: placement@elitecrewintl.com

Facebook: www.facebook.com/elitecrewintl

Elite Crew International, Inc. specializes in the placement of professional, qualified crew for luxury mega yachts of 100 feet (30 meters) and above. Elite currently works to staff over 900 yachts worldwide. Because of their specialization in coordinating crew onboard the larger, more sophisticated vessels, Elite prefers that candidates have a minimum of one year's experience in the industry. In some cases, they will represent crew without previous yachting experience, but novice candidates must have necessary skills.

Elite's registration process requires that initial contact be made via email, fax, phone, mail, or in person. To determine if you qualify for registration, they will ask you to supply your full résumé/CV, a photo, and a minimum of four verifiable references for review by a crew agent. If you meet the Elite standard, they will advise you to complete an application and schedule an interview. A daily crew check-in form is available to registered applicants via the agency's website.

➥ **IMA Yachts Crew Solutions**

Contact: Beverly Grant

500 SE 17th St., #224, Fort Lauderdale, FL 33316

Tel: 1-954-583-1377, ext. 212, Fax: 1-954-522-2886

Website: www.imayachts.com, Email: b.grant@imayachts.com

As a professional yacht consultancy, IMA Yachts is also a highly specialized crew-recruitment agency that places crew for all positions, from deckhands to stewards and from yacht chefs to engineers to yacht masters. IMA leverages their extensive experience and personal relationships with owners, captains, and interior and exterior crewmembers throughout the worldwide yachting community to match the right person with the right position. IMA's systematic approach to crew recruitment is borne out in our achieving ISO 9001 accreditation—unique among industry professionals.

IMA Yachts has one staffing advantage that no one in the industry can match: Beverly Grant. Beverly served for 20 years as a superyacht charter chef and operated her own crew agency, Culinary Fusion, from 1997 until she joined the Grateful Palate for two years where she developed, crew placement, catering and provisioning, and the restaurant and wine bar. In 2012 Beverly joined IMA Yachts as the Director of Crew Solutions. Because of her background, Beverly is a wonderful resource on how to get started in the industry.

Scope of Services: Full-time Crew, Part-time Crew, Relief Crew, Day Workers, Estate Staffing, and Special Events Staffing

➼ **Northrup & Johnson Crew Services**
17 Rose Drive, Fort Lauderdale, FL 33316
Tel: 1-954-522-3344, Fax: 1-954-522-9500
Website: www.northropandjohnson.com, Email: crew@northropandjohnson.com
Facebook: www.facebook.com/njyachts

The Crew Services division of Northrup & Johnson is based in Fort Lauderdale. Northrup & Johnson is a global brokerage firm with six additional offices around the world. The company deals in everything from the sale, purchase, charter, management, and new construction of luxury yachts, to placing the crew that work on them.

For crew, Northrup & Johnson provide career advice, help with your résumé/CV, and overall guidance to optimize your chances of finding the right opportunity. You can create an account on their website where you will be able to manage your profile. Your background and qualifications will receive careful review upon registration. If they have a suitable opportunity, a representative from Northrup & Johnson's Crew Department will contact you.

➼ **MTS Yachts**
1041 S.E. 17th St., Ste. 100, Fort Lauderdale, FL 33316
Tel: 1-954-671-0003, Fax: 1-954-727-5206
Website: www.mtsyachts.com, Email: info@mtsyachts.com
Facebook: www.facebook.com/pages/MTS-Yachts-Crew/376729391506

MTS Yachts has been placing crew since 1998. It is an independent agency with a placement staff that are extremely experienced in yacht operations and supported by qualified marine officers. MTS Yachts places specialized and experienced crew, whether it is for temporary or permanent positions. Register online, answering all questions and attaching your résumé/CV. A personal interview will then be set up, ideally face to face where feasible, or otherwise by "Skype" with video or by telephone.

➼ **SPORTAble Crew Inc.**
501 SW 20th Street, Fort Lauderdale, FL 33315
Tel: 1-954-522-9954
Website: www.sportablecrew.com, Email: sporta@ablecrew.com

SPORTAble Crew facilitates employment opportunity for crews, vessels, and companies in the marine industry worldwide. Their mission is to match the best professionals with exactly the right placement—from engineers, pilots, and able-bodied seamen to chefs, butlers, and technical sales managers—whether at sea, in air, or on land. SPORTAble Crew is owned and operated by Suzanne Porta (a.k.a. SPORTA), a former yachtie with background in communication, sales, and marketing.

You may register with SPORTAble Crew via its website. Complete the registration form and upload your credentials, then call to schedule a face-to-face interview. Suzanne personally interviews, screens, and otherwise verifies suitability for the company to facilitate work. She then uses all reasonable and professional judgment to select the best candidate available at the time a job order is received, based upon the agency's experience with the candidate, information available, and the applicant's professional history.

→ **Nautic Crew International Inc.**

777 SE 20th St., Ste. 280, Fort Lauderdale, FL, 33316

Tel: 1-954-453-0097 or 1-954-453-9402, Fax: 1-954-530-2598

Website: www.nauticcrewintl.com, Email: info@nauticcrewintl.com

Facebook: www.facebook.com/pages/Nautic-Crew-International-Inc/32273941712

Founded by former yacht crewmembers, Linda and Darryl Leatheart, NauticCrew International offers its placement services out of Fort Lauderdale. You may register on their website.

Crew Agencies in Antibes, France

As you scan through this list of agencies, you'll notice that many of them are located in La Galerie du Port, a grouping of businesses in town similar to an office complex or shopping center. Let that be a hint that if you are looking for work out of Antibes, it pays to hang out in this area (pubs included). With many crew placement agents around though, be sure to be on your best behavior.

→ **Bluewater Crew**

7 Boulevard d'Aguillon, 06600 Antibes, France

Tel: 33 (0)4 93 34 47 73, Fax: 33 (0)4 93 34 77 74

Website: www.bluewateryachting.com, Email: crew@bluewateryachting.com

Facebook: www.facebook.com/pages/Blue-Water-Yachting/81710752968

Bluewater Crew is a traditional crew placement agency, with an Internet-based database of over 46,000 candidates that not only tracks career moves, but also lists qualifications, current situations, locations, references, and even personal information about what each candidate is ideally looking for. This online database of potential crew is accessible 24 hours a day for captains and owners to search, as well as for crew to make updates to their files.

Bluewater began as a crew agency in 1991 and subsequently has grown into one of the largest and most successful yacht crew recruitment agencies. The agency is centered in the main yachting hubs in the Mediterranean, with offices in both Antibes and Palma. As a company, Bluewater also provides yacht charter, yacht brokerage, crew training, and yacht management services. Be sure to visit its website for a wealth of good information about working on yachts.

To register with Bluewater Crew, fill out an online registration form. You can also call or visit the Antibes office to meet a member of their placement staff weekdays between 9:00 a.m. and 12:30 p.m.

→ **Camper & Nicholsons France SARL**

12 Avenue de la Libération, 06600 Antibes, France

Tel: 33 (0)4 92 91 28 90

Website: www.camperandnicholsons.com, Email: Use the website to send enquiry

Facebook: www.facebook.com/camperandnicholsons

Camper & Nicholsons Crew Placement Division provides professional crew for its renowned fleet of managed yachts. You are welcome to register online at the agency's website, which also contains very useful information for crew and is worth checking out.

↔ **Crew Unlimited (April 15 – October 15)**

La Galerie du Port, 30 Rue Lacan, 06600 Antibes, France

Tel: 33 (0)4 92 38 05 58

Website: www.crewunlimted.com, Email: france@crewunlimited.com

Crew Unlimited's summer office is open from April 15 through October 15 in Antibes, France. The same registration process listed for the head office in Fort Lauderdale applies.

↔ **Edmiston Crew**

17 Avenue du 11 Novembre, Antibes, 06600 France

Tel: 33 (0)4 93 34 09 30, Fax: 33 (0)4 93 34 69 96

Website: www.edmistoncompany.com, Email: crew@edmiston.com

Facebook: www.facebook.com/EdmistonCrewRecruitment

Founded by Chairman Nicholas Edmiston in Monaco in 1996, Edmiston is a yacht-management and yacht-sales company with offices around the world, and they offer crew recruitment services as well. As it states on their website, the company encourages new and fresh talent into the yachting crew industry. They will provide career guidance and advice on courses and will coordinate training to enable crew to obtain the essential operational certificates and licenses to ensure career advancement. You can register on the website.

↔ **Luxury Yacht Group**

La Galerie du Port, 8 Boulevard d'Aguillon, 06600 Antibes, France

Tel: 33 (0)4 89 12 09 70, Fax: 33 (0)4 97 21 37 84

Website: www.luxyachts.com, Email info@luxyachts.com

This is the Antibes office for Luxury Yacht Group. You are welcome to register online at www.luxyachts.com. (See the Luxury Yacht Group's full description under the previous Fort Lauderdale office listing).

↔ **Peter Insull's Crew Agency**

La Galerie du Port, 8 Boulevard d'Aguillon, 06600 Antibes, France

Tel: 33 (0)4 93 34 64 64, Fax: 33 (0)4 93 34 21 22

Website: www.insull.com, Email: crew@insull.com

Facebook: www.facebook.com/pages/Peter-Insulls-Crew-Agency/171423606225153

As the first Mediterranean-based crew agency, Peter Insull's Crew Agency was created in the late 1970's and can draw on nearly 40 years of experience to offer a superior service. Register online.

↔ **ReCrewt**

18 Rue Aubernon, 06600 Antibes, France

Tel: 33 (0)4 93 34 22 97 or 33 (0)615 40 01 34 (mobile)

Website: www.recrewt.com, Email: crew@recrewt.com

Sarah Plant originally came into yachting from a Merchant Navy background. After a three-year career in yachting, she held a four-year position in crew recruitment with a well-known and established yacht agency. With this knowledge and experience behind her, Sarah has since launched ReCrewt, her own company, where she specializes in crew placement that offers clients straightforward, impartial advice, and personalized service. Initial contact is best made by email, and you may fill out a registration form on the ReCrewt website.

↦ The Crew Network Antibes

12 Avenue Pasteur, 06600 Antibes, France

Tel: 33 (0)4 97 21 13 13, Fax: 33 (0)4 97 21 13 14

Website: www.crewnetwork.com, Email: antibes@crewnetwork.com

This is The Crew Network's first satellite office, which opened in 1998. You are welcome to register online at www.crewnetwork.com. (See The Crew Network's full description under the previous Fort Lauderdale office listing). Check-in any weekday morning between 9:30 a.m. and 12 p.m. at the Antibes office.

↦ Y.CREW (part of YCO Group)

1-3 Place de Revely, 06600 Antibes France

Tel: 33 (0)4 92 90 92 90

Website: www.ycrew.com, Email: antibes@ycocrew.com

Facebook: www.facebook.com/pages/YCREW/155100784613759

Y.CREW is part of YCO Group PLC, a collection of specialist companies providing services to the superyacht community, including yacht management, yacht sales and charter, project management, and crew placement. With crew placement offices in both Antibes and Palma, Y.CREW welcomes you to register for free on its website.

↦ YPI CREW

Résidence de la Mer, 6 avenue de la Libération, 06600 Antibes, France

Tel: 33 (0)4 92 90 46 10, Fax: 33 (0)4 93 34 47 08

Website: www.ypicrew.com, Email: info@ypicrew.com

Facebook: www.facebook.com/pages/YPI-CREW/179738895453836

YPI CREW is the result of the fusion between Yachting Partners International's 30 years' experience in first class yacht management, brokerage, and charter service, and Laurence Reymann's wealth of recruitment experience in and outside the yachting industry on the Côte d'Azur and abroad. Laurence manages the recruitment office. YPI's mission is to work in accordance to MLC 2006 to ensure that seafarers have access to efficient and well regulated seafarer recruitment and placement system. Registering on the YPI website is easy and straightforward.

Crew Agencies in Palma de Mallorca, Spain

↦ Dovaston Crew

Joan de Saridakis 2, Edificio Goya, Local 1A, Marivent, 07015 Palma de Mallorca, Spain

Tel: 34 (0)971 677 375, Fax: 34 (0)971 677 785

Website: www.dovaston.com, Email: info@dovaston.com

Fred Dovaston served as a yacht captain for 25 years. When he started this agency in February 1996, he knew from firsthand experience the needs of the industry's employers as well as those of the employees. While Fred passed away in 2008, his agency, Dovaston Crew, carries on.

With head offices in Palma de Mallorca, Dovaston Crew uses a unique database system, specifically geared to matching crew with specific job description criteria. Their screening process includes a structured interviewing technique in order to build a detailed picture of each individual's qualifications, level of abilities, character and personal needs. You can register online at the agency's website, which also allows you to view their current list of job requests without being registered first.

⤏ **Bluewater Crew**
Calle San Juan 4, La Lonja, 07012 Palma de Mallorca, Spain
Tel: 34 (0)971 677 154, Fax: 34 (0)971 676 993
Website: www.bluewateryachting.com, Email: crewpalma@bluewateryachting.com
This is Bluewater Crew's satellite office in Palma. (See Bluewater's full description under the previous Antibes listing.)

⤏ **Y.CREW (part of YCO Group)**
Calle San Magin 12A Bajos, 07013 Palma de Mallorca, Spain
Tel: 34 (0)971 402 878
Website: www.ycrew.com, Email: palma@ycocrew.com
This is Y.CREW's Palma office. (See Y.CREW's full description under the previous Antibes office listing). Register by visiting the website.

⤏ **Van Allen Group Recruitment**
Palma de Mallorca, Spain
Tel: 34 (0)871 960 694
Contact: Leticia Van Allen
Website: www.vanallengroup.com, Email: info@vanallengroup.com
Facebook: www.facebook.com/VanAllenRecruitment
Founded by industry veteran Leticia Van Allen, Van Allen Group Recruitment has built a web-based application to assist in matching the right candidate with the right yacht. The agency provides a quality service, without losing sight of the need for individual contact.
Van Allen Group of companies provides professional marine services to superyachts. Van Allen Group Recruitment is based in Palma de Mallorca and services yachts around the world.

⤏ **Crew and Concierge**
Palma Address: Paseo del Born 1, Apt 2a, 070012 Palma De Mallorca, Spain
Based out of St. Maarten during winter season.
Tel: 34 (0)608 228 242
Website: www.crewandconcierge.com, Email: info@crewandconcierge.com
Facebook: www.facebook.com/pages/Crew-Concierge/57981098068
Crew and Concierge (C&C) is an independent crew and concierge service based seasonally in Palma de Mallorca and St. Maarten. Not only can C&C assist with crew placement, but they can also help match crew with apartments in Palma. Crew and Concierge also offers a stew training course. With regard to crew placement, you can register on the website.

Crew Agencies in Newport, RI and West Coast, U.S.

↔ **Ship to Shore Crew Placement**

The Newport Shipyard, 1 Washington St., Newport, RI 02840

Tel: 1-401-846-3816, Fax: 1-401-845-8909

Contact: Sarah Baines, Skype: shiptoshoreglobal

Website: www.shiptoshoreglobal.com, Email: info@shiptoshoreglobal.com

Facebook: www.facebook.com/pages/Ship-To-Shore-Crew-Placement-Agency/199737426727925

Ship to Shore Crew Placement was started in 1999 by professional crew to respond to the ever increasing need for crew placement, services, and support in the busy harbor of Newport, Rhode Island. The agency places crew on luxury power and sailing yachts both in Newport and worldwide, with experience in the New England area to follow the careers of the crew and the progress of the luxury yachts that operate there.

Ship to Shore's office is based in The Newport Shipyard, a busy megayachting center, providing easy access for crew, captains, and owners. All crew are interviewed.

↔ **LaCasse Maritime, LLC**

Seattle Office: P.O. Box 1975, Edmonds, WA 98020

Seattle Tel: 1-206-545-2201, Fax: 1-206-260-3821

San Diego Tel: 1-619-523- 2318

Website: www.lacassemaritime.com, Email: info@lacassemaritime.com

LaCasse Maritime is a full service global crew and vessel support agency based on the West Coast of the United States and has been the answer for visiting superyachts for over 22 years. LaCasse Maritime has been in the marine business for more than 40 years and was one of the world's first full service professional yacht crew placement agencies. You can register online on its website.

Crew Agencies in the U.K. and Australia

↔ **Viking Recruitment Limited**

Viking House, Beechwood Business Park

Menzies Road, Dover Kent, CT16 2FG, United Kingdom

Tel: 44 (0)300 303 8191, Fax: 44 (0)130 482 7710

Website: www.vikingrecruitment.com, Email: info@vikingrecruitment.com

Facebook: www.facebook.com/pages/Jobs-at-Sea/121770547906020

Viking Recruitment is a well-known agency for crew placement aboard both superyachts and cruise lines. You may register on the Viking Recruitment website. Viking is very good about sending job vacancies out via Twitter. Find them at @ VikingRec. A full list of vacancies can be found at: www.jobs-at-sea.com.

↔ **Crew Pacific**

22 Minnie Street Cairns QLD 4870

Tel: 61 (0)7 4041 7243, Fax: 61 (0)7 4041 3163

Web: www.crewpacific.com.au, Email: crew@crewpacific.com.au

Facebook: www.facebook.com/crewpacific

Crew Pacific is based in Cairns, Queensland, Australia and provides crew to superyachts throughout the world, both motor and sail, and for all sizes ranging from 20-173m. In addition to listing job vacancies on its website, Crew Pacific also posts many of these on Twitter: @CrewPacific.

Originally established in 2001 by owner/operator Joy Weston, Crew Pacific is also a crew training school that specializes in servicing the needs of the international and national super yacht industry.

Crew Pacific also offers "Free Career Nights" throughout Australia, offering information about working on superyachts. Visit the website for dates and times.

→ **SuperCrew (Superyacht Crew Academy)**
Newport Anchorage Marina, Office 10, Marina level
79-81 Beaconsfield St., Newport NSW 2106, Sydney, Australia
Tel: 61 (0)2 9979 9669, Fax: 61 (0)2 9979 3463
Website: www.supercrew.com.au, Email: info@supercrew.com.au
Facebook: www.facebook.com/superyacht

SuperCrew is based in Sydney, Australia. Through SuperCrew's association with Superyacht Crew Academy, yacht crew undergo programs for professional career training on superyachts, insuring that owners and captains of foreign-flagged vessels have access to quality crew with IYT international commercial qualifications recognized by the Maritime Coastguard Agency (MCA).

Training Schools Placement Assistance

Many of the training schools listed in Chapter 7 also offer crew placement services for students having completed their courses. Listed in the previous section, some examples are Bluewater in Antibes and Palma, and both Crew Pacific and Superyacht Crew Academy (their agency being SuperCrew) in Australia.

International Crew Training in Fort Lauderdale is another training school that has an in-house recruitment and placement division, CREW.ICT. Registration is possible for anyone going through ICT's courses. You can find them at www.crew-ict.com. And while many of the other schools don't have officially named crew placement divisions, a lot of them can also assist with helping you get your first job. For example, MPT has a Student Services Staff and career counselors to help its students land a job after training.

The benefit of placement services being offered through the training schools is that the agents there have a great opportunity to get to know candidates. Do not underestimate the degree to which administrators and instructors can assist you with job leads. (Need I stress again just how tight-knit an industry this is?) Demonstrate your enthusiasm and eagerness to learn while taking your training courses, and it will no doubt pay off—the word will get out about you. Just remember that this word-of-mouth phenomenon can have the opposite effect as well, so give it your all when the eyes are on you.

The Online Job Hunt

Outside of the official crew agency websites, there are a handful of yacht-crew job listing/searching sites for all levels of crew positions. A couple serve as résumé/CV hosting sites, and their goal is to provide captains/owners and crew with a means to connect directly with each other during the hiring process, without an intermediary (crew agent). I definitely recommend giving these types of "cyber agencies" a shot. The three that I list in this section are Crew4Crew.net, JF-Recruiting. com, and FiveStarCrew.ca. Not only are these verified, but I've received very positive feedback with regard to all three. Crew4Crew.net has a physical office in Fort Lauderdale and gets my highest recommendation for a number of reasons, which you can read about under its listing. I recommend subscribing to the RSS feeds of these sites and following them on social media to keep an eye on job postings.

Beyond that, there are a couple online job-search sites where you can register and apply for specific jobs that catch your eye. They work slightly different and are separated out for that reason. Yacht Crew Register, while based online, operates more like traditional agencies. And SuperyachtJobs.com is more of a job aggregator that will then funnel you over to the traditional agency that has posted the job—from there you must register with the respective agency to apply. Either of these options are a great way to learn about job opportunities.

I round out this section with some additional information about online forums and other types of job boards, as well as a couple things to be aware of with regard to online scams.

Internet-Only Crew Agencies

Here's how these agencies work: Crew are able to register for free, whereby they can post a résumé/ CV and then view active positions on the site, applying to any position for which there's a fit. Note that you'll be replying directly to the employers; in other words, there's no middle man. It's the employers—likely captains and owners—who are paying for the service (and are how these agencies make money). So, with that in mind, know that this method of securing employment is not going to be as useful for novices. And here's why: The benefit of having your résumé/CV viewed by captains and owners around the world means you would need to be qualified enough to stand out. You would also typically need to be in the same hiring port where a captain can arrange to meet you, and even then, experienced crew will definitely have the most luck. Since it's a free service, it couldn't hurt to give it a shot, but you should still attempt using traditional crew agencies and trying to find day work.

What I DON'T recommend is that you take part in any similar type of yacht-crew jobs website where YOU are the one who must pay to register. (As I explained earlier, you should never have to pay a recruiter of any kind to offer you placement services, especially since the passing of the MLC 2006.) I address this further on in this chapter, but most of these sites are fly-by-night: here today, gone tomorrow, and predominantly filled with spam. You can check for updates on my website to see if I've uncovered any additional Internet-based agencies that are legit, but for now, I'm warning you not to get sucked into some online "service" where you have to pay to have your profile and CV hosted, or even to search jobs. Again, the three recommendations I make below are funded by the hiring parties—employers—and the employers benefit by not having to pay more expensive agency fees when crew are placed. There are advantages and disadvantages there, but it is now an option for employers, and many crew are finding jobs this way.

Here are the four agencies that I do recommend registering with; although, again, be realistic in doing so if you are brand-spanking new to the industry with zero experience and no certifications yet:

➻ Crew4Crew.net—www.Crew4Crew.net

1093 SE 17th St., Fort Lauderdale, FL 33316 (Next to Waxy's)

Tel: 1-954-764-8995

Website: www.crew4crew.net, Email: support@crew4crew.net

Facebook: www.facebook.com/pages/Crew4Crew/134608359943733

Twitter: @Crew4Crew_net (worth following for notice of job postings)

Crew4Crew.net was created for yacht captains and owners hiring crew to have direct access to all professional yacht crew available for employment without having to paying commission. Employers pay a subscription fee to access professional yacht-crew CVs and employment files. It was also created to give crew an equal opportunity to be considered for positions without being fielded by an agent (there is no interview requirement). The agency offers commission-free online crew placement and a wide range of job opportunities worldwide.

How Crew4Crew differs from the other online-only placement services (and why it gets my highest recommendation among agencies of this sort) is that they have a physical location in Fort Lauderdale. They offer a serene crew lounge with work stations and Wi-Fi access, where you can go hang and take advantage of in-office crew support, including crew business card production, document scanning, and résumé/CV writing services. Crew4Crew also offers a Managed Qualified Profile service where they create your profile, scan documents, resize and convert files, offer résumé/CV feedback, and update content for six months.

Another cool benefit is that you choose to complete either a "Standard" or "Qualified Profile." Standard Profile is the basic option and the default when you first register and upload your résumé/CV resume and profile photo. After that, you are made available to employers immediately. A Qualified Profile is the more advanced, professional option that will allow you to set yourself apart from other crew by indicating that your profile meets a certain professional standard. Employers are more likely to find crew efficiently with a Qualified Profile. There is no fee for either option, but with Qualified, you'll need to get a checklist of the requirements and submit all of their requested information and documents. It's much more time-consuming, but worth the effort.

Aside from choosing the Qualified Profile option, here are some quick tips for using Crew4Crew.net:

- Log in regularly to keep your profile at the top of the available crew list for the position you are seeking. This also lets employers know you are available.
- Check the Job Posting Board and apply directly to posted positions. The employer's profile maintains a record of your application and provides a direct link to your profile and all of your uploaded files.
- Do not apply for a job if you do not meet the minimum requirements listed. Employers report crew that abuse the job posting system and those crewmembers are no longer allowed to use the site.

➡ **JF-Recruiting—www.JF-Recruiting.com**
Tel: +1 954 604 6298 or 34 (0)971 57 09 67
Website: www.jf-recruiting.com
Facebook: www.facebook.com/pages/JF-Recruiting/153708861306034
Twitter: @JFRecruiting (worth following for job postings)

Owned and operated by Jonathan Franklin, this is another Internet-only crew recruitment database for yachting jobs worldwide. Register online where you then post a résumé/CV and provide two references. From there, you'll be able to view active positions on the site's Job Board page. Candidates can then apply directly to employers. Once you've registered, you must maintain your active crew status by logging into your account every 14 days.

Judging by the Job Search listings I've seen, there are some pretty good opportunities available through this service. I would try it. You can also register for the RSS feed to keep tabs on the postings.

➡ **Five Star Crew—FiveStarCrew.ca**
Website: fivestarcrew.ca, Email: karen@fivestarcrew.ca
Facebook 1: www.facebook.com/pages/Five-Star-Crew/158314280855254
Facebook 2: www.facebook.com/pages/Five-Star-Crew-II/229490427090501 (crew bios only)
Twitter: @FiveStarCrewca

Five Star Crew is a professional megayacht crew-job listing site for both experienced crew as well as newbies internationally. Register at www.fivestarcrew.ca; the site has about the shortest registration process out there (no photos) and allows megayacht crew to post and manage position postings. The ads appear on the main page in the chosen category. The agency keeps an eye on who is registering and applying, and crew benefit from a two-click application process once registered.

Run by Karen Murray, Five Star Crew also communicates with crew through its Facebook page. It even has a second Facebook page dedicated to letting crew post biographies for all hiring parties to peruse. Both pages are very popular. The website also has an RSS feed you can subscribe to, and the agency is active on Twitter. The site does not accept non-yacht positions (so no land-based jobs), nor are cruise or commercial ship positions permitted.

The final thing I'll say about the type of agencies just mentioned is that they do offer a more direct way of both searching for jobs and being sought out by employers. That can be useful, but the downside is that, without a crew agent intermediary, both employers and job seekers carry a lot more risk. Without proper screening on both sides, you never know what you're going to get. This can make things more time consuming, especially on the side of employers, who are the ones typically benefitting from having the more professional agencies checking references, pre-interviewing, and getting to know the candidates. From the crew perspective though, without knowing who's behind these jobs (especially for those new to the industry), you might be playing with fire a bit. Proceed with caution. And also know that this type of job search option will likely be much more valuable to you once you've been in the industry awhile and know what to look out for (and also have enough experience to attract good employers).

Online Job Search Sites

Now, here are two additional options for you, at least in terms of searching out available job openings and applying if you see a fit. I highly recommend looking at both:

➻ **SuperyachtJobs—SuperyachtJobs.com**
Operated by the very reputable The Superyacht Group, which publishes The Crew Report magazine
Facebook Page: www.facebook.com/superyachtjobs
Twitter: @SuperyachtJobs1 (a great feed to follow)

SuperyachtJobs.com provides a space for crew at all levels to explore the superyacht jobs market. It is a portal for all recruitment companies, managers, agents, and yachts to promote vacancies and secure the most experienced teams for new and existing yachts. Jobs available, jobs wanted, day worker vacancies, relief crew, training courses, and career advice form the backbone of this website, with a view to encouraging new people to explore the large-yacht world and see it as a professional career and not a short-term opportunity. Think of it like a content aggregator, gathering up jobs from partnered agencies and making them available to job candidates in one place. You can also register on the site to allow employers to access your profile and accompanying résumé/CV.

If you wish to apply for any positions though, you'll be linked over to the agency that has posted the listing. From there, you'll have to go through the actual agency, not directly with the employer. Still, as you move to decide which agencies with whom you might register, this is a great way to go in with a purpose—that is, by having spotted that job you know you're perfect for.

➻ **Yacht Crew Register—yachtcrew.ca**
Website: www.yachtcrew.ca
Facebook: www.facebook.com/YachtCrewRegister
Twitter: @yachtstews (for stews)

Yacht Crew Register is an independent yacht-crew placement agency focused solely on crew placement for the maintenance and operation of private and charter yachts. Owned and operated by Darcy Narraway, Yacht Crew Register has been successfully placing crew since 1995 while providing personalized service with the same clients for close to twenty years.

This Internet-based agency operates a bit different from the others. View listings of available jobs, and to apply to ones where you see a fit by sending your résumé/CV, photos, and references to the specially designated email addresses for your position. Darcy will arrange to interview applicants if there's a match. Note that he specializes more in the placement of captains, so stew jobs may not be as plentiful.

To keep an eye on job postings, follow the Yacht Crew Register Facebook page or look on the website for Twitter feeds that are specific to positions sought. For stews, that is @yachtstews.

Online Bulletin Boards, Forums, and Scams

As I mentioned in the previous section, if a service makes you pay upfront for a direct link to employers, I advise you to run in the other direction. 1) That's no longer allowed with the passage of the new MLC 2006 in August of 2013. And 2) Over the last seven years since this book first came out, I have seen more of these websites come and go than I have seen become successful.

The same holds true for sailing forums and "boat job" searching sites. Many of them are trying to operate in a similar way to Crew4Crew.net and JF-Recruiting, but they are failing miserable at it. I often find that links on sites like this lead to error pages and messages saying they've been removed. Either that, or I can't find much hint of recent activity. On the few sites that do show signs of life, they only carry job postings for either high-level professional marine crew or hardcore, temporary sailing positions, the latter of which are most likely unpaid anyway. And I do not recommend online bulletin boards where people can just post items freely with no moderation, as most of them are out of date. Hanging out in any of these types of forums will very likely be a waste of your time.

There are only two services similar to these bulletin board sites that I *do* recommend you try:

1) The first is the online classified ads site run by *The Triton* (mentioned previously).

2) The second such site is YachtForums.com—an online forum dedicated to the yachting industry. Unlike many of the other industry forums on the Internet, YachtForums.com is moderated, up-to-date, and widely read. Visit the website at www.yachtforums.com and look under the section "CAPTAINS & CREWS." From there, the subsection "Yacht Crews" is where crew are able to find work, network, find accommodations, and get help and advice from other yachties. This site is also a wonderful resource to learn about the entire yachting world, in general. Especially the boats themselves. (Beware of salty dog captains with chips on their shoulders; they'll be rude just for the sake of it. Keep your posts straightforward and professional.)

Of course, I'm always hearing about new websites and forums to check out, so I will gather feedback, and if it's worth adding them to this list, I will add them to my website. Be sure to check www.WorkOnAYacht.com to see if any new ones have turned up since this book was published.

Lookout for Yacht-Crew Recruitment and Training Scams

Finally, be on the lookout for online scams, not only with regard to crew placement and recruiting, but also with "online training certification" offers. I've uncovered a number of these over the years. In many cases, it is former crew trying to make a quick buck by offering "how to get a yacht crew job" advice, much of which you're reading here in this book anyway. Certainly, purchasing a quick e-book guide can't hurt—and for anyone seeking out more specific information on deck and engineer jobs, they could benefit from advice catered to those positions. (Although, outside of some additional entry-level coursework, the second half of this guide is about all individuals need to begin a job hunt.) More important, you shouldn't have to spend more than what you paid for this book to get that education.

And by no means is it necessary to sign up for a subscription-based website that charges you monthly for access to jobs and "how to" information. They just want your money, and many of them charge a small amount so that you register and then forget about it. With such minimal fees, you may not notice $4.99 or $9.99 hitting your bank account each month; but believe me, it adds up. (And for the people running the site, it certainly adds to the lining of their pocketbooks when they get hundreds of eager crew fooled into thinking it's useful for them to do.) Take it from me: I've been working in Internet marketing since 2004, and I know how these sites work. Don't fall into the trap. This information is available all over the Internet for free anyway. (Just look at all the job-listing and crew-recruitment sites I offer you earlier in the chapter.)

The worst scam I've seen up to now is one offering a "superyacht crew diploma," whereby you pay several hundred dollars/euros for access to an online portal of information, again, most of which you're reading in the very book you have in front of you now. These websites will try to tell you their "diploma" is internationally-recognized, but that's a load of B.S. As it is, the official governing bodies of this industry have a hard time agreeing upon what coursework and training is required and recognized, so there's no way any online certificate is going to be worth any value to you when you arrive in a hiring port. Crew agencies and current crew will laugh you off the dock if you turn up with one of these in your hand, bragging that you've been endorsed by some sketchy website run by people who don't even post their official names. Run the other direction.

Unfortunately, it doesn't stop there. Edmiston Crew Recruitment Agency has reported that there are some scams out there offering crew jobs that even go as far as to issue bogus appointment letters. After that they get wanna-be crew on the line, they are charging up to 900 euros to arrange for a U.K. visa—for a job that doesn't exist. This is another one to look out for.

Day Working

Day work is short-term, freelance work. You don't live aboard the yachts that hire you for day work; rather, you stay in a crew house while you are working. Prior to, and even during peak seasons, day working opportunities are plentiful in the various hiring ports because a lot of vessels require extra help beyond what their full-time crew can provide.

There are a variety of reasons why a need for day workers can arise. A vessel may be trying to get out of a shipyard and could use additional workers to assist in completing projects; the crew may be rushed because an owner is coming onboard a few days later and they need help getting the boat ready on time; or maybe a crewmember was just given a vacation, and the captain wants someone to stand in. Regardless of the reasons, a yacht's demand for day workers equals an opportunity for you.

And yes, day working pays off in many ways. First of all, this is a way you can make some quick, cash-in-hand money to help cover your living expenses and training costs while you job hunt. Regardless of how much money you bring with you when you move to a hiring port, you don't want your bank account to be whittled down by the costs of everyday needs such as food, shelter, cell phone bills, and entertainment. If you initially bring enough to live for one month, chances are you aren't going to tap into that savings too far until you find some day work to keep you going (or until you find the right permanent job).

Doing day work while job hunting and taking training classes is also a way to gain skills and become more comfortable with how the industry works. I honestly cannot imagine having interviewed for a job without ever having stepped foot on a yacht beforehand. You will want to take on as much day work as you can to add to your résumé/CV, because this will prove you've had at least some experience working on a boat. Day work can also lead to permanent jobs.

"Any day work is good experience because it shows that you are keen to work in the industry. Not to mention, it will keep the wolf from the door while you are looking for a job."
—**Lynne Cottone**, Crew Placement Specialist at Luxury Yacht Group

Day Work Pay

As a day worker, you will be paid an hourly or daily rate, and lunch with the rest of the crew is typically included. When being hired to handle simple interior or deck work, wages tend to range from $12–$15 an hour, with $12 per hour being standard (perhaps a bit more in European ports) for entry-level crew. If it's a job that requires special skills, you could find it's higher, but that is mostly for work done by engineers or experienced deck crew. For the shorter-term jobs, this money is also tax-free and most always paid in cash. Therefore, a couple days' work can actually cover your accommodation costs for the week.

As a day worker, you will typically put in a full, eight- to nine-hour day, which includes a lunch break, along with usually two additional short breaks (what the British call "tea breaks"). As stated above, most all boats will cover your lunch, but you never know what to expect, so be sure to ask ahead of time so as not to feel slighted if they don't invite you to eat onboard.

Using Day Work to Network

Day working is very useful for the purpose of networking. Every boat you accept day work on will provide you the opportunity to meet and work alongside current professional crew, some of whom may have great advice, or even the ability to help get your name out there. If you can befriend these veterans, you never know how it might pay off.

Be sure to be on your best behavior and to work your very hardest in every day working situation—even if you're just onboard for one day. Dress appropriately, show up on time, be eager to learn, and always go above and beyond what is required of you to demonstrate that you will make an excellent crewmember on that, or any, yacht.

It is important that you bring a copy of your résumé/CV when you show up for day work. There are some boats that will actually require you to present this document just for the day work job. The beauty of day work is that it's a free ticket into some of the otherwise restricted shipyards and marinas, so once you're in the gates, be ready to hand your résumé/CV to other boats if the opportunity should present itself. More importantly, you never know when a yacht may be looking for a permanent crewmember (or when someone on that boat knows someone else who is).

❖ **INSIDER TIP:** Your résumé/CV is your main networking tool. Don't leave home without it—especially when heading off to day work. I recommend carrying some copies that are sealed in an envelope marked "Captain" or "Chief Stew" so that lower-ranking crew are more likely to pass it along to the appropriate person. (Otherwise, they could look at you as a potential job-stealer and toss your résumé/CV into the bin as soon as you've walked away.)

How Day Work Can Lead to a Permanent Job

A lot of yachts use day workers in order to find new crewmembers, since they can try someone out and test his or her compatibility with the rest of the crew. You might not even be aware that you are being considered for a full-time position. The crew could already be short on staff or trying to find a suitable replacement for someone whose last day is approaching.

Really, any day working opportunity could end up leading to a full-time job offer, whether planned or not. A disgruntled crewmember could suddenly quit or get fired the day after you are brought on to work. You just never know what is going to happen in the yachting industry. When you manage to get onboard as a day worker, this is your chance to strut your stuff. Approach each one of these opportunities with the mindset that a crew position could open up at any moment. If a captain or chief stew is really impressed by you, he or she will either make room for you onboard or refer you to associates who may be looking for crew.

How Day Work Can Help Build Your Portfolio

Day working allows you to obtain work references. If a particular job lasts longer than three days, be sure to ask for a reference letter on how you performed. Captains are accustomed to writing these letters and oftentimes have pre-written versions on file where they simply have to change the name. If they feel you've done an extra good job, they may even go out of their way to personalize it to reflect your enthusiasm and hard work. Captains are not required to write references for you, but again, you should always ask (especially if you've been employed for two weeks or longer). When doing so, approach him or her a day or two before your work onboard is set to finish, and be sure to ask in a polite and professional manner.

If you have only been working on the boat for three days or less, the captain may not have met you, nor would he or she have had a chance to assess your skills. In such instances, at least ask for a letter stating that you did, in fact, complete the work. Just be upfront. Explain that because you are trying to break into the industry, you could use some proof that you now have some onboard experience. If asking the captain does not seem like a possibility (and captains are usually very busy), then going to the highest ranking crew member who oversaw your work, such as the chief stew or 1st mate, is the next best thing to do. Having watched you complete tasks, they will often be the best to comment on your performance, anyway. Additionally, these crewmembers might be flattered by your request for their reference and will put a lot more time and effort into it.

Finally, all day work experience is something you can (and will!) add to your résumé/CV. Consider this a living document. For each day working job, you need to have an addendum that says what yacht you worked on, the amount of time you were there, who your supervisor was, and include a phone number to contact that person. You'll find that day working allows you to improve your level of competency with new or existing skills. Be sure to make note these accomplishments on your résumé/CV as well (and update all online versions accordingly!).

How to Find Day Work

There are many ways to find day work. One of the easiest, as I mentioned in the last chapter, is staying in a popular crew house, where calls often come in from yachts needing crew. In fact, a lot of the crew houses now offer services to assist crew in finding these opportunities.

Fort Lauderdale-based The Neptune Group offers an Internet-based day work database where crew can both post their own availability, as well as search day work job requests that come in on a daily basis. Once offered only to residents of their crew houses, The Neptune Group has recently extended this service outside of Lauderdale to cover all of the main crew hiring ports around the world. Now, anyone looking for day work opportunities can visit www.theneptunegroup.com and click on the "Day Work" link to register (this will redirect you to www.daywork123.com). You are also able to upload your résumé/CV to be listed under the Available Crew section. You can also check the site for job announcements that employers have posted. I highly recommend you look into this.

Additionally, make your availability to day work known by posting notices on some of the online crew-publication sites. You'll want to consider the Dockwalk.com forums and The-Triton. com's online classified ads section. (See the Trade Publications section further in this chapter.)

Another way to find out about day working jobs is through the crew agencies. Alert the agencies to the fact that you are willing to accept day work at a moment's notice if they get requests. The more jobs you take through them, the more they will continue to recommend you—that is, provided the feedback is good. It is important when taking a job through an agency that you really go all out to make it a good experience.

Getting leads through the network of contacts you'll be making at your crew house, in yachtie hangouts, and after other day working experiences are common ways to obtain day work. Here again is why you want to get to know and befriend as many people in the industry as possible. Whenever you meet fellow yachties, even if it's on Las Olas Boulevard in downtown Fort Lauderdale or at the Provencal Food Market in Old Antibes, tell them you are looking for day work. Public job posting notice boards, which I will discuss later in this chapter, are also a place to advertise your availability to accept these short-term positions.

And finally, there is dockwalking—a job hunting method that deserves its own section:

Dockwalking—For Temporary or Permanent Positions

One of the most common ways to find day work, and also permanent positions on yachts, is what those in the industry refer to as dockwalking.

The concept: You head down to where you know the boats are, whether that's the marinas, the shipyards, or the nearest port. You walk along the dock near these boats and boldly walk up to each passerelle/gangway and ask if a) they have any day working vacancies for the day, or b) they are looking to hire a new stew. (I suggest beginning with the day work question.)

Yachts in need of day workers tend to be on the lookout for dockwalkers. Most current crew have all done dockwalking at some point in their lives, so you should not feel silly or shy about approaching them. If anything, you will be networking just by talking to whatever crewmember happens to be standing out on deck in the morning.

To be successful at dockwalking, you must make a commitment to start early in the morning because it does tend to get competitive at times. Most yachts officially begin their work day at 8:00 a.m., so I suggest getting started prior to this, at 7:30 a.m. Go out dressed for work—khaki shorts, deck shoes, and a polo shirt are your best option, but a nice t-shirt will also do (after all, whatever you wear is likely to get dirty). And bring your résumé/CV, which you will want to have printed on nice stationery and placed in some type of see-through presentation folder to protect it from water (or spilled coffee).

Be discreet when walking up to these yachts, because there could be guests onboard. Don't lurk around waiting for someone to come out on deck. You must also never step foot on a yacht without permission. If you don't see anyone within a close enough distance to grab his or her attention, you can ring the intercom button (if one exists) on the end of the passerelle. However, if guests are onboard, this could backfire. My suggestion is that you make your first walk-through of the area looking for yachts with crewmembers on deck. If there are none, move to the next yacht down and come back later, or another day.

Once you start talking to someone onboard about what opportunities exist, if you are completely new, tell the person that. He or she may empathize with you and want to offer you a break by having you on for the day. Or, sometimes they'll say, "Well, we need someone who knows how to do such and such." Here again, if you cannot do what it is they require, be honest. Don't take on jobs you can't handle, because that will only frustrate people and earn a strike on your reputation. Finally, even if you get turned down for day work, be sure to ask if the yacht is looking for permanent crew. If they say no, make sure you follow up by asking them if they know of any yachts that are.

Do not be discouraged if you try many boats and still haven't had any luck. It could take awhile. Make sure to hit different places. If you have no results in one marina, then by all means, go to another one the following day. If marinas are not working, head to the shipyards; if the shipyards are not working, try the docks along the port. And remember, you can always check back with the agencies.

And be sure to leave a business card behind, for while a boat may not need anyone that day, they may two weeks later. While they may lose track of a bulky packet of résumés, your card may just get passed along or set in a place where they'll run across it later.

Challenges for Dockwalkers

Some marinas and shipyards prohibit dockwalking. This has become even more and more common in recent years, and it's only likely to get worse as security measures continue to increase. Make sure you know the rules before you try to enter any marina (and I don't recommend trying to climb any gates either). At the very least, you might be able to leave your CV with the dockmaster and hope it gets passed along.

Alternatively, if you have trouble getting access into the marinas and shipyards, try lurking around some of the coffee shops and breakfast restaurants just outside the gates of these facilities during the early hours of the morning. You will easily be able to recognize crew coming in by their yacht t-shirts; perhaps you can strike up a conversation, then just casually mention that you're new to town and looking for day work. Hell, buy 'em a coffee and tell them you'll work for free that day. Let the stewardess know you're willing to take her least favorite task for that day off her plate, even if it means ironing sheets or polishing silver (maybe that will remind her that the silver hasn't been polished in months).

Either way, know that dockwalking isn't as easy as it used to be due to stepped-up security at these dock facilities. So get clever, be eager, and have persistence.

❖   **INSIDER TIP:** If you are very sincere, offer to work a day for free to show what you can do! You'll probably learn something and you can add the experience to your résumé/CV.

Non-American crew, beware: It is illegal to accept day work while in the U.S. There were even rumors of non-U.S. crew being deported when they were caught dockwalking at the 2010 Fort Lauderdale International Boat Show, even though they were only calling upon foreign-flagged vessels. (If true, it doesn't sound fair—but hey, rules are rules.) In fact, as backwards as it sounds, you are able to come to the U.S. as a non-American citizen and look for a permanent job on a foreign-flagged vessel based here (which you can do via the crew agencies), but it is illegal for you to dockwalk and look for day work on those same vessels. Hmmm (scratches head)... go figure.

As for American crew, you might want to steer clear of seeking out day work on islands such as St. Martin/St. Maarten and Antigua. I encourage you to do a search online for updated information on how difficult this has become in recent years. While these island are both yachting hot spots during the winter, if you're not already networked well enough to find work "behind the scenes" (via existing crew by phone or text), you can get into some serious trouble if caught looking for work. If you've exhausted your search in Lauderdale past mid-December and feel you must head to the islands, seek out online how you might apply to get a work permit before buying a ticket to these places.

Make Business Cards

To step-up your efforts, try making up business cards to hand out, letting people know you are available for day work (and for permanent jobs, too). These are great to take to networking events, or even just out to the yachtie bars. Anymore, you can make these on your own online and send them to a local print shop. Some crew houses may also have printers. Information to include:

- ➥ Name
- ➥ Citizenship
- ➥ Contact info (mobile number and email address)
- ➥ Bullet-pointed certifications, qualifications, and any other pertinent information from your résumé/CV.
- ➥ Be sure to also include the words: "Looking for Full-Time Stewardess Position: Entry-Level. **Also Available for Day Work.**"

I Must Confess...
I screwed up my first time day working...(and I even took my toothbrush!)

When I first started looking for a job in the industry, I accepted an offer for day work. I was hired by a 140-ft. yacht to help the full-time stewardesses get the vessel ready to exhibit at the Miami Boat Show coming up a week later. The boat was going to be shown off to potential buyers and charterers, so it was essential that every inch of the interior be spotless.

Nervous for my first day of day working (or working on any yacht, period, for that matter), I turned to the more experienced crew staying in my crew house for advice. There was one thing everyone agreed upon as for how to make a killer first impression:

"Take a toothbrush," I was told.

That's right, a toothbrush. And no, it's not because I was to expect a last minute invite to an onboard slumber party. Rather, I was advised to use it as a cleaning tool. One experienced stewardess I lived with referred to it as "a magic weapon," and another called it, "a stew's best friend." As silly as I felt (*are they playing a joke on me?* I wondered), I showed up for my first day work job with my trusty toothbrush in tow.

My assignment on the first day was to clean the master cabin and its accompanying bathroom (the most elaborate "head" on the yacht). Well, I got right to it… I scrubbed, and I cleaned, and I polished, and along the way, I came to understand what the stews back at my crew house had been talking about. What better way to get into every possible crevice when cleaning something than to use a toothbrush? Ridges in the ceilings, build-up around tiny faucet fixtures, discoloration in the grout surrounding marble floor tiles…right down to the toilets. The only cleaning utensil that may give the toothbrush a run for its money as far as attacking those hard-to-reach places would be a cotton swab.

In the end, I thought I did what would be deemed an impeccable job. (But *thought* is the key word there.)

I still remember the disappointed look on the chief stewardess's face as she scanned the results of my labor. Surveying my mirrors and floors, and all around the knobs and door handles, she scrunched up her nose the way people do when the smell of something is not to their liking. She was obviously not happy with my work.

As she turned to me to comment, I swear she took on the image of Miss Hannigan in the musical *Annie*, when she shouts to the orphan girls, "You'll stay up 'til this dump SHINES like the top of the Chrysler Building!" Or maybe it was the movie *Mommy Dearest* and the "No more wire hangers!" routine. Either way, she suggested quite sternly that I pay more attention to detail. I realized then there was definitely a lot more to learn in this line of work.

The moral of this story? The toothbrush alone does not the good stew maketh. (But use it anyway.)

Trade Publications—Online and Offline

I highly recommend becoming an avid reader of the industry trade publications that are available in your chosen hiring port (and also now online), and keep a close eye on the classified ad sections for stew job listings. If you have gone several weeks with little response from the agencies, and you are feeling your momentum lag, taking out your own classified ad to market your availability is a terrific idea.

All of the industry publications have online editions, and many have websites that not only contain additional news and information, but also feature public forums, job listing boards, and even some online networking opportunities. Of course, don't forget to connect with them online via Facebook, Twitter, and other social media platforms, too.

Publications Based in the U.S.

The Triton and *Dockwalk*, listed in this section, are also available in Mediterranean ports. They are published out of the U.S. though, so they will tend to have a stronger emphasis on news and events happening in Fort Lauderdale, Newport, and the Caribbean. *The Crew Report*, which you'll find listed under the Mediterranean section, is also distributed in the U.S., as is *Yachting Pages*. (And of course, you can get them all online.)

⇥ *All At Sea – Southeast*
Website: www.allatsea.net
Facebook: www.facebook.com/AllAtSeaSoutheast

A monthly, full-color magazine that is literally *All At Sea* with full coverage of yachting, fishing, cruising, sailing, and the waterfront lifestyle. Truly is the pulse of the Southeast region's boating scene, *All At Sea* is distributed throughout nine coastal Southeast states from the mouth of the Chesapeake Bay down through the Carolinas, Georgia, Florida, and the Gulf Coast to Texas. Found at over 1,500 marinas, boatyards, marine service providers, and boating haunts throughout the region.

⇥ *Dockwalk*
Website and Social Network: www.dockwalk.com
Facebook: www.facebook.com/pages/Dockwalk/37807917475
Twitter: @dockwalk

Dockwalk comprises *Dockwalk* magazine, Dockwalk.com and Dockwalk events—crew parties and The Captains' Hideout at two of the largest boat shows. Around since 1998, Dockwalk has its finger on the pulse of the yacht-crew community.

A monthly, full-color glossy magazine, *Dockwalk* magazine is an excellent resource for all kinds of superyacht-crew news. With lots of articles and photos to browse through, you'll gain a closer look at the yachtie lifestyle in this magazine; it entertains, informs, and, above all, helps crew pursue their chosen career. Written by both current and ex-crew for crew, *Dockwalk* really gets under the skin of the industry from the crew's perspective. Published out of Fort Lauderdale, the magazine is widely distributed around key superyacht ports in the USA and Europe. Pick up a free copy the first day you are in town. (Most likely, there will be plenty of copies lying around any crew house you choose to stay in.)

Better yet, a digital version of the monthly magazine is made available online if you have a Dockwalk.com account. And I highly recommend creating one, as the website also features additional content and news not found in the magazine. Furthermore, the site also operates as a social network, allowing captains and crew to keep in touch with their friends and colleagues around the world. With a profile on Dockwalk.com, you can include a résumé/CV, list past and current yacht jobs, add photos and videos, create blogs, participate in forums (another job-hunting bonus), and even connect with other crew by adding friends and using the internal messaging function (a great way to start networking, mind you!). The majority of the content on the site is "user-generated," and the forum is one of the most active in the industry; members can view the latest jobs available (posted by crew agents and other members), and browse upcoming training courses from the leading training schools around the world. It's definitely something you want to check out!

In addition to various Dockwalk-organized parties throughout the year, the publication also hosts The Captains' Hideout during the two biggest superyacht shows in the world—the Monaco Yacht Show and the Fort Lauderdale International Boat Show. This venue offers a VIP area for captains and crew to network and relax away from the show. Once you become a crewmember, you'll qualify to attend. Meanwhile, you can look for parties open to a wider audience but staying informed on Dockwalk.com.

⇥ *The Triton*
Website: www.the-triton.com
Facebook: www.facebook.com/tritonnews
Twitter: @TritonNews

This is a monthly yachting news (their tagline is "Nautical News for Captains and Crews") publication that is online and in print. You can find it the Fort Lauderdale area and seasonally in the Mediterranean, Caribbean, as well as other yacht ports in the United States like Newport, R.I. and on the west coast. You can pick up a free copy at nearly any crew agency and many local yachting businesses. Thousands of crew also follow their Facebook page (listed above) for up-to-date news. They also publish a daily *Triton Today* at the Fort Lauderdale International Boat Show, Miami Charter Show, and Palm Beach International Boat Show.

The Triton includes a section known as "Earning Your Stripes—Career News for Captains and Crews," where yacht crew can find information to help them manage their yachting careers. You will find articles from working crew like stews and chefs, as well as information tailored to crew's needs on international laws, regulations, certifications, medical issues, finances, travel, and more. Search online at www.the-triton.com for topics of interest.

You can also place classified ads online, for free, stating that you are looking for work (or peruse available jobs). You read that right: The-Triton.com allows crew looking for jobs to place FREE classified ads. To do this, you need to sign-up on the website and create a profile. For your ad, you are able to create a brief overview (250-character limit), and a longer description for employers to read once they click on your profile. Be sure to add a photo and a catchy title so that you stand out. Remember, these will only appear on the website (which does get a lot of targeted traffic), not in the printed paper.

While I recommend this opportunity, I would not do it until you can state that a) you have your STCW certification (or that you are taking it that week), and that b) you have taken a stew training course. As someone with no previous experience on a yacht, you need to have those two qualifications to get noticed in the public classifieds. Be sure to also state your citizenship and some small fact about you that helps compensate for a lack of yacht-job history.

Here is something you could try for the brief 250-character overview (although, don't use this verbatim; you are probably not the only person reading this book):

American female seeking entry-level stew position aboard M/Y. STCW, ENG 1, PYA intro stew-training certificate; detail-oriented, strong work ethic, restaurant service experience; non-smoker w/ no tattoos. Ft. Lauderdale-based. Available for day work.

Notice I did not state much about what I, as the job seeker, am looking for, other than that I specified my desire to work on a motor yacht (M/Y) as opposed to a sailing yacht. The reason I left out details such as whether I wanted to work on a private or charter yacht, whether I had any itinerary preferences, or what type of vessel I wanted to work on (American or foreign flag) is that you don't want to sound picky. You're the humble, new kid on the block, and you want all the leads you can get. After all, you could get a call from a captain whose job opening isn't a match, but that person could prove to be a good contact for other job leads. In the beginning, you take all interviews you can get.

Here is an example of what this might look like for a more experienced stew (notice the caps for emphasis of specific training):

Australian charter-yacht stewardess seeking long-term stew position. I have my B1/ B2, STCW, SILVER SERVICE, BARTENDING, FLORAL ARRANGING, and ENG1 certificates. Non-smoker w/ no visible tattoos. Available for Skype or in-person interviews in Antibes.

The-Triton.com also lists job openings posted by captains and owners. Check this weekly! Here is the type of entry-level posting you should look for:

Stew needed for busy 130' charter yacht. 6 crew and up to 8 guests. Foreign flag; based in Miami. Headed to the Med for the summer. Immediate start. Non-smokers only. Will accept entry-level with some proven skill. Must have STCW & ENG1.

Note that you quite often don't find mention of salary or pay packages in these public notices. Those are more likely to be found on the online list of jobs posted by the crew agencies (which require registration with the respective agencies to access).

Signing up at The-Triton.com will also allow you to receive a weekly email with the most current and pertinent information specifically for yacht crew (you can opt-out of that if you want to, but give it a chance, it's full of events, courses, and links.) And then there's The Triton's crew networking events—attending these is a must!

❖ **INSIDER TIP:** If you are job hunting in Fort Lauderdale, you will want to attend *The Triton's* crew networking events, held on the first Wednesday of every month, and usually on the third Wednesday also. These events bring several hundred captains, crew, and industry professionals together at different locations (chosen by the businesses that sponsor them) and have light food and beverages. *The Triton* also hosts an Expo several times a year around boat shows. These usually have about 30 vendors in the industry including crew agencies, schools, and other companies that help in being a successful crewmember. Usually *The Triton's* events are in Fort Lauderdale, but they are sometimes held in Newport , R.I. and Antibes. See their website or check out the latest issue for information on where the next event is being held.

↔ *Waterfront Times*

www.waterfronttimes.com

Facebook: www.facebook.com/pages/Waterfront-Times/119864491389555

Twitter: @WaterfrontTimes

Waterfront Times is a monthly publication that is a good source for news on what's going on in the yachting world, but it is geared more toward the local boating community. It covers the issues, challenges, and trends of South Florida's coastal neighborhoods, including Broward Country (Fort Lauderdale), West Palm Beach, and Miami. Printed versions of the paper are distributed to marine businesses, marinas, and restaurants in Broward County. The online edition features listing of marine resources for Broward, Dade and Palm Beach counties.

Most of the classified ads placed here are for captain positions or crew on smaller vessels, but if you're looking for a creative way to look for work, you could try placing one (or at least check it for "help wanted" ads). You can check this resource for various types of local boating events to attend, too.

↔ *Yachting Pages*

www.yachting-pages.com

Facebook: www.facebook.com/captainsbible

Twitter: @YachtingPages

See listing under the Mediterranean section. While *Yachting Pages* is based in the Med, they publish three separate editions: (1) USA, The Americas & Caribbean; (2) Mediterranean, Europe, Africa & Middle East; (3) Australia, Asia Pacific & Far East. All directory information can also be accessed online from anywhere in t he world.

Publications Based in the Mediterranean

The Triton and *Dockwalk*, listed in the previous U.S. section, are also available in these Mediterranean ports. Likewise, in this next listing, *The Crew Report* is also distributed in the U.S., as is *Yachting Pages;* they are published out of Europe though, so they will tend to have a stronger emphasis on news and events happening in the Mediterranean ports. (And of course, you can get them all online.)

↔ *The Crew Report*

Website: www.crewreport.com

Facebook: www.facebook.com/TheCrewReport

Twitter: @TheCrewReport

The Crew Report appeals to every yacht crewmember and all those in the industry who want to be kept up to date with issues facing today's large yacht crew. Editorially it offers invaluable information on key subjects such as safety, security, attitude, technology, operations, guest services, and other mentoring topics are covered, coupled with regulatory and career-based knowledge.

The Crew Report is a must-read publication and totally free of charge. You will find it distributed at various yachting businesses and hangouts in the key industry ports on both sides of the Atlantic, although it is published in the U.K. Once you are on a boat, *The Crew Report* is also sent to superyachts free of charge; if superyacht crew do not receive the magazine onboard, they need only contact the publication, and they'll make sure it's received.

I recommend registering on the website at www.thecrewreport.com (where you will also be able to download a PDF copy as soon as it's published); it as a valuable resource for industry news and networking opportunities.

↔ ***Yachting Pages***
www.yachting-pages.com
Facebook: www.facebook.com/captainsbible
Twitter: @YachtingPages

Since 2004, *Yachting Pages* has been firmly established as the most comprehensive superyacht purchasing resource for Captains and crew, shipyards, refit yards, and all superyacht businesses. *Yachting Pages* is available either in its original printed form, or online.

- **Yachting Pages Printed Directory:** Often referred to as the "Captains Bible," the annual A5-sized, high quality print directory is the superyacht industry's first point of reference for contact details of over 13,000 superyacht companies around the world. Broken down into headings and then into countries, the directory couldn't be easier to use. Yachting Pages is available in three separate editions: (1) Mediterranean, Europe, Africa & Middle East; (2) USA, The Americas & Caribbean; (3) Australia, Asia Pacific & Far East.

- **Port Maps:** The Port Maps section at the front of every edition totals over 350 detailed maps of the world's superyacht marinas. The port maps can also be found online, complete with description, images, promotional offers, news, and reviews.

- **Yachting Pages Online:** Yachtingpages.com is a tremendously useful online resource for Captains, crew, and superyacht industry professionals. The comprehensive search engine helps users to quickly find exactly what they're looking for. You can refine searches by country, port, category, product, brand, and service to find contact details, reviews, and promotions from superyacht businesses all over the world. The website also has a wealth of interactive information for the industry, providing daily news, reviews, and up-to-date information on boat shows, industry events, port maps, and much more.

↔ ***The Riviera Reporter* Magazine—Antibes**
Website: www.rivierareporter.com

This publication is geared toward the English-speaking population living in the French Riviera (a haven for British expatriates). There is very little directed at the yachting industry, and no classifieds pertaining to yacht work. However, it is a good resource for local products and services information while you are staying in this area. You can view the most recent edition online.

Publications Based in the Caribbean

↦ *ALL AT SEA* – The Caribbean's Waterfront Magazine

Website: www.allatsea.net

Facebook: www.facebook.com/ALLATSEACaribbean

All At Sea has been covering the marine industry in the Caribbean for 20 years. Who would have thought that the small little "fish wrapper" newsletter would evolve into what it has become—the voice of the Caribbean Marine Industry. From Jamaica throughout the island chain to Aruba, *All At Sea* is a community magazine providing local news and entertainment, and promoting this nautical paradise to the world. *All At Sea* is distributed throughout the Caribbean, as well as in geographic areas that are staging points for yachts coming to the region, including over 400 distribution locations in South Florida alone.

↦ *Caribbean Compass Newspaper*

Website: www.caribbeancompass.com

Southern Caribbean-based monthly newspaper with feature articles and news on cruising destinations, regattas, events, the Caribbean environment, and marine-related businesses.

↦ *La Regata*

Website: www.laregatapr.com

Facebook: www.facebook.com/pages/La-Regata/167048387288

Spanish-only newspaper covering the fishing and sailing scene in Puerto Rico. Great on the scene coverage of the Puerto Rico lifestyle. Truly in the heart of things.

Networking—Making Connections and Meeting the Right People

Networking is going to be crucial to your job search. No matter what port you are in, make an effort to meet people, talk to people, gather information, and keep track of who you meet. Network with people in your crew house. Network with other students in your STCW and stew training courses. Network with the instructors at the various training centers. Get out there and dockwalk at local marinas and shipyards, and even if you find there is not much work available, try hard to make connections with the people you speak with on the dock.

My one piece of advice is this: everyone you meet in the yachting world opens up an opportunity; *but*, it works the other way, too. The more people you turn off, the more it can come back to haunt you. The yachting community is very tight-knit, despite the fact that its reach spans the globe; and when something happens, it doesn't take long for word to travel. I worked with a first mate on a yacht in the Mediterranean who cheated on his girlfriend—she was on a boat in the Caribbean. It took less than 24 hours for her to find out about his escapades "through the grapevine." And it was later determined that it was a very crazy series of conversations—many yachting ports were involved along the way.

My point in that little anecdote demonstrates why I give you this advice: the second you step foot in Fort Lauderdale, Antibes, Palma, or wherever your job search takes you, you must mind your P's and Q's at all times. This industry is HUGE, and also very, very small. Especially when living in a crew house, it is crucial to not create any drama or get involved in any activities that could come back to haunt you in your quest for a job.

Public Job Boards in Yachtie Bars (and other places people post)

Internet cafés and other popular places where yachties hang out may just have a designated jobs board, and I would be sure and use these. They are great places to pin up those business cards I told you to make. Funny enough, I used to find job-wanted postings in the bathrooms of the yachtie bars. I suppose it can't hurt to try this, but I would only do it if there's a designated board for it. Otherwise, the bar staff will only take it down.

I also recommend frequenting (but not hassling!) local businesses that cater to the yachting community, such as crew uniform shops, private mailbox and postal/shipping service centers near the marinas and shipyards, nautical book and map stores, and specialty food and wine shops where yachts are known to provision. These are excellent places to network.

Get Out and About in Port

Oftentimes jobs are found just by being in the right place at the right time or through contacts in the industry. Some of the right places are the businesses where current yacht crew are circulating. Do not pester these places, but if you casually drop in and just keep your ears open, you never know what opportunity may pop up.

Following are some suggested places to visit, or even frequent, in order to get yourself connected within the yachting community:

Networking in Fort Lauderdale

Big hint: Attend *The Triton's* crew networking events, held on the first Wednesday of every month, and usually on the third Wednesday also. See back under their listing for more details.

Yachtie Bars and Restaurants in Fort Lauderdale

- ↔ **TAP42 Bar & Kitchen**—Tap42 is one of the newest and hottest spots for the yachtie demographic to meet up. Opened in 2011, it also has one of Fort Lauderdale's finest selections of American craft beers, hand-crafted cocktails, and also craft beer cocktails. Located near Maritime Professional Training and within walking distance to many popular crew houses, Tap42 has a huge patio with plenty of tables and space to enjoy the fresh air, plus tons of free parking: 1411 South Andrews Ave. Fort Lauderdale—Tel: 1-954-463-4900—Website: www.tap42.com.
- ↔ **Waxy O'Connor's Irish Pub**—Authentic Irish bar and restaurant offering traditional music and international rugby matches via satellite TV. Waxy's (as most yachties call it) has been very popular with the yachting community for over well over a decade and is a great place to be on Friday and Saturday evenings. Located at the intersection of SE 10th and SE 17th next to Smallwood's and Crew4Crew: 1095 SE 17th St., Fort Lauderdale—Tel: 954-525WAXY—Website: www.waxys. (There's also a location in Miami, along the Miami River.)
- ↔ **15th Street Fisheries**—Plan to head here via the world-famous Water Taxi (look for the 'Cruise & Save" symbol and save with your ticket)! A restaurant offering fresh fish

and seafood, the Fisheries is situated on a prominent point directly inside the city's most famous nautical landmark, Lauderdale Marina, just north of the 17th Street bridge, Port Everglades, and Fort Lauderdale's inlet to the Atlantic Ocean: 1900 SE 15th St.—Tel: 954-763-2777—Website: www.15streetfisheries.com.

➻ **The Village Well**—This is a bit more of a dive bar, but a favorite among yachties, especially those who like to shoot pool. A bigger bonus is that it stays up until 2 a.m. on weeknights and 3 a.m. on weekends. Located in the same parking lot as Waxy's: 1023 SE 17th St.—Tel: 1-954-524-2531.

➻ **Tarpon Bend** Open daily, Tarpon Bend serves up lunch, dinner, and a legendary happy hour. The menu consists of America classics, highlighted by daily fresh catches and an array of raw bar items. Located in a fun part of downtown Fort Lauderdale just one block from the Broward Center for The Performing Arts: 200 SW 2nd St.—Tel: 1-954-523-3233—Website: www.tarponbend.com.

➻ **Bimini Boat Yard & Grill**—Restaurant serving lunch and dinner. Fresh local seafood; a great spot for Sunday brunch. Located on the water—1555 SE 17th St.—Tel: 954-525-7400—Website: www.biminiboatyard.com.

➻ **Hyatt Regency Pier Sixty-Six Resort & Marina**—Visit the Pelican Landing that is located dockside, overlooking the Intracoastal Waterway. This is a spot for catching a sensational sunset. 2301 SE 17th St. Causeway—Tel: 954-525-6666—Website: www.pier66.hyatt.com.

➻ **Chuck's Steak House**—Restaurant serving dinner seven nights a week from 4:30 p.m., and lunch from 11:30 a.m. Also features a lounge with full bar. Located at 1207 SE 17th St.—Tel: 954-764-3333—Website: www.chucksflorida.com.

➻ **Southport Raw Bar**—Restaurant offering fish, oysters, clams, and more. A local and crew favorite. Located just off SE 17th St. on the Intracoastal Waterway: 1536 Cordova Road—Tel: 954-525-CLAM—Website: www.southportrawbar.com.

➻ **The Quarterdeck Seafood Bar & Neighborhood Grill**—Family-style seafood restaurant, also very popular with the local yachtie community, especially for lunch. 1541 Cordova Road—Tel: 954-524-6163—Website: www.quarterdeckrestaurant.com.

➻ **Elbo Room**—A Lauderdale institution (it celebrated 75 years in business in 2013), the Elbo Room has the rare distinction of being a two-level dive...with a patio and balcony, too. Located along the A1A: 241 S Atlantic Boulevard, Fort Lauderdale Beach—Tel: 1-954-463-4615—Website: www.elboroom.com.

➻ **Casablanca Café**—While not flooded with big groups of yachties, the Casablanca Café is on one of Fort Lauderdale's scenic beach areas and is a perfect place for cocktails at the bar or a romantic dinner overlooking the ocean. If you dig piano bars, this is your spot, with live entertainment seven nights a week. Conveniently located on Fort Lauderdale Beach at Alhambra Street between Las Olas Boulevard and Sunrise Boulevard on A1A: 3049 Alhambra St.—Tel: 1-954-764-3500—Website: www.casablancacafeonline.com.

Other Fort Lauderdale Businesses with a Yachting Connection

➻ **Liquid Yacht Wear**—Yacht Uniform Shop—Liquid Yacht Wear is a boutique specializing in updated, fashion forward, and functional yacht-crew uniform. Having catered to the yachting industry for over 10 years, Liquid has created its own brand of uniform to meet the needs of today's crew. (For examples, see my book promotional pictures—and might I recommend the adorable scarves!).

Owned and operated by designer Theresa Morales, Liquid Yacht Wear's mission is "to help create unique and practical uniforms that are distinctive to each yachts character; incorporating both Liquid's own uniform and other major brands." And they certainly do just that. Thanks to Theresa's vision, stew uniforms have become much more fashionable since I was working onboard.

I highly recommend dropping in the shop if you're in Lauderdale. They carry super cute tees you'll want to wear around the town. And be sure to ask about the discount offered to new stews needing a uniform for interviews.

Located right off U.S. 1: 1512 South Federal Highway—1-954-523-8875—Website: www.liquidyachtwear.com.

➡ **Smallwood's Yachtwear**—Yacht Uniform Shop—Located at the corner of 17th St. and 10th Ave., directly across from the Embassy Suites Hotel, Smallwood's Yachtwear is a crew uniform shop that provides a free listing of job opportunities in the yachting industry. The staff at Smallwood's invites job-hungry crew to drop by the store to peruse what is known as "The Jobs Book." This book lists crew job openings posted by captains or owners. New listings are added almost daily, so it's a good idea to check in often. Smallwood's also allows crew searching for jobs to add their résumé/CV to their "job-wanted" books, which are organized according to crew position.

Please note: This service is only offered to those coming into the Smallwood's storefront. Under no circumstances will the staff offer this service over the phone. If you decide to take advantage of this free job-finding method, be courteous when visiting the shop. Dress appropriately (not only is this a place of business, but it's quite possible you could meet your future employer while looking through the books) and do not interrupt the sales staff while they are with customers. Do take a pen and paper for copying down contact information on job leads.

➡ **Big Blue Yachtwear**—Yacht Uniform Shop—Another great uniform to check out. Big Blue was founded by Amanda Connor in 2000, primarily as a reaction to the extreme lack of attractive and properly-fitting uniform options for women working in the yachting industry. The staff at Big Blue are great, too. Located at 1366 SE 17th St.—Tel: 1-954-525-7840—Website: www.bigblueyachtwear.com.

➡ **Bluewater Books & Charts**—A 5,000 square foot retail bookstore with more than 35,000 nautical books and charts in stock, Bluewater Books & Charts has been in business since 1986 and is America's largest seller of nautical books, paper charts, and electronic charts. (The first edition of my book was a bestseller there for several years in a row.) With an incredibly helpful and friendly staff, this is certainly a great place to see and be seen. Located in The Harbor Shops: 1811 Cordova Road—Tel: 954-763-6533—Website: www.bluewaterweb.com.

➡ **Brownie's Yacht Diver**—Scuba Diving Shop— Brownie's Southport Divers is a top of the line scuba equipment and gear provider in Fort Lauderdale. Located at 1530 Cordova Road—Tel: 1-954-524-2112—Website: www.yachtdiver.com.

Networking in Antibes

Yachtie Bars and Restaurants in Antibes

- **The Drinkers Club**—A popular hangout for superyacht crew, this is also a great place to watch sporting events. Located at 12 Rue Aubernon.
- **The Blue Lady**—In the heart of the yachtie area of town, this is an English-style pub. You'll find many a crew interview happening here by day. It is an excellent spot for networking by night, too. Located in Galerie du Port at Blvd. d'Aguillon.
- **The Hop Store Irish Pub**—Located off the busiest pedestrian street in Antibes, The Hop Store Irish Pub's enormous terrace is hard to miss, especially since it's usually overflowing with yachties: 38 Blvd. d'Aguillon.
- **The Quay's**—English pub and very popular yachtie bar. Formerly was Le Gaffe. They have karaoke on Thursdays, which while fun, tends to attract more local people than yachties (not that that's a bad thing).—Located at 6 Blvd. d'Aguillon.
- **The Colonial**—Yachtie bar.—36 Blvd. d'Aguillon.
- **The Lincoln Bistrot**—34 Blvd. d'Aguillon, next door to The Colonial.
- **Stars 'N' Bars**—American sports bar, restaurant, nightclub, and cyber café, offering game arcade and televised English and U.S. sports. Menu includes American and Tex-Mex specialties and weekend brunch. Located at 6, Quai Antoine 1er, in the port of Monaco.

I've also received word that Happy Face and Latino Bar have also been quite popular as networking spots in Antibes. Another tip is that you can get free Wi-Fi at the Grand Cafe de la Gare opposite of Gare d'Antibes (the railway station), which attracts a lot of yachting professionals like crew agents on their lunch break, captains, and other crew looking for work.

Other Antibes Businesses with a Yachting Connection

- **Dolphin Wear**—Yacht Uniform Shop—12 Blvd. d'Aguillon—Tel: 33 (0)4 93 34 03 08—Website: www.dolphinwear.com.
- **Sea Design**—Yacht Uniform Shop— 3 Avenue Tournelli—Tel: 33 (0)4 93 74 74 53—Website: www.sea-design.com.
- **Liquid Yacht Wear**—Yacht Uniform Shop. See the listing under Fort Lauderdale. This is Liquid's Antibes Showroom …An easy walk from Port Vauban: 23, rue de General d'Andreossy—Tel: 33 (0)6 83 94 91 78—Website: www.liquidyachtwear.com
- **Workstation Internet Café**—A fabulous place to post job-wanted information—Offers high-speed Internet access, email, printing facilities, faxing, telephone, translations, and UPS shipping. Located at 1 ave Saint Roch, near Port Vauban—Tel: 33 (0)4 92 90 49 39.
- **ASA Internet Café**—High-speed Internet connections, e-mailing, and word processing—6 Rue du Marc—Tel: 33 (0)4 93 34 55 84.
- **Geoffrey's of London**—English & American specialty grocer located in La Galerie du Port, rue Lacan—Tel: 33 (0)4 92 90 66 40—Website: www.geoffreysoflondon.com.

↔ **Heidi's English Bookshop**—Large range of English books, cards, stationery, and videos. Located at 24 rue Aubernon—Tel: 33 (0)4 93 34 74 11.

Please visit my website for more listings in both Fort Lauderdale and Antibes, as well as popular networking spots for yacht crew in other key hiring ports around the world, including Palma de Mallorca and Newport, Rhode Island.

Events to Attend

Yachts will sometimes need additional help to prepare for being exhibited at large boat shows. This can mean an abundance of day working opportunities in the weeks leading up to these events. By being in the area during these shows, you may also find boats being sold where the crew will change over completely.

Following is a list of some of the more popular boat shows taking place in the hiring ports I have suggested to you. If you happen to be in these ports during the time these events take place, great, but do not go out of your way:

↔ **Fort Lauderdale International Boat Show (FLIBS)**—The World's Largest Boat Show—Late October. If you are currently trying to decide where to head when, I certainly recommend being in Fort Lauderdale in time for this boat show at the end of October. For more information, visit www.showmanagement.com.

↔ **Miami International Boat Show & Strictly Sail—(followed by The Yacht and Brokerage Show)**—Mid to Late February. The Miami Boat Show is held a bit earlier than when you ideally want to arrive in Fort Lauderdale to begin looking for work into the summer; however, if you do end up making it down to the area in time, do not miss this event—it would make a good kick-off to your search due to the networking you could manage. For more information, visit www.miamiboatshow.com and www. showmanagement.com.

↔ **The Palm Beach Boat Show**—West Palm Beach, Florida—Late March—A great time to be headed to the Fort Lauderdale area to look for summer work. For more information, visit www.showmanagement.com.

↔ **Cannes International Film Festival**—Cannes, France—Mid-May—While I don't necessarily mean expect to attend any film screenings or celebrity soirees, this is a great time and place to be positioned in the Med to look for work. The summer yachting season truly kicks off with this event. For more information, visit www.festival-cannes.org.

↔ **The Newport International Boat Show**—Newport, Rhode Island—Mid-September, just before yachts head back to Fort Lauderdale from the summer season. This is usually a huge extravaganza. For more information, visit www.newportboatshow.com.

↔ **Monaco Yacht Show**—Monaco, France—Late September—This event is held just as boats are wrapping up the Mediterranean season and heading into a transitional phase. If you are jobless in the Med at this time, definitely attend and look for work on yachts heading back across the Atlantic for the winter. For more information, visit www. monacoyachtshow.com.

- **Antigua Charter Yacht Meeting**—Antigua, West Indies—Early December—If you have been in Fort Lauderdale for a couple months with no permanent job offer, but you have taken your training courses and have met face-to-face with all the placement agencies, you may consider repositioning yourself to the Caribbean for the winter. It will be much easier to secure a position because you will be where the boats are. Antigua, during this charter yacht show, or St. Martin/St. Maarten, are both great options. For more information, visit www.antiguayachtshow.com.

- **Newport Charter Yacht Show**—Newport, R.I.—Mid June—A showcase of luxury charter yachts alongside a display of ancillary boating goods and services for the charter-yacht industry, this event is heavily attended by charter brokers and vendors. More importantly for crew, this event kicks of the New England Yacht Charter Season. Just prior to and after this show is a great time to obtain work. Visit www.newportchartershow.com to learn more.

And finally, a great crew-oriented event to attend just after the Fort Lauderdale International Boat Show, put on by Crew Unlimited crew agency:

- **Annual Fort Yachtie-Da International Film Festival—Fort Lauderdale—Early November**—Each year, Crew Unlimited hosts a video contest for yacht crew to write, direct, and produce 5-minute video shorts to compete for up to $1,000 plus their own "Oscar" trophy. The awards ceremony, similar to the Academy Awards, will announce the winners and provide an opportunity to celebrate each year's productions. If you're in Fort Lauderdale just after the boat show, get tickets for this event! For more information and to view past entries (a fun way to learn more about the people who work in this industry), visit www.fortyachtieda.com or the official Facebook page here: www.facebook.com/FortYachtieDa.

10

FIT TO BE HIRED
—RÉSUMÉS/CVS, INTERVIEWS, AND
ACCEPTING YOUR FIRST JOB!—

If you'll recall from the Quick Guide at the beginning of Part II, compiling your résumé/CV made the top of the job-hunt checklist. So, now that you know all the possibilities of where to distribute this document, let's backtrack a bit and cover how you are going to construct it. This chapter explores how to prepare a knock-'em-down, bowl-'em-over résumé/CV, as well as how to compile a list of quality references. I recommended that you begin to work on this project before pursuing any of the other suggested activities.

Beyond that, our next order of business is going to be interviewing. I will tell you all you need to say and ask during an interview and how to best market yourself to captains, or anyone who handles the hiring.

Finally, because we know that the preparations you are making now will have you screened and ready for hire in no time, I am even going a step further in this chapter. After we've taken you through the interviewing process, you are likely left wondering, *Okay, what type of job is it that I really want to take?* I've included a mini guide to walk you through this decision-making process, giving you specific advice on how to be selective when accepting your first, full-time position.

So, enough of just sitting back and reading, it's time to do some work. Get out a pen and a clean sheet of paper—probably several—because by the end of this chapter, I hope to have you just that much closer to luxury-yacht heaven! Let's just say we're writing you your ticket. (And for that matter, open up a Word document or equivalent word processing application and start constructing your first draft.)

Résumés/CVs

Make no mistake about it, the résumé/CV you put together, no matter how you choose to distribute it, is the single most crucial element to getting hired onboard a yacht. Oh sure, there will be interviews that follow where you will have the chance to elaborate upon your repertoire of skills and present your irresistible personality. But first, you need to make the cut. Your résumé/CV is your showpiece for introducing who you are and what type of work you seek. Along with your list of quality references, it is the key to getting your foot in the door.

Do not put off creating this necessary document. In fact, get it done NOW, before you head off to any hiring port, and most certainly before you bother calling upon any of the recruitment agencies. I guarantee that the first thing any of the crew-placement agents will ask you is, "Do you have a résumé or CV, and can you send it over for review?" Be ready.

Don't worry if it's not perfect (although, hopefully by the end of this chapter, it'll be close). By having it done in advance, the agencies will have something to critique. The crew agents have your best interest in mind (getting a job!), and you can count on them to suggest changes or additions before they begin sending it out to captains. However, you do have a chance to make a good impression here, and that's by coming up with a humdinger of a first try!

Is It a Résumé or a CV, and What the Heck Is the Difference?

A CV and a résumé are *almost* the same thing; in fact, in some cultures, the concept is used interchangeably. In the U.K. and Australia, for example, the word CV simply replaces the word résumé, regardless of the document's content. Within the yachting industry job market, the term résumé will be used occasionally (more often than not when you are speaking with an American), but in actuality, what people are referring to is a certain type, or genre, of résumé that is known in its formal definition as a CV.

For those of you unfamiliar with the term CV, this is the abbreviation for *curriculum vitae*—a style of résumé that is traditionally used within the academic community. The literal translation for this Latin term is "life's path" or "course of life," and like a résumé, it is a comprehensive, biographical statement emphasizing your professional qualifications and activities. A CV should include past work experience, job-related skills, education, and any other evidence to prove that you have the specialized abilities and attributes required for the job you are seeking—in this case, a position as a yacht stew.

Here is how they differ: A CV tends to be longer and more informational (rather than promotional) in tone. While a résumé is expected to focus on specific achievements and results-oriented responsibilities, a CV should go into extensive detail with regard to your chronological work history, applicable education, and even your non-work-related history, in order to provide evidence to back up your said skills and abilities.

A CV will also include personal information that you don't typically find in a standard résumé, such as your hobbies, personality traits, and special interests. When applying for yacht jobs, you will even be expected to list your nationality, passport number, and age on this document. (It's not unusual to find a person's marital status included.)

Hmmm, you might be wondering, *so why is it that I should use this CV form when applying for a yacht job?*

A CV is more appropriate to use in yachting when it comes to applying for higher-ranking positions, such as captains, engineers, chief stews, and first mates. As you move up the ladder of this industry, the licenses and schooling you have become more important, as well as the types and numbers of yachts you have worked on, and for what duration. As we've learned, a captain also must log a certain number of nautical miles to legally work aboard certain types of vessels. The fact that education and work-related experience are highlighted in CVs make them the more common type of résumé to use in yachting.

For entry-level positions, you are not going to have those same types of educational requirements. Yes, the STCW '95 Basic Safety Training certification will need to stand out—whether you have it, are in the process of getting it, or are about to take the course—but otherwise, non-maritime schooling is not as big a draw. You still, however, should use a CV format.

A CV's more extensive personal biography is pertinent, since you are not only applying for a job, but for a position where you will live together with your co-workers. The more a captain can learn about you to confirm that you're a good fit within the current onboard environment, the better. In fact, some of the data you are expected to put down may seem odd to you, as things you normally wouldn't think a prospective employer should want, or even need, to know.

Alas, that is how the game is played. Some people have even asked me, "Is it legal to ask some of this stuff?" You could opt not to include such details; however, when a captain is considering hiring a new crewmember, these are the first things he or she is going to review. This is not to say that a captain is going to discriminate based on certain pieces of information, but in the best interest of both you and the other crew, he or she wants to find the best match.

For example, if a male captain is married and has his wife onboard, and there are also other couples working onboard—say, a chef-engineer team and a stew-deckhand team—then most likely, if a new stew and deckhand position come open, he would prefer to hire another couple. I am sure that you, as a single person, would rather not go work with three other couples. In the same sense, if the captain is older and has a crew that has been working together for the last 10 years, and the age range of most of them is 32–42, you might again feel slightly out of place stepping onboard as, say, a 21-year-old.

Therefore, you are not simply listing all of your background experiences in a yachting CV; rather, you are painting an accurate picture of who you are as a person, and the value you can add to a yacht crew. It's in everyone's best interest that you get hired somewhere where you feel welcomed and are as comfortable as possible among your co-workers.

From here on out, I will use the word CV to refer to a résumé or CV.

CV Strategy

The strategy behind your CV is to highlight and play up any and all experiences in your background—work-related or otherwise—that demonstrate your skill set and give a solid impression of the type of attributes you possess. Your CV will also be a living document, and you should add to it any time you acquire new training, an additional skill, or onboard work experience.

There is no one "right" way to construct a CV. No matter how you do it, there will always be someone who will suggest you change it or do something different. The following set of guidelines on how to best put together your first yachting CV comes from numerous crew agents and yacht captains, as well as an analysis of many different CVs put together by current stews who've had proven success with their respective formulas. This information is the best advice I have found on how to increase the chances of getting hired (and getting hired quickly), even as a novice. Please tailor these guidelines to meet your needs and create a CV that represents YOU in the best possible way.

Getting Started: Reflect and Brainstorm

Before preparing the main content for your CV, take some quality time to evaluate your skills, thinking about the ones you need to highlight. Who are you, and what in your background best illustrates your ability to fit with this job?

If right now you are saying to yourself, *Oh, but I have never waited tables or worked in a hotel or bartended, or any of that,* then just wait right there. Even without that direct service background, I'll bet if you dig a little deeper, there are experiences from your past that could quite easily lend themselves to the functions required of a yacht stew.

Start by writing down the various skills you currently have or ones in which you can demonstrate some knowledge or exposure. As you learned in Chapters 4 and 5, there is a laundry list (which includes laundry!) of different technical skills you need to have or be willing to learn, so you want to include information about those and tell where or how you acquired them.

I also suggest you review Chapter 6 ("The Recipe for a Great Stew"), where I discuss the various personal attributes a yacht stew should possess. List all of the qualities you have that could be useful or contribute to an eventual job as part of a yacht crew.

You may know you have certain skills, but what is the evidence in your past to back them up? Reflect upon all of your life experiences up to now, work-related or not. Go back five or six years. Write them all down. List every job or position you have ever held—paid or unpaid. Here are the types of experiences mentioned back in Chapter 6 that you need to keep in mind as you take a walk down memory lane:

- hotel/hospitality
- restaurant, bar, or catering
- culinary training or cooking background
- nanny or babysitting
- water-sports proficiencies or lifeguarding
- event planning
- cruising or sailing
- work- or study abroad or an extensive leisure-travel background
- patient care or medical field
- massage or fitness
- domestic-arts background

➔ administrative, customer-service, or personal assistant job

➔ living with a large number of people

Now it's time to combine your lists in order to show how each of the experiences you've had has led to the skills you possess. You'll need to present the information in such a way as to make the connection obvious. Pretend you are an advertising executive coming up with an award-winning campaign to sell an amazing product: you!

What are the benefits in having you around? C'mon, this is salesmanship in print.

Advice: Consider Your Audience

There are a couple types of individuals you should expect to eventually view and analyze your CV. If you register with the crew agencies, the placement agents themselves will be some of the first to see it. Beyond that, even if you choose an alternative job-finding route, such as posting your CV online, handing it out while dockwalking, or just passing it along through someone in your crew house, all of these roads end up in the same place: Your CV will ultimately make it into the hands of the captains. It is always the captain or chief stew, and sometimes also the yacht owner, who will use this document to gain a quick glance, but hopefully a long-lasting impression, of you. These are the people you must impress!

As you prepare to begin listing all the things about yourself that make you the best candidate for the job, it is wise to first put yourself in the shoes of a captain and chief stew. Ask yourself: *Who is it that I would be looking for to be a part of my team?*

Captains are busy individuals, and with crew turnover being as high as it is, they are all too familiar with the tedious process of scanning and contemplating CVs for every type of crewmember onboard. If a captain or chief stew relies on a crew agency, he or she may end up receiving 5 to 10 different CVs (or more, depending on how many agencies were called upon) to look through before deciding which candidate to interview. Your goal is to stand out and capture his or her attention immediately so you get the chance to shine in person. Therefore, your information should therefore be stated in clear and concise fashion and in an easily-read format.

Anatomy (What to Include)

Below are the various sections, or headers, you should include in your CV, followed by an explanation of each:

➔ Include a headshot (photo) in the upper-right-hand corner of the page

➔ Contact Information and Personal Details

➔ Objective and Summary Statement

➔ Qualifications or Skills Summary (you may also merge it with the Summary Statement above and title this "Profile" instead)

➔ Education and Training

➔ Employment History/Work Experience (you can separate this out to show yachting vs. land-based work experience)

➔ Honors/Activities/Leadership/Special Skills (optional)

➔ Interests

→ Reference Letters or References List (it's recommended to submit these separately, but a list of references also can be placed at the bottom of the page).

Headshot

Most every CV floating around the yachting industry includes a photo, so you are hurting your chances of getting noticed without one. (In other words, leaving it off is a good way to get weeded out of a stack of CVs awfully quick.)

Here are some tips for what to include:

→ A head and shoulders shot is all you need, and it should be passport size (which means a picture of you standing with the Eiffel Tower in full view behind you is out of the question).

→ NO glamour shots! You want to keep your appearance conservative, professional, and tactful—this will make the best impression. If you wear make-up, keep it to a minimum; no excessive jewelry; no revealing or outlandish clothing; and have a neat and tidy hairstyle, which includes being clean shaven if you are male.

→ Use good lighting and a neutral or light background. This will ensure that the photo is suitable for photocopying or digitizing. It does not really matter whether the original is black and white or color, so long as it comes out clear on your CV.

→ Consider having your photo taken especially for this purpose rather than just playing cut and paste with your vacation photos. Note that if you wear a white polo shirt, you'll definitely look the part.

→ Since the photograph will need to be digitally uploaded and distributed to crew-agency sites, make sure it is in JPEG format (jpg).

→ Oh, and the most important thing to include: a smile on your face!

Note: Some of the crew agencies offer photo services. Be sure to ask about this when you are calling around.

The Basics: Contact Details and Personal Information

Following is the information that you must include at the top of your CV. You can use the header Personal Details to block it off from the remainder of the document. It is also acceptable to use no header at all for this section.

→ **Name:** State your full name, plain and simple. You might also include your name in a larger font as the header of the document.

→ **Current Location:** You do not need a current or permanent address, but rather, simply a location city (or hopefully, a location port). Fort Lauderdale? Palma? Sydney? That is the crucial part crew agents and captains will want to know—how convenient it will be to interview you, and, if you're hired, get you to where the yacht is located.

→ **Cell Phone (preferably) or Crew House Number:** Don't worry if your cell phone number isn't local to the hiring port where you will be searching—captains and crew agents are used to placing calls all around the world. This is also why it's a good idea to include a country code when you list the number. For the United States, the country code is 1, as in: 1 (555) 555-5555. Using a phone number at the crew house or other location where you will be staying during your job hunt is also acceptable.

↦ **Email Address:** Make sure to include an email address! Nowadays, some crew candidates also include a Skype address, which can be handy for captains who might wish to do a phone or video chat interview first from a different location.

↦ **Date of Birth (D.O.B.):** Self-explanatory. And yes, this needs to be there.

↦ **Nationality and Hometown:** Nationality is a major determining factor as to whether or not a yacht can employ you. (Remember, U.S. boats can often only hire American crew.) There will be other situations where specific nationalities are either required or forbidden, due to the boat's upcoming itinerary and the visa requirements involved. Captains do not like to discriminate, but in many cases, a yacht's circumstances—the itinerary, flag it's registered under, preferences of the owner—may come into play. Bottom line: Put your nationality down, and put it at the top.

You can also include your hometown here. This certainly isn't mandatory, but captains like to see where people hail from originally; it might help you to stand out if the captain has a connection to that place.

↦ **Passport Number and/or Expiration Date and Visa Status (if applicable):** In addition to a valid passport, non-U.S. citizens must have a valid B1/B2 visa to work on a foreign-flagged yacht within United States waters. If you are American or Canadian, because many international crew are putting down what visas they hold, you should indicate that you have a valid passport. The best way to do this is to put down its number, or at the very least, its expiration date. (If you are applying to work on a yacht, you need to have a passport, so this is just a way of emphasizing that you are able to travel.) Some nationalities, such as South African, will also require Schengen Visas to work on foreign-flagged vessels cruising Europe; that information should also be indicated here.

Optional Information Under Personal Data
The following personal details are optional. If you choose to include them, use the following headers on their own, or group the data together under something more general, like "Other Details."

↦ **Marital status:** This is really only used by crew who are looking to be hired as a couple or team.

↦ **Health status or Presentation:** This is a common listing on many yachting CVs due to the fact that most British and Australian citizens include it. This is often where crew will list their smoking habits.

Are you a smoker or a non-smoker? If you are wondering whether or not you should be honest, the answer is yes. Some yachts do have a rule about only hiring non-smokers, and the owners usually dictate this. If you are just an occasional smoker, with no intention of pursuing your habit when you are physically onboard the vessel, then you can consider putting non-smoker (or just not putting anything at all).

The types of responses people put down here are things like, "Excellent Health, Non-Smoker" or "Excellent Health, Physically Fit, Active." (This last one is good for smokers who wish to leave that information off.)

I should mention here that I do know of some yachts where all the crewmembers smoke, so do not think that it's a habit that is prohibited in this industry. If you are a smoker, you can simply leave this off your CV, but be sure to bring it up in an interview to make sure the captain is aware. Also be sure to invest in electronic cigarettes or nicotine gum or patches in order to get your "fix" when you can't get off the boat.

I've recently noticed a new trend is to title this bit of information "Presentation," as opposed to "Health Status." Not only are crew indicating their non-smoking habits here, but also whether or not they have visible tattoos. It can be a positive for some captains or chief stews to know this ahead of time if the owner has expressed a desire for crew sans visible body art.

→ **Foreign-language abilities:** You can simply head this "Languages." I only recommend including this information if you do, in fact, speak more than one language. Otherwise, it draws more attention to the lack of a skill. Also be sure to state whether you are fluent or conversant, or simply have a basic understanding of the said languages. (And know that any and all language abilities are useful in this industry.)

One further suggestion I have is to include a line stating your STCW certification status. Even though you will be listing it again under Education and Training, stating it in the top section is also a good idea. As an entry-level applicant, this is something you want to really stand out on your CV. Alternatively, if you are going to include a Skills/Qualifications Summary at the top, you can list it there.

→ **STCW certification status:** If you have taken your STCW Basic Safety Training Course, include the date of completion: "STCW '95 (as amended) BST, July 2013."

→ If you are registered but have not yet taken the course, use something like the following: "STCW '95 (as amended) BST: **Currently enrolled. Date of Completion: July 12, 2013.**"

Please note that having the "(as amended)" portion is not 100 percent necessary; no person reviewing your CV would call you on it. Simply having "STCW BST" should suffice. The way it is written above is simply to make note of the fact that, as of 2013, there are a few changes in what is taught in the course modules in order for them to be compliant with the 2017 shift. All of this is explained in Chapter 7.

Now, with all of the mandatory details out of the way, let's get into the real meat of the content.

Objective Statement and Summary

Your **Objective Statement and Summary** is where you present the true introduction of who you are. The personal details preceding this section are merely logistical facts; this is where you now have the opportunity to stand out. It is common with yachting CVs for this objective to actually be a two-part statement. The goal is to state what position you are looking for and give a summary of who you are. The paragraph should run three to five lines.

Your objective portion of this statement should answer the question, *"What do I want to do?"* And yes, you want to put down the position you are seeking. However, simply stating, "I want an entry-level stew position onboard a motoryacht—private or charter" is only telling the person reading it what YOU want to gain out of this relationship.

Don't underestimate the power of having some type of quick, polished, and non-self-centered statement to give the captain an overall impression of your character. This will also demonstrate you understand that the selection process is about what you can offer in order to enhance the onboard experience for the guests, captain, and crew. You can also use this space to give a brief explanation of what your goals are and what you hope to accomplish in the position for which you are applying.

Here are some examples of the first part of this statement—your objective sentence:

- To secure and sustain a position as a 3rd or 4th Stewardess on a heavily booked charter superyacht, where I can go above and beyond all expectations of first-class service and provide the guests with memorable experiences onboard.
- To secure a position as an entry-level Stewardess on a private or charter motoryacht, where my customer-service background, organizational skills, and overwhelming desire to work in the yachting industry will make me a valuable team player when it comes to delivering impeccable guest service.

The second part of this paragraph is where you continue to give an overview, or summary, of your more relevant personal qualities. Do not use more than two sentences, as anything beyond that would be better suited for a cover letter (which is optional) or for a more experienced crewmember.

Following are some examples of good personal statements to include in your Objective and Summary statement:

- I seek a challenging work experience that will allow me to further develop the professional competencies involved in being a top-level yacht stewardess.
- With my background in customer service, I am skilled in problem-solving and peace-making, and I have excellent interpersonal skills.
- As a former administrative assistant, I am incredibly organized, detail-oriented, and skilled at time management.
- I am extremely adaptable, flexible, and easy-going, which allows me to get along well with people in a team-oriented environment.
- My experience as a live-in nanny for a family with four children under the age of 10 and my certification in massage therapy from an accredited school give me a unique set of skills that could be an asset to a superyacht crew and its guests.

So now that you've made all these glorious statements about yourself, it's time to back them up.

Qualifications/Skills Summary (Alternatively, "Profile")

When captains see a straight-to-the-point CV, it's a huge relief to them. You don't want to overwhelm them with information, but rather, give them key points. A quick opening skills summary where you spotlight everything you can and state it simply, yet with a stroke of pizzazz, will allow you to jump off the page. Make this a bulleted list, and be careful not to repeat what you just stated in your Objective Statement/Summary above.

Your STCW BST and interior crew training certifications would go at the top of the list, even if they get stated again later on (unless you also listed them under Personal Details, which I discussed earlier as one option). Have you been a waitress, bartender, hostess, busser, or customer-service rep? What about your international travel experiences or any professional work experiences in the hospitality, medical, or event-planning industries? Computer skills are good to note here, too. And if they are impressive, you may also want to include your language proficiencies here rather than under your personal details.

Here are some examples of things to include in a bulleted Qualifications/Skills Summary or Profile:

➡ Hospitality and service-industry experience: hotel desk clerk at XYZ Hotel in Toronto, Canada; bartender and cocktail waitress at upscale, fine dining establishments, including ABC Restaurant in Chicago, Illinois.
➡ Extensive travel experience throughout Australia, Canada, and Eastern Europe, including one year teaching English in Hungary.
➡ Professional background in travel marketing, travel sales, tour directing, and destination management.
➡ Water-sports background: former competitive swimmer, advanced water skier and wakeboarder, experience on Jet Skis and WaveRunners, snorkeling, and deep-sea fishing.
➡ Professional background in public relations and event/party planning.
➡ Six years Italian-language study with conversational speaking ability/read fluently.
➡ Computer literate: proficient in Microsoft Word and Excel.
➡ Certified hospice patient-care volunteer, Littletown, USA, June 2011-April 2012.

Education and Training

Here is where you will specifically list all of your professional certifications, licenses, and training, and education—even if information gets repeated from your profile above. The most crucial to list will be the status of your STCW Basic Safety Training. Also be sure to put down any courses you have taken in massage, wine and food service, etiquette, childcare, event planning, floral arranging, computers, and cooking, along with any additional first aid, medical, or safety training. Be sure to list the institutions where your training was received, and the date of completion.

Captains are not as interested in your non-marine or non-stew-related training; however, if you have a degree or some college experience, you should mention it. Captains should be impressed and feel confident that candidates with college degrees will have a good head on their shoulders. Here is what to include:

- Institution: city or country
- Degree or certification obtained
- Dates attended or graduation date
- GPA (if proud of it)
- Major/minor/emphasis area

Employment History/Work Experience

Experienced crew will normally break this down into two parts:

1) Yachting/Boating Experience
2) Land-Based Work Experience

You will not have any yachting experience to put down at first, but you may eventually. Once you acquire day work and temporary jobs, you can go back and create a listing for them.

As far as the land-based experience goes, I hope you've got it! What qualifies to go here are any other work-related experiences, either relevant to yacht jobs or ones that you simply put down to cover employment gaps during the previous five years. Furthermore, this section of your CV may include volunteer experiences, internships, community service, student teaching, college-campus leadership, and any other significant unpaid work experience.

For each position, briefly describe:

- your title or position, dates of employment, and the name and location of the employer or organization
- the duties and responsibilities of the job, using action words to describe situations and achievements

There are three format structures commonly used in CVs when presenting your work experience. These are:

a) chronological
b) functional
c) a combination of the two

- **Chronological**—A chronological format presents work experience in chronological order by listing the most recent events first. This is the style most commonly used in the yachting industry, since crew typically want to demonstrate their upward career growth and continuous experience on boats. Even without previous yachting experience, this is still a beneficial format for showing a solid work history.

- ❖ **INSIDER TIP:** Make sure that you document at least your last five years of employment or school-related work experiences. Captains and crew agents will want to see explanations for any gaps in employment and reasons why you left certain positions. As Luxury Yacht Group states on its website, "Yachting jobs are generally given to candidates with similar experience and to candidates who show a solid career path. Please include the real reason for leaving a job. We do check references, and any inconsistencies will restrict our ability to place you." (www.luxyachts.com)

- **Functional**—If you do not possess a solid work history, or much of any previous job experience at all, the functional format is for you. It is skills-oriented, de-emphasizing when and where you acquired your abilities and instead putting the focus on what you can transfer to this new field.
- **Combination format**—This is the best way to get to the point quickly. If you have included a profile at the top of your CV, spotlighting your most applicable skills, you will then elaborate on where and how you obtained these abilities in this "Work Experience" section farther down (at which point you move to a chronological timeline of your experiences).

Honors/Activities/Special Skills (Alternatively "Other Relevant Experiences")

Groupings of other past achievements or experiences can enhance your CV. Here is where you would list any honors, scholarships, or recognition awards that you've received. If you were actively involved in any clubs, teams, or committees while in college, those may also be mentioned. Consider listing any professional organizations you've been a member of or leadership positions you've held. The key to this section is keeping it brief, and only include those experiences most relevant to your objective.

Interests

This isn't something we typically think of including in a traditional résumé, but for yachting CVs, it's expected that you will include a line or two about your personal interests. Consider highlighting hobbies that show your adventurous side or that present you as a well-rounded person. Water-sports activities are a big plus here, as are previous travel experiences.

Examples: surfing, guitar, hiking, swimming, yoga, rollerblading, knitting, billiards, horseback riding, sailing, wakeboarding, theatre, reading, skydiving, stained glass, music, and travel (perhaps specify a favorite area of the world or a desire to explore another).

Tips for CV Construction

It's time to put everything together. Following are some tips for laying out your CV content in an attractive and well-organized fashion.

Layout

- **Page limit**—Limit your CV to two pages. As for that common piece of advice about sticking to one page, ignore it. Trying to pack all of your information on one page usually ends up having a disorganized and non-reader-friendly effect. Two pages are necessary for a CV, given the amount of extra information you're expected to include, such as in the personal details section.

    Do NOT, however, go over two pages. Captains, engineers, and maybe 1st mates, chief stews, and chefs can get away with three pages if they have an extensive history aboard yachts. For a novice, anything over two pages is overkill. Important: Put your name at the top of each page in case the two get separated.

→ **Margins and spacing**—White space is a good thing! The more of it there is, the more inviting your CV will be to the eye. That doesn't mean to skimp on information; it just means to balance the type on the page, spread your words out, and say things as concisely as possible. Use wide margins and space in between items and sections. Remember, you have two pages here, so allow for as much white space as possible.

→ **Printing**—You may initially email your CV around to agencies (or in some cases, you will manually enter the content into online registration forms), but at some stage, you will be hand-delivering your CV to someone. You want it to look as impressive as possible. Once you've completed your final draft, print it, and print it well. The final hard copy of your CV should be laser printed on quality paper or professional stationery.

Style

→ **Font type and size**—Do not use unusual fonts, or those that are too small to be easily read (10 to 12 point is acceptable). All text should be the same font size, with the exception of your name and possibly your headers, which can be a couple font sizes larger.

You should use either a standard serif or sans serif typeface, such as Times New Roman, Arial, Helvetica, Garamond, or Verdana. Alternatively, you might try a combination of two, such as a Times New Roman 12-point font for the main text, and an Arial 14-point for your headers (but never use more than two fonts in your CV).

→ **Visual formatting**—Is it really all about words? I mean, just words? NO. The look of the copy is just as important as the words themselves. You want to direct the reader's eyes and drive important points home. Use consistent visual elements and formatting to attract attention and boost readership and response. I'm not talking about going crazy with different fonts and colors. But you can jazz up the visual appeal of your CV with strategically placed bolds, italics, underlining, and font sizes to keep the reader engaged. Make sure you apply these format approaches in a consistent manner, with the end result being that you highlight, rather than clutter, your information.

→ **Use Bullet Points**
- I cannot emphasize enough…
- how the use of bullets can help organize information.
- Use them!

Writing Quality

→ **Clarity**—Use clear, concise, and easily understood language (in other words, no bloviating or grandiloquence). Also avoid the use of slang terms.

→ **Word Choice**—Action verbs are direct and emphatic: USE a variety of them to describe situations. When stating a previous job responsibility, let that action word lead your statements:

"Provided fine dining service"
not
"I was responsible for providing fine dining service"

A few more good action verbs to discuss your work-related activities (already in their past-tense form for you to plop right in!):

Accommodated, Administered, Arranged, Budgeted, Cared, Catered, Cleaned, Communicated, Coordinated, Counseled, Created, Delivered, Developed, Displayed, Employed, Enabled, Enhanced, Ensured, Facilitated, Filed, Finished, Fixed, Formed, Fulfilled, Gathered, Greeted, Guided, Implemented, Improved, Initiated, Inventoried, Led, Maintained, Monitored, Navigated, Negotiated, Optimized, Ordered, Organized, Participated, Performed, Planned, Prepared, Prioritized, Produced, Provided, Reorganized, Repaired, Represented, Retained, Safeguarded, Scheduled, Secured, Solved, Spoke, Specified, Streamlined, Submitted, Succeeded, Supervised, Supplied, Supported, Taught, Trained, Traveled, Typed, Unified, Volunteered, Won

- ↔ **Consistency**—Be consistent in your phrasing. If using complete sentences to describe your previous job responsibilities, stay with complete sentences. If you use short phrases, stick with short phrases. Keep your tense consistent, too. When you are writing about your past jobs, discuss them in past tense throughout:
  "Supervised team of four"
  not
  "Supervising team of four" or even "I was supervising a team of four"
- ↔ **Pay attention to the details**—Remember that you are expected to be detail-oriented, so be it! Pay attention to the small things on the page. A detail-oriented person would not allow typos, spelling errors, or grammatical mistakes in a document representing him or her. Go over your final draft with a fine-tooth comb, and for goodness' sake, run spell check. Better yet, have someone else proofread your work; preferably someone with good grammar and spelling abilities.

Content

- ↔ **Stay positive**—Use only positive statements. Don't make excuses for skills that you do not have, but rather, punch up those that you do. Sell your value with a 100-percent can-do attitude!
- ↔ **Focus**—Make sure your CV contains only objective-related information. (Hint: you're applying for a job as a yacht stew.) If it doesn't apply, don't include it. The only exception to this rule is if you just want to plug in a previous job to avoid having a gap in the chronological order of your work history. If you do list irrelevant experiences, do just that—list them, quickly, and move on to the next.
- ↔ **Accuracy**—While it is okay to spin an experience to show how it applies to becoming a yacht stew, it is not okay to exaggerate or make up details. Be sure you are creating an accurate reflection of you and your experiences.

Sample CV

Jane Jobseeker

Name:	Jane Jobseeker
Current Location:	Fort Lauderdale, Florida
Cell Phone:	1-555-555-1234
Email:	janejobseeker@gmail.com
D.O.B.	June 10, 1989
Nationality:	American (Originally from Atlanta, GA)
Visas:	U.S. Passport, expires 08/20
Marital Status:	Single
Health Status:	ENG1 certificate; Non-Smoker; No visible tattoos.
Languages:	English, Spanish (fluent), and French (conversational)

OBJECTIVE

To secure a position as an entry-level Stewardess on a substantial motoryacht—private or charter—with the goal of providing excellent service and complete customer satisfaction. I am a highly-motivated and hardworking person whose previous hospitality-industry experience has prepared me to communicate effectively and offer top-notch, quality service to all types of clients and guests.

PROFILE

- STCW BST Certification, completed October 2012
- PYA Yacht Interior Introduction Course; PYA Yacht Interior Basic Food Service Course; PYA Wine & Cocktail Introduction Course, December 2012
- Food Hygiene Course to be completed January 2013—will then have earned the PYA Yacht Junior Steward/ess Certificate of Competence
- Broad hospitality and service industry experience: hostess, waitress, and catering experience at first-class, fine dining establishments; and front desk clerk at the prestigious Hotel Ritz in Miami, Florida
- Extensive travel experience throughout the U.S., Mexico, and South America, including one semester studying abroad in Ecuador (Winter/Spring 2010)
- Previous lifeguard training and experience
- Computer literate: Proficient in all Microsoft Office programs and Adobe Photoshop

EDUCATION and TRAINING

- STCW Basic Safety Training—Maritime Professional Training (MPT), Fort Lauderdale, FL, October 2012
- PYA Yacht Interior Courses: Introduction, Basic Food Service, and Wine & Cocktail Introduction at International Crew Training (ICT), Fort Lauderdale, FL, December 2012. Food Hygiene Course to be completed January 2013—will then have earned the PYA Yacht Junior Steward/ess Certificate of Competence
- California State University, Los Angeles, California—B.F.A., May 2011; G.P.A.: 3.5; Major: Theater
- American Red Cross lifeguard training—Los Angeles, California, July 2010

Jane Jobseeker—CV—Page 2

YACHTING/BOATING EXPERIENCE

Oct 2012–Dec 2012   **M/Y Dreamer, 188' Feadship**

Position: Day Worker—Interior Department

Assisted chief steward in preparing the yacht for the Fort Lauderdale Boat Show

Performed interior detailing and cleaning in all main guest areas and cabins

Reason for leaving: temporary worker while vessel was in shipyard

LAND-BASED WORK EXPERIENCE

Front Desk Manager   **Hotel Ritz**

July 2011–September 2012   Miami, Florida

- Oversaw guest/customer relations
- Supervised and trained staff of four

Catering Staff   **XYZ Events Company**

September 2007–May 2011   Los Angeles, California

- Provisioned fine-dining service for high-profile clientele
- Supervised and managed up to 60 staff, ensuring the highest standard of unobtrusive, five-star food service
- Exhibited and applied knowledge of both French and Russian service
- Worked seven shifts a week while attending school full-time

Lifeguard Attendant   **XYZ Country Club**

July-November 2010   Los Angeles, California

- Worked at local country club; direct supervision of pool swimmers during recreational and fitness swim, insuring safe operation of all activities on the grounds of the pool; held valid lifeguard certification; certified in CPR/AED and First Aid

Restaurant Hostess   **XYZ Restaurant**

Summers between 2006–2009   Atlanta, Georgia

- Supervised and coordinated activities of dining-room personnel to provide fast and courteous service to patrons; Scheduled dining reservations and arranged parties and special services for diners
- Greeted guests, escorted them to tables, and provided menus
- Addressed complaints of patrons
- Handled preparatory service of silver and utensils throughout meals

INTERESTS

Reading, travel, yoga, water skiing, and photography

REFERENCES

Submitted separately

References

As should be expected, references are essential in the yachting industry, and they can work wonders in helping you land your first job. Your prospective employer will want to find out from your previous bosses how you handle yourself in a work environment. Yacht-industry professionals are all connected and can get in touch easily. Therefore, since you're coming in as a novice, with no former captains to call upon in the industry, having quality references from previous employers or supervisors will make a captain feel more comfortable about hiring you.

You will need to provide **three to five professional references** who you are certain will speak highly of you. If you do not have three to five people who can comment on your professional skills, it is okay to also include character references from former teachers, athletic coaches, leaders from your church or community who know you well, or even supervisors from non-work environments, such as leaders of clubs or groups to which you belong. Your best bet is to find the most "official" individuals possible to comment on your character and/or work ethic. Again, preference goes to former employers, if you have enough to put down.

The Power of the Written Word

Here is where you can score major points: Get written letters from your references! Providing a list of references is required by all the crew agencies. But if you can also get each of your contacts to you write letters of recommendation, it would not only save everyone a lot of time, but also be more powerful!

You may already have written letters on file from previous employers. If not, it's time to start contacting them. Do your best to get their statement about you on company letterhead and with their signature, and let them know that by doing so, they are cutting down on the number of people who may otherwise contact them.

The crew agencies may still call each contact even with a letter in hand. It is their responsibility to verify the legitimacy of your references so that captains don't have to bother. But, if you have a noteworthy letter of recommendation, it can easily be forwarded alongside your CV directly into the captain's hands. (And what a great way to stand out in a crowd!)

When asking someone for a reference letter, show the list of questions I've included at the end of this section as good ideas on what to cover. Depending on your comfort level in dealing with this person (and in what they might say about you), ask him or her to briefly discuss your character, what kind of person you are, and whether or not you are responsible and trustworthy. Comments regarding your work ethic and level of enthusiasm are also helpful. Having the person add a note such as "Feel free to call me" is also a nice touch. (Such a statement might actually do more to avoid calls than it will to invite them.)

How to Submit Your Reference List

You will include your list of references on a separate sheet of paper—none of this "References Available Upon Request" business that we so often see snuck in at the end of a traditional résumé.

The format is simple. Title the page "References for [Insert Your Name]," and center that in bold at the top of the page. You could make a statement beneath this heading to officially introduce the list (example below). Next, list and number each reference. Here is the information to include:

1)   Name of reference
     Title
     Company or organization name
     Address 1
     Address 2
     Telephone number
     Email address
     *A sentence or two describing your relationship to this individual and the duration of
     time you worked for or with him/her
2)   And so on... again, providing three to five contacts total.

Here is how this may look:

References for Suzie Stew

The following is a list of my professional references, each of whom is able to discuss my work habits, personal character, and professional background in detail. Each of these individuals is a former employer/supervisor. Please feel to contact any of them at your convenience.

1)   John Doe
     Kitchen Manager
     Bob's Steakhouse
     123 Cattle Drive South
     Anywhere, CO 88888
     Tel: (111) 555-5555
     Email: JohnDoe@BobLovesSteak.com
     * My former manager when I worked as a line cook at Bob's Steakhouse; 5/1/11–4/28/13.

An opening statement or closing comment is not required, but I think it's a nice touch. Alter it to fit your own situation. For example, if you do not have an extensive work history and need to rely upon other types of references, a short opening statement is a great time to explain that. Consider saying something along the lines of, "The following is a list of personal and professional references..." And later, "I have included two former work supervisors who can discuss my work habits in detail. I have also listed one former college professor and a former athletic coach—each of whom can discuss my personal character and work-related skills."

That's yours to play with. If you are under the age of 21 or just out of college, it may be that you've only had one job. You may need to think out of the box on this one. If you've never held a paid position before, captains can be equally impressed by what other types of individuals you are able to list as personal references. Here are some sources to consider for your reference list:

•   Former supervisors, managers, bosses from paid positions or internships
•   Former professors and/or teachers

- Youth ministers or leaders at your church
- Former athletic coaches/trainers
- Former volunteer work supervisors
- Former sorority or fraternity house Moms/Dads
- Community leaders
- Close family friends
- (NOT your parents!)

Finally, don't just list people as contacts because you worked under them. Make sure the individuals you put down will speak positively about you! If you left on bad terms, leave that contact off the record.

Prepare Your Contacts

It is your job to contact your references first to alert them to what you are doing and get their approval to give out their contact details. Call them in advance, fill them in on what you are doing, and confirm that they will improve—and not harm—your chances of getting hired.

Beyond it being a professional courtesy, you also want to make sure they are prepared to discuss you. If you have been out of touch for a while, it would be horrible if they were not able to instantly recall who you are when contacted for their comments on your character.

Aside from simply asking, "Did this person work for you, and for what dates was he/she employed?" a crew agent or captain could possibly ask any number of things about you. Below is a list of information that may be requested from your reference contacts. You can also use this as a guideline to send the people who will be crafting statements about you, whether it be a written or verbal reference:

- How were his/her organizational skills?
- How well did he/she take direction?
- Did he/she follow through with projects?
- Was he/she on time for work and/or meetings?
- How was he/she as a team player?
- How was his/her attention to detail?
- Was he/she expected to work long hours or take on extra projects, and if so, what was the reaction?
- Discuss this individual's strengths and weaknesses.
- Describe his/her temperament and attitude.
- Rate his/her level of responsibility and conscientiousness.

Some Final TIPS on Obtaining References

- You do not want 10 different people calling your former boss in the period of one month. Save your reference list for the important people: the agencies and captains or chief stews who are interested in hiring you (checking your references should be his or her final task in the consideration of hiring you).

➥ Do not make up a reference! By now you know: References will be checked. You make up a reference, and you will get burned.

➥ Keep adding to your list! If you are pursuing day work in your hiring port, add captain references. Preferably, get them writing, but at the very least, ask the person if you can list his or her name and number for contact.

Interviews

There are two types, or levels, of interviews that you must be prepared to go through. The first will be with the crew agents. (Remember, as a novice, there is no question you need to utilize these placement services to find work.) The second type of interview will be with an actual hiring party, which will most likely be a captain, but could also be a chief stew, yacht owner, or yacht manager. Much of the advice I am about to impart will apply to both scenarios; however, I discuss them independently in order to point out different things to emphasize during each stage.

Interviewing With Crew Agents

Your interviews with the crew agents are equally as important as the ones you will have with potential employers. Consider this a screening process, the result of which will determine whether you even get to partake in the next level of interviews—the ones where you actually have an opportunity to be offered a position.

Because you rely on crew agents to put you forward for jobs, if you impress them, you are golden. They will want to learn about your background and relevant skills, of course, but this job is just as much about personality and attitude as it is skills sets. The really professional agents will get to know you personally. They will make an assessment of your character and inquire about your interests in order to determine what job best suits you (or to determine if you're even suited for this industry).

If you've taken the effort to submit your best possible CV and a list of quality references ahead of time, you are halfway there. This will show the agents that you are detail-oriented, prepared, enthusiastic, and serious about finding work in this industry. Captains are looking for longevity from their crew. If you aren't able to demonstrate commitment, that's a red flag to crew agents. Keep in mind that a lot of individuals turn up on the agencies' doorsteps (especially in Europe, where Antibes is a major stop on the backpacking circuit) because they hear about all the amazing benefits that come with working on a yacht, and they want to "give it a try." Crew agents know to be wary of this category of job candidate. These types of people will usually talk most about how they want the job for the travel benefits. Most are interested in either a seasonal position or "gap year" work (meaning they only plan on working one year in the industry—which, hey, is fine, but not really something you should admit to when trying to find a job). It's not that these people won't ever find work, but most likely, the agents will see right through their intentions and won't feel comfortable recommending them for many interviews.

To show crew agents your intentions are genuine, you should be able to say that you're already enrolled in your training courses or, better yet, that you've recently completed them.

Also be ready to explain any chronological gaps in your work history that might indicate you are not a dedicated person. You want to convey your most positive attitude and present yourself as someone who is discreet and has a strong work ethic. Answer questions honestly and thoughtfully, and stay away from any negative comments about your past working experiences. Tell them about any special ways you've prepared to come into this industry, such as having taken a quick bartending course or wine seminar before you moved to your hiring port. And be sure to express that you are eager to begin day working right away.

During your agency interviews, it will also be important to communicate that you are wise to the demands of this job, such as the long hours, top-quality service expectations, and the high level of skill it takes to become a great stew. Prove to them you've done your research (in fact, tell them you've read this book), and demonstrate that you know what you're getting yourself into. But don't sound like such a know-it all that you come across overconfident and arrogant. As a novice, you need to remain somewhat humble—eager and informed, but well aware that you have a lot to learn. And when agents ask about jobs you might be interested in, do not be too specific. You have no right to be picky as an entry-level candidate, and you want to show you are willing to get started however you can.

And finally, but probably most important, be friendly and easy to talk to. Converse, laugh, chat, and even ask questions of your interviewer to engage them in conversation. The more positive of an impression you make, the more easily you'll be remembered when great job opportunities come along.

Interviewing With Captains or Other Hiring Representatives

Once a captain or hiring rep has expressed interest in meeting you for a personal interview, he or she will either contact you directly or have the crew agent assist in arranging for a time and place to meet. My advice to green job candidates is to accept every interview invitation that comes along. You can use all the practice you can get, and even if you don't think you're interested in the job, it's a chance to perhaps make a good connection.

Another suggestion I have is to always be conscious of giving a good first impression. When you receive your initial phone call from an interviewer, stand and smile during the conversation. These actions translate in a way that makes you sound friendly and alert. Be flexible on the meeting place, and don't ask a lot of questions. Just go for the interview!

Once you get yourself into an interview, it's up to you to sell your skills and experience for the job. The following tips are based on those offered by Ami Ira of the crew placement agency, Crew Unlimited. The same advice will also apply to crew agent interviews, and for any other hiring representative you are required to meet.

➥ Do your homework, and know with whom you're meeting. If you are told the name of the yacht in advance, use Google to find out more about how big it is, what special features it has, who the owners are, and any other pertinent information. The interviewer will be impressed by your motivation and interest, and you'll be able to better explain what you can do for the vessel.

➥ Dress smart and respectably by looking the part: khaki shorts or pants and a polo or dress shirt, with deck shoes or flats. Women might also consider wearing a navy skirt and low-heeled navy pumps. No blue jeans, sleeveless shirts, flip-flops, or bathing suits.

➤➤ For women: Wear your hair up or pulled back, and keep your make-up to a minimum. No excessive perfumes.

➤➤ For men: Be clean-shaven or with a neatly trimmed beard/mustache, and have clean cut, short hair.

➤➤ Do not show up smelling like alcohol or cigarettes, and allow for no visible tattoos or piercings.

➤➤ Bring your CV portfolio to the interview, with all your relevant information enclosed: your photo, copies of references and certificates, and your passport/visa.

➤➤ Show up on time (10 minutes early is even better), and call if you are going to be late. This shows commitment, dependability, and professionalism. Bring the interviewer's contact information (cell/boat number) with you and a cell phone so you can call him or her for directions if you get lost.

➤➤ Have prepared questions with you, and bring a note pad and pen to take notes.

➤➤ Listen to the interviewer first and see if you're interested in the position (and do not interrupt!). As the person is talking, make eye contact and lean forward just slightly to show your interest. Once he or she has finished, then it is your turn to let them know how you can fulfill the needs of the job.

➤➤ Don't fidget, and try not to be nervous. A lot of what captains are looking for when they hire is someone who will have good chemistry with the rest of the crew. Just be yourself, because once you get the job, they will get to know the real you anyway.

➤➤ Do not waste an interviewer's time. If you realize that you are not interested in the position, be honest. You will gain more respect for being upfront and sincere than if you make the person think you want the job and then let him or her down later.

➤➤ Be willing to talk and be interesting. Don't just respond to questions with "yes" and "no." Show enthusiasm, and let your personality shine!

➤➤ At the end of the interview, reaffirm your interest in the position, if it is genuine. If not, be diplomatic about it and say that you will continue interviewing until you find the right position. (Remember, we don't burn bridges in this industry.) Shake hands confidently and firmly, making eye contact, and thank him or her for the time.

➤➤ Send a thank-you note after the interview. Hiring happens fast in this industry, so if you really want the position, get this out immediately. Use this opportunity to continue pursuing the job as well; this is your chance to confirm your interest and re-emphasize your key qualifications.

Interview Questions for Crew to Ask Captains or Other Interviewers

When given the opportunity to ask questions of your interviewers, do it! Just keep in mind that, at this stage, you're still selling yourself. Rather than jumping right into topics such as money, benefits, or perks, start off by asking thoughtful and probing questions in order to achieve a better understanding of the captain's and the owner's needs and how you can fulfill them.

As an entry-level stew, it is crucial to mention anything that qualifies you as unique, and which might also counter a lack of skills in other areas. Pose questions that demonstrate your interest in being a good fit for the entire crew. For example, if you were not given the chance to adequately discuss the talents or attributes that you feel make you the perfect candidate for the job, ask something like, "Well, I have a strong background in party planning, and I am curious as to how much emphasis your crew places on theme dinners and parties to help entertain the guest. Is that something you think you might have a use for?"

Next, it's time to go after the information that's necessary for you to determine if the job is right for you. Remember, you are interviewing them, too. *How do you feel?* You need to make sure you get the full scoop on what a job entails, because you're not only about to become immersed in a working environment, but a living situation as well.

Following is a list of questions to use as checklist while you are listening to your interviewer's presentation of the job details. For anything that is not covered, you should feel free to ask these questions next.

You will most likely know the basics going into the interview, but any of the following **yacht details** that have not been disclosed should be inquired about:

- The yacht's name, registry, make, size, and the year it was built
- Is it a motoryacht or a sailing yacht?
- Is it strictly private, or a charter yacht as well?
- Is the vessel MCA compliant?

Find out about the **type of owners and guests** you will be working for:

- How busy is the boat? How many weeks/months per year will there be guests onboard?
- If chartering, how many trips will there be per season?
- How much time do the owners spend onboard?
- When the owners are onboard, how do they spend their time: water-skiing, book reading, taking excursions ashore? What is their daily schedule like? What time do they get up, and when do they like to eat breakfast/lunch/dinner?
- What levels and styles of service do the owners and/or charter guests typically prefer: silver service, plated meals, buffet or casual lunches?

It is important that you learn as much as you can about the **existing crew:**

- How many total full-time crewmembers are there?
- What is the breakdown of their nationalities?
- What is the longest tenure out of the current crew, and what position does that person hold?
- Which is the highest turnover position onboard?
- What is the chief stew that you will be reporting to like, and will you have a chance to meet him or her during the interviewing process? (This applies only if the chief stew is not the person interviewing you; if he or she is, inquire about the captain.)
- With whom will you be sharing a cabin? (Another stew? The chef? Same sex?)
- Who cleans the crew quarters, crew mess, and the captain's cabin?

You will also want to ask about **how the yacht is run** and what its schedule is like:

- What is the vessel's upcoming itinerary, and is it subject to change? (In place of this, you could ask what the past 12 months were like and inquire if upcoming seasons are expected to be similar.)
- Is there any yard time planned and for how long? If so, what happens to the crew? (Are they laid off, is vacation allowed, is living ashore provided, or does the crew live onboard with minimum A/C and water facilities?)
- What is the schedule for the workweek when no guests are onboard: 5 days, 5½ days, 6 days?
- Is there a document of crew terms and conditions? (If there is, you might ask to review it.)
- Do you have a training program for career development?
- Is there any time allowed for training and upgrading licenses?
- Does the boat run regular drills—man overboard, fire, flood, and abandon ship?
- What is the uniform?
- Is there a designated crew vehicle, and will you ever have access to it?
- Does the company conduct background and criminal checks?
- Does the company require random drug testing?
- Does the company have a social media policy—for example, one that prohibits usage of Facebook and Twitter, or regularly screens crewmembers' profiles for release (intentional or otherwise) of information related to the owner and/or yacht?

Generally speaking, **salary and benefits** are not discussed during an initial job interview; however, that's not the case in yachting. You will usually always be told the pay and benefits being offered during this first meeting. In fact, a crew agent may even reveal this information to you prior to the interview. If not, here are the appropriate (and fair) questions to ask:

- What is the salary for this position? How is it paid (direct deposit, check, or cash), and how often?
- Is there medical and/or dental coverage? Is the premium covered, or is it split? When does the coverage start?
- Are there regular performance evaluations and bonuses? And is there a trial period?
- Are there tips or other perks that can come along, and if so, how are those handled?
- What will the income-tax situation be like? (Note that this will often depend on a variety of circumstances, including your citizenship, the flag of the vessel, and where the yacht will be cruising; therefore, it might not be a question that is easily answered at this stage. You could start by asking where and whom the employment contract is with.)
- After what employment time frame and for how long is vacation time? Is your return airfare covered?
- Does the boat cover the cost of training and upgrading licenses?
- Is all food provided? What about basic toiletries?
- Would you be under contract to the owners as part of the crew?

Please note that you will ask the above questions in order to gain information, not to lay the groundwork for salary negotiations. With little or no experience to back you up, you won't really have much room to negotiate anyway. Making an attempt to do this could even end up hurting your chances at being offered the job.

And finally, if an interviewer makes you a job offer, it is fair to ask if you can meet the rest of the current crew onboard before making your decision. It's in the captain's best interest to allow you this opportunity—and to let the other crew meet you, too—in order to test the chemistry. If the captain or a chief stew seems offended by your request, then you should be wary, because it may mean they're trying to hide something. The most important thing, though, is that you get the chance to meet with the chief stew—even if it's a brief introduction. This is the person you want to click with the most. After all, he or she will be your direct supervisor and could even end up becoming your roommate.

Deciding Which Type of Job You Want

> *"It's not the boat that makes the experience, it's the owners and the crew."*
> —**Ami Ira**, owner and operator of Crew Unlimited

In trying to consider which type of yacht you want to work on, or which position you should accept, there are many things to consider. My biggest piece of advice is, don't hop on the first thing offered to you. Research the vessel, make an attempt to meet potential crewmates, and take care that your own needs and interests are also being satisfied.

Following are some criteria you will want to consider when determining the most rewarding job for you:

Motoryachts vs. Sailing Yachts: Which Do You Choose?

For novices to the yachting industry with little to no previous boating experience, motoryachts are the way to go. There are more luxury motoryachts in existence that will be actively searching for crew, so ruling out sailing yacht positions shouldn't really affect your chances of finding a job.

There are major differences between these two types of onboard experiences. First of all, living and working on a sailing vessel typically takes a strong love of the sea. Sailors tend to be real purists, and they enjoy the sense of "being exposed to the elements" that comes from hoisting those sails and letting the wind take them where they want to go. Travelers aboard powerboats, on the other hand, enjoy a life at sea that feels as comfortable as the one they have on land. With all the latest technology in stabilizers to keep them Steady Eddie as they power across oceans, many of today's motoryachts give the passengers onboard the illusion that they are not even on water.

Service is sometimes more formal on motoryachts than it is on sailing yachts, but not always. You encounter a Jimmy Buffet type aboard a big motoryacht just as easily as you can a Thurston Howell type aboard a sailing yacht. Regardless, I tend to advise people new to the industry to shy away from sailing yachts in the beginning. I have had many fellow crewmembers in the past who actually preferred working on sailboats. I worked with them all on motoryachts, but I'd often listen to their tales as they reflected fondly upon their sailing experiences. Many swore they'd seek a sailing-yacht crew position again in the future.

Perhaps you come from a boating background and don't find the idea of working aboard a sailing yacht daunting at all. Perhaps it's exactly what you're looking for. One former yacht stewardess I interviewed came into this industry 12 years ago solely to work on a sailboat, as her family had vacationed on them growing up, and she had been a member of the sailing team in college. She later fell into motoryachts, accidentally, much in the same way you might come down to join a power yacht and later grow into sailing. Who knows, one day you might drop me a postcard from some island in the Caribbean, saying, "Thanks, Julie. Not only did I have a successful five-year career as a yacht stew, but I ended up falling in love with life at sea and saved up to buy a sailboat... I am now sailing around the world with my new French lover, and we are planning on buying a racing sailboat next year!" Crazier things have happened.

Finally, while there will be some exceptions, for the most part, salaries tend to be slightly higher on motoryachts. One reason is due to the more high-end service expectations. But also, since sailors work more for their love of boating, sailing yachts can get away with offering less pay.

Charter Yachts vs. Private Yachts

If money is your priority, your best bet is to work on a chartered vessel. A busy charter yacht may mean you receive less downtime, and there is typically more hard work involved (some charter boats are so busy, they have rotating or alternating crew), but the pay off is in the TIPS. You are paid your salary whether there are guests onboard or not, but the extra tip money that comes at the end of a charter trip can mean some hefty sums of money going straight into your pocket. Just remember, gratuities are at the discretion of the charter guests, and they are not something to rely on.

Salary-wise, private yachts may pay a little more. Again, you are paid your salary whether the owner is onboard or not, but when guests do come aboard, the tips are not necessarily going to be there. Another downside is that the itinerary may not be as exciting. Unless you have a real adventurous owner, it's the charter yachts that frequent the more popular yachting ports and constantly move around from hotspot to hotspot.

For the crew, working on a charter yacht means different people on a regular basis and a changing tide of faces. That can be fun from a monotony vantage point. Meanwhile, a yacht that is only used privately is more intimate because you get the same people all the time (or friends of the same people). One of the bonuses there is that the more time you have with the owner and his or her entourage, the more of a rapport you can establish with them. It isn't always the case, and be aware that I'm not telling you to get into this industry just to schmooze with and gain favor from some wealthy owner. However, I have heard some pretty heartwarming stories of owners who have taken crewmembers under their wings. Establishing these kind of relationships can lead to many more opportunities down the road.

If simply gaining your first onboard experience and getting the opportunity to build your skills is the most important thing to you, my recommendation would be to look for a private-only yacht. The schedules on these vessels are usually more relaxed (but not always—so ask!), and you will likely have a more stable chance to learn from your chief stew. And while you will work hard when the owner is onboard, you may end up with more downtime.

Ami Ira of Crew Unlimited also suggests private yachts as the place to start: "Entry-level stews need time to gain their sea legs and learn their way around a yacht—just to get it down pat before they take work on a busy charter boat where people are paying big money for professional service."

In fact, Ami points out that a majority of the busy charter yachts require their crew to have some previous onboard experience. But again, there are always exceptions, and the stronger your service background in other industries, the more likely you'll do just fine jumping right into charters (and of convincing the hiring party that you can handle the task).

Bigger Yachts vs. Smaller Yachts

You will have opportunities to interview for positions on yachts ranging from just under 80 feet (24 meters), all the way up to the gigayachts of 300 feet (91 meters) or more. For purposes of this discussion, I refer to a "small" yacht as roughly 70 to 120 feet (21.4 to 37 meters). Storage space is at a premium on any yacht, and it is especially true on these smaller vessels. Some other downsides are that the crew accommodation can be a tight fit, and the crew-to-guest ratio may make things a bit stressful (between two and six crew positions, but anywhere up to eight to 10 guests).

One of the bonuses to smaller yachts is that the atmosphere is a bit more intimate (and hopefully drama-free), since you work with fewer crew. You will also have the chance at getting a more well-rounded introduction to yachting, as you'll be expected to help out more in other departments as well as take on more advanced tasks. However, it is for this reason that a small yacht is probably not where you want to start out. Most of them only operate with one, possibly two, stews, and that typically requires more experience.

Large yachts, 125 feet to just over 200 feet (38 to 60 meters), are great sizes to work on for entry-level stews. There is adequate living space for the crew, and the balance of staff to guests is usually more manageable (between six and 16 crew, but in most all cases, only up to 12 guests). These vessels aren't so big that you get stuck doing only monotonous and unvaried tasks (such as being confined to the laundry room, ironing for days on end), but they are large enough that you can come in as a third or fourth stew and receive adequate training, with the ability to progressively take on more advanced responsibilities while under the direction of a well-qualified chief stew.

Anything over 200 feet (60 meters) is where we now begin to see crew numbers swell. This can be good and bad. There will be more diversity among the crew and a larger friend selection; however, the feel of working as a team will be less intimate. On a yacht this size, an entry-level stew is probably not going to have much of a varied list of responsibilities. But, it at least gets you onboard and learning; therefore, accepting a job on such a vessel is not necessarily a bad place to start.

For practical purposes, it is somewhat of a misconception that a bigger yacht equals greater pleasure. The size of a vessel can restrict a yacht from what ports it can enter. If a yacht is too large to fit into a berth (a parking space for boats) in a port or marina, it must anchor out off of that port town and thereby rely upon tender or dingy boats to shuttle the guests ashore. Another downside to the larger yachts, based on their larger volume: stricter rules and regulations. For example, megayachts available to the charter market are restricted to carrying a maximum of 12 guests at a time. Once we hit gigayacht size, around 280 to 300 feet, more guests can be accommodated, and hence, more crew are needed. The extra guests and extra crew usually mean that the vessel is also likely to be run in a stricter fashion, with a lot more rules in place to manage the crew.

Level of Service

If you are new to the industry, a yacht where the level of service verges on the side of super-high-end (such as having an owner who demands silver service for a majority of the meals), this might not be the best place to start. You will have the opportunity to ask about service expectations in your interview. No matter what, you are going to be expected to perform at a five-star level; however, the more formal the owner likes it, the more advanced your skills need to be. With charter guests, it can vary, but the owner will have his or her habits. I once interviewed for a job where I learned it was silver service straight down the line, and I did not feel I was ready to perform at that level on a consistent basis, so I turned it down.

American Flag vs. Foreign Flag Yachts

As we've been over, only American crew can be hired to work on American-flag vessels. However, this does not mean that if you are a U.S. citizen, you don't have other options. And foreign-flag vessels do have their benefits. First of all, there is a tax issue that might be to your advantage. American crew working on foreign-flag vessels typically don't have to pay income tax. This is not a cut-and-dry rule, however, so your best bet is to inquire about this during your interview, and to check with a tax specialist to confirm that your situation qualifies. You will also most likely have a diverse mix of crewmembers from many different nationalities on a foreign-flag vessel, so if that is important to you, then there's another advantage.

My final piece of advice on choosing a job: If you receive several offers at one time, yes, take in everything you just read… but at the end of the day, go with your gut instincts.

11

ALL ABOARD!
—LIFE "OUT THERE"—

"This is more than a job for any one of us; we live where we work and work where we live… Our lives—our jobs: they are so intertwined."

—**Me**, from my journal

S o you got the job… *Now what?*

Well, it's time to hop onboard! In this final chapter, I offer you some basic guidance for settling into crew life and your new, live-aboard way of being.

Moving Onboard

Setting off on any new career—any new job—comes with a period of adjustment to industry-specific issues and stresses…but, unlike many other industries out there, going into yachting also entails taking on a completely new lifestyle. You must understand in advance that by becoming a yacht stewardess, you are also becoming part of a society of people for whom work life and personal life are elaborately intertwined. You will be living among your fellow crewmembers in extremely tight quarters—eating with them, sleeping with them (you know what I mean), partying with them, running errands with them, and working long, hard, stressful hours with them, with little time off and, of course, with every conversation revolving around the topic of the boat or the next charter.

Mind you, this is not necessarily a bad thing—it's just different than what most people are accustomed to when taking on a new professional endeavor. Job—Life: There is very little separation in yachting, and yes, that takes some adjustment.

What to Bring

Everything I recommended you bring with you when you move to a hiring port is going with you onboard (refer back to Chapter 8 for packing suggestions). That is, unless you want to move a few items into storage, which you should only do if you expect to end up back in your hiring port at some later stage. Bear in mind you could get a job on a yacht and board the vessel in, say, Fort Lauderdale, but when you decide to move on and seek different employment a year later, that boat could be in Europe. Therefore, my rule of thumb is to take with you only what you can manage to carry on your own, in case you should suddenly find yourself "out on the dock."

Take it easy on how many personal possessions you bring onboard, such as your books, photos, laptops or tablet PCs, and knickknacks. These items are important—especially if homesickness ever kicks in—but you don't want to wind up with a bunch of unnecessary clutter that will annoy your cabin mate. You shouldn't have to worry in such a small and close-knit group that one of your fellow crewmembers is going to get into your things, but I still recommend purchasing locks to put on your bags and backpacks. Some vessels allow you to store more valuable items in the ship's safe, so this may also be an option.

Please recall from Chapter 8 that soft, collapsible luggage is a must. You will also need to have any prescription medications filled and written orders for them ready in case you have to obtain them overseas. (Oh yeah, and don't forget your passport and/or visa!)

Cabin Fever (Crew Accommodations)

Here is one of the drawbacks: You will be living within pretty confined quarters as far as your actual cabin goes. To give you a good idea of what I mean, I used to refer to my cabin as a "cabinet." (Yes, that means there is limited space.)

Generally, crew live two to a cabin, with the exception of the captain, and possibly also another crewmember with high rank or longevity onboard. When you move in, since there will likely be someone already in your cabin, you will take the bed that is designated for you. Rest assured that most captains do all they can not to mix genders (like a female chef and a male first mate sharing a cabin).

Be aware that bunk beds are the norm in shared cabins. The beds are typically narrow, so don't expect to roll around a lot. In fact, I became used to sleeping on my back, and since I was almost always on the top bunk, I quickly got over my habit of sitting straight up in bed when I awoke from a nightmare (POW!). Yeah, no more sitting up in bed.

Despite being small, most crew cabins do feature some nice amenities: iPod docks and reading lights next to each bed are common, and quite a few yachts also have either DVD players or TVs connected to the onboard movie server in each of the crew cabins. On a vast majority of vessels, the crew quarters are found in the lower deck (beneath the water). In these instances, you may have porthole windows, which are not really meant for sightseeing. When the vessel is underway, these are locked closed; but, when at dock or on anchor, you will be able to see at a level above the waterline…and gain a little access to sunlight.

Each cabin should have its own head—again, with a small amount of room available for moving around: Showering can be a royal pain, especially for the ladies when it comes to shaving your legs. You will also have your own closet, but space is slim, so do not bring a lot of extra clothes. Keep in mind you'll have a lot of uniform pieces to fit in there as well (and these will be given to you when you first arrive).

The good news is that you spend very little time in your cabin aside from sleeping, showering, changing, and perhaps reading (lying down). Outside of your actual cabin, there is a common area known as the "crew mess"—a living room-type of setup. Here you will typically find: a dining table with seating wrapped around it that will fit all crewmembers at once; a mini kitchen with microwave, dishwasher, sink, fridge, ice maker, and lots of cabinet space for crew snacks (loaded with every type junk food imaginable); and a TV with satellite access for news, sports, and entertainment as well as a DVD player or a connection to the onboard movie server, for all to share. The crew area is also where the laundry room is usually located.

Needless to say, it doesn't take long to get to know your new crewmates… Quite often, you can't escape them.

Fitting in With the Crew

As I've said throughout this book, good crew chemistry is crucial to having a positive work experience. Life onboard is similar to a dorm type of situation, and dealing with multiple personalities in such a confined area is one of the hardest things crewmembers will ever do. Learning to get along with everybody is the name of the game.

First and foremost, each crewmember's personal space must be respected. For example, I once had the bottom bunk in my cabin, and my roommate would throw her shirt on my bed while she was in the shower…and then she'd forget about it. It drove me crazy!

Beyond physical space, be mindful of your fellow crewmembers' *mental* space. If someone is not in a very good mood and doesn't want to chitchat, don't push him or her on it. In situations like this, people have a tendency to say things such as, "Oh, we want to cheer you up…what's wrong?" Resist this temptation. Just give that person his or her space.

And if you have a conflict with your fellow crewmembers—say, their shoes are at the bottom of the crew mess stairs every night, and you are always tripping over them—mention it nicely and diplomatically when it *first* starts aggravating you. If you let your frustration build, then it is apt to get blown out of proportion when everyone is tired and stressed. And a rift between two of you can try the patience of every crewmember.

It's important to remain open-minded and always willing to see another crewmember's point of view…and tell people how you feel before any tension can build. If every crewmember keeps the lines of communication open, then there should never be a need for the captain to become involved.

Uniforms

Every yacht should provide several uniform sets, including shoes. During guest-free periods, the crew (both interior and exterior) will typically wear casual attire: Work t-shirts with a picture of the boat on back and the vessel's name on the front breast pocket are standard, along with Bermuda-style shorts in khaki, navy, or white.

When guests are onboard, a boat's dress code will most commonly be as follows:

Bermuda shorts will still be worn during the day, while most yachts then swap the aforementioned boat t-shirts for more professional-looking polo shirts that have the yacht's name or logo embroidered on the front. Exterior crewmembers will wear deck shoes, and while stews should try to do the same, they oftentimes end up barefoot, since the majority of their day is spent parading about the fine carpets inside. Crew may also have a designated uniform for docking the boat (when you've got an audience at the docks), or one specifically set aside for owner's visits (vs. charter trips).

In the evenings, crewmembers change into more formal service apparel. Female stews might wear culottes or skorts, skirts, or nice dress slacks (navy or black is standard), and vest blouses or nice button-down shirts (typically in white). Male stews will wear nice dress slacks and button-down shirts. A more formal vessel may ask that stews wear tuxedo shirts with Eton or Spencer jackets. In the evenings, the interior staff may also opt for loafers or dressier, slip-on shoes (but it's also possible that everyone will simply remain barefoot; after all, the guests will be, too).

Most every yacht will also require another crew uniform set to be worn on both the day the guests arrive and when they disembark. On really formal vessels, such uniforms may even be worn at all times when guests are onboard. Here, I'm referring to traditional, button-down epaulet shirts. Epaulets are strap-like shoulder ornaments (such as what are seen on military uniforms) that indicate both rank in the crew based on the number of stripes that appear on them, as well as what department an individual works within, which is represented by a symbol. For example, a steward/ess epaulet features a silver crescent emblem to indicate the service staff. Rank in the crew is then conveyed by the use of one (the highest-ranking member, such as the chief stew), two, three, or four silver stripes. Crew may also be required to wear double-breasted jackets during these more formal periods.

Finally, all crew will be issued a set of foul-weather gear. This includes items such as waterproof, breathable, and lightweight jackets for spray protection in warmer climates, and fleece-lined, hooded coats and pants for colder conditions.

There are a few yachts out there that will stray a bit from the traditional attire I just described. In fact, I once interviewed for a job on a yacht where the owner was a well-known fashion designer. He apparently outfitted his entire crew with uniforms designed by Versace (but no, the owner was not himself Versace).

Once again, you have to keep in mind that, as a member of the crew, you are a representative of the vessel upon which you live and work. Therefore, your appearance is part of the overall presentation. It will be expected that you take pride in all uniforms and in the proper wearing of them. (This means shirts tucked in.) If one crewmember is wearing his or her uniform in a sloppy manner, then the entire crew looks sloppy. Remember this even when you're off-duty and just casually hanging out on deck (but are within public view).

Romantic Relationships Onboard

This can be a tough subject. Many yachts frown upon romantic relationships among the crew, and for a good number of vessels, they are forbidden altogether. On the other hand, there are also yachts out there where the entire crew is made up of couples (or "teams," which is what they are most often referred to in the industry, such as a first mate-chief stew team).

Much of this is determined by the captain (and in some case, the owner). If a captain is himself or herself a member of a team, then it is likely that the boat will be happy to hire couples to fill other positions on the crew. (And when the captain has a partner, it tends to work out better.)

Other captains won't hire couples because of bad experiences in the past. For example, if one of the team is fired or quits, the other goes, too. And if there is an argument with a member of the pair, then that can easily result in a feud with "the couple" as a whole (where the remaining crew feel they must choose sides). Captains don't have time for the sort of pettiness that can result from soap opera drama among the crew.

It can be difficult to find work as a team, unless you are a captain. Captains don't have trouble if they have a chief stew or chef partner, but for other crew—especially lower-ranking positions, such as a deckhand-junior stew team—it can be incredibly tough.

I interviewed one captain about this, and his response was that he doesn't have a problem hiring couples, yet they must realize that he views them as individuals, and they will be treated as such. They should never expect that if one of them has the day off, the partner gets to join him or her. Couples may also not be guaranteed a shared cabin. This captain also admitted that, to hire a team, each member of the pair would need to have a good deal of previous yachting experience. Some captains may even inquire as to how long a couple's been together, assuming that relationships in their early stages are a much bigger risk.

Crew Placement Specialist, Heather Adams, from Crew Unlimited had this to say about what it's like trying to place couples aboard superyachts as team:

> This is a real thorn for me to deal with in placing crew. Think about it, what other jobs in the world hire employees as teams? This is what I regard as a legit team: Two people at the top of their respective positions who have worked together for many years on yachts. None of this crew house hook-up, boyfriends/girlfriends who change with the seasons, or 'I would feel less scared working this job if I had a teammate on board with me.' Insecurity and being a yacht crew do not mix—a sure bet for failure. Captains are more hesitant than ever to hire teams for permanent positions because of the uncertainty. And most of these teams out there are the less experienced, less mature, with less longevity, but certainly have that love bug.... Every (new) crewmember [should] strive to advance on their own, get certification and experience, create their own reputation, and if they really feel it necessary to become one of two, then be sure you are working with someone at the same level of experience in his/her respective position.

So, if you are new to the industry, and you're entertaining the idea of coming in as a couple—say, you've read this book and think it would something cool for you and your guy or girlfriend to come do—I'd think again. I doubt any captain in his or her right mind would hire a team where both individuals are green. At least one of you has to have experience (and lots of it, for that matter). Note: This is one of the reasons you find the yachting industry filled with so many young, single, and unattached individuals.

Now, it's one thing if you are hired on as a couple…but hooking up once you're onboard is an entirely different scenario. Becoming romantically linked with a fellow crewmate is not uncommon, it's just not recommended. As with traditional office politics, partnering up with one of your co-workers can lead to disaster. Obviously, though, these things can't always be planned, so my advice is this: When it's mid-charter, you're feeling lonely, and that hunky new Dutch engineer starts making goo-goo eyes at you from across the crew mess table, just think twice before you react.

<hr>

I Must Confess…
I dated a fellow crewmember.

What would a confessional book be without an element of romance? Well, while I can't promise to dish all the details, what I can tell you is that, yes, I once dated a fellow member of my crew. As for the juicy part: We sort of had to keep our relationship a secret at first! (Note: I do **not** condone this despicable type of behavior.)

Here's how it went down: There was an official rule on this particular yacht I was working on that NO COUPLES were allowed to be hired onboard, nor were they allowed to become couples after the fact. Well, we (my onboard lover and I) obeyed this…for a while, anyway. This person and I actually worked together for nearly a year before any sparks developed…but once they did, there was no denying it (which is probably why we dated for a year and a half after that).

The good part was that three months into our relationship, a new yacht-management company was hired to oversee our boat, and they wanted to bring on a new captain. The person they wanted for the job came complete with a girlfriend, who would also be our new stewardess. So, they did away with the "no couples" rule. (And wasn't that convenient?)

Apparently, many of our fellow crewmates had begun to pick up on subtle hints of our romance anyway, so fortunately, before my "friend" and I were outed, we got the chance to come clean on our own—and with no repercussions (such as having to quit our jobs). He and I continued to work on that same yacht for another season…before quitting together to pursue life on land for a change. (And there you go…that's why most yachts don't like hiring couples in the first place: You lose one half, you lose 'em both.)

Perhaps in a future book I will dish out more details…but for now, I will employ the good ol' excuse that "I never kiss and tell."

Dealing with Seasickness

You may or may not know whether you're susceptible to seasickness. However, if you are prone to equilibrium problems or inner-ear infections, then it's quite possible you'll experience nausea on rough seas. The good news is that it is conquerable.

I suggest doing what I did, which was to wear acupressure travel wristbands. You can purchase them at most pharmacies, and they only cost under 10 dollars. However, the wristbands will not CURE seasickness; if you get seasick, you pretty much have to ride it out, whether that means throwing up or just feeling miserable for several hours (which will feel like days). For prevention, you need to start wearing them *before* the boat actually goes into motion. I would put them on right before we set sail and simply leave them on the entire time—whether in motion or at anchor. I think I actually did a good thing in that respect, for the guests didn't feel stupid wearing them when they saw that one of the crew was doing it, too. In fact, I made sure that every guest cabin had at least two pairs in its toiletry basket.

For more advice on managing seasickness, refer back to Chapter 5 where I discuss it in relation to guests. I think it's fair to say that a majority of your guests don't want to expose themselves to the possibility of getting ill, either, so they typically request only to travel short distances and on flat water. And if they do wish to journey far, they'll usually ask that it be at night while they are sleeping. Therefore, the only times you will likely experience seasickness is when guests are not onboard and you are traveling long distances to relocate the vessel.

◆━━━━━━━━━◆

I Must Confess...
I got seasick on a couple occasions.

My first bout with seasickness, while horrific to endure, was pretty uneventful. One trip to the toilet and several hours of feeling incredibly disoriented and nauseous, and I was done with it. Fortunately, there were no guests aboard, so I spent the day attempting to sleep it off.

The second time, however, was a much different scenario. We were in the middle of a charter, and while I'm still not sure what planet these guests were from, the group came complete with stomachs of steel. Their wishes were to keep the boat at sea, travel tremendously vast distances, anchor out in the rolliest of places—and to carry on all the while as though we were docked in a calm, quiet port.

One night, while making the voyage from Turkey to Mykonos, Greece (in the middle of a rainstorm, might I add), the head guest requested to have dinner served in the main dining room. This was the only instance I can recall where my trusty travel wristbands failed me. Mistake number one: The chief stew and I had had soup for dinner (not the best thing to have rolling in your tummy when out at sea). Mistake number two: We didn't try and talk the guest out of his decision.

Midway through the meal, it hit me. I was leaning over to pour wine for one of the guests, and suddenly, I felt "that urge" coming on. I somehow managed to complete my task, but then immediately ran into the galley to let the chief stew know I was running for the bathroom... But she was nowhere to be found. With no time to spare, I darted downstairs to my cabin, hand cupped to mouth the entire way.

Upon opening the door to our cabin head, lo and behold, I found the chief stew. Judging by the smell of things, she'd beaten me by only a minute or two. So there we were, left to take turns ridding ourselves of the evening's fare. Not a pretty scene, but certainly one we were able to laugh about later...(and that would be *much* later).

Work Schedules

No Guests Onboard—Work Hours, Breaks, and Meals

Work hours and breaks without the owner or charter guests are much more flexible. As I've mentioned before, a typical work day will likely be 8:00 a.m. to 5:00 p.m., Monday through Friday. Some yachts also work half days on Saturdays, while for all vessels, weekends will be added if the captain feels work projects are behind schedule.

Here is a typical crew meal schedule when there are no guests onboard:

- 0700–0800: Breakfast, which is usually every man for him- or herself, with plenty of options made available.
- 0800–0805: The workday begins.
- 1030–1045: Take tea break #1.
- 1200–1245: Lunch (prepared by the chef) is served.
- 1500–1515: Take tea break #2.
- 1700–1730: Clean up daily projects.
- 1830–????: Dinner (prepared by the chef) is served.

Without guests, you also have more run of the ship than just the crew mess. Most boats discourage use of the guest cabins; however, if someone is using the crew mess TV for Xbox or Playstation games, the captain may let you watch a movie in a guest area of the vessel (unless you can do so in your own cabin). The outside decks are also open terrain.

Guests Onboard—Work Hours, Breaks, and Meals

It will vary, but the average owner or charter trip ranges from 10 to 14 days (although, month-long trips are not unheard of!). If you work on a yacht that doesn't charter and instead is used only by the owner, you never know. There are yachts out there where the owner actually lives onboard.

Work hours with the owners or charters guests onboard will be on a "whatever it takes" basis. Breaks will usually be determined by the department head (who should try to arrange for up to a two-hour break per day for each person in his or her department). Positive energy from all crewmembers is expected at all times, so you should use your breaks wisely. In other words, soak in all the relaxation time you can; it's at a premium when guests are around.

Service is the number one concern with guests onboard, so crew meal hours may vary. Since each crewmember's work hours will differ, there may also be times when you are unable to eat with everyone else. This is part of the job and should not become an issue. (And someone will always save you a plate.)

With guests onboard, crew are often confined to the crew mess and their cabins when not on duty. Two yachts I worked on actually let us spend time on the bow of the boat when we were on break, which allowed for sleeping and sunbathing. It won't be every day, but captains (and guests) understand that you need to get some time off the boat, too. With the captain's permission, crewmembers can sometimes journey ashore on their breaks if the yacht is in port—go for a run, explore the town, or head to a beach for a swim. We actually had guests invite us with them to the bars or casinos at night (although, accepting those invitations is not always a wise choice, for you're the one who needs be up early in the morning and can't afford a hangover).

Getting time ashore with guests onboard is a lot more common on a private yacht or when an owner is onboard. Charter guests might not like it as much, for they feel they are paying for your service 24/7. It all depends on the guests. Crew should tag team to make sure everyone gets some sort of break ashore to keep their sanity—especially on a lengthy and demanding charter.

I Must Confess...

I played hooky from work one afternoon, while we were on charter.

Most people wouldn't consider accidentally slicing one's finger with a paring knife to be a lucky break, but one particular morning, it was for me. We were in the middle of a three-week charter, and our entire crew was in full-on work mode. I hadn't stepped foot on land for days, except to run ashore in Monaco to buy some eggs for the chef. I was feeling very worn down from the go, go, go.

It wasn't a deep cut, so all that was needed was a Band-Aid (a "plaster" for those of you playing along at home in the U.K.). Three mornings later, however, my entire finger was throbbing; I had good reason to believe the wound was infected.

"Let's send her to a doctor to have it checked out," was the captain's order.

The doctor? Wait, that means going off the boat. As much as I hate going to emergency rooms, I was all over this plan.

The yacht was docked in Gocek, Turkey—a paradisiacal place to be sent ashore. I stepped off the boat, and a guy pulled up on a scooter and told me in a thick, Turkish accent that he had been hired to take me to the hospital. I must admit, the captain had found me a very cute (and also very married) chaperone for the morning.

In the end, my finger was not infected. The doctor who saw me did, however, think it was a bad enough cut to prescribe me an antibiotic. After all, my position onboard left me "in the line of fire" for picking up germs. The trip to the doc was otherwise uneventful, and I was in and out in less than 45 minutes.

As we walked out of the building, my Turkish companion turned to me and asked if I felt like returning to the boat or if I'd rather come join him and his wife at their travel agency to hang out and enjoy some coffee and baklava (a sweet pastry made of chopped nuts and layered with phyllo, popular in the Middle East and the Balkans).

Gee, let me think a minute.

I spent the next two hours laughing and swapping "culture differences" examples with my two lovely hosts. They told me all about the sailboat charter business they ran there in Turkey. It was unbelievable just how cheap it was for a group of people to charter their own boat for a week, which included a captain to sail them around as well as all of their food. I realized this was a hidden secret that obviously few spring breakers knew about. In fact, years later, after I had left yachting and was operating my own travel agency business back in Indianapolis, I actually looked this couple up and booked a family of five from Indiana to fly to Turkey and charter one of their boats. (Note: Don't miss the opportunity to make these kinds of connections when you get the chance—you never know when you can call on a friend from afar.)

Oh yeah, and I did make it back to work by noon that day. I was gone less than three hours. For all my captain and crew knew, there was a long wait in the emergency room.

Behavior Guidelines

Every yacht should issue you a manual of crew guidelines when you first come aboard. Read this thoroughly to make sure you understand all the dos and don'ts on that particular boat, for rules will vary with each vessel. Following are some examples, adapted from actual onboard crew manuals:

Personal Hygiene

Living in close proximity with other individual personalities demands a high awareness for personal cleanliness, grooming, and hygiene. The "odd couple complex," where one crewmember is less tidy than the other, can cause animosity between the crew. It is expected that all crewmembers keep themselves in a sanitary manner.

The crew cabins and crew mess onboard are expected to be presentable at all times in readiness for the occasional owner, guest, or broker visit. Each crewmember is responsible for neatly making his or her bed every morning before reporting to work. Bed linens must be laundered and crew cabins vacuumed at least once a week. Crewmembers' cabin desktops and shelving should also be clutter-free.

Smoking

There are boats that allow smokers, and there are those that don't. If this is a habit of yours, it should have been indicated on your CV. One thing is for sure, if you are allowed to smoke, it will be outside (smoking is not allowed on the interior of most vessels); and with guests onboard, it will be out of their view, with no traces of ash left behind.

An alternative to consider is electronic cigarettes. Most convenient stores sell these now, and there are a ton of options you can purchase online. When I was in Fort Lauderdale just last month, I saw tons of crew out smoking these in bars. As for on the boat, whether the captain or owner have a problem with it or not, they won't really ever know if you are smoking e-cigs in your cabin—there's no odor since they only put out water vapor, not smoke. Hey, they cure the nicotine craving. For that matter, you could consider Nicorette gum.

Alcohol Consumption

Without guests onboard, crewmembers are normally allowed to consume alcohol freely outside of working hours, so long as all drinking is controlled and not disruptive, destructive, or embarrassing to the yacht or her owner (and never done before driving any of the yacht's water or land transportation). Many boats will pay for crew liquor up to a certain point, so a cabinet of spirits is usually available, along with beer and wine. However, when guests are onboard, crew should refrain from consuming alcoholic beverages—especially while at sea.

Drugs

At no time should any crewmember employed on a luxury yacht use illegal drugs or bring them onboard. A majority of yachts do require drug testing, and should you either refuse to participate or test positive for drugs, you will be relieved of your duties.

Keeping in Touch with "Back Home"

Phone & Skype

Crewmembers are encouraged to keep in touch with family and friends; this is one of the reasons why, as I recommended in Chapter 8, you should have your own personal cell phone. Make sure your calling plan includes international roaming, too. You'll be glad you have a cell, especially for giving out the number to people you meet in port so you can keep in touch. Just be careful with the international calls. I know many crew who've received $500+ cell phone bills from talking on the phone too much to people back home. Also check back to Chapter 8 to read my tip for using either Skype VoIP and/or Google Hangouts to keep in touch with people far away.

E-mail

Most yachts today use their satellite systems for not only telephone calls, but Internet connections as well. And even though you're working in an industry where a lot of money is being spent to maintain the boat, not all owners want to pay for their crew's personal e-mail time. Therefore, while out at sea, the captain may only go online for a few minutes at a time. A lot of boats now have e-mail accounts set up for the crew so that you can receive messages (for example, Julie@ theyacht.com). Then, when the boat goes online, your e-mails can be downloaded along with everyone else's, printed off and given to you. You can't necessarily guarantee a lot of privacy in this instance; however, your friends and family can be made aware to watch what they say when using your boat account, and you can just use that to stay in touch when you don't have access to a personal e-mail account.

If you have a personal computer, Skype and Facebook are popular ways to stay in touch. (And as we've been over, just be careful of what you post publicly.) Some yachts even have their own crew Internet café —an area in the crew's quarters set aside with a PC or two. If you can't use the yacht's Internet connection, look for an Internet café next time you're on land. You are never far from shore, unless you are crossing to another part of the world; therefore you will have a lot of opportunity to access Internet cafés, which are everywhere in ports.

You want to make sure you have a personal email account set up. As mentioned back in Chapter 10, G-mail and Yahoo are some good options.

Banking and Bills

There are several ways you can handle managing your life back home while off working on a yacht. You should definitely look to consolidate your life before heading out to sea. Keep in mind that you won't have as many bills when working on a yacht. As for the bills you do need to keep paying, I recommend online banking as a good place to start. Most yachts will pay you by direct deposit into your bank account, so you can set up an automatic bill pay system and not worry about it. Having a contact (parents or close friends) back home who can assist you if need be could also prove handy.

Another option is to look for businesses in the main hiring ports that specialize in taking care of a yacht crew's personal business while they are away. The boat you work on will have a mailing address from which all mail and packages are forwarded once or twice a month whenever the yacht is around the world. You can set up a similar system as an individual. I highly recommend looking into such services when you get to a hiring port (there are plenty around that cater specifically to yacht crew), because you can set up a "home base" and get all your bank and mailing information straight before you head out on a job.

Changing Jobs and Crew Turnover

Changing Jobs

While it can be easy to find jobs in the yachting industry, be aware that job security is not a guarantee. Anything can happen at anytime when you're dealing with the wealthy: You could get fired because of bad chemistry with the captain or owner, the crew could get scaled down before heading into a shipyard period, or the boat could get sold to a new owner who wants an entirely new crew. On the other hand, it might be you who makes the determination that the job is not a fit.

Following is the protocol for job termination, as it is explained in a sample crew contract on Crew Unlimited's website (www.crewunlimited.com): "The Collective Crew Agreement provides that your employment may be terminated if, in the opinion of the Company of the Captain, your continued employment would be likely to endanger the Yacht or any person onboard. …You are entitled to a single economy flight paid by the Company to your place of domicile at the end of your service with the Company, whether the period of employment is completed or not, save only where your employment is terminated in accordance with the summary dismissal provisions of this Agreement or the Collective Crew Agreement, or by your resigning your position; and if not withstanding this proviso, the Company is obliged by law to provide for your repatriation in the case of the termination of your employment is such circumstances, it may be entitled to deduct repatriation costs so incurred from your final remuneration."

Boat Hoppers

The hospitality industry, more than any other industry I can think of, has frequent job turnover—and the yachting industry is no different. Due to the aspects of crew life, such as having to live and work peacefully among so many different types of people (and usually very independent types), keeps many boats struggling to find that perfect "crew formula."

Despite the fact that it's common, I recommend you don't get into the routine of frequently switching jobs. Most yachts will give 30-day trial periods, which is for the newly hired crewmember and the captain/crew/owner to (forgive the pun) "test the waters" with one another. After this initial 30 days, many of the employment benefits will kick in (although it may take longer on health insurance), and at that point, you should be willing to stick the job out for *at least* six months to a year before you decide to seek a different vessel. Of course, if things prove to really not be working out, you may have to cut that timeframe shorter; but just don't make a habit of it. Being dubbed a "boat hopper" is a terrible reputation to have. If captains learn that you have changed jobs frequently in a short period of time, they will likely avoid hiring you.

Money Management

I mentioned this briefly in Chapter 2, but it's worth reiterating: SAVE your money, and don't get carried away with the fact that your bank account may start building faster than you can even notice. When you start out in this industry, you will really have to be diligent about setting guidelines and resisting the temptation to try and emulate the lifestyles of those whom you serve. I know many current and former yachties who would be a whole lot better off financially now if they'd only been conscious about this sudden money they began to make.

❖ **INSIDER TIP:** Keep this in mind from Day 1: Open a bank account. Your income will most likely be wired to you; because you are out on the ocean, a land-based office or corporate head will wire money into your account. Use an ATM card to pull out exactly what you need when you need it. Also, tips are often paid in cash. It may be a nice feeling to hold a few thousand dollars in your hands for a minute or two, but I advise you not to carry that cash around with you on the yacht. As soon as you can, get it deposited into a bank—even wire it to your account if that's possible. Trust me: It is way too easy to spend those dollar (or euro, or what have you) bills when they're that accessible. Also, you lose out on any potential interest you could gain from having it in the bank.

Life After Yachting

"Working onboard yachts is an awesome job. It offers opportunities that most people don't even realize exist. It doesn't only have to be a short term or 'gap year' job. It can lead to a lifetime career in an amazing industry. Work onboard, work hard, take it seriously, and travel the world. When you are ready to go 'land-based' you can still have a home in the yachting industry. I always say that after almost 10 years on yachts, I started my second career in yachting. I love what I do, and because of my years on yachts, I have a unique perspective working with my clients and truly understanding who they are and what they do."

—**Julie Liberatore**, Regulatory Liaison Maritime Professional Training (MPT)

"When you feel the need to go back on land, there are plenty of opportunities in and around the marine industry—if you choose to stay in it. I began with crew placement, then I went on to work for yacht and charter brokers, and then I worked for Yachting Magazine *until the training school became available."*

—**Kristen Cavallini-Soothill**, owner and operator of American Yacht Institute

One of the chief questions I hear from people I recruit into this industry is this: "But what would I go do *after?*"

For some yacht stews, the job represents a long-term career path where they can work up to chief stewardess status and stay in the industry for 10 or 20 years. (With those high-paying salaries for top-quality chief stews, who can blame them?) Others decide they want to work in a different capacity onboard, and they go on to culinary school to become yacht chefs, or even to captain's school. Becoming a yacht purser is another option (refer back to Chapter 3 for a job description). Purser positions only exist on the larger boats, and openings are hard to come by (and are oftentimes held by the captains' wives), but they're out there, and they pay well.

Then there are those stews who get burnt out after a time—they want to plant some roots ashore, start a family, or transition into another line of work. If you are wondering what type of jobs being a yacht stew can prepare you for, I honestly think the list is endless.

Future Possibilities

When you decide to leave your life at sea behind, the most likely career path is to stay in the yachting industry by parlaying your onboard expertise into a land-based job. There are many exciting careers to be pursued in this arena:

- **Become a crew-placement specialist**—Assist yacht crew in finding jobs (and vice versa: assist the yachts in finding crew). Another name for this occupation is crew agent or crew recruiter.
- **Work for a yacht-management company**—Yacht managers serve as liaisons between the owners and the captains, helping manage the overall operations of vessels that have chosen to enlist third-party management services (which many now do). There are a number of both small and large yacht-management companies where you could serve in this capacity.
- **Work for a yacht-provisioning business or a yacht chandlery**—Yacht-provisioning businesses are located in nearly every major port, and their job is to provide the boats with food and beverage items, which, in the case of luxury yachts, means supplying the freshest products, specialty items, and gourmet goodies of all types. Orders are often delivered directly to the yachts. Yacht chandlers are similar, only they supply boats everything from uniforms to mechanical parts to marine accessories and equipment.
- **Become a yacht agent**—Yacht agents are land-based contacts, situated near the areas where yachts travel, who offer all kinds of support services to the crew. Things such as advising on customs procedures in the nearby ports, obtaining products or provisions that the crew can't find on their own (or don't have time to look for), and even receiving and signing for shipments that arrive when the yacht and crew are at sea.
- **Become a charter broker or a yacht broker**—As the names suggest, yacht brokers serve as agents in negotiating the sale of yachts, while charter brokers handle the chartering of them. For ex-stews carrying all that previous onboard experience, becoming a charter broker is a wonderful career option.
- **Study to become an interior designer for yachts**—This doesn't happen overnight, but it's a great vocation to aspire to if you have a flair for decorating.

↔ **Work for the yachting media**—When it's tough to leave the yachting world behind, you can consider working for one of the many publications and/or websites that covers the industry. Write for them, or even sell advertising space using all the great contacts you'll have made. You will find a list of the more popular industry publications and websites in Appendix F, with additional yachting magazines mentioned in Chapter 9. Related to this, you can start your own blog.

↔ **Get a job at one of the crew-training schools**—Teach others to become professional crew. As the industry grows, enrollment levels at the maritime and specialized training facilities will become increasingly important. Teach or aim to become an administrator at one of these schools.

But don't think you'll be bound to boating for life. There are a multitude of careers that make perfect follow-ups to yachting, and which are completely unrelated. I've seen so many unique jobs come out of this. You'll walk away with the demeanor and the quick-thinking ability that makes you adaptable enough to work with any kind of person and in a variety of environments.

If you've never been before, you could go on to college, or finish up a degree you once started. If you are already a college grad, you might choose to pursue a graduate degree or professional certification program. Regardless, you can go back to school confident that you will do well because you will have a whole different worldview—and you can pay for it.

Naturally, there's always the possibility that you'll make a connection through an owner or guest that will lead to a job outside of yachting. A lot of yacht stews go on to become estate managers, working at the homes of the yacht owners and managing their private affairs...or, they may want to put you to work in one of their companies. You may meet someone who gives you their card and says, "If you ever leave this industry, give me a call"—like Mark Cuban, for example! I know of a former stew who went to work as an event coordinator for one of the major television networks in New York City. An executive staying onboard took note of her superb attention to detail when throwing last-minute dinner parties, and she snatched her up.

You will leave this industry with extreme skills in hospitality, so you could do nearly anything in that field, such as work in hotels or restaurants. Event planning is also an excellent career choice, as is catering. I've heard of former stews who've set up their own businesses just running errands for people.

Below are some outstanding follow-up careers for which stewardessing can prepare you:

↔ Estate manager (this is very common)

↔ Event planner

↔ Personal assistant or personal shopper

↔ Sales representative for a wine or spirits company

↔ Bar or restaurant manager (or better yet, open a wine bar!)

↔ Etiquette consultant

↔ Hotel manager

↔ Bed and breakfast owner

↔ Travel consultant or agent

↔ Florist

- ↔ Professional organizer
- ↔ Tour director
- ↔ Flight attendant (although you will want to probably stick with private jets at that point)

Note: If you are already in one of the occupations or industries I've listed above, you are sitting on skills that are perfect for transferring over to yachting.

Some people even get married to fellow crew. And with that, there's a possibility you might settle down in another country.

The list is endless!

"The more knowledge you have of the industry, the better. That gives you transferable skills into the land side. For example, I became a crew agent. Former stewardesses also go on to become yacht brokers, managers, or provisioners. There are all kinds of outside services that work with the marine industry."

—**Lynne Cottone**, Crew Placement Specialist with Luxury Yacht Group

I Must Confess...
I worried about what I would do "after."

I'll admit it: I worried how taking time out to travel the world as a yacht stewardess would affect my future job prospects. I had two college degrees under my belt, and they carried a lot with them—namely, the pressure of having to get "a real job" in some corporate setting at some stage in my adult life. I've now grown to understand that the "have to" part of that sentiment is just one big myth, and that there is no direct correlation between holding what others deem a prestigious job—and happiness. And still, while I worked as a stewardess, I often wondered, despite the great money I was earning and how much I loved my job, if I might be harming any potential for a serious corporate career down the road.

I later discovered that, in fact, the opposite was true. Soon after leaving my career as a yacht stewardess, I sent my résumé out to companies in marketing, advertising, and media sales, and immediately, people were calling me to interview. At the time, I attributed this to my academic accomplishments and all of the professional internships I'd held in college.

On the contrary!

When I got into these offices for face-to-face Q&A, all my interviewers wanted to hear about was the time I'd spent on yachts: "So, tell me more about this yachting thing you did…like, who was it traveling onboard?" (That's where I'd fantasize saying, "Well, I could tell you, but I'd have to kill you.") And in rattling off the types of people I served (keeping names confidential, since it could have been a test of my integrity) and everywhere I'd traveled, I made some of these no-nonsense executives' jaws drop on the floor. This is when I'd begin to spin my specific functions as a stewardess to cater to the particular job I was there to land.

And surprisingly, it was easy to do: "When they're spending that kind of money to be onboard, you can never say no to a request—no matter how impossible it might seem to fulfill. Remember, these are the richest people in the world, and it's not easy to always please them. Our mentality had to be 'if there's a will, there's a way.' It's taking customer service to a whole new level."

And: "Stewardesses keep these vessels meticulously cleaned and organized, using highly complex inventory-control systems. It's like managing a five-star boutique hotel, you see. And we could have royalty onboard for the week—or a world leader. That's a lot of pressure. You don't want to run out of necessary items while out in the middle of the ocean. We had to be overly prepared and ready to jump through hoops to accomplish some seemingly impossible tasks."

And one that always seemed to impress: "The attention to detail that must be paid is difficult to describe. We were often wearing four or five hats at one time, juggling all types of responsibilities and making it look effortless. Talk about multi-tasking! Well, you can see on my résumé the types of things we were responsible for on the yacht." And they did. (And don't hesitate to borrow from the following yourself someday; it's on my LinkedIn.com profile as we speak!):

Yacht Stewardess, Motor Yacht "X": Date X to Date Y

Managed the interior of this "five-star hotel on water," hosting $25,000-per-day charters for celebrities and dignitaries. Responsibilities included, but were not limited to, guest and crew provisioning, taking full accountability for interior cleanliness, meal presentation (silver service), stock management and budgeting (developed an inventory-control system), theme-night planning and decorating, arranging guest excursions ashore, assisting in docking maneuvers, and supervising two other stewardesses. Trained in sea survival, fire-fighting, basic first aid, and onboard-safety procedures.

In addition to the above, I also served as the captain's office assistant (purser) when needed. Responsibilities included accounting, communications, ordering, and broker relations.

If you were looking to hire someone in a customer-relations or a sales position, ask yourself if you'd be interested in a job candidate who was "detail-oriented," "results-driven," and a "multi-tasker," accustomed to dealing and communicating with all types of people, and experienced at completing even the most difficult of challenges (a.k.a. "a problem-solver"). Throw in the "trained in high standards of etiquette and well-traveled" part, and you have a pretty impressive applicant for most jobs—corporate or otherwise. And that's exactly what steward/essing can make you!

"Experience, travel—these are as education in themselves"

—Euripides, Greek playwright, c. 480-406 BC

CONCLUSION

Thoughts on Being a Yacht Stew

"I soon realized that no journey carries one far unless, as it extends into the world around us, it goes an equal distance into the world within."

— **Lillian Smith**, American novelist and civil rights activist

It is an unusual workplace... an unconventional occupation. The work can wear you down, and having normal relationships with a significant other or your family back home is nearly impossible.... And yet, crew live with a freedom that does not exist in "normal life."

While yes, work in this industry can make you a lot of money, it is not necessarily about the financial rewards. Certainly, when a charter is onboard, you are aware that your performance could mean the difference between $2,000 and $5,000 extra in tips for those two weeks of labor. However, when you are not coming home to a lifestyle, like a home, a car, heaps of personal belongings—things that remind you of your "status"... when you can go weeks on end without wearing anything but a crew uniform... when piles of bills are not streaming into your mailbox on a daily basis... when few constants are faced to make you feel stagnant... when an influx of newness and difference envelops you each day... when you are living a life in a "place" that is always changing... Well, when you have all of that, you hardly have time to think about the money. I remember checking my bank statement after not having thought about it for nearly three months one summer, and I was in shock: I had money that seemed to have just appeared. Not once during the course of those back-to-back charter trips had I even considered anything outside of the tip that might be coming.

For me, life on yachts, unlike what I later experienced working in Corporate America, wasn't a rat race. Despite the fact that we were surrounded by wealth, the job itself was not about chasing money, attempting to gain status, or climbing a ladder of success or social hierarchy. My life felt so free of those concerns. The work I did, while yes, for financial gain, did not seem to carry the same weight of "have to."

Working on a boat, you are free of possessions, unattached to anything truly defining but some choice photos, scraps of letters and postcards, and then the things you accumulate along the way… things that have a story attached to one day remind you… things later difficult to let go of.

As I said before, while so many yachties are out there in pursuit of their own individual adventure and are the types to enjoy this life of uprootedness, what you find underneath is that they are trying to establish roots in any way they can. They open up much more quickly; a closeness or bond can be established with another crewmember or someone you may meet in port much more quickly than in "normal life."

I joke that life on boats is akin to indentured servitude. I downplay the job when I refer to my former stewardess role by saying, "Oh yeah, I cleaned rich people's toilets." This is my modesty and my effort not to sound like I'm "bragging." What I really want to say is that it was the most incredible experience of my life, and it changed me forever. And yes, it was hardcore. I likened some of our charter experiences to being in the armed forces: rigorous days of blood, sweat, and tears. It's certainly not for everyone… it takes a unique kind of individual, and the passion has to be there. Whether it's an addiction to the travel and adventure, the excitement of living in an awe-inspiring environment, the thrill of constant activity and an always-unexpected future—or all that and more—the common thread is passion for this lifestyle. When you have all of that, the workload and the need to put so many others before yourself… it all becomes worth it.

I Must Confess…
I grew to love the sea.

Just like with any job, we the crew would occasionally end up asking ourselves, "What is it we are doing… what is it that we're working for?"

One of my former captains provided perhaps the most adequate answer to this question when he said that he felt safer in a tilted sailboat out at sea than anywhere else in the world, adding that he took comfort in listening to the water beneath him as he slept. It almost seems like a contradiction, doesn't it: To feel the most secure in one of the most mysterious, least explained and explored "places" on Earth—out at sea…so exposed to the elements? And yet, when you think about all of the "back homes" we each carried with us, it seemed to make sense that we found a new comfort in the simple rhythm of waves and thought…and of feeling oneness with something grander.

To this day, I'll re-read a journal entry from my time in yachting, and I'll hear just how clear my thoughts were. I'll remember that, on any given day, despite whatever frustrations I might have had with a guest, a fellow crewmember, or even my work schedule, I always found something to remind me of why I was there. Even if it was just that 15 minutes at the end of a long guest dinner when I could sit up on the bow, sip a glass of wine, and gaze up at a starlit sky; or that brief glimpse I might catch of a group of dolphins playing alongside us as I carried a plate of caviar to a deck filled with demanding guests—in moments such as these, I was reminded of why I was there, and I learned to appreciate the experience in full...realizing one would not come without the other.

"As I gaze upon the sea! All the old romantic legends, all my dreams, come back to me."
—Henry Wadsworth Longfellow

Mark Twain once said, "Travel is fatal to prejudice, bigotry, and narrow-mindedness, and many of our people need it sorely on these accounts. Broad, wholesome, charitable views of men and things cannot be acquired by vegetating in one little corner of the earth all one's lifetime."

I couldn't agree with him more. Taking the time to explore oneself and the world outside of our "comfort zones" not only benefits us as individuals, but ultimately, it can make us more globally minded citizens.

Those years I spent traveling are priceless. I live now with a faith that the world is filled with infinite opportunities and possibilities. If anything, it was my years spent vagabonding around the world that contributed most to the development of my entrepreneurial spirit. Talk about inspiration...talk about self-empowerment...talk about learning to rely on one's own instincts and developing a desire to chart one's own course in life! Risks are necessary in life, and sometimes, you do need to leap in the dark to transform. Once you've experienced that, it's addicting.

The yachting industry is a wonderland of life-altering experiences and could be the greatest thing you ever do. If you are standing at the fork in the road right now, this might be the path that makes all the difference. I guarantee that the skills you acquire will empower you for the rest of your life.

You've taken step one by reading this book. So now the question becomes: Are you ready to leap?

"A mind that is stretched by a new experience can never go back to its old dimensions."
—**Oliver Wendell Holmes**, American poet and physician

APPENDIX

A

—

UNDERSTANDING YACHT MEASUREMENTS

The international makeup of yacht builders, owners, crew, and policymakers dictates that yacht measurements be referred to in metric terms as well as American feet and inches. Learn the conversion between the two systems of measurement now so if you are offered a job on a 24-meter yacht, you can quickly decipher that as being an 80-foot vessel. For example, I once worked on a 164-footer. Some referred to it as just that; however, I also had to know my boat was a 48.8-meter yacht (and for my British cousins, that "meter" is spelled "metre"). Again, it is good to learn these equivalents, since you may only have the vessel's size given to you in one or the other term of measurement.

Here are some helpful conversions to know for "bilingual" yacht talk:

Metric to American Standardized Measurement Conversions

- ↔ 1 meter (metre) = 3.28 feet
- ↔ 1 meter (metre) = 39.27 inches
- ↔ 1 foot = 12 inches
- ↔ 3 feet = 1 yard (which is quite close to 1 meter and is a good way to think of it when "rounding")

APPENDIX

B

A SAMPLE
MEDITERRANEAN ITINERARY

Below is a sample itinerary that I wrote for a yacht that was chartering in the Mediterranean during summer 2005. This is a great example of a typical seven-day yacht charter voyage in this region. I have changed the name of the boat to M/Y *Stew Voyager* (to protect the not-so-innocent):

M/Y *Stew Voyager* Itinerary—7-Day Cruise—Naples to Porto Cervo

We welcome you to spend seven days of luxurious relaxation aboard the magnificent M/Y *Stew Voyager*. From the legendary Bay of Naples, we will explore the enchantment of Italy's dramatic Amalfi Coast, visiting the chic destinations of Capri and Positano. We will later sail on to experience the more remote Mediterranean islands of Ponza and Palmarola, part of Italy's Pontine Archipelago.

From there, we venture to the dramatic islands of Corsica and Sardinia—one French flavored, the other unmistakably Italian. Each of these renowned islands has a multitude of small fishing villages and protected, tranquil anchorages not accessible by land and ideal for the enjoyment of the water sports onboard *Stew Voyager*.

A visit to the Maddalena archipelago on the northeast coast of Sardinia and a stop near stunning Cala di Volpe precedes disembarkation in the fashionable Porto Cervo.

Keep in mind that itineraries are only guidelines, and unlike Pompeii, they are not etched in stone! The following outline for your journey is subject to change, as we are dependent upon favorable winds and seas. However, we know the area well and will have a contingency plan.

Our *Stew Voyager* crew will ensure you see all the highlights while offering the ultimate in personal service and guest care.

Welcome aboard!

Day 1—Pick-up: Naples/Isle of Capri

On arrival at the Naples International airport, a host from the *Stew Voyager* crew warmly welcomes you to Italy's third-largest city, located at the foot of Mt. Vesuvius. Within 15 minutes you will be onboard the M/Y *Stew Voyager*, moored in the Port of Napoli.

After your journey there will be time to relax, explore your surroundings, and meet the entire *Stew Voyager* crew before our departure to the **Isle of Capri**—a breathtaking area of natural beauty in the Bay of Naples.

We will dock in Capri for the night. After dinner, you can wander through the winding streets, where you will find chic shopping boutiques. Enjoy some leisure time to explore the Piazzetta, the center of attraction for the many international visitors who grace the island each year.

Day 2—Capri and Positano

This morning our crew will serve breakfast alfresco as the skipper sets sail for an afternoon cruise along the back side of Capri. During our excursion, we will reach parts of the island completely inaccessible by other means. Discover the Grotta Bianca, the Natural Arch, the Faraglioni rocks, and the bay of Marina Piccola.

We will then take a short, one-hour hop to **Positano,** known as "The Gem of the Divine Coast." Gaze out at the town of Positano rising up vertically from the sea and following the steep incline of the mountains. This is quite possibly the only place in the world where the panoramic view of the town facing away from the sea is more beautiful than the sea horizon behind you.

Stew Voyager will remain at anchor near Positano all afternoon, allowing you to relax on the sundeck or participate in some of the numerous water sports we offer. For the more adventurous, your crew will delight in teaching you the basics of water skiing or wakeboarding!

This evening we will remain at anchor off Positano. You can dine under the stars and enjoy the view or head ashore to dine at one of the many fine restaurants located in port.

Stew Voyager will depart late in the evening for an overnight run to our next destination, the remote islands of Italy's Pontine Archipelago.

Day 3—Palmarola/Ponza (The Pontine Islands)

You will awaken this morning to find *Stew Voyager* anchored between the islands of **Palmarola** and **Ponza.** Welcome to the Pontine Islands.

If you love solitude, Palmarola is one of the most charming places you will find. Today, we cruise the island's transparent blue waters while admiring its extremely craggy coast, dotted with grottos, bays, and cliffs.

We can anchor in a bay off Palmarola for a light lunch and the opportunity to take advantage of the crystal-clear waters to relax, play, or both! This is a sunbather's paradise, and a wonderful area for snorkeling.

If time allows, we will run to Ponza, the largest island of Italy's Pontine Archipelago. Charmingly fringed with dramatic coves and cliffs, the main town features colorful houses and is seen by its visitors as a less-spoiled version of Capri.

If you care to take a tender boat ashore, the island's main settlement is Ponza Porto, around the harbor. There aren't many tourist sights or monuments on Ponza, but there are some excellent restaurants as well as a few options for late-night drinking and dancing.

This evening, *Stew Voyager* departs for an overnight run to Bonifacio.

Day 4—Bonifacio (Corsica)

By morning, we have made our way to the southernmost tip of the French island of **Corsica.** We will moor overnight here in the town of **Bonifacio**—also known as "the City of the Cliffs."

Enjoy an afternoon at leisure meandering through the medieval lanes, touring the walled fortress area, or strolling along the bluff high above the harbor. On the tip of the promontory is the marine cemetery and windmills that date from the 12th century, but best of all is the view stretching right across the straits to Sardinia.

Terrace bars and restaurants, ice-cream parlors, and fancy boutiques welcome you to this enchanting spot, which you can enjoy into the night.

Day 5—La Maddalena Group of Islands (Sardinia)

From the lively town of Bonifacio, we depart this morning for a quiet sail up to **La Maddalena Archipelago** on the northeast coast of **Sardinia**—a charming and largely uninhabited area that includes the islands of Maddalena, Caprera, Santo Stefano, Spargi, Budelli, Santa Maria, and Razzoli.

The many secluded coves and bays throughout this region offer exclusive spots to discover. Let this natural haven be your sanctuary!

We may choose to spend the afternoon anchored in a remote, tranquil bay near one of the islands, where you can relax, sunbathe, and enjoy a buffet-style lunch. You can also opt to take advantage of more water-sports activities.

This evening, we anchor for the night near one of these enchanting islands.

Day 6—Cala di Volpe

We awaken this morning to enjoy a short cruise past the numerous islets and inlets of Sardinia en route to the beautiful **Cala di Volpe.**

The day and evening are whiled away in the renowned Cala di Volpe Bay, well protected from the Mistral wind and surrounded by beautiful sandy beaches. Enjoy a leisurely lunch, water ski, snorkel, or take the Jet Skis for a spin.

The line of picturesque beaches along Cala di Volpe provides a stunning backdrop to the evening's anchorage. End your day with a wonderful Sardinian meal and nighttime celebration.

Day 7—Porto Cervo (noon drop off)

We continue our cruise of Sardinia's rugged Costa Smeralda to reach our final destination, the fashionable **Porto Cervo.** A recreational Sardinian fishing village, Porto Cervo, can be described as active, sporty, chic, and popular with royalty and movie stars alike.

After breakfast or a late lunch onboard the yacht, your journey aboard M/Y *Stew Voyager* comes to an end. You can be certain that you have enjoyed both a relaxing and eventful experience. Please visit us again soon!

APPENDIX

C

CULINARY TERMS

Pronunciations are given in brackets.

Agneau—Lamb [ah-NYO]

à la Mode—Served with ice cream [ah laa MOWD]

Anguille—Eel [ahn-ghee-YUH]

Apéritif—Alcoholic drink served before a meal [ah-pehr-uh-TEEF]

Aubergine—Eggplant [oh-bear-JHEEN]

Béchamel—Savory white sauce made with milk [bay-shah-MEL]

Béarnaise—Sauce of tarragon, shallots, egg yolk, and butter [behr-NAYZ]

Beurre—Butter [BURR]

Bisque—Cream soup, usually of shellfish [BIHSK]

Blini—Mini buckwheat pancakes typically served alongside caviar [BLEE-nee]

Boeuf—Beef [BUHF]

Calamari—Squid [kal-uh-MAHR-ee]

Canard—Duck [kah-NAHR]

Charlotte—Molded dessert, containing gelatin or pudding [shar-LOHT]

Charcuterie—Pork products, such as hams, sausages, and pâtés [shahr-KOO-tuhr-ee]

Chateaubriand—Double tenderloin; think filet mignon [sha-toe-bree-AHN]

Chaud—Warm or hot [SHOW]

Chèvre—Goat [sheh-VRUH]

Consommé—Beef broth [kohn-soh-MAY]

Côte de boeuf—Prime rib [coat duh BUHF]

Côtes de veau—Veal chops [coat duh VOH]

Coq au vin—Chicken, stewed with wine and mushrooms [kohk oh VAHN]

Coulis—A thick sauce made of puréed fruit or vegetables [koo-LEE]

Crème—Cream [KREHM]

Crêpes—Very thin pancake, often stuffed and served with sauce [KRAYP]

Crevettes—Shrimp [kruh-VET]

Dauphine—With roasted potatoes [doh-FEEN]

Entrecôte—A cut of steak taken from between the ribs [ahn-treh-KOHT]

Épinard—Spinach [ay-pee-NAHR]

Escargots—Snails [ehs-kahr-GOH]

Filet—Tendorloin steak [fee-LAY]

Flambé—To flame, with alcohol as the burning agent [flahm-BAY]

Florentine—With spinach [floor-ehn-TEEN]

Foie—Liver [FWAH]

Fraise—Strawberry [FREHZ]

Framboise—Raspberry [frahm-BWAHZ]

Froid—Cold [FRWAD]

Fromage—Cheese [fro-MAHJZ]

Fruits de mer—Seafood [frwee duh MEHR]

Fumé—Smoked [fyoo-MAY]

Gambas—Prawns [gahm-BAH]

Gâteau—A cake [ga-TOE]

Glace—Ice cream [GLASS]

Gratin—Browned baked with cheese [GRAH-tun]

Haricot Verts—Green beans [ah-ree-KOH vaire]

Hollandaise—Sauce made form melted butter, egg yolks, shallots, and vinegar [oh-lahn-DAYZ]

Homard—Lobster [oh-MAR]

Hors d'oeurves—Savory pre-dinner tidbits; appetizers [or DERV]

Huitre—Oyster [wee-TRUH]

Jambon—Ham [jahm-BOHN]

Lait—Milk [LAY]

Lapin—Rabbit [lah-PAHN]

Légumes—Vegetables [lah-GUHM]

Marron—Chestnut [mah-ROHN]

Menthe—Mint [MAHNT]

Meringue—A topping of beaten egg white and sugar for pastry or pies [muh-RANG]

Moules—Mussels [MOOL]

Noisette—Hazlenut [nwah-ZEHT]

Oeufs—Eggs [OUFS]

Omelette—Omelet [ohlm-LET]

Pain—Bread [PEHN]

Pâte—A paste made of finely mashed and seasoned fish, meat, or liver [pah-TAY]

Pâtisseries—Pastries [pah-tees-REE]

Pêche—Peach [PAYSH]

Petits Fours—Tiny cakes that are served after a meal, along with coffee or after-dinner drinks [PEH-tee fohrs]

Poisson—Fish [pwah-SOHN]

Poivre—Pepper [PWAH-vruh]

Poire—Pear [PWAR]

Pomme de Terre—Potato [pom duh TEHR]

Polenta—The Italian version of cornmeal mush [poh-LEHN-tah]

Porc—Pork [POHR]

Poulet—Chicken [poo-LAY]

Profiteroles—Cream puffs with chocolate sauce [proh-FIH-ter-ohls]

Rôti—Roast [roh-TEE]

Saumon—Salmon [sow-MOHN]

Sorbet—Lightly frozen water ices, often based on fruit juice; sherbert [sor-BAY]

Saint-Germain—Made with fresh green peas or pea purée [san-zhehr-MAHN]

Tarte—Pie [TART]

Thon—Tuna [THON]

Torte—Round cake, usually containing fruit or nuts [TOHRT]

Truite—Trout [tru-EET]

Veau—Veal, a flesh of a milk fed calf up to 14 weeks of age [VOH]

APPENDIX

D

SAMPLE LUNCH
AND DINNER MENUS

Lunch Buffet

Chilled melon and ginger, fresh figs and prosciutto ham
Couscous salad
Fusilli pasta with tomato and Italian sausage sauce, flavored with fennel seeds
Italian buffalo mozzarella and Roma tomato salad with basil Salade Niçoise
Deep-fried calamari with baby spinach
Freshly baked bread
Dessert: fresh strawberries with a vanilla and balsamic sauce served à la mode

Dinner Menu

Canapés Assortis: lumpfish caviar, smoked trout pâté, and Westphalian ham
Cream of mushroom soup with truffle oil
Oeufs brouillés au saumon fume
Terrine of confit Canterbury duck and organic pork belly, toasted brioche, crisp apple and Riesling jelly
Grilled langoustine with marjoram and lemon
Sorbet de melon et d'abricot au Pernod
Carré d'agneau—rosemary stuffed with steamed rice and sultanas served with aubergine caviar
Arugula, endive, and mixed leaves with French dressing
Sweet options: chocolate torte with compote of cherries served à la mode
Fromages—a selection of French cheeses
Café; truffles au chocolat et petits fours

321

APPENDIX

E

GUEST PROFILE:
CHARTER REVIEW EXAMPLE

Dates: 1/10–1/20/2012

Persons: 11

Locations: St. Thomas, USVIs, Anguilla, St. Martin, St. Barts, St. Kitts, and Nevis

In General: A very nice group of guests. The Riches and their four children are from Los Angeles, and Mr. Rich's parents and Mrs. Rich's brother and sister-in-law are from Boston. They also brought along their nanny. This was their first charter on a yacht. They seemed to love it. No one got seasick, but they did choose to sleep or lie down when the yacht was moving. They had very young kids, so we had the boat "baby-ready" upon their arrival.

They were very routine in their meal habits. Breakfast was always between 8:00 and 8:30 a.m., and everyone ate together. Lunch was around 1:00–1:30 p.m., and again, everyone joined as a group. For dinner, the four kids ate with the nanny at approximately 6:00 p.m., while the adults preferred to have cocktails and canapés beginning at 7:30 p.m., with dinner at 8:00 p.m. sharp every night. The kids ate inside at the card table for all three meals. We had a baby chair that hooked onto the table for the little girl. (It can get quite messy!) The adults enjoyed eating breakfast and lunch outside, but they liked dinner in the A/C. This group did not drink beer. The liquors they enjoyed were vodka and rum. They had maybe one bottle of wine with dinner and never anything at lunch.

Activity-wise, the men and boys enjoyed the WaveRunners, snorkeling, and learning to ski. The women were more into reading, relaxing, and watching the kids in action. None of them were in the sun too much, and they all enjoyed playing in the Jacuzzi—hot or cold. We had a Luau-style dinner for them one night, which they loved. We played volleyball, did the limbo, and made up some games for the kids. We also took the boys "night shell-finding" with flashlights, and they had a blast!

This group gives you quite a bit of laundry. They really over packed but now realize all the amenities on a yacht and understand that they don't have to bring so much next time.

Mr. Rich (John):

Slept in master cabin. He is a record producer from L.A. Very nice man—asked lots of questions about yachts. Mr. and Mrs. Rich played games with the kids at night. They constantly praised the chef's cooking and were very appreciative of everything. For breakfast they all ate lots of French toast, waffles, and eggs.

They asked us to order Marlstone Meritage, Duckhorn merlot, and Cristal champagne, but he prefers chardonnay. He also likes strong coffee and will have 3–4 cups after every meal. Throughout the day, he drank iced tea (with lemon and Splenda) or Diet Coke. He likes light desserts, such as sorbets.

Mrs. Rich (Jane):

Incredibly nice! She didn't spend much time in the water, as she claims she is not very outdoorsy. She likes to be docked and loved shopping in St. Barts. They did eat two dinners off the boat. She was easy to please, and as long as the kids were happy, she was as well.

She drinks lemonade and water, and loves red wine. She is very petite and does not eat much. Likes fruit in the morning. She only likes desserts at lunch every other day.

Kids—Joey (13), Mary (10), John, Jr. (5), and Katie (2):

Joey and Mary slept in the lower starboard forward cabin, and John, Jr. slept port forward. The nanny slept in the starboard aft with the baby in a crib. The nanny watched over them all very closely but spent most of the time with the baby (and fixed all the baby's meals).

Very fun kids. They played tons of Xbox and Wii games and watched 2-3 movies a day. They loved the WaveRunners and kneeboarding, and while they can't quite get up on skis yet, the deckhands tried to teach them every day.

In general, they ate "kid" food such as mac & cheese, plain pasta, grilled cheese, and pizza. Joey and Mary love crepes and probably ate three to four a day. John, Jr. is very quiet and a very picky eater. Joey and Mary are very adult-like and love talking to the crew. They snack on lots of dry cereal throughout the day and drank Coke for every meal. They never pick up after themselves but always say please and thank you.

This was an easy charter; they were easy to please and very pleasant to have onboard. They seemed very happy at end of charter, and their tip expressed the fact that they enjoyed their week. They said they plan to make yachting part of their yearly vacations.

APPENDIX

F

WORLDWIDE YACHTING PUBLICATIONS, WEBSITES, AND BOOKS TO CHECK OUT

I recommend the following yachting industry publications as valuable resources for learning more about luxury yachts, how they operate, their owners and captains, the issues facing the industry today, and even specific port and destination information. Topics related to crew are sometimes covered, but where I think you will benefit the most is in discovering more about the actual vessels that exist and gaining familiarity with their names and features.

- ↪ *CharterWave*
  Website: www.charterwave.com
  The first—and only—website devoted to the charter market, CharterWave is the brainchild of Kim Kavin, a highly regarded journalist who specializes in this segment of the industry. Besides reviews of charter yachts (both motor- and sailing yachts, and some smaller than 80 feet), CharterWave interviews the leading charter brokers and charter yacht captains, giving readers insight into why these professionals are at the top of their game. It also has sections educating newcomers to the lifestyle as to what differentiates yacht charter from cruise ships. Kavin is further the author of the book *Dream Cruises: The Insider's Guide to Private Yacht Charter Vacations*.

- ↪ *Dockwalk*
  Website: www.dockwalk.com
  As mentioned in Chapter 9, this monthly publication is helpful for all kinds of crew news, distributed in the Fort Lauderdale area. If you register at its website, you can download a copy for free. The website further provides regularly updated news, blogs written by and for crewmembers, salary surveys, polls, and details on upcoming events for captains and crew. Be sure to register on the site to engage in a little online social networking with other crew.

➻ *Megayacht News*

Website: www.megayachtnews.com

Founded in 2007, Megayacht News is an online media outlet owned and operated by Diane M. Byrne, a longtime superyacht journalist. While targeting the needs of American yacht owners and buyers, as well as their circle of influential advisors, Megayacht News is read by individuals in the U.K., Europe, and other regions as well. It includes a daily, diverse mix of original articles, videos, and slideshows, featuring onboard reports, details of new launches, interviews with prominent owners, and more. And note: every year Diane does a wonderful calendar featuring incredible megayacht shots. I've gotten it every year since 2011. It's excellent!

➻ *Power & Motoryacht*

Website: www.powerandmotoryacht.com

An enthusiast publication, *Power & Motoryacht* is committed to one topic: powerboats 24 feet and larger, providing details readers seek about large boats and onboard gear—and all the information they need to more fully enjoy their time on the water. *Power & Motoryacht* provides its readers with product and lifestyle editorial exclusive to this top end of the powerboat market.

➻ *ShowBoats International*

Website: www.showboats.com

Founded in 1988, *ShowBoats International* is a premier luxury-yacht publication. From its base in Fort Lauderdale, the international yachting capital, *ShowBoats International* delivers the definitive inside stories on the remarkable boats, significant events, outstanding people, and exceptional wealth that shape this multibillion-dollar industry.

➻ *The Superyacht Report*

Website: www.thesuperyachtreport.com

The Superyacht Report is a valued journal with rich, sharp editorial content, offering reports on yacht construction, operation, and maintenance. The publication applauds design initiative and excellence of engineering, construction, and design, while also criticizing safety breaches and ergonomic failures. *The Superyacht Report* stands behind the statement that a good yacht will not only work well for the owner and his guests, but more importantly will provide a safe and efficient working and living environment for the captain and his crew. Nine issues a year. *The Superyacht Report* is the sister publication to *The Crew Report,* mentioned above.

➻ *Superyacht Business*

Website: www.superyachtbusiness.net

Superyacht Business is the b-to-b magazine for the superyacht industry. It provides highly qualified analysis and comment on the market, covering industry trends, legal issues, and more. Among the regular features are country-by-country spotlights on yacht builders, providing details on what they have under construction, what they have delivered in recent years, and interview with their general managers, discussing how they are responding to today's challenging business environment.

⊷ *SuperYacht World*

Website: www.superyachtworld.com

An international magazine, *SuperYacht World* delivers yachting and lifestyle editorial to owners. From helping readers choose the best charter vessel for that holiday of a lifetime, to highlighting designer watches made out of recycled steel from the *Titanic*, *SuperYacht World* provides the access for readers to share in the privilege of being onboard the world's finest yachts.

⊷ *The Triton*

Website: www.the-triton.com

As mentioned in Chapter 9, *The Triton* is a monthly yachting news publication targeting captains and crew. A must-read, the paper is available in print, but the website is current and has tons of links to just about any topic from course requirements to life as a crew. Be sure to register on the website to post free classified ads and get weekly emails (optional). *The Triton* also hosts monthly networking events for crew and posts news on their Facebook page (www.facebook.com/tritonnews). Watch for their Expo several times a year around boat show times in Fort Lauderdale.

⊷ *Yachting*

Website: www.yachtingmagazine.com

Yachting is a monthly magazine devoted to informing readers about the best of today's powerboats, sailboats, and gear and how to optimize their use, as well as inspire and entertain them about destinations, the sport, and the lifestyle. *Yachting* considers itself to be the authority in the marine industry on yacht charter.

⊷ *Yachting World*

Website: www.yachtingworld.co.uk

Founded in April 1894, *Yachting World* is the world's oldest sailing magazine. Published monthly from London in the U.K., today *Yachting World* is the most widely distributed and most international sailing magazine in the world, reaching over 100 countries. Coverage includes the latest news stories and features on blue-water cruising, global sailing epics, international yacht racing, superyachting, international events, and charter.

⊷ *Yachting and Boating World*

Website: www.ybw.com

This U.K.-based publishing house offers a variety of yacht-related magazines, including *Motor Boat & Yachting*, *Motor Boats Monthly*, *Practical Boat Owner*, *Yachting Monthly*, and *Yachting World*. Yeah, it certainly seems like they've got it all covered!

⊷ *YachtForums.com*

Website: www.yachtforums.com

An online chat forum dedicated to the sharing of knowledge, news, and information about yachting, this site is a terrific way to learn more about the industry and the overall yachting community. Not only can you post "job wanted" details here (in the Yacht Crews Forum), but also you can research particular motor- and sailing yachts that are looking to hire you (complete with photos!). Registration at YachtForums.com is free and highly recommended.

➼ *Yachts International*

Website: www.yachtsmagazine.com

Yachts International has English- and foreign-language editions, giving it global reach. It's written for knowledgeable and passionate yacht owners, designed to help them make better-educated decisions when buying, servicing, or outfitting their yachts. Regular articles include yacht reviews, designer profiles, charter trips, and more. *Yachts International* further hosts high-profile events and has an exclusive partnership with Show Management, the producer of the industry's leading boat shows.

➼ *The Crew Report*

Website: www.thecrewreport.com

Launched in May 2006, *The Crew Report* offered invaluable information, from career advice to financial planning and contract issues, as well as stories from the lighter side of yachting. In autumn of 2012, *The Crew Report* combined with its sister company SuperyachtJobs.com and was revamped to be even more advisory, supportive, and guiding, becoming a conduit between owners, managers, the authorities, senior captains, and other leading experts who want to see the world's superyacht crew grow in quality and professionalism. Key subjects such as safety, security, attitude, technology, operations, guest services, and other mentoring topics are covered, coupled with regulatory and career-based knowledge.

➼ *Yachting Pages*

Website: www.yachting-pages.com

Yachting Pages is a marine directory that lists over 13,000 yachting businesses, including yacht brokers, yacht management, builders, shipyards, refit and repair facilities, yacht painters, and services worldwide. Crew training, crew housing, and crew placement information is included. It's distributed throughout the Mediterranean yachting ports, as well as in Fort Lauderdale. The website also features all of the directory listings and advertisers.

Other Books About Yacht Crewing

➼ *The Yacht Service Bible*

By Alene Keenan

Alene Keenan has stewed on yachts since 1981 and offers expert advice on everything from high-level service instructions to linens and upholstery care. Once you get onboard a yacht, this is what you're going to need to know. It's a bit pricey and contains information you'll get in stew-training courses, but once you land your first job, this guide is chock-full of incredibly detailed information. This will be a tremendous resource and reference tool to have onboard. Alene also offers stew training courses in Fort Lauderdale and aboard vessels through her company Yacht Stew Solutions: www.yachtstewsolutions.com.

➼ *The Marine Cookery Bible: A Specialist Cookery, Training, and Employment Guide for Interior Crew Working on Yachts and Superyachts*

by Malcolm Alder-Smith

This book has everything you need to know about working in the galley of a yacht or superyacht. Not only are the pages full of essential recipes and menu ideas for chefs, but there is information on how to apply for a yacht-chef job, the qualifications one needs, where to provision, and how to cook for different nationalities and diets. As Victoria Allman, another superyacht chef-turned-author has said: "[Malcolm] has a firm knowledge and complete understanding of what it takes to run a galley on a yacht and how to succeed at it. This book is a must for anyone who cooks, or wants to cook, onboard a pro-crewed yacht or superyacht." Available on Amazon and BN.com.

➥ *Chef Peter Ziegelmeier's Dreams of A Yacht Chef – Food For Thought*
By Chef Peter Ziegelmeier

An interactive style cookbook, where you can post your journal style responses, change Chef Peters recipes, post your own photos 4 x 6, figure out how to make some of the recipes using ingredient lists and pictures, develop your own food for thought so to speak it is motivating and surprising, it will allow your inner chef to come out and play. Find it at www.dreamsofayachtchef.com; also available on Amazon and BN.com

➥ *SEAsoned: A Chef's Journey with Her Captain* (2011) and *SEA FARE: A Chef's Journey Across The Ocean* (2009)
By Victoria Allman

I absolutely loved both of Victoria Allman's books. Sprinkled with over 30-mouthwatering recipes and spiced with tales of adventure, *SEAsoned* is the hilarious look at a yacht chef's first year working for her captain-husband while they cruise from the Bahamas to Italy, France, Greece and Spain, trying to stay afloat. I laughed out loud at some of the stories she told about her experiences with other crew on large charter yachts. *SEA FARE* is for readers who enjoy travel writing and exotic cuisine. Culinary trained at the Statford Chef's School in Canada and the Culinary Institute of America, Victoria shares her nine-year cooking odyssey as a yacht chef. I highly recommend them both, but if you're going to choose one, SEAsoned gave the best crew stories. Find it through most all online book merchants such as Amazon.com and BN.com, or visit Victoria's website at www.victoriaallman.com.

ABOUT THE AUTHOR

 **Julie Perry spent three years** as a megayacht stewardess, which took her to over 40 different ports in 18 countries. And she can tell you how to do it, too. The first edition of her book, *The Insiders' Guide to Becoming a Yacht Stewardess,* has been a must-read guide for yacht crew since 2006. With the release of her updated, second edition, Julie hopes to continue to help wannabe "yachties" get into this awe-inspiring industry—if not simply entertain those intrigued by such a career path.

Currently a digital-marketing executive and freelance writer living ashore, Julie stays connected to the yachting community by attending megayacht shows year-round and speaking at marine industry events. She doesn't miss cleaning toilets for the world's wealthiest, but she does miss traveling the high seas with them… Instead, she writes about it.

CPSIA information can be obtained
at www.ICGtesting.com
Printed in the USA
JSHW020715160720
6705JS00005B/318

9 781614 487852